Rethinking Disability

Now in its second edition, *Rethinking Disability* introduces new and experienced teachers to ethical framings of disability and strategies for effectively teaching and including students with disabilities in the general education classroom. Grounded in a disability studies framework, this text's unique narrative style encourages readers to examine their beliefs about disability and the influence of historical and cultural meanings of disability upon their work as teachers. The second edition offers clear and applicable suggestions for creating dynamic and inclusive classroom cultures, getting to know students, selecting appropriate instructional and assessment strategies, co-teaching, and promoting an inclusive school culture. This second edition is fully revised and updated to include a brief history of disability through the ages, the relevance of current educational policies to inclusion, technology in the inclusive classroom, intersectionality and its influence upon inclusive practices, working with families, and issues of transition from school to the post-school world. Each chapter now also includes a featured "voice from the field" written by persons with disabilities, parents, and teachers.

Jan W. Valle is Professor of Inclusive Education at The City College of New York (CUNY), USA.

David J. Connor is Professor of Special Education and Learning Disabilities at Hunter College (CUNY), USA.

Rethinking Disability

A Disability Studies Approach to
Inclusive Practices

Second Edition

Jan W. Valle and David J. Connor

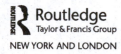
Routledge
Taylor & Francis Group

NEW YORK AND LONDON

Second edition published 2019
by Routledge
52 Vanderbilt Avenue, New York, NY 10017

and by Routledge
2 Park Square, Milton Park, Abingdon, Oxon, OX14 4RN

Routledge is an imprint of the Taylor & Francis Group, an informa business

© 2019 Taylor & Francis

First edition published by McGraw-Hill 2010

Library of Congress Cataloging-in-Publication Data
A catalog record has been requested for this book

ISBN: 978-1-138-08584-8 (hbk)
ISBN: 978-1-138-08586-2 (pbk)
ISBN: 978-1-315-11120-9 (ebk)

Typeset in Sabon
by Newgen Publishing UK

To the educators who taught and supported us through our first year of teaching

Carol Sunderman, Dickie Hitch, and Lesley Quast
—Jan

Jayson Fansler, Iris Davidow, Tom Williams, and John Treadwell
—David

Contents

PART III
How Talk Changes Knowledge and Practice   225

List of Contributors

Diane Berman has been teaching for 28 years and has written two books, *Beyond Words, Reflections on our Journey to Inclusion* and *A Child, a Family, a School, a Community* (co-authored with David Connor).

Dr. María Cioe-Peña is a former elementary school teacher whose passion for children and social justice in education pushes her to fight for equity and full inclusion for children of diverse backgrounds and abilities.

Kristen Goldmansour has been an educator in New York City for 30 years. For the past 15 years she has owned G&R Inclusive Group, which provides inclusive professional development to school communities.

David I. Hernández-Saca is an assistant professor at the University of Northern Iowa. His research agenda problematizes common-sense assumptions about learning disabilities.

Keriann Martin teaches in a first-grade integrated co-teaching classroom at P.S. 300 in the Bronx.

Jonathan Mooney is a dyslexic writer, speaker, and activist. His work has been featured in the *New York Times*, *Los Angeles Times*, *Chicago Tribune*, *USA Today*, *New York Magazine*, *Washington Post*, *Boston Globe*, and on HBO, NPR, and ABC News, and he continues to speak across the nation about neurological and physical diversity, inspiring those who live with differences and advocating for change. He is the author of *The Short Bus* and *Learning Outside the Lines*. His forthcoming book, *Normal Sucks*, will be published in March 2019.

Louis Olander is a doctoral candidate in urban education at the City University of New York (CUNY) Graduate Center.

Jody Polleck teaches both adolescents and pre- and in-service teachers in New York City and has published several articles in academic journals on culturally relevant and responsive pedagogies.

Carrie C. Snow is a teacher in the Seattle public school system. In 2015, she published a book with Teachers College Press titled *Creativity and the Autistic Student: Supporting Strengths to Develop Skills and Deepen Knowledge*.

Meric Gulum Weinkle is an elementary school teacher at the Greenwich Village School in New York City, who taught for seven years in an integrated co-teaching classroom. She is dually-certified in special and general education and holds a master's degree in literacy.

Foreword

On Little Books and Big Ideas

"Uhm, do you mean the little book?" the pre-service teacher, a student in my class, asked. Her confusion in response to the writing prompt I assigned at the beginning of class was amplified by the fact that her peers appeared fully engaged by the question, "How might you explain the various models of understanding disability considered by Jan W. Valle and David J. Connor in the first three chapters of *Rethinking Disability: A Disability Studies Approach to Inclusive Practices*?" I have used this text every semester in my undergraduate education courses since its initial publication in 2010. My writing prompts often came directly from the "Questions to Consider" section at the end of each chapter. However, on this occasion, I hoped students would weave across the chapters to complicate their thinking and to deepen the reader reflexivity encouraged by Valle and Connor. When I asked the student if she read the assigned reading, she did not say "No." Instead, she explained that, in her other education classes, only textbooks were required purchases and that the other "little books" sometimes listed on the syllabus were optional. Given the length of the line at the bookstore, the student made an executive decision convinced that Valle and Connor's "little book" was optional because of its size.

The "measured" approach taken by this undergraduate student provided a unique twist on Ellen Brantlinger's (2006) critique of the overreliance on "the big glossies"—textbooks that convey the ideological framework of special education as indisputable. Brantlinger held that textbooks, with their outdated approach to understanding disability, merely served to rehash the assumption that teaching amounted to little more than technicist and reductionist practice. Their framing of unproblematized content and approaches posed a fundamental obstacle in the preparation of critical reflection among future and practicing educators. I was amused to consider that Brantlinger would somehow appreciate the irony of this exchange with my former student who, to be fair, was successfully conditioned to dismiss the authority of Valle and Connor's "little book."

As an educator and scholar who claims disability studies as my academic home, I, not unlike many of my peers, anxiously awaited the initial publication of *Rethinking Disability*. Prior to its release I organized course packets that captured the essence of my introduction to disability studies for the future or practicing general or special educators I taught. The promise of a text that could replace course packets was long overdue. As noted by Valle and Connor, the "view from disability studies" begins with the argument that the way disability is understood within special education is problematic and far "too restrictive, even fundamentally flawed" (2010, p. xi). In practice, the application of knowledge becomes a huge project of unlearning all that has been previously understood and uncritically accepted about disability in schools and society. *Such a huge project for such a "little book."*

Valle and Connor are to be congratulated for their willingness to tackle the myriad ways in which disability studies disrupts unproblematized notions of the very meaning that schools make of disability and, by default, the ways in which such meaning is reified by teachers through the embrace of policies and practices sanctioned by "institutional ableism" (Beratan, 2006). The demand for "rethinking" nearly every aspect of status quo teacher education preparation in an effort to promote inclusive practices as the norm in K-12 education is carefully unpacked by the authors, who not only explain the impact of historical and cultural claims that impede inclusion, but also keep the conversation they seek to promote alive through the dynamic examples that succeed in translating their call for inclusive reform into actual practice. *Rethinking Disability* provides a cogent structure in three parts. In Part I the authors discuss how knowledge guides practice, in Part II explore how practice deepens knowledge, and in Part III conclude by considering how talk changes knowledge and practice. Readers will find that the authors have succeeded in presenting the kaleidoscopic influences of the culture of public schools, the origin of readers' beliefs about difference, the nature of inclusive practices, and the endless ways to promote inclusive school communities—none of which require investment in glossily packaged programs or curriculum materials that claim to "celebrate" diversity and inclusion.

To be sure, there are many complicated concepts and theories contained in this book—many will challenge teachers as they travel with the authors to familiar and unfamiliar contexts and conversations. Understanding that the challenge to unpack complexity and abandon previously uncontested notions about disability in schools and society begins with recognition that unexamined attitudes and beliefs about disability have shaped schools and schooling practices that inevitably interfere with inclusive philosophy and practice. *Rethinking Disability* serves to assure readers that complexity need not be feared and that a movement inspired by disability studies will prove more enduring and meaningful for educators and the students they support in ways that were previously unimaginable. Together, we can imagine disability otherwise.

Linda Ware
SUNY Geneseo

References

Beratan, G. D. (2006). Institutionalizing inequity: Ableism, racism and IDEA 2004. *Disability Studies Quarterly, 26*(2).

Brantlinger, E. (2006). The big glossies: How textbooks structure (special) education. In E. Brantlinger (Ed.), *Who benefits from special education? Remediating (fixing) other people's children* (pp. 45–76). Mahway, NJ: Lawrence Erlbaum.

Valle, J. W. & Connor, D. J. (2010). *Rethinking disability: A disability studies approach to inclusive practices.* New York, NY: McGraw-Hill.

Preface

Almost a decade ago we decided to write a short, practical book on inclusive education, primarily aimed at pre-service teachers yet hoping in-service teachers would also see the value of what we shared. In brief, we wanted to write the type of book we wished we'd had when in graduate classes and teaching children. We are delighted that the book struck a chord and is now in its second edition.

It is worth noting that the topic of inclusion has long been incorporated into teacher education courses, as well as into general and special education textbooks. Yet inclusion remains more of an ideal than a widespread reality within public education. Although movement toward more inclusive practices has been made in recent years, we are still far away from schools that *really* include all of America's schoolchildren. Intense debates about inclusion continue to persist among educators, parents, and the general public alike.

So how is a new teacher to make sense of the discrepancy between educational theory and the multiple belief systems and practices of real people who inhabit public schools? Or, for that matter, how can a seasoned teacher engage with a familiar topic in new, even radical ways? The inspiration for this book comes from our ongoing classroom conversations with teachers who struggle to reconcile theory with the practice of inclusion within their classrooms and school communities. The typical inclusion textbook focuses upon how-to strategies for teachers without much consideration of the "bigger picture" that inclusion represents in a democratic society. Thus we address not only teachers' questions about *how* to do inclusion, but also the fundamental question of *why* to do inclusion, given that special education already exists for children with disabilities. By foregrounding historical, social, and cultural issues inextricable to ongoing debates about inclusion, we focus upon the *context* where teaching and learning take place—a context that has been and continues to be influenced by beliefs and values regarding "who belongs" and why. We hope to inspire readers to reflect upon what they believe in and why, what they teach and why, how they teach and why—and to recognize the power of an individual teacher to make school a place where everyone belongs.

Why Read *This* Book on Inclusion?

There is no shortage of inclusion textbooks available to teachers. And not unlike those books, we, too, offer classroom strategies for best practice. So how does this text differ from all the others?

Inclusion in a Different Light

We frame inclusion through the lens of Disability Studies in Education (DSE), a constantly growing academic discipline that helps us unlearn restrictive notions of ability, recognize difference as natural human variation, and better understand the complexities underlying the implementation of inclusion. In other words, we have not written "the same old book" in which inclusion is presented as simply another iteration of special education services for children with disabilities. It is our intention to offer teachers new ways in which to think about disability and inclusive practices.

Disability in Context

We do not shy away from difficult issues often ignored, glossed over, or swept under the rug in special education texts. For example, we challenge readers to consider the material consequences inherent within a medical model of disability—the model upon which all of special education revolves. We offer readers an opportunity to understand the human experience of disability as it intersects with race, class, gender, and other markers of identity, as well as to consider the meaning that such a perspective holds for inclusive practices.

Authors with a Voice

Most textbook authors posit inclusion in one way or another as "the right thing to do," hoping that *telling* readers what to believe will increase the likelihood that their how-to advice will make its way into classrooms. Based upon our experience as teacher educators, we know that merely extolling the virtues of inclusion does little to shift anyone's thinking. Inclusion is not the latest teaching technique to learn and apply. It is a fundamental philosophy about how we perceive and respond to human difference. Why a person holds particular beliefs is highly specific to the life experiences of that individual. We believe that our task as teacher educators is to present ideas that inspire reflection upon the meaning of human difference as well as new ways of thinking.

We chose to approach this text in much the same way that we teach. Rather than present a disembodied narrative as "the omniscient authority" on inclusion, we write in a voice that makes transparent to the reader the perspectives, experiences, and situatedness that we bring to the text, as well as questions for which we still seek answers and clarity. Moreover, we share moments from our own lives that have changed how we think about human difference. This kind of "storytelling" invites reflection in a way that assertions about inclusion cannot.

A Participatory Text

We mean to engage the reader in what feels more like a conversation than a typical one-sided transmission of information. It is our hope that the text invites self-reflection, generates more questions on the part of the reader, and provides a framework for (re)envisioning classrooms and school communities.

In Defense of "Pie in the Sky"

Change never happens while people are busy being sensible and realistic. It happens when we dare to imagine a world that is otherwise and take risks to make it so. To critics who might accuse us of "pie in the sky" thinking, know that we choose to err on the side of imagination and bet on the chance to make a difference.

The View from Disability Studies

Based upon our experiences as former special education teachers and what we know from our current vantage point as teacher educators, we agree with a relatively small but increasing number of scholars who believe that the way disability is understood within special education is too restrictive, even fundamentally flawed. Given that the field of special education grew out of medicine, science, and psychology (disciplines rooted in the understanding of human difference as dysfunctional, disordered, deficit based, and abnormal), it is unsurprising that schools appear unable to conceptualize students with disabilities in any other way than in need of a "cure"—rendered through "appropriate services" meant to restore normalcy, or at least approximate it as closely as possible (Danforth & Gabel, 2007). This particular way of conceptualizing disability significantly impacts how schools are structured. The organizing principle for educating American children revolves around the presence or absence of disability, which determines how and where a student is taught and by whom (Brantlinger, 2003). Historically, it is widely known that once labeled as having a disability, children have a high chance of being segregated from their original peers and placed in separate special education programs (Gartner & Lipsky, 1987).

Disability Studies (DS) provides a counterbalance to the deficit-based understanding of disability that permeates education. It is an interdisciplinary field in which disability is studied as a marker of identity—like race, ethnicity, class, gender, and sexual orientation (Gabel, 2007). Disability is viewed primarily through a social lens, as a series of historical, cultural, and social responses to human difference. In contrast to the medical model that centers the individual as its unit of analysis, DS focuses on social relationships among people and the interpretation of human difference. In other words, how we choose to respond to disability shifts significantly depending upon whether we perceive that "something is 'wrong' with disabled people" or "something is 'wrong' with a social system that disables people." Thus, how we educate students with disabilities has everything to do with how we *understand* disability. Without wishing to oversimplify, we might think of the medical model as primarily concerned with identifying and changing the student who does not fit the school context (i.e., based upon a perception that a child is intrinsically disabled), whereas the social model focuses upon adapting the school context to fit the student (i.e., based upon the perception that the environment can disable a child).

In contrast to special education literature primarily written by non-disabled scholars *about* students with disabilities, the growing body of DS literature represents the perspective of scholars *with* disabilities and their allies. Simi Linton describes DS as "an organized critique on the constricted, inadequate, and inaccurate conceptualizations of disability that have dominated academic inquiry. Above all, the critique includes a challenge to the notion that disability is primarily a medical category" (Linton, 1998, p. 2). DS scholars argue that the seemingly omnipresent understanding of disability within a medical model is sustained by non-disabled people's fixation with prevention and cure, and the need to reinforce notions of normalcy. The powerful and unyielding medical model that undergirds much of society's understanding of disability contributes to the ignoring of social conditions that are actually causing or increasing disability among people with impairments (Wendell, 2001). Scholars and activists within the field of DS view disabilities as natural human variations that become categorized as disabilities by a society unwilling to reconfigure itself in terms of removing barriers and restrictions. Or, disability as meaning something is wrong with a person becomes disability as something wrong with society (Oliver, 1996).

Education: Going Forward or Awry?

In discussing these and other issues, we wish to clarify that our intention is not to vilify special education, but rather to broaden our current understanding of disability in an effort to promote deeper dialogue among scholars and teachers alike (Baglieri, Valle, Connor, & Gallagher, 2011). It is without question that the Education for All Handicapped Children Act (P.L. 94–142), passed by Congress in 1975, remains one of the most significant steps forward for persons with disabilities in this country. Currently known as the Individuals with Disabilities Improvement Education Act (IDEIA), the law guarantees a free and appropriate public education for *all* children—providing hope and services to innumerable American families whose disabled children, prior to 1975, would have remained homebound or institutionalized.

Our critique of special education is not meant to negate or dismiss any positive outcomes that have resulted from the current system. On the other hand, we do believe that failure to respond in any meaningful way to the unforeseen, yet well-documented, negative consequences of special education is, in a word, unethical. Over the past 50 years, the structure of special education has been implicated repeatedly for stigmatizing difference (Harry & Klingner, 2006), maintaining racial segregation in schools (Blanchett, 2006), separating many migrant and indigenous children (Gabel, Curcic, Powell, Khader, & Albee, 2009), diluting curriculum (Brantlinger, 2006), limiting post-secondary opportunities (Connor, 2008), and contributing to the "school-to-prison" pipeline (Annamma, 2017). And yet, the special education system remains, for the most part, intact and seemingly impervious to critique.

From as early as the 1960s, scholars emerged who criticized special education for its commonplace institutionalization (Bogdan & Taylor, 1989), stigmatizing labeling (Carrier, 1986), institutional structuring (Gartner & Lipsky, 1987), reductionist pedagogy (Iano, 1990), and separate professionalization (Skrtic, 1991). However, their attempts at a constructive critique of special education from within the profession's journals met with ongoing resistance from those who rejected any challenge to the orthodoxy of a positivistic field grounded within science (implying, of course, that science is above reproach) (Gallagher, Heshusius, Iano, & Skrtic, 2003)—thereby effectively maintaining a medical model perspective of disability. In much the same way, most teacher education programs present special education as grounded within "scientifically-based" research that renders it largely unproblematic. In the absence of any meaningful critique of special education, it is little wonder that new teachers struggle to reconcile what they learn in university classrooms with what they experience in public schools.

As DS scholar Michael Oliver suggests, people with disabilities have ample reason to mistrust the medical framework of disability and the research it generates. He characterizes such research as, at worst, oppressive and, at best, irrelevant (Oliver, 1996). Oliver's perspective reflects the beliefs of a growing group of critical special educators who continue to foreground issues such as special education's insular, reductionist approach to research (Danforth, 1999), an overreliance on the remediation of deficits (Hehir, 2005), sustained use of intelligence testing despite critiques (Flynn, 2000),[1] commonplace segregation based on disability and/or race (Ferri & Connor, 2005), the professionalization of school failure (Ferguson, 2002), and the continued medicalization of disabled people (Hayes & Hannold, 2007). Taken together, these critiques illustrate limiting, oppressive understandings of disability within special education as well as the role of contemporary society in actively disabling people through social practices, beliefs, attitudes, and expectations.

Disability Studies in Education: Rethinking What We Know and How We Do It

Within the last ten years, critical special educators have not only gravitated to the field of Disability Studies as a framework for rethinking disability, but have also seen the possibility for a subfield dedicated to the study of disability *and* education. The resistance, even intolerance, within the field of special education toward historical, cultural, and social understandings of disability, along with its fierce embrace of medical, scientific, and psychological frameworks, compelled these scholars to forge a new, more inclusive discipline known as Disability Studies in Education (DSE). Its mission statement, purpose, and tenets have been featured in the *International Journal of Inclusive Education* (Connor, Gabel, Gallagher, & Morton, 2008). See Appendix A and the website of the American Educational Research Association (www.aera.net/).

We ground this book within the discipline of Disability Studies in Education. As DSE scholars and practitioners, it has long been our desire to write a book on inclusion that draws upon pertinent DSE research as well as our own experiences as special education teachers and teacher educators. It is our hope to have written a book that speaks to the everyday reality of classroom teachers and offers clarity not only about how to support inclusive education but—perhaps more importantly—why it is ethical to do so.

Organization of the Book

The book is divided into three broadly-defined sections. Part I, "How Knowledge Guides Practice" (Chapters 1–4), asks the reader to pause and reflect upon the origins of his or her knowledge about disability and the beliefs and values that undergird it. We invite readers to consider what they know, how they know it, and—most importantly—how it impacts their own decision making as teachers. Part II, "How Practice Deepens Knowledge" (Chapters 5–8), looks at how to create and sustain classrooms in which all children can participate. These chapters describe and illustrate many different tools for teachers to use in crafting engaging lessons and evaluating student progress. Part III, "How Talk Changes Knowledge and Practice" (Chapters 9–10), presents disability as an aspect of diversity to be represented, talked about, and celebrated in the classroom and school community. Ideas for challenging normalcy and promoting school change are also discussed.

We open each chapter with a question posed to us by students in our graduate education classes. Every chapter closes with a series of questions to promote individual reflection and/or discussion within venues such as a school-based study group, faculty meeting, professional development workshop, or graduate education class.

Chapter 1, "Making Sense of Public School Culture and Context," sets the stage for understanding public schools as a culture shaped by patterns of human activity and social structures that embody its history, beliefs, attitudes, and values. We explore the purpose of public education and the ongoing role of social, political, and economic factors in shaping its purpose. Examples of how federal policy becomes enacted at the local level are examined, particularly in regard to *Brown v. Board of Education* (1954) and the Education for All Handicapped Children Act (1975). We argue that whether or not the *spirit* of a law is carried out depends upon the commitment of teachers to the ideals of public education in a democracy.

Chapter 2, "Contemplating the (In)visibility of Disability," unpacks commonplace misperceptions of disability and juxtaposes real-life experiences of people with disabilities. Our purpose here is to challenge cultural assumptions and widespread stereotypes of disability that lead to and sustain segregated practices. Focusing upon representations of disability found in ordinary artifacts of popular culture, we contrast such understandings to representations that come from within "disability culture." We explore the history of educating students with disabilities in the United States, highlighting events leading up to federal legislation that changed the structure and operation of public schools. The chapter closes with a discussion of the unintended consequences of special education and the rise of a counter-movement—inclusive education.

Chapter 3, "Examining Beliefs and Expanding Notions of Normalcy," begins with a comprehensive analysis of the medical model of disability that undergirds special education, followed by illustrations of how disability becomes socially constructed through society's *response* to difference. By extension, we show how disability materializes through school practices, including the implementation of laws, cultural expectations around what is considered "normal," and teacher beliefs about ability. By foregrounding the concept of normalcy, we seek to undermine many taken-for-granted practices within special and general education, arguing that disability is best understood as contextual. Through real-life scenarios, we illustrate how individuals become socially constructed as disabled in particular contexts but not others. We close by suggesting that resisting inclusion on the basis of "not being ready" may be symptomatic of unexamined attitudes, beliefs, and fears about disability and restrictive notions of normalcy.

Chapter 4, "Practicing Educational Equity in a Democracy," offers examples of what inclusion is and what it is not. Defining inclusion as a matter of social justice, we look at disability through a civil rights lens (in contrast to a medical lens) and raise questions about who holds the power to decide which children are included in or excluded from general education and who benefits from such an arrangement. We include personal narratives of teachers with disabilities who share "insider perspectives" about the response toward difference within public schools. In asking readers to consider what constitutes ethical practice, we explore the consequences of *action* or *inaction* when working within existing school structures. The chapter closes with classroom illustrations of inclusion and creative collaboration among school professionals.

In Chapter 5, "Selecting Approaches and Tools of Inclusive Teaching," we look at how to create a classroom community that is both respectful of and fair toward all learners. Getting to know students is the first step toward building a community of learners. We suggest practical ways to determine each student's strengths, challenges, interests, preferences, and learning styles for the purpose of creating "student profiles" to use in planning instruction. Drawing upon theories of multiple intelligences, learning styles, and differentiated instruction, we demonstrate how it is possible to plan a curriculum that provides multiple entry points for all learners.

Chapter 6, "Creating a Dynamic Classroom Culture," underscores the importance of synthesizing *all* components of a lesson. We emphasize sharing goals and objectives with students (academic, social, behavioral), connecting previously taught concepts to new information, using students' background knowledge, and utilizing teaching techniques that lead to student interest and motivation. Accepting differentiated expectations for students within the same classroom is explored, along with real-life illustrations. We present multiple ways for students to process what they are learning—as individuals, pairs, triads, and small groups, as well as through whole-class configurations. A list of classroom activities is discussed, along with anticipated benefits and potential drawbacks of each.

Chapter 7, "Assessing Student Knowledge and Skills in the Inclusive Classroom," examines the multiple purposes of student assessment. Within the context of assessing what students *can* do, we discuss how to use this information as the basis of instruction.

By relying upon both formative and summative assessments, we illustrate how teachers can come to know and understand students' abilities as they progress through the curriculum. Issues are raised and discussed regarding the tension between standardized testing generated by the federal legislation No Child Left Behind and the requirements of the Individuals with Disabilities Education Act. In closing, we highlight test accommodations and modifications available to students with disabilities, along with ways for teachers to prepare students for state examinations without falling victim to a "teach to the test" classroom environment.

In Chapter 8, "Drawing upon the Power of Two," we discuss the increasing trend within public schools to offer inclusive classrooms co-taught by a full-time general education teacher and a full-time special education teacher. Potential benefits are outlined for what is often referred to as "the four constituents" of collaborative classrooms: general educators, special educators, general education students, and special education students.[2] Team teaching is portrayed as an ongoing collaboration that, like all relationships, cannot be taken for granted, and requires constant reflection and assessment to ensure its continued success. In closing, we outline ways in which to collaborate effectively with auxiliary professionals (e.g., school psychologists, guidance counselors, occupational therapists, paraprofessionals, and speech/language pathologists).

In Chapter 9, "Actively Challenging Normalcy," we broach the subject of silence about disability in the classroom (presumably an effort not to draw attention to difference)—a stance that, ironically, contributes to ongoing misperceptions and assumptions. In contrast, we encourage all kinds of differences to be acknowledged and embraced and suggest practical strategies for engaging children in thinking about disability as natural human variation. In that the experience of disability is not likely to be represented within school curriculum in any intentional way, we draw upon the emerging discipline of DSE to suggest ideas about how teachers might integrate a "disability lens," when and where appropriate, into instruction. The chapter closes with examples that range from incorporating suggested texts into the curriculum to entire elementary- and secondary-level units that infuse DSE into the curriculum.

In Chapter 10, "Promoting Inclusive Beliefs and Practices," we ask readers to (re)consider the meaning of human difference within their own schools. Is inclusion conceptualized as a current trend in educational practice or an ethical choice that embraces natural human diversity as a resource for all? Acknowledging that inclusion is always a work in progress and never a "one model fits all" endeavor, we describe "inclusion" as a fluid concept that reflects a commitment to larger societal issues of access and equity. Although advocating for any change within a resistant school climate can feel like a Herculean task, the choice to make no response is to tacitly accept the status quo. For readers up to the challenge, we close with suggestions for promoting inclusive beliefs and practices within classrooms, schools, and communities.

What has changed since the first edition? We're almost a decade older and have seen some of the changes we wished to see, taking heart from how inclusive education is an integral—and expected—part of the educational landscape. In a recent edition of *Educational Leadership* entitled "Differences, Not Disabilities," featuring a young girl with Down syndrome on the cover[3] and asking the rhetorical question "Where do U.S. students with disabilities learn?", the following statistics, provided by the National Center for Education Statistics (2016), were revealed:

- 81.2% regular school, more than 40% of the day in a general classroom
- 13.8% regular school, less than 40% of the day in a general classroom
- 2.9% separate school for students with disabilities

- 1.1% parentally placed in regular private school
- 1% residential facility, correctional facility, or homebound

From these numbers it is clear that more students with disabilities than ever are being educated in general education settings. Yet many of the "old ways" of thinking still stick to these children and youth, oftentimes through our field's insistence, prompting Armstrong (2017) to suggest, "At some point, the field of special education needs to rid itself of its negative baggage and embrace a more progressive way of educating students who learn differently. The concept of neurodiversity provides the catalyst for such change" (p. 11). Indeed, we have seen a shift, both at grass roots and some professional levels, to rethinking disability as diversity. To reiterate a positive point, we have witnessed progress in many realms. At the same time, we realize there is far to go. For example, it was recently reported that only 20 percent of special educators' time is spent on academic instruction, and four out of five secondary special educators feel they are not ready to teach the "what" of content matter in high school (Ashby & Cosier, 2016). Defining the nature of inclusive education is clearly an ongoing process.

In terms of what has physically changed in the text, among other things we have:

- Extended several chapters, incorporating important areas such as working with parents and transitioning from high school
- Provided additional recommended teaching resources
- Added "Featured Voices" of educators, students, family members, teacher-friendly researchers, and activists, all with a view to them sharing some of their knowledge
- Provided explicit references to disability studies literature
- Incorporated recent research findings
- Expanded the appendices
- Made visible some connections among theory, research, and policy—to daily practices of teachers

In full disclosure, we did not seek to change the original text substantially, but rather to focus on keeping the content current, incorporating actual voices in education, and enhancing the content in a few selected ways. Finally, it is sincerely hoped that you will find this text interesting and, above all, useful. That was, and still is, our primary goal.

Notes

1 For a systematic scientific, historical, and cultural critique, see Gould (1981).
2 While we acknowledge these existing categories, we also feel compelled to point out that maintaining such labeling systems is counterproductive to dismantling a segregated education system.
3 *Educational Leadership*, 74(7).

References

Annamma, S. A. (2017). *The pedagogy of pathologization: Dis/abled girls of color in the school–prison nexus*. New York, NY: Routledge.

Armstrong, T. (2017). Neurodiversity: The future of special education? *Educational Leadership*, 74(7), 10–16.

Ashby, C. & Cosier, M. (2016). The work and history of special education. In M. Cosier & C. Ashby (Eds.), *Enacting change from within: Disability studies meets teaching and teacher education* (pp. 21–38). New York, NY: Peter Lang.

Baglieri, S., Valle, J., Connor, D. J., & Gallagher, D. (2011). Disability studies and special education: The need for plurality of perspectives on disability. *Remedial and Special Education, 32*(4), 267–78.

Blanchett, W. (2006). Disproportionate representation of African American students in special education: Acknowledging the role of white privilege and racism. *Educational Researcher, 35*(6), 24–8.

Bogdan, R. & Taylor, S. (1989). Relationships with severely disabled people: The social construction of humanness. *Social Problems, 36*(2), 135–47.

Brantlinger, E. (2003). Confounding the needs and confronting the norms: An extension of Reid and Valle's essay. *Journal of Learning Disabilities, 37*(6), 490–9.

Brantlinger, E. (Ed.). (2006). *Who benefits from special education? Remediating (fixing) other people's children*. Mahwah, NJ: Lawrence Erlbaum.

Carrier, J. G. (1986). *Learning disability: Social class and the construction of inequality in American education*. New York, NY: Greenwood Press.

Connor, D. J. (2008). *Urban narratives: Portraits-in-progress: Life at the intersections of learning disability, race, and social class*. New York, NY: Peter Lang.

Connor, D. J. & Valle, J. W. (2015). A socio-cultural reframing of science and dis/ability in education: Past problems, current concerns, and future possibilities. *Journal of Cultural Studies of Science Education, 10*(2), 1103–12

Connor, D. J., Gabel, S. L., Gallagher, D., & Morton, M. (2008). Disability studies and inclusive education: Implication for theory, research, and practice—Guest editor's introduction. *International Journal of Inclusive Education, 12*(5–6), 441–57.

Danforth, S. (1999). Pragmatism and the scientific validation of professional practices in American special education. *Disability and Society, 14*(6), 733–51.

Danforth, S. & Gabel, S. (Eds.). (2007). *Vital questions for disabilities studies in education*. New York, NY: Peter Lang.

Ferguson, P. M. (2002). Notes toward a history of hopelessness: Disability and the places of therapeutic failure. *Disability, Culture and Education, 1*(1), 27–40.

Ferri, B. A. & Connor, D. J. (2005). Tools of exclusion: Race, disability, and (re)segregated education. *Teachers College Record, 107*(3), 453–74.

Flynn, J. R. (2000). The hidden history of IQ and special education: Can the problems be solved? *Journal of Psychology, Public Policy, & Law, 6*(1), 191–8.

Gabel, S. (Ed.). (2007). *Disability studies in education: Readings in theory and method*. New York, NY: Peter Lang.

Gabel, S., Curcic, S., Powell, J., Khader, K., & Albee, L. (2009). Migration and ethnic group disproportionality in special education: An exploratory study. *Disability & Society, 24*(5), 625–39.

Gallagher, D. J., Heshusius, L., Iano, P., & Skrtic, T. M. (2003). *Challenging orthodoxy in special education*. Denver, CO: Love Publishing.

Gartner, A. & Lipsky, D. K. (1987). Beyond special education: Toward a system of quality for all students. *Harvard Educational Review, 57*(4), 367–95.

Gould, S. J. (1981). *The mismeasure of man*. New York, NY: W. W. Norton & Company.

Harry, B. & Klingner, J. (2006). *Why are so many minority students in special education?* New York, NY: Teachers College.

Hayes, J. & Hannold, E. M. (2007). The road to empowerment: A historical perspective on the medicalization of disability. *Journal of Health and Human Services, 30*(3), 352–77.

Hehir, T. (2005). *New directions in special education: Eliminating ableism in policy and practice*. Cambridge, MA: Harvard Education Press.

Iano, R. P. (1990). Special education teachers: Technicians or educators? *Journal of Learning Disabilities, 23*(8), 462–65.

Linton, S. (1998). *Claiming disability*. New York, NY: New York University Press.

National Center for Education Statistics. (2016). Fast facts. Retrieved from https://nces.ed.gov/fastfacts/display.asp?id=59

Oliver, M. (1996). *Understanding disability: From theory to practice.* New York, NY: St. Martin's Press.

Skrtic, T. M. (1991). *Behind special education: A critical analysis of professional culture and school organization.* Denver, CO: Love Publishing.

Wendell, S. (2001). Unhealthy disabled: Treating chronic illness as disabilities. *Hypatia, 16*(2), 17–33.

Acknowledgments

We offer special thanks to:

Alex Masulis, Lauren Frankfurt, and Misha Kydd for the production of this book.

Dr. Linda Ware for contributing a foreword.

Sarah Bickens, Fran Bittman, Colleen Cruz, Jody Buckles, Kristin Fallon, Kate Garnett, Jen Taets, and Rob van Voorst for their classroom-based contributions.

María Cioe-Peña, Kristen Goldmansour, David Hernández-Saca, Diane Linder Berman, Keriann Martin, Jonathan Mooney, Louis Olander, Jody Polleck, Meric Gulum Weinkle, and Carrie C. Snow for sharing their words of wisdom and expertise as "featured voices."

Lastly, Jan would like to thank Paul Valle for his technological assistance, and David would like to thank his family and friends for their support.

Part I
How Knowledge Guides Practice

1 Making Sense of Public School Culture and Context

"Why didn't somebody tell me that teaching is so complicated?"

Cartoon #1 The juggler

Given that you are reading this textbook, you are most likely approaching your first year of teaching, or perhaps you already are experiencing (or have recently experienced) the rite of passage through which all first-year teachers must pass. If you want to start a lively conversation among veteran teachers, wander into the teachers' lounge and ask your colleagues what they remember about their first year of teaching. Be prepared to sit and stay awhile. Notice how your colleagues bond over the retellings of their early days of teaching. Surviving the first year of teaching is akin to an initiation rite—a feat confirming one's worthiness for membership into hallowed ranks—in this case, the teaching profession. What is one of the best parts of being a first-year teacher? Knowing that you are only a first-year teacher *once*.

Yet experienced teachers, ourselves included, also look back on that first year of teaching with a blend of sweet nostalgia and pragmatic appraisal of our younger selves in the classroom. For most of us, our very first students are unforgettable. They are, after all, the original cast in the long-running production of our teaching careers. From our vantage point in the present, it is tempting to reminisce about the "good old days" when we were both young and eager to change the world…but we will spare you our memories that, we admit, are polished by the passage of time, and instead reassure you that your first year of teaching likely is typical of most people's who enter the profession.

It is natural to feel overwhelmed during your first year of teaching. Right about now, you are probably wondering why your teacher education program failed to instruct you in traffic management (e.g., bus duty, carpool supervision, monitoring hallway and cafeteria activity), business strategies (e.g., organizing and managing field trips, fund-raising activities, materials fee collection), office skills (e.g., collection, analysis, and storage of assessment data; student file maintenance; general record-keeping; special education paperwork; phone, text, and e-mail correspondence; classroom website maintenance); human resources (e.g., collaborating with colleagues, administrators, and paraprofessionals; responding to and engaging with parents and caregivers; creating warm relationships with school secretaries, custodians, lunchroom staff, and security officers). Need we go on? As you have no doubt concluded on your own, teaching is a complex act that requires constant shifting among multiple and simultaneous skill sets—not all of which are, or can be, taught in schools of education.

And if it is not enough to think about all of the above (while you are, of course, constructing curriculum, organizing your classroom, delivering motivating lessons, establishing and sustaining classroom routines, meeting the academic and social needs of all students, preparing students for standardized assessments, reflecting thoughtfully on your classroom practice, and exercising self-restraint toward friends, family, and strangers who suggest that teaching is a breeze because of all the vacation days), we are about to ask that you consider the historical, political, and social stage upon which public education takes place, how the role of teacher is played, and the material consequences (intended and unintended) for *all* students performing in our national drama of schooling.

The Historical Complexity of Public Schools

Surely a ritual ought to occur that officially marks the transition of Student to Teacher—a ritual apart from successful completion of student teaching or college graduation. After all, it is a passage to "the other side" of sorts. Among the benefits awaiting on "the other side" is freedom of access to formerly forbidden territory, such as the teachers' lounge, student records, parent–teacher conferences, the teacher lunch table, faculty meetings, the teacher workroom, and the storage closet. Whatever the myriad reasons are that inspire us to become teachers, we share the headiness that comes with legitimate border crossing into Teacher Territory for the very first time. Once on the inside, new teachers find answers to questions long held ("So *this* is what teachers do in here!") or confirmation of old suspicions ("I *knew* they talked about students!").

For others, border crossing represents a kind of loss of innocence brought on by close exposure to the humanness and foibles of teachers. As teacher educators, we are privy to the reactions and reflections of new teachers regarding their work in public schools. Certainly, we hear positive reports from the field. Yet, most new teachers also experience varying degrees of incongruity between their idealism and the realities of public schools. They might question administrative responses to students and their families that "don't feel right" or feel uncomfortable when colleagues label their beliefs about children as naïve and temporary. And in speaking about such struggles, they inevitably muse, "You know, it's never about the kids—it's all this *other* stuff!" It seems that the complex, and often contradictory, *context* within which teachers work is anything but stress-free.

Remember those foundation courses you took at the beginning of your education program? You know—courses that covered topics such as the history of public schools in American society, political and legislative aspects of public education, issues in urban education, and the like? If that material did not seem particularly relevant then, now might be the time to reread those textbooks and articles (as well as those copious notes you no doubt took) to shed light on the complexity of school culture. Okay, maybe you *might* not have the time right now to dig through your college boxes (or perhaps you sold those textbooks back to the university bookstore long ago), so we offer a critical (albeit brief!) historical review of public education as a reminder of the major points to consider about "all that *other* stuff."

The Purpose of Public Education

Every reader of this text has a personal narrative about what led him or her to choose the teaching profession. Some of us, inspired by teachers who opened some aspect of the world that forever changed our lives, wish to ignite passion for learning among students. Others of us may be motivated by negative school experiences and commit ourselves to making a positive difference in the lives of children. Whatever particularity of experience led to entering the profession, it is reasonable to assume that teachers generally do so because of a genuine devotion to the nurturance of children and commitment to the ideals of education.

Enter the new teacher. Freshly graduated. Brimming with the latest theories of child development and instruction. Eager to guide and inspire all children to achieve beyond what they believe is possible. Committed to making a difference in the world. Surely the context into which the new teacher is about to step corresponds to such ideals. The stage is set with the accoutrements of schooling—tables, bookshelves, chairs, computers, maps, smartboard, books, bulletin boards—all awaiting the entrance of the principal actor who will make this set come alive. What could be afoot in this benign setting where teachers and students meet to do their work? Plenty. And most of it unseen and unspoken.

Most new teachers survey their very first classrooms and imagine the future they will construct there. They see a neutral canvas upon which they will paint their best dreams and hopes for children. Yet the context of schooling is anything but neutral. That classroom, like all other classrooms in America, is deeply embedded within a *culture* that is public education. And like all other cultures, public education has been and continues to be shaped by patterns of human activity and social structures that embody its history, beliefs, attitudes, practices, and values. Understanding "all that *other* stuff" requires acknowledgement of and awareness about the ways in which this culture actively influences everyday life in schools.

Let's start with a seemingly simple question. What is the purpose of public education? An obvious answer might be that public education is the means by which a civilized society uses public funds to teach its young people the academic and social skills necessary to become responsible, productive, and self-fulfilled citizens. Certainly, public education is one of the major cornerstones of our democracy. Textbooks have long referred to America as "the melting pot"—a land of opportunity for *all* people. And undeniably, a free public education is one of America's greatest opportunities. Given that teachers participate in the legacy of one of America's greatest opportunities, why do they continue to report disillusionment and frustration? Perhaps we can more clearly understand where we are if we return for a moment to where we came from—in other words, how did we get here from there?

How We Got Here from There

Consider the historical context within which compulsory schooling originated during the early twentieth century. Despite romanticized notions of "the melting pot of America" described in history textbooks, the dominant culture of the time (Anglo-Saxon Protestant) actively sought to preserve itself within what was rapidly becoming a diverse and sputtering societal stew (Kliebard, 1995). By 1918, all states had passed compulsory schooling laws. Recognizing the potential of compulsory schooling for creating a common citizenry, reformers targeted public education as a *means* by which to preserve the position and values of the dominant culture. Thus, the arena of public education became "part and parcel of a national morality play in which those hopes and fears were enacted" (ibid., p. 291). It is worth noting that political and social agendas became embodied early on within the institution of public education—a pattern, we might point out, that is unmistakable in the current context of public education.

Let's revisit the social, political, and economic landscape of early twentieth-century America. Major population shifts occur as industry lures rural citizens into urban areas. Overtaxed cities strain to accommodate the heavy influx of immigrants as well as social and economic challenges. Science penetrates American society giving rise to "scientific management" of factories, a new class of scientific professionals, and scientific study of human beings. American nationalism increases in the aftermath of World War I, heightening suspicion and distrust of immigrant populations as well as governmental targeting of political radicalism. Industrial democracy theories emerge that promise greater control over workers. Low-status groups, such as African-Americans and Indigenous peoples, face an increasingly hostile society that controls access to cultural and economic collateral (Anderson, 1988).

So where does public education figure into this historical landscape? In response to the complexity and multiplicity of social issues in the early twentieth century, public education is conceptualized as a social institution through which to enculturate the nation's young (immigrant children in particular) into the dominant culture. How to accomplish enculturation, however, becomes the subject of intense debate among four major interest groups with differing ideas on curriculum: *humanists* (supporters of a classical education in the tradition of the Western canon), *developmentalists* (advocates for curriculum grounded in the new science of child development), *social meliorists* (champions of schools as agencies of social change), and *social efficiency experts* (proponents of operating schools by industry principles) (Kliebard, 1995). In the end, no single group controls the American curriculum; however, it is noteworthy that social efficiency emerges as a major and long-lasting influence upon public education. Indeed, the footprints left by social efficiency experts explain much of the taken-for-granted assumptions and values that circulate within schools today. As you read on, you might recognize vestiges of social efficiency lingering within your own school context.

The Factory Model of Education

Let's consider the early twentieth-century milieu in which science and industry reign supreme. Social efficiency proponents, influenced by mechanical engineer Frederic Taylor, who applied scientific methods to industrial management, believe that scientific rationality and technology are the answer to public education. Drawing upon Taylor's notions of scientific task analysis and scientific training of individual workers to perform industry tasks according to ability, social efficiency proponents likewise support school curriculum designed to educate each class of individuals according to their *predicted* social and vocational roles. Public schools embrace the factory model as an efficient response to educating the nation's diverse student population (Mondale, 2002). Thus, we see perhaps the first instance of business principles applied to public school management—an application, we shall see, that has significant material consequences for certain groups of children.

But how might predictions be made about a student's future social and vocational place in society? Enter the emerging field of mental measurement at the turn of the twentieth century. Intelligence testing provides the scientific technology for classifying children according to ability. These classifications, in turn, give rise to a differentiated curriculum with five educational tracks ranging from accelerated to atypical. A report for the National Society for the Study of Education in 1924, for example, provides evidence of curriculum adaptation for gifted children (e.g., special classes, grade skipping, enrichment, acceleration). At the opposite end of the educational spectrum, low-performing students (labeled "backward children") are segregated into ungraded classes for drill and skill instruction (Kliebard, 1995).

It is worth considering for whom social efficiency yields the least social and educational benefit. Immigrant children, unable to adequately demonstrate their native capacity for learning because of language and cultural barriers, are placed disproportionately in slow-track classes. Girls, regardless of ability, are tracked into the curriculum to prepare them for a domestic role in society. By far the most marginalized groups are children of African-Americans and Indigenous peoples. Fueled by "scientific evidence" proffered by social Darwinists, members of the dominant culture regard these two groups as inferior and primitive races who require segregated education outside the realm of public schooling. Thus, segregated schools (such as the Hampton Normal and Agricultural Institute, for African Americans, and the Carlisle Indian Industrial School, for Indigenous peoples) train students to adopt the Protestant work ethic in preparation for their subordinate roles in society (Fraser, 2014).

We Said All That to Say This

What goes on inside public schools reflects the social and political climate on the outside—a phenomenon established from the inception of public schools and maintained throughout their history. If you were reading the discussion of the factory model with an eye on your current context, you might have sensed a familiarity among some of the now *century-old* issues, such as reliance on "scientific" assessment of children, "efficient" sorting of students according to ability, and the intended or unintended marginalization of students deemed "diverse." As suggested earlier in this chapter, public education can be understood as a culture shaped by patterns of human activity and by social structures that embody its history, beliefs, attitudes, practices, and values. What happened in the past lingers, to one degree or another, in the present culture of public schools. It is also worth considering how inhabitants of public schools experience the winds of political and social change within their everyday context. How might children understand the impact of such issues upon their school experience? Or do they notice at all?

If, for example, I (Jan) reflect back upon my own experiences as a white, middle-class American public school student, what stands out most about my primary grade years is the intensifying crisis between the United States and Cuba during the early 1960s. Along with exposure to television commercials featuring modern conveniences for bomb shelters and interruptions of television programming intended to refresh the public on what to do in case of an "emergency" (i.e., a nuclear missile headed our way), American school-children of this era regularly practiced diving under desks at the directive of teachers. As I huddled under my desk with skinned knees up to my chin, I wondered if my teacher really believed wooden desks were a reliable means of nuclear protection, but it was simply less frightening to believe that she did.

Beyond routine safety drills, the Cold War insinuated itself into the American school curriculum. My first-grade teacher reverently passed out our New Math textbooks. I do not remember the particulars of our introduction to New Math, but I came away with the vague idea that New Math was the means by which we would fend off the Russians. Thus, in a post-Sputnik era, world politics landed in my first-grade classroom along with the directive to master math and science skills as our active contribution to the space race (i.e., world domination). It seemed that learning New Math was what I could do for America.

By the time I reached junior high school, the defining feature of my public education became desegregation. Perhaps no other political event had as significant an impact upon American public schools as the Supreme Court's 1954 decision to overturn *Plessy v. Ferguson*'s "separate but equal" doctrine that supported racially segregated public schools. Emerging out of the civil rights movement, *Brown v. Board of Education* challenged the legal basis for segregated schooling in Kansas as well as 20 other states. The Supreme Court declared racially segregated public schools unconstitutional and in violation of the Fourteenth Amendment, which guarantees all citizens equal protection under the law (Urban & Wagoner, 2008). As a result of this landmark decision, states were required to comply with desegregation policy "with all deliberate speed." Formal compliance, however, transpired only after years of resistance, particularly among the Southern states. Integration of most public schools in the South occurred under the Nixon administration in 1970 (Ogletree, 2004)—as was the case of the public school that I attended.

To many residents of the small Southern town where I lived at that time, desegregation represented government imposition upon an established way of life. It proved to be a contentious process that predictably evoked public fear, anger, and anxiety on both sides of the issue. School faculties were integrated first, followed by full integration of student bodies. I remember bomb threats and the sudden disappearance of white friends into hastily opened private schools. Yet, it is the silence that stands out most in my memory. Against the backdrop of one of the most significant social shifts in American history, teachers carried on the business of schooling as if what was happening was not happening. No discussion. No preparation. Awaiting the inevitable. And it came on buses. Lots of buses.

I admit that I was relieved that it was not me making the transition to an already inhabited school in a neighborhood not my own. *How must that have felt?* I was left to imagine in the sanctioned silence that separated us. Administrative efforts toward maintaining separation within integration were not lost on either faculty or students. The unspoken agenda hung heavily within our hallowed halls—Minimal Interaction Begets

Maximum Control. There were no forums and no community-building efforts. That year, there were two homecoming queens. One white. One black. There were two student councils. One white. One black.

Let's stop for a moment to consider this leg of our historical jaunt. We have just passed by several images that illustrate how social and political agendas settle heavily into the business of reading, writing, and arithmetic. Although these images reflect my experiences of American public schooling, they belong to a common history that I share with my generation of schoolmates. And that history contributes to the history of all other generations of schoolchildren, including *yours*, whose experiences make up the legacy that is American public education. As a new teacher, you are stepping knee-deep into a river of history rushing a watery past over the present and beyond. The past is a sensible place to look for clues to the present. Looking to the educational past is akin to picking through family stories to better understand who you are in the world. And in a sense, you have entered a family of educators connected through a shared history.

Given that it is not our intention to write a history of public education, we close by visiting one last stop on our historical itinerary—the origin and outcome of perhaps the greatest legislation for persons with disabilities in American history—and the focus of our textbook.

We Can Legislate Policy, but We Can't Legislate Attitude

Schools are populated by human beings who come with myriad values, cultures, ethnicities, languages, beliefs, histories, and behaviors. As illustrated in the "separation within integration" example of my early desegregation experience, legislative policy that precedes attitudinal shifts can meet insidious resistance that remains just inside the letter of the law. Despite undeniable social progress that has occurred since the early days of desegregation, there are some who maintain that the spirit of *Brown v. Board of Education* has yet to be fully realized (Minow, 2010). Perhaps it is somewhat unsurprising, then, that the landmark legislation Public Law 94–142 or *The Education for All Handicapped Children Act* (now known as the Individuals with Disabilities Education Improvement Act or IDEIA) — another example of legislative policy preceding attitudinal shifts—likewise met resistance (Ferri & Connor, 2006).

Let's return to the years preceding 1975. From the standpoint of the present, it seems rather shocking that public education was not a given for students with disabilities. While some public schools chose to offer segregated classes for students with disabilities, others did not. Private facilities served affluent parents seeking educational options. It was not uncommon for children with disabilities to remain at home. Building upon the momentum of the civil rights movement and *Brown v. Board of Education*, parents of children with disabilities and their advocates claimed violation of the Fourteenth Amendment (which guarantees all citizens equal protection under the law) and pressed for legislation that would guarantee a free and appropriate public education for *all* children. Their efforts were rewarded in 1975 when Congress passed P.L. 94–142. States were given three years to create institutional frameworks to support assessment and services for students with disabilities as outlined in the law—or face withdrawal of federal funding for public education. (Perhaps the imposed three-year limit reflects lessons learned from the earlier federal directive to integrate public schools "with all deliberate speed.")

In the fall of 1978, the year in which states were required to have implemented P.L. 94–142, I began my career as a first-year teacher in a middle school learning disability (LD) resource room. I imagined entering an educational context that embodied the spirit of the law. Instead, I met a school community—not unlike most of this era—that viewed the new law's complex requirements for institutional structures and regulations as a considerable intrusion. It was a transition marked by resentment and resistance on the part of many school administrators and teachers. Not unlike the public response to desegregation, P.L. 94–142 generated fear, anger, and anxiety among public school stakeholders, thereby begging the question: Who are American public schools *really* intended to serve, and for what purpose?

Who Belongs and How Do We Know?

Brown v. Board of Education and the Education for All Handicapped Children Act (later renamed the Individuals with Disabilities Education Improvement Act, or IDEIA) established that "separate and unequal" is unconstitutional under the Fourteenth Amendment. In other words, federal law mandates that *every* American child has the right to a free and appropriate public education. However, as established earlier in this chapter, public schools are highly politicized spaces where human beings compete for material resources as well as social and educational benefits. The persisting inequities between suburban and urban public schools are legendary. Jonathan Kozol, among the most well-known critics of public school inequality, has written prolifically on the subject (e.g., *Savage Inequalities: Children in America's Schools*, 1992; *Amazing Grace: The Lives of Children and the Conscience of a Nation*, 1995; *Ordinary Resurrections: Children in the Years of Hope*, 2000; *The Shame of the Nation: The Restoration of Apartheid Schooling in America*, 2005). And yet, Kozol's critique persists in such current works as *Inequality in the Promised Land: Race, Resources, and Suburban Schooling* (Lewis-McCoy, 2014) and *Despite the Best Intentions: How Racial Inequality Thrives in Good Schools* (Lewis & Diamond, 2015). We are not suggesting that there is some grand scheme orchestrated by members of the dominant culture to ensure their advantage over others, but rather that inequities—highly correlated with race and socioeconomic status—are naturalized within the practices of American public schooling. Let us illustrate with an example about the origins of one of IDEIA's disability categories.

The Learning Disability Phenomenon: Scientific or Political?

The history of the field of learning disabilities (LD) is well documented in college texts and educational journals. It is a history most often told as a continuous tale of scientific progress leading to the discovery of an identifiable and treatable childhood pathology. During the early to mid-twentieth century, children with seemingly "normal" intelligence who exhibited significant difficulty learning to read and write became the subject of study for ophthalmologists, neurologists, doctors, psychologists, and educators. In response to this burgeoning scientific research, the LD field was officially established in 1963 at a conference sponsored by the Fund for Perceptually Handicapped Children. Samuel Kirk, a prominent speaker at the conference, is credited with having introduced the term "learning disabilities" to differentiate children with learning difficulties from other children with disabilities (e.g., mental retardation, hearing and/or visual disabilities) (Kirk, Gallagher, & Coleman, 2014). What could possibly be afoot here—after all, this is science, right?

In the years preceding the 1963 conference at which Samuel Kirk first used the term "learning disabilities," Postwar America stewed with uneasiness over the threat of communism. Following the successful launch of Sputnik in 1957, the steadily mounting competition for control of worldwide military and business interests intensified between the United States and the Soviet Union, as did the idea that American schools must prioritize education for the academically gifted, who will become our nation's scientific, business, and technological leaders (Spring, 2002). In 1957, Rear Admiral H.G. Rickover informed the nation that it was an urgent matter of national security to raise educational standards and implement a tracking system to provide a *specific* kind of education for students of *specific* ability levels (e.g., college-bound, general, slow), with the most talented teachers being assigned to the college-bound track (Rickover, 1959). Thus, it quickly became natural within American public education to track students according to ability and to assign the highest value to gifted and college-bound students.

Within the naturalized idea that students can and should be sorted within the ranks of bright, average, and slow is the assumption that not all students will meet average educational standards. To explain this "necessary" failure, educators of the 1960s identified deficiencies within children and/or their home environments to construct four student categories—the mentally retarded, the slow learner, the emotionally disturbed, and the culturally deprived. As Sleeter (1986) points out, these four categories explain school failure of "minority" children from disadvantaged backgrounds but leave unexplained why some white middle-class children are not able to keep pace with higher academic standards. Thus, "learning disabilities" was created as a category to explain school failure when explanations of mental, emotional, or cultural deficiency did not fit. Compared with other labels for low achievers, the label of "learning disabilities," applied more often to white middle-class children who struggled academically, affirmed intellectual "normalcy" and innate potential for academic success (ibid.).

Perhaps a more accurate rendering of the birth of the LD field is one that accounts for the *interaction* between the educational discourse of the day and newly available scientific information. In other words, might it also be possible that white middle-class parents of the early 1960s drew upon the latest medical research—namely, a neurological condition called a learning disability—to offer educators an explanation for why their children (considered to be among those students *expected* to perform well) were unable to meet increased standards? This is not to say that white middle-class parents consciously sought a distinction that would set their academically struggling children apart from others; however, we might acknowledge that white middle-class parents possessed the social and cultural capital that enabled them to: (1) avail themselves of the latest medical research; (2) seek out and pay for private diagnostic services; (3) garner the attention of educators regarding this newly identified neurologically-based learning problem; and (4) expect school personnel to regard their academically struggling children as capable of obtaining an educational level and occupation at least commensurate with the family's current socioeconomic status. It is worth noting that the majority of students identified as learning disabled between 1963 and 1973 were, in fact, white and middle class or higher.

We offer you this example not to challenge the biological basis of learning disabilities, but rather to illustrate the complex nature of public schools and the people who inhabit them. The moment teachers step into this context, they begin to engage with the "world already there"—the history, politics, economics, race/culture, social stratification, language, values, and belief systems tightly woven into the intricate tapestry that is American public school. You know—"all that *other* stuff" about which our students routinely lament? *This* is that "stuff"—ever present and mostly unnamed.

Special Education: A Parallel System

With the 1975 passage of P.L. 94–142 (now known as IDEIA), a free and appropriate public education was guaranteed for *all* children. Public schools could no longer choose to educate only children without disabilities. Now *everyone* belongs. Well, sort of. Central to IDEIA is the notion of least restrictive environment (LRE) for students with disabilities. The LRE means that, to the greatest extent possible, students with disabilities are educated with their non-disabled peers, given access to the general education curriculum as well as noncurricular activities, and provided with services and supplementary aids as needed to achieve at a level commensurate with non-disabled peers. A continuum of service options is also available to meet the learning and social needs of those students whose severity of disability may necessitate a more restrictive environment than a general education setting. Decisions regarding the most appropriate student placement are made by parents and school personnel in collaboration.

As noted elsewhere, I began teaching in 1978—the same year that states were required to implement P.L. 94–142. Although students with disabilities won the right to a free and appropriate public education in the least restrictive environment, I observed during those early years that not all school administrators, teachers, or parents of children without disabilities agreed that students with disabilities *belonged* in general education classrooms. In my role as a middle school resource teacher, I saw each of my students in the resource room for one class period a day. Despite spending the other six class periods in general education classrooms, these students were routinely referred to by most teachers as "Jan's kids" (as if I were hosting some sort of unending school telethon), reflecting the belief that it was I alone who was responsible for their education. At that time, it was not uncommon for a teacher to dismiss collaborative efforts on my part with some iteration of the following: "I did not go to school to teach children with disabilities. If I had wanted to do that, I would have majored in special education." Allow me to fill in the unspoken implication: "Therefore, it is your job and not mine."

Having experienced public school desegregation, I recognized a strikingly similar response to the integration of students with disabilities. As required by law, school districts erected the infrastructure that would support special education. Yet little to no preparation of teachers and students occurred at the school level. No discussion. Awaiting the inevitable. And it came again on buses. Small yellow minibuses.

As the institution of special education moved into public schools and "set up shop," a cadre of professionals followed—special education teachers, school psychologists, special education paraprofessionals, speech/language pathologists, special education administrators, physical and occupational therapists, and special education clerks. Materials purchased with federal dollars allotted for special education were indelibly marked P.L. 94–142 and designated for use *only* with students identified as disabled. Special education classrooms opened within school buildings and took over book closets, auditorium stages, library reading rooms, and unused basement spaces. Small villages of portable special education classrooms dotted the backs of school properties.

Reminiscent of the "separation within integration" phenomenon of my public school years, students with disabilities were integrated into general education classrooms if they demonstrated the ability to perform like students *without* disabilities—a practice called "mainstreaming" (see Chapter 2); otherwise, they were placed in segregated classrooms where their "special needs" could be met through the expertise of "special" teachers and "special" instructional materials. Again, we are not suggesting that there was any conscious strategy on the part of school personnel to exclude students with disabilities. Rather, school personnel, operating out of long-held cultural beliefs about children with disabilities being qualitatively different from children without disabilities, conceptualized the newly implemented special education system as the place where students with disabilities *belonged*—essentially a parallel system of education.

In retrospect, it seems that such a response to special education might have been anticipated, given that the law's implementation preceded any large-scale attitudinal shifts or increased understanding about disabilities among public school personnel. Rather predictably, research began to mount regarding negative academic and social outcomes for students in segregated classrooms (see Chapter 2). Inclusive philosophies and practices eventually emerged to bring support services to the general education environment in lieu of segregation—an approach to students with disabilities that is the focus of this book.

Back to the Present

Look around at your current school context. You do not need us to point out that you are teaching in the Age of Standards and Accountability—an era that gained momentum during the 1990s. By 2002, President Bush had signed the education law, No Child Left Behind (NCLB), that enforced the most intense surveillance of student and teacher performance in the history of public education. NCLB (2002–2015) extended the reach of Washington into American classrooms with a national system for evaluating schools based on math and reading test scores and required schools to raise scores every year or endure intensifying consequences (e.g., school closures). Remember the first application of business principles to public education during the early twentieth century when public schools adopted the factory model? There is no mistaking a second wave of business principles applied to public education during the NCLB era. To meet escalating standards, many school districts around the country looked to young Ivy Leaguers with MBAs to "save us from ourselves" by bringing the practices and language of corporate America to public school administration.

In the middle of the NCLB era, growing concern arose among politicians and business leaders regarding America's capacity for competition in a global economy. In 2009, the Common Core State Standards (CCSS), a public education initiative sponsored by the Council of Chief State School Offices (CCSSO) and the National Governor's Association (NGA), emerged as a voluntary program for states with two major goals: (1) to prepare college and career-ready graduates by emphasizing reasoning and critical thinking within school curricula; and (2) to align high standard public education across the states (Layton, 2015). Although CCSS sets common standards for schools across the country, states and local districts choose their own curricula and materials to achieve the standards (Linnell-Olsen, 2018). To motivate state adoption, the United States Department of Education offered competitive federal grants under its Race to the Top initiative to states that proposed educational reforms (including but not limited to college and career-ready standards) as well as waivers from NCLB requirements for states willing to adopt reforms consistent with Race to the Top (Peterson, Barrows, & Gift, 2016)—tactics that prompted outcries from teachers' unions. Public concerns soon emerged regarding federal intrusion into states' rights, the Bill and Melinda Gates Foundation's role in bankrolling CCSS and its subsequent partnership with Pearson to develop and market K-12 materials aligned with CCSS, the nature of standards to reinforce official myths and ignore diverse perspectives, the cost of training and materials, no pilot testing of standards, inadequate input from teachers in creating standards (Karp, 2013/ 2014) ... and so the century-old struggle for control over American public school curriculum persists. Despite its controversy, CCSS was adopted by 40 states and the District of Columbia in 2010, with five more states joining shortly thereafter. As of 2017, eight states have repealed CCSS and 21 states have made revisions or are in the process of revising the standards.

In 2015, the era of NCLB ended when President Obama signed a new K-12 education law, the Every Student Succeeds Act (ESSA), shifting responsibility for school accountability from the federal government back to the states. Although ESSA retains requirements to test students annually in reading and math (grades 3–8) and once during high school, as well as to publicly share test scores according to race, ethnicity, socio-economic status, disability, and language, the states now bear responsibility for responding to underperforming schools, developing holistic forms of accountability, and evaluating teachers. For the time being, standards and accountability appear to be part of the foreseeable future. However, it is worth noting that there is a growing movement among parents to exercise an "opt out" option that releases their test-weary children from standardized assessments (McArdle, 2014).

So how might current students experience the high-stakes testing that defines their public school education? Even the youngest of children appreciate tests as something curiously important to adults. They quickly understand that test performance has something to do with the way in which other people—namely, teachers and peers—think about them. We routinely overhear children in New York City public schools refer to themselves and others as 1s, 2s, 3s, or 4s (referencing standardized test scores)—reflecting not only the internalization of these rankings but also the *value* attributed to the scores. Given the increased attention to "minority populations" under both NCLB and ESSA, English Language Learners as well as students with disabilities experience both intended and unintended consequences of heightened surveillance. It is worth noting that, within a climate of intense accountability, students are likely to become positioned, to one degree or another, as more or less desirable.

As teacher educators, we regularly engage in conversations with public school teachers about their daily work. We hear concerns about the time and energy directed toward formal assessment (see Chapter 8) as well as the capacity of standardized measures to reflect academic growth of children as individuals within local contexts. Some of our new teachers tell us that experienced teachers admit to choosing grade levels in which less formal assessment is required. We might ask ourselves what might result from the least experienced teachers working in grade levels requiring the most extensive formal assessment. Still others acknowledge resistance to co-teaching in inclusive classrooms (see Chapter 4) for fear that test scores of students with disabilities might reflect poorly on their teaching. Clearly, the context within which teachers do their daily work can be described as anything *but* neutral.

Featured Voice of Carrie C. Snow

A View from Inside School Conformity and Democracy

Supporting Autistic Youth

Public schooling straddles at least two opposing poles: conformity and democracy. Its structures demand both compliance to well-established rules and norms, and engage a dream that, in gathering communities of divergent youth, we invest our future with elemental and essential tools for getting along in the world—learning to be with and work with people who come to school representing very different life experiences.

As a system that is rooted in order and rule-following, public schools can be awfully challenging places to be autistic; or to be any person who finds it difficult to control impulses, to do things in a way that is not uniquely of his or her own conception or in ways that offer the stimulus (i.e., tactile, mobile, visual) one needs to feel his or her best self. I have found in my years of teaching autistic youth[1] that it is imperative to use various means of support that enable attentive participation in school. Sometimes, for autistic youth, the order and rule-following predicate of public schooling can be a nice fit, provided other qualities are in place. Because many youth, and very frequently autistic youth, show an affinity for routine and predictable experience, the structure that is inherent to public schooling can be used to scaffold students' learning and experience. Teacher support of autistic youth takes creativity, flexibility, collaboration, and the ability to use all of our senses to tune in to the changing needs of students.

If I am to support my students in the best way I possibly can, I have to acknowledge that conformity is a central tenet of public education, but I do not need to privilege it. Rather, I steadfastly focus on the belief that public schooling is, above and beyond everything else, a driving force of democracy—insofar as democracy is defined as the equitable coming together of voices in a diverse community of people. Public schooling has a weighty role in shaping youths' most formative impressions of diversity. While I am always wary of the strong element of conformity that public schools impress, undoubtedly what holds me in the public sector is the promise and hope that students' experiences of being, playing, and learning with any child that happens to be in his or her class will culminate in a force that resonates deeper than the conforming powers that the system upholds.

Here, I share some of the elements, followed by short illustrative anecdotes, which in my experience as a teacher have supported the educational and personal growth of autistic youth within the public school system.

1. General education and special education teachers have a good, communicative, and honest relationship built on mutual respect and respect for the wellbeing of students, and use the students' special interests to guide their work.

    A general education teacher with whom I work reflects on an autistic student, Jason,[2] in her class, and his recent disagreements and physical aggression with a classmate at recess. Together, we ask Jason to use one of the dozens of musical compositions that he writes as an offering of apology to the student he'd been bothering. Jason likes the idea, chooses a composition, offers it as an apology to the student, and names the piece for him. We walk down the hallway to the music teacher's room, where the music teacher agrees to allow Jason to play the piece on the piano for the other student. Smiles emerge on both boys' faces, as well as on the music teacher's and on my own. We all leave delighted.

2. Students are given flexibility to move, process, respond in time, and make reparations later.

    Felix throws an eraser at his teacher, who sends him down to a resource room to take a break. In the resource room, Felix sits quietly with me, using a blank comic strip template to illustrate what happened leading up to the throwing of the eraser. He includes thought bubbles in his illustrations and then discusses each cell of the strip to me, in a far more detailed way than he did when I initially asked him to recount the incident. After our discussion and break, Felix returns to class calm and ready to focus on classroom learning, and apologizes to his teacher.

3. Teachers make time to individually focus on autistic youth, especially to discuss those topics that are near and dear to their hearts.

    Emeline is a quiet girl, and she rarely speaks in school. In an effort to get to know her better at the beginning of the school year, I interviewed her about the ways she sees herself as a student. Emeline was reluctant to answer most of my questions directly related to her school-based learning (i.e., "What do you think you are very good at/What do you think you still need to work on?"), and she looked down at her lap. But then we somehow fumbled upon the topic of candy. Her face lit up and she made immediate eye contact with me as she began speaking in a quick cadence, sharing how in Japan, where she often spends time, there are dozens of categories of Kit-Kat bars. Our conversation meandered from there, but centered on Japanese culture, of which I learned a lot that day. Namely, traveling to Japan in the summer months will ensure a zillion mosquito bites! Now, Emeline shares a smile and a hello with me whenever we pass in the hallways.

4. Teachers make time to nurture relationships among peers in natural settings and suit these social settings to meet students' interests.

    Mrs. Johnson runs a whole-class morning meeting for her fourth graders several times a week. The students share in a circle, first stating where they are on the mood meter, with green being calm, yellow being a bit energetic, red being frustrated or angry, and blue being a bit sad. They then share something about their week if they choose to, or simply share why they are feeling the way they are on the mood meter. Some kids share quickly and some take quite a bit of time, such as Peter, an autistic boy, who gives precise and comprehensive detail on the events of his recent trip to another state. Mrs. Johnson and the class wait patiently, until the entirety of Peter's turn. Peter then takes any questions that his classmates have, and the turn moves to the next person in the circle. Never is there a sense of hurry during this process, and over the course of the school year, I have learned a great deal about each student in that class, as a result of this enriching weekly sharing circle.

5. Adaptive measures are made universal and available to all students in a given classroom.

    It's September, and it's the beginning of third grade for Austin, whose struggle with transition and change amplifies at the beginning of any new school year. Third grade is notorious for being a huge leap in terms of the academic and behavioral demands students are expected to have mastered in the earliest elementary years. Kids know that work will get harder, and the learning postures (sitting still, not blurting out, waiting one's turn to speak, listening respectfully, keeping hands and feet to oneself, etc., etc.) are no longer expected to be a part of their learning curve. Austin jumps up from his seat, blurts out when a classmate says something he doesn't agree with, gets up at unexpected times to sharpen his pencil. His teacher, who will get to know him over the course of the year, grows frustrated, and asks him to leave the classroom to take a break.

    Later, Austin's teacher and I reflect on measures that will give Austin a chance to work with his energy in the classroom. We consult with Austin, and decide on trying a Kore stool, which allows him to swivel as he sits and completes his work; noise-cancelling headphones for quiet work time; scheduled movement breaks; and the freedom to get snacks when he's hungry. As we put these measures in place, we notice several other students who benefit from these as well, and in particular the noise-cancelling headphones. I send out a school-wide request for any unused noise-cancelling headphones, and once collected, create a box for them in Austin's classroom so that all students can benefit from their use. In addition, we obtain a Kore stool specifically for Austin, which he can take with him throughout his elementary school years. His teacher has a small collection of swivel stools for students to use on a rotating basis, and most kids look forward to their turn.

As the years tick on, these and other moments in my growing stockpile of memories allow me to work with a strong sense of assuredness that we can successfully support autistic youth to participate democratically in a system that expects a degree of conformity. The practices, routines, and strategies shared here breathe an ethos of building trust and relationship with students, teachers, and families. This ethos and the practices that illuminate it give me the confidence to say that a successfully inclusive school community, and one in which autistic youth can thrive, is one that expects difference of perspective and ways of being, anticipates learning from these diverse perspectives, and looks out for one another—and especially one another's vulnerabilities—in responsible, kind ways.

What You Believe and Why You Believe It = How You Teach

We hope that our first chapter has not sent you searching through the want ads for an easier career path. Rather, our intention is to affirm that the school context within which you teach is *predictably* complex, contradictory, and changeable—a mirror of the political, social, and economic times in which we live. Moreover, it is a context within which multiple, simultaneous, sometimes conflicting human interactions occur in every moment. Teaching is a messy business—and gloriously so. To be entrusted with the minds and souls of America's young is to accept a profound, exhilarating, and sometimes daunting privilege.

Throughout this chapter, we have noted the impact of legislation upon the everyday lives of teachers and students. We have related examples of federal policy enacted at the local level that lead us to contend that "we can legislate policy, but we can't legislate attitude." Whether or not the *spirit* of a law is carried out depends upon teachers committed to the ideals of public education in a democracy. Thus, what you believe and why you believe it has everything to do with who you are as a teacher. And who you are as a teacher has everything to do with how you think about and teach children.

It follows, then, that what teachers believe about disability determines how students with disabilities are *really* educated. Federal law creates the infrastructure and procedures for identifying and serving students with disabilities, but the spirit of this revolutionary law happens (or not) in the relationship between teacher and student. Let's consider the following example. A new fourth-grade student arrives. He has a documented learning disability. His parents bring a copy of his Individual Education Plan (IEP). Teacher A reads the IEP with an eye to how well the student will fit into her classroom. Skeptical that her classroom is the least restrictive environment (LRE) in which to meet his educational and behavioral needs, Teacher A carefully documents behaviors that support her belief that a more restrictive environment is warranted. She presents her documentation to special education staff, expressing concern that she is not the best qualified to teach this student. Teacher B reads the IEP with an eye to what the student needs to succeed in his classroom. He proactively supports the student's transition. Teacher B carefully observes the student and focuses upon developing strategies to support his inclusion within the class community. Teacher B regularly engages with the child's parents and consults with special education staff.

What is noteworthy about the preceding example is that the student with disabilities remains constant. What shifts is the *conceptualization* of that student depending upon who is looking. And *how* a teacher conceptualizes a student with disabilities has everything to do with the educational outcome for that student. What interests us as teacher educators is *when* and *where* teachers develop beliefs about disability (as well as *why*) and what these beliefs have to do with classroom practice. Having established within this chapter that public education has been and continues to be shaped by patterns of human activity and social structures, we turn now to an examination of beliefs about disability within American culture (past and present) and the impact of those beliefs upon educational outcomes for students with disabilities.

Questions to Consider

1. As a new or experienced teacher, what do you find most challenging about your school context?
2. How do *you* define the purpose of education?
3. Are vestiges of social efficiency evident within your school context? Explain.
4. Think back to your own school experience. What social and political issues impacted your education? As a child, did you notice anything about these issues within your schooling? Explain.
5. What are the most salient social and political issues today? How do you see these issues impacting your work as a teacher?
6. Do you agree with our assertion that "we can legislate policy, but we can't legislate attitude?" Why or why not?
7. What parallels do you see between racial integration in schools and the integration of students with disabilities?
8. How do you know "who belongs" in your school community? Explain.
9. How might students in your classroom understand the current political and social issues that impact schools today? How do you know?
10. Do you agree that disability can be constructed differently depending upon the viewpoint of the observer? Why or why not?

Notes

1 I use identity-first language rather than person-first language in alliance with many autism self-advocates who find autism to be a welcome and significant aspect of their identity.
2 All names are pseudonyms.

References

Anderson, J. (1988). The education of blacks in the South, 1860–1935. Chapel Hill, NC: University of North Carolina Press.

Brown v. Board of Education. (1954). 347 U.S. 483. Retrieved from https://supreme.justia.com/cases/federal/us/347/483/

Education for All Handicapped Children Act. (1975). P.L. 94–142, amending Education of the Handicapped Act, renamed Individuals with Disabilities Education Act, as amended by P.L. 98–199, P.L. 99–457, P.L. 100–630, and P.L. 100–476, 20 U.S.C., Secs. 1400–1485.

Every Student Succeeds Act (2015). P.L. 114–95, 114 Stat. 1177. Retrieved from www.congress.gov/114/plaws/publ95/PLAW-114publ95.pdf

Ferri, B. A. & Connor, D. J. (2006). *Reading resistance: Discourses of exclusion in desegregation and inclusion debates.* New York, NY: Peter Lang.

Franklin, B. M. (1987). The first crusade for learning disabilities: The movement for the education of backward children. In T. Popkewitz (Ed.), *The formation of the school subject-matter: The struggle for creating an American institution* (pp. 190–209). London: Falmer Press.

Fraser, J. (2014). *The school in the United States: A documentary history.* London: Routledge.

Karp, S. (2013/2014, Winter). The problems with the common core. *Rethinking Schools.* Retrieved from www.rethinkingschools.org/articles/the-problems-with-the-common-core

Kirk, S., Gallagher, J., & Coleman, M. R. (2014). *Educating exceptional children* (14th ed.). Boston, MA: Cengage.

Kliebard, H. M. (1995). *The struggle for the American curriculum, 1893–1958* (2nd ed.). New York, NY: Routledge.

Kozol, J. (1992). *Savage inequalities: Children in America's schools*. New York, NY: Harper Collins.

Kozol, J. (1995). *Amazing Grace: The lives of children and the conscience of a nation*. New York, NY: Harper Collins.

Kozol, J. (2000). *Ordinary resurrections: Children in the years of hope*. New York, NY: Harper Collins.

Kozol, J. (2005). *The shame of the nation: The restoration of apartheid schooling in America*. New York, NY: Three Rivers Press.

Layton, L. (2015). Obama signs new K-12 education law that ends No Child Left Behind. *Washington Post*. Retrieved from www.washingtonpost.com/local/education/obama-signs-new-k-12-education-law-that-ends-no-child-left-behind/2015/12/10/

Lewis, A. & Diamond, J. (2015). *Despite the best intentions: How racial inequality thrives in good schools*. Oxford: Oxford University Press.

Lewis-McCoy, R. L. (2014). *Inequality in the promised land: Race, resources, and suburban schooling*. Stanford, CA: Stanford University Press.

Linnell-Olsen, L. (2018). Causes of common core controversy. VeryWell Family. Retrieved from www.verywellfamily.com/causes-of-common-core-controversy-2601484

Lomawaima, K. T. (1995). Domesticity in the federal Indian schools: The power of authority over mind. In J. Terry & J. Urla (Eds.), *Deviant bodies: Critical perspectives on differences in science and popular culture* (pp.197–218). Bloomington, IN: Indiana University Press.

McArdle, E. (2014). What happened to the common core? *Harvard Education News*. Retrieved from www.gse.harvard.edu/news/ed/14/09/what-happened-common-core

Minow, M. (2010). *In Brown's wake: Legacies of America's educational landmark*. Oxford: Oxford University Press.

Mondale, S. (2002). *The story of American public education*. Boston, MA: Beacon Press.

National Governors Association Center for Best Practices & Council of Chief State School Officers. (2010). *Common core state standards*. Washington, DC: Author.

No Child Left Behind Act (2001). P.L. 107–110, 20 U.S.C. 6319, 2002. Retrieved from www.2.ed.gov/policy/elsec/leg/esea02/107-110.pdf

Ogletree, C. (2004). *All deliberate speed: Reflections on the first half century of* Brown v. Board of Education. New York, NY: W.W. Norton.

Peterson, P., Barrows, S., & Gift, T. (2016). After common core, states set rigorous standards. Education Next. Retrieved from http://educationnext.org/after-common-core-states-set-rigorous-standards

Rickover, H. G. (1959). *Education and freedom*. New York, NY: E.P. Dutton.

Rousmaniere, K. (1997). *City teachers: Teaching and school reform in historical perspective*. New York, NY: Teachers College Press.

Sleeter, C. E. (1986). Why is there learning disabilities? The social construction of a special education Category. *Exceptional Children, 53*(1), 46–54.

Sleeter, C. E. (1987). Why is there learning disabilities? A critical analysis of the birth of the field in social context. In T. Popkewitz (Ed.), *The formation of the school subject-matter: The struggle for creating an American institution* (pp. 210–37). London: Falmer Press.

Spring, J. H. (2002). *Conflict of interests: The politics of American education* (4th ed.). New York, NY: McGraw-Hill Education.

Urban, W. & Wagoner, J. (2008). *American education: A history*. London: Routledge.

2 Contemplating the (In)visibility of Disability

"Why can't I remember going to school with kids with disabilities or having a teacher with a disability?"

Cartoon #2 Everywhere and nowhere: The (in)visible disabled

Depending upon when and where you were born, the answers to the question posed beneath the title of this chapter may differ significantly. I (David) was born in the United Kingdom and attended school from the mid-1960s through the end of the 1970s. I remember few children with disabilities. For example, there was Kelvin,[1] who was transferred to a segregated setting in sixth grade, a place called the Glebe School. In hindsight, I recall him as cognitively impaired. Yet, to that point, he participated in all classes, played sports with everyone, ate lunch with us, and hung out. The school to which he was sent was ridiculed as a place for "stupid' students. In local terms, to be referred to as "a Glebe" was the ultimate put-down. There was also Chrissie, nicknamed "Dumb-dumb," who had difficulty socializing. There was Daniel, slow in all content areas and chronically asthmatic, making him one of the last to be picked for a sports team. Finally, there were two girls with twisted limbs that required the use of permanent leg braces ("calipers"). The first, Deidre, attended our school from day one. The second, Mary, transferred at age 16 from a private school for her last two years.

Becoming an educator who specializes in working with students with disabilities has often made me think of my former peers. I did not hear about Kelvin again until many years later at a high school reunion, when his sister asked why he had not been invited. The truth was that everyone had forgotten him, even though he still lived in the same community. When recalling Chrissie, I cringe at the way most people teased her before leaving her alone much of the time. Daniel drifted through school, largely accepted by our peer group as he came from a large family of tough brothers who always looked out for him. However, he did miss a lot of his education, and this meant Daniel always stayed in the lower academic track. Occasionally when I visit back home, I bump into Deidre and Mary, both of whom are now married with children.

While these memories may appear substantial, bear in mind that my recollections span 12 years of school experience, meaning that I can count the number of students with disabilities on my fingers (on one hand). If students with disabilities account for approximately 15 percent of the population, where were the others? Since then, of course, major laws have been passed in the United States and the United Kingdom that provide children with disabilities access and support (discussed in the section of this chapter titled "A Brief History of Disability in American Public Schools"). Students formerly overlooked, neglected, and/or placed in segregated settings now have the right to be educated with their non-disabled peers. Yet, despite legislative efforts, many students with disabilities still remain in segregated settings.

On a related note, I do not recall any teachers with a disability except one. She had curvature of the spine, and—in the shameless world of high school—was unkindly nicknamed Quasimodo. Once again, given the numbers of people with disabilities in society, I ponder the absence of teachers with visible disabilities. Where were/are role models for students with and without disabilities?

Disability and Society

We begin by foregrounding personal memories because they reflect the relative absence of people with disabilities in general education classes. By absence, we refer not only to an underrepresented physical presence in classrooms (as teachers or students), but also to the absence of realistic representation within the school curriculum and, perhaps more significantly, within society at large.

This chapter addresses four broad but related areas of interest. First, in order to provide a greater context for the work of inclusion, we look at the often-hidden histories of people with disabilities as we believe this helps undergird a human rights approach to inclusive education. We then look at common perceptions of disability and compare them to the lived experiences of people with disabilities in our society, thereby challenging cultural assumptions and widespread misperceptions that often stereotype people with disabilities. Next, we examine representations of disability found in everyday artifacts of popular culture (e.g., books, films, television, charities, news media, superstitions, language) and contrast such understandings with representations from within "disability culture." After that, we briefly trace the history of the education of students with disabilities in the U.S., highlighting the parental advocacy that led to legislation which would change the structure and practices of public schools. Here, we also discuss the problematic growth of special education as a place rather than a service, the growth of disability labeling, and the counter-movement of inclusive education that has challenged these phenomena. Last, we explore unintended consequences of the special education system through an overview of research that points to troubling outcomes for students with disabilities, such as the persistent overrepresentation of students of color in segregated special education classes, social and academic stigma, inaccessibility to the general education curriculum, low graduation rates, and adult underemployment and unemployment.

Some Mysteries of Histories

The history of people with disabilities is complex and just beginning to be (re)claimed. For many cultures around the world, from ancient Mesopotamia to the present, a child with a disability represents displeasure of the gods. In ancient Greece, disabled infants were left in deserted locations to die—an act of returning them to the deities. Within influential texts such as the Bible, most people with disabilities were outcasts who were cured and redeemed as a way of glorifying God. Disability therefore signified a status of not being fully human, displeasing God, and/or being touched by evil. For example, deaf people were believed to be unable to enter the Kingdom of Heaven because they were unable to hear the word of the Lord; people with epilepsy were believed to be possessed by devils (Stiker, 1999). The attribution of less-than-human status, subsequent marginalization, and the belief that eradication of disabled people "serves the better good" echoes throughout the centuries from ancient to modern times.

In the twentieth century, such beliefs became embodied within the eugenics movements in the United States and Europe. Proponents of eugenics actively promoted the notion that selective breeding would yield a healthier and stronger American population by encouraging "fit" classes to procreate while curtailing procreation within "unfit" classes through involuntary sterilization and/or institutionalization (O'Brien, 2011). During the rise of eugenics, many groups were deemed "unfit" and the cause of social problems (e.g., the poor, the mentally ill, persons with physical, sensory and/or cognitive dis/abilities criminals, prostitutes, epileptics, and immigrants). By the turn of the twentieth century, however, it was "feebleminded" persons in particular who became the target of social control "as the presumptive primary source of dysgenic evil within society" (O'Brien & Bundy, 2009, p. 156). Influenced by the practices of American eugenicists, leaders in Nazi Germany initiated approximately 400,000 sterilizations between 1934 and 1937, among them people with mental illnesses, physical and sensory disabilities, and alcoholism (Shapiro, 1994). By 1939, "under the ruse of compassion and mercy for the physically and mentally disabled" (Childress, 2003, p. 162), Hitler escalated from sterilization to the unthinkable large scale T-4 euthanasia program intended to "free Germany and the Third Reich of disabled people" (Grue, 2010, p. 33).

It is important to recognize that, in the wake of American eugenics, scientific paternalism continued to dominate how the public understood disabled bodies. Well into the latter half of the twentieth century, disabled persons were routinely placed into institutions run by the state. Michael Grossberg (2011) describes the era of "disability as personal responsibility" as follows:

> Most critically, all of the initiatives in the era remained based on a medical model that defined disability as an individual failing. Consequently, even as the focus of policies drifted from protecting society from the feebleminded to protecting families from their own offspring, intellectually disabled children remained objects of fear and apprehension and thus subjects of segregation and other exclusionary policies of protection.
>
> (p. 746)

In brief, the history of disability is intimately connected to many forms of exclusion manifest in families, communities, and, in extreme cases, death. Even today, socially sanctioned medical practices encourage termination of fetuses determined to have Down syndrome, while advocates with Down syndrome assert their basic right to life—rejecting the majority consensus of able-bodied people that a person is better off dead than disabled.

Disability Rights Movement

When teaching disability history, we most often find that students have no awareness whatsoever about the disability rights movement in the United States. Born decades after the Vocational Rehabilitation Act of 1973 as well as the Americans with Disabilities Act of 1990, most students do not know that curb cuts did not always exist and they do so now as a result of activism to gain disability access. After being shown news clips of demonstrations by disabled activists barricading buildings, out of their wheelchairs lying on the streets, or crawling awkwardly up the steep steps of inaccessible buildings to make a public statement, students are bewildered that they have never heard of the disability rights movement, unclear as to why it was never taught in schools along with other civil rights movements of the same historical era.

Soon after deinstitutionalization and the rise of the independent living movement, disabled activists and their allies changed the conversation from *the individual burden of disability* to one about *disability as a public issue* "dedicated to such goals as physical accessibility of buildings and transit systems, community-based services, access to education and work, and the right to vote and make medical decisions" (Richards, 2009).

While space limitations prohibit an extensive analysis of disability history here, and we make some suggestions in Chapter 9 about ways to teach about the disability rights movement, we do encourage readers interested in this area to explore the website of the University of California, Berkley for information on the Disability Rights and Independent Living Movement (http://bancroft.berkeley.edu/collections/drilm). Audio-recordings of pioneers of the disability rights movement are available on the website; thus, visitors have the opportunity to listen to first-person narratives of disability and begin to construct understanding of what it means to be disabled within our culture. Additionally, the Smithsonian's online exhibit (http://americanhistory.si.edu/disabilityrights/welcome.html) features memorabilia in the form of t-shirts, bumper stickers, posters, and badges, together with photographs from the dis/ability rights movement.

(Re)claiming Disability

While much of the subsequent content of this chapter calls attention to ways in which disability is present yet unseen, often in derogatory and marginalizing ways, it is important to highlight that disability historians have studied the topic from alternative perspectives, framing issues in new and insightful ways (see Box 2.1). In addition, disability activists have made major contributions in terms of creating new laws, rethinking how society can view human differences as natural, and that everyone should have a right to access all aspects of society (see Box 2.2).

Box 2.1 A Sample of Work by Disability Historians

Douglas Baynton, *Defectives in the Land: Disability and Immigration in the Age of Eugenics* (2016)
Susan Burch and Michael Rembis (Eds.), *Disability Histories* (2014)
Paul Longmore, *Why I Burned My Book and Other Essays on Disability* (2003)
Michael Rembis, Catherine Kudlick, and Kim Nielson (Eds.), *The Oxford Handbook of Disability History* (2018)
Susan Schweik, *The Ugly Laws: Disability in Public* (2010)
Henri-Jacques Stiker, *A History of Disability* (1999)

Box 2.2 A Sample of Disability Activists

Rosemary Garland-Thomson

A public intellectual and Professor of English and Bioethics at Emory University, Thomson has written extensively on the interrelated topics of disability and (ab) normalcy, including influential books such as *Freakery: Cultural Spectacles of the Extraordinary Body* (1996), *Extraordinary Bodies: Figuring Physical Disability in American Culture and Literature* (1997), and *Staring: How we Look* (2009), as well as co-editing *Disability Studies: Enabling the Humanities* (Snyder, Brueggemann, & Garland-Thomson, 2002) and *Re-Presenting Disability: Activism and Agency in the Museum* (Sandell, Dodd, & Garland-Thomson, 2010).

Judith Heumann

An internationally recognized leader in advocating for civil rights for the disability community from the 1970s to the present, Heumann was originally denied access to public school in New York City because she was a wheelchair user. As a result of her parents' advocacy, she was placed in a public school classroom in fourth grade. Later, Heumann was denied access to employment as a public school teacher and fought to become the first wheelchair-using teacher in New York City. She maintained an interest in education and became Assistant Secretary of Education for Special Education and Rehabilitation Services (1993–2001) under President Clinton, and Special Advisor for International Disability Rights (2010–2016) under President Obama.

Simi Linton

Considered one of the founding voices of the academic field of Disability Studies in the United States, Linton's first book, *Claiming Disability* (1998), made a powerful contribution in terms of questioning the academy's fear and negation of disability as an integral part of the curriculum. In her memoir, *My Body Politic* (2006), and the documentary film *Invitation to Dance* (Linton & von Tippelskirch, 2014), she shares her life and experiences as a woman who uses a wheelchair.

Lynn Manning

The late Lynn Manning was a poet, playwright, actor, co-founder and artistic director of Watts Village Theater Company, and world champion of blind judo. Manning created multiple works, most notably his play *Weights*, first performed in 2001, in which he explored being disabled, black, and male, forging new ground in intersectional representations.

Ed Roberts

As the first student with multiple and severe disabilities to attend the University of California at Berkeley, Roberts ultimately became known as "The Father of the Independent Living Movement." He slept in an 800-pound iron lung and fought to participate in all aspects of classroom and dorm life, developing a political understanding of disability that he engaged with and pushed for recognition of at the federal level. Roberts became California's Director of the Department of Vocational Rehabilitation, then co-founded (with Judy Heumann and Joan Leon) the World Institute on Disability, and led successful protests occupying government buildings in San Francisco to demand that the Californian government enforce the rights of people with disabilities.

Marta Russell

As her own cerebral palsy progressed, Russell tried to navigate the poor and barely existing social system of support for people with disabilities. A fearless writer with a fierce turn of phrase, Russell's book, *Beyond Ramps: Disability at the End of the Social Contract* (1998), looked at the problematics of disability, social class, and unfettered capitalism in the United States. It stands as a biting critique of topics such as healthcare, ableism, poverty, physician-assisted suicide, and the prison–industrial complex.

Irving Zola

Zola was one of the founding members of the Society for Disability Studies and the first editor of the organization's journal, *Disability Studies Quarterly*. He developed a sociological perspective of disability that informed the development of a social model of disability, wherein attitudes and beliefs, systems and structures, became the locus of "the problem" rather than individuals with congenital differences.

Assumptions versus Realities of Life for People with Disabilities

Scholars in disability studies (DS) have called attention to how non-disabled people perceive individuals with disabilities. Joseph Shapiro's landmark book, *No Pity* (1994), opens with the line, "Nondisabled Americans do not understand disabled ones" (p. 3). He goes on to tell the story of hearing several eulogies about a disabled person. At the funeral, several people commented, "He never seemed disabled to me" or "He was the least disabled person I ever met." Such intended compliments, however, negate disability as an integral part of a person's life experience and identity. (Would the same things be said about other minorities, e.g., "He never seemed black to me," "He was the least gay person I ever met," or "She never really acted like a woman"?) The funeral comments do betray, however, the awkwardness in thinking and talking about disability. People with disabilities do agree that, in general, society automatically underestimates their capabilities. Thus, to be capably disabled appears a contradiction, when in fact, it is commonplace.

Forms of *ableism*—the belief that able-bodied people are superior to disabled people—range from subtle to blatant. In general, considered "less than" by their non-disabled counterparts, people with disabilities are ascribed second-class status, and experience a different sense of reality. A luxury of privilege is not having to think about one's status. Just as European-Americans rarely think about the benefits of their skin color, able-bodied people are privileged in not having to think about things that disabled people must contemplate. For example, when planning a simple trip to a restaurant, an able-bodied person does not have to think about accessible public transportation, doorways, table seating, and restrooms because the world is configured with able-bodied people in mind.

The majority of people with disabilities are either unemployed or underemployed largely due to a mixture of a lack of opportunity, an unwillingness to provide reasonable accommodations, and largely negative attitudes toward the disabled. Gaining increased access to all aspects of society is of prime importance to the disabled community. For example, the frequency and quality of public transportation influence participation in all aspects of community life. If you cannot reach a destination because the means is not provided, everyday events such as seeing a movie, using a swimming pool, meeting friends at a bar, observing a sports event, watching a concert, or participating in a service at a church, synagogue, mosque, or other place of worship are simply not possible. The low visibility of people with disabilities means that a majority are out of sight, remaining segregated in most aspects of social experience. As Marta Russell (1998) points out, unlike civil rights bills of other minorities, major laws such as the Americans with Disabilities Act were not followed up with affirmative action, thereby severely lessening their impact and not significantly improving the lives of people with disabilities.

Challenging Cultural Assumptions and Widespread Misperceptions

There are many paradoxes around the idea of disability. For example, consider the aforementioned absence of people with disabilities in all aspects of society, contrasted with the many representations of people with disabilities within our culture. While knowing few people with disabilities, non-disabled individuals are, at the same time, marinated in a culture where disability is portrayed in children's books, novels, films, television, history, humor, language, and customs (e.g., superstitions, beliefs, and fears). Moreover, disability has been historically tied to charity, including acts of begging, therefore shaping attitudes of patronization, benevolence, superiority, and the common disposition, "There but for the grace of God go I." These sources mold the thoughts of many non-disabled people, leading them to believe they know what it must be like to be disabled in contemporary society. However, if non-disabled people are unfamiliar with actual people who have disabilities or their first-hand accounts, it usually means not understanding the world they experience at all.

A clear example of not understanding the world from the viewpoint of persons with disabilities is the perpetuation of "Awareness Days" during which non-disabled people sit in a wheelchair, or tie on a blindfold, or are required to write with their non-dominant hand to simulate physical impairment, blindness, or dysgraphia. Simulations actually trivialize disability as something that can be "tried on" and "taken off." While these commonplace exercises exist in many education classes, a similar exercise of non-black students wearing blackface, males dressed as females, and straight same-sex students holding hands in a public place could hardly give them meaningful and accurate insights into being African-Americans, women, or gays and lesbians. It would at best give them the experience of a non-black temporarily pretending to be black, a man pretending to be a woman, a straight person pretending to be gay. At worst, it reinforces deeply rooted stereotypes. For example, a sighted person feels blindness as a loss, an incapacity, in contrast to a congenitally blind person who feels complete, having known the world only without vision. As has been pointed out, a more accurate simulation exercise is actually not doing something, such as boycotting inaccessible restaurants, restrooms, and transportation systems (Blaser, 2006).

Commonplace Representations of People with Disabilities

Commonplace representations of disabilities usually reinforce the overwhelmingly negative connotations associated with disability. Because they are so widespread, yet ironically hardly noticed, we believe it is worthwhile to recognize representations and highlight how problematic they are in perpetuating stereotypes, distortions, and misunderstandings of disability that, in turn, perpetuate the marginalization of people with disabilities.

Books

Classic literature is full of representations of disability that confine characters to a limited number of "types." Oversimplified notions of evil are usually signified by physical deviance; in contrast, the concept of good is portrayed through physical beauty. In traditional fairy stories, witches, trolls, and ugly sisters reinforce outward physical characteristics that symbolize psychological traits (just as Snow White and Sleeping Beauty celebrate idealized attractiveness as unblemished whiteness). The messages in fairy tales similarly echo throughout classical literature. For example, Shakespeare purposefully created Richard III with a hunched back to serve the same end—to illustrate an outward depiction of inner corruption, Disability also characterizes a vengeful desire in response to what a person has lost. In *Moby Dick*, Captain Ahab's missing leg fuels his relentless pursuit of the whale. Similarly, in *The Phantom of the Opera*, the title character's distorted appearance drives his revenge for the loss of a happy, public life.

Representations of children with disabilities in classic literature often posit them as weak and pitiful, lifelong liabilities to their families. In *A Christmas Carol* (1843), Dicken's young Tiny Tim exemplifies this phenomenon as a fragile, weak boy on crutches who hovers near death. Tennessee Williams' Laura Wingfield in *The Glass Menagerie* (1944) is typical of an older child, portrayed as an introverted, "on the shelf" daughter, disappointing her desperate mother by thwarting the family's future. Characters with disabilities in children's literature are largely represented as "brave little things" and "poor little souls" and decidedly monocultural. Such portrayals incite associations of inspiration and pity for disabled children, who are almost always European-American (Ayala, 1999). On a positive note, some recent books, such as *It's Okay to be Different* (Parr, 2001), portray children with disabilities as three-dimensional characters—everyday people in everyday situations—thereby emphasizing the normalcy of disability. Likewise, *Happy in Our Skin* features disability as part of human diversity writ large—kids who use a wheelchair, have facial birthmarks, and have vitiligo along with gay, interfaith, and mixed-race families. Sometimes the message is clear, such as in *Ernest, the Moose Who Doesn't Fit*

(Lozoff, 2002), where the book—not the moose—has to change. However, even ostensibly progressive stories such as *The Fly Who Couldn't Fly* (de Serres, 2014) can unwittingly reinforce limited understandings of disability.

Films

More people watch films than read books; therefore, our culture largely receives messages about disability through cinematic representations. Once again, while disability is always present in some shape or form, it is overwhelmingly portrayed in inaccurate and damaging ways, upholding long-standing stereotypes and circulating misinformation.[2] Some of these stereotypes include being pitiable, pathetic, sweet, and innocent, awaiting a miracle cure (*The Elephant Man*); a victim or object of violence (*Whatever Happened to Baby Jane?*); evil or sinister (*Unbreakable*); a curio, comic, or horror (*Freaks*); a triumphant "super-crip" (*My Left Foot*); an object of humor (*There's Something About Mary*); an aggressive avenger (*Black Panther*); a burden or outcast (*Of Mice and Men*); asexual and/or unworthy of a relationship (*Born on the Fourth of July*); incapable of participating in everyday life (*Children of a Lesser God*); and suicidal (*Million Dollar Baby*). Accurate portrayals of ordinary people with disabilities and their ability to function in an often inhospitable world are rarely witnessed in mainstream cinema. However, some independent movies do offer the opportunity to analyze and discuss the accuracies of living with a disability in thoughtful and more accurate and meaningful ways, such as *Untouchable*, *Rust and Bone*, and *The Sessions*, and arguably blockbuster movies such as *Avatar* have helped shift disability imagery. Perhaps the most progressive of all genres is the documentary, with many films reflecting the reality of living with disabilities (see Box 2.3).

Box 2.3 Recommended Documentaries

Documentaries can be an incredibly powerful tool with which to examine the issue of disability, particularly from the point of view of people with disabilities. The following are 12 of our recommendations (from a much longer list) that vary in content, length, tone, and "teachability." What they all have in common is their clear interpretation of disability as just another way of being, not as a deficit, disorder, or dysfunction.

Including Samuel (2007)

Photojournalist Dan Habib documents the life of his family, including his child Samuel who has cerebral palsy. Admitting that he seldom thought of the inclusion of people with disabilities in society until raising his son, Habib's film focuses on the educational and social inclusion of children and youth with disabilities as a civil right. The documentary also features other families who have children and youth with disabilities, sharing multiple perspectives on inclusion.

Educating Peter (1992)

Considered a "classic," this Oscar-winning documentary is about a boy with Down syndrome who is included in his local school and the multiple perspectives of all those involved. Its success generated an equally interesting sequel, *Graduating Peter* (2001), also focusing on how he adapted to a school community and a school community to him.

Ennis' Gift (2000)

An anthology of famous people and "ordinary" students describe the impact of what they prefer to term "learning differences," rather than learning disabilities, on their lives. James Earl Jones, Charles Schwab, Danny Glover, Lindsay Wagner, Robert Rauschenberg, and Henry Winkler are among those who share personal memories of school experiences and ways in which they self-strategized in order to survive.

Emmanuel's Gift (2005)

Narrated by Oprah Winfrey, this film documents a Ghanaian man born with one leg. While Emmanuel's father's sense of shame led him to abandon his family, his mother was determined to fight for the dignity of her child. Utilizing a prosthetic leg, Emmanuel participates in all aspects of Ghanaian life. Intent on showing his country that people with disabilities were more capable than non-disabled people believed them to be, Emmanuel rode a bike across Ghana, and in doing so challenged many Africans' perceptions of disability.

Misunderstood Minds (2002)

Known for his neurodevelopmental framework to help understand the diversity of human minds, Dr. Mel Levine interviews students from all grade levels with learning, social, and/or emotional difficulties in an attempt to better understand how they think and what they can do to negotiate the academic, social, and emotional demands of school.

What the Silenced Say (2001)

Best-selling author, with David Cole, of *Learning Outside the Lines* (2000) and *The Short Bus* (2008), Jonathan Mooney tells of his struggles as a child who could not read at the expected developmental level, and consequently grew to understand school as an agonizing and alienating experience. Additionally, and importantly, Mooney shares ways in which teachers can assist students who are faced with managing their learning difficulties.

When Billy Broke His Head … and Other Tales of Wonder (1995)

Award-winning journalist Billy Golfus traverses America to meet other people with disabilities. Humorously calling attention to the seriousness of the disability rights movement and the need for increased accessibility in all aspects of life, the film illustrates the challenges posed by cultural norms and institutions that cause unnecessary absurdities for people living with disabilities.

Refrigerator Mothers (2003)

Not so long ago, in the 1960s and 1970s, scientific theory laid the groundwork for blaming mothers of autistic children for their offspring's "condition." Viewed as being coldly indifferent instead of warmly loving, mothers movingly explain how such knowledge influenced their self-perception and how they viewed their children for decades.

The Sound and the Fury (2000)

Also an award winner, the film highlights the deep dilemma faced within and outside of the deaf community: should deaf infants, toddlers, and children undergo surgery to have cochlear implants to facilitate greater levels of hearing? Families present multiple points of view as they weigh the decision of whether to accept or reject cochlear implants.

On a Roll: Family, Disability and the American Dream (2005)

This powerful portrait is of a 65-pound African-American man, Greg Smith, who created *On A Roll* talk radio from his electric wheelchair in 1992. While visiting countries around the world to speak on civil rights, he finds the capital city of his own country inaccessible.

Murderball (2005)

Another Oscar-nominated film charts a team of wheelchair-using football players as they roll their way to the world championships. Much of the film is set behind the scenes, revealing accounts of individual players' personal lives, family situations, and understandings of disability.

Autism Is a World (2004)

This documentary is about a woman called Sue who is autistic. Diagnosed and treated as mentally retarded until age 13, Sue then began to communicate via a keyboard. Sue does not make eye contact, but she does reach for people's buttons. She also stands at the sink with water pouring over her hand, revealing that it makes her feel better. The film guides the viewer through Sue's mind, her world, and her obsessions, as well as explores her writings and social relationships forged in college.

Journey into Dyslexia (2004)

Academy award winners Alan and Susan Raymond created a documentary that explores what dyslexia is, from the perspective of people who have managed living in a print-dominant society throughout their lives. Through interviews with students in K-12 and college settings, along with professionals who proffer various points of view, the viewer comes to understand the complexities involved in being dyslexic and the implications for social, psychological, and emotional realms of experience.

Who Cares About Kelsey? (2012)

This film focuses upon the life of a teenage girl who deals drugs, breaks the rules in school, and has difficulty managing her emotions and behavior. With ADHD, and prone to self-mutilation, Kelsey challenges even her most supportive teachers and appears as the poster child for becoming a high school drop-out, or even juvenile incarceration. The film chronicles her school team's response to their charge of supporting her and, after a few bumps in the road and some turbulent times, Kelsey makes it to graduation.

Wretches and Jabberers (2012)

Larry and Tracy, two American men with autism, aged 42 and 52, respectively, travel to Japan, Sri Lanka, and Finland to challenge people's notions of disability and intelligence. Culturally-specific and global perceptions of human differences are illuminated through their interactions with many people they meet on their journey.

Television

Television offers a wide variety of programs, including news, talk shows, sitcoms, made-for-TV films, dramas, and documentaries. Like cinema, television often portrays disability in highly predictable, circumscribed ways.[3] Many of the stereotypes in film are paralleled in television programming, with disability usually portrayed as something tragic or needing a cure, or programs featuring a person with a disability who has overcome enormous obstacles. It is common for news items to feature disabled children coming from faraway places around the world to have corrective surgery, or to highlight a disabled hero, such as a man rolling across the country to raise money for charity. These "feel good" stories tend to portray disability as a personal tragedy that can be fixed or risen above. In television dramas, we find some portrayals of characters with disabilities, such as the brilliant surgeon House or the quirky detective Monk, that reveal complex personalities with impressive abilities. Yet, at the same time, one wonders if chronic pain (eased by the use of a cane and prescription drugs) might be the root of House's bitterness, or if the viewing audience laughs at, rather than with, the obsessive-compulsive Monk. Former television characters, such as Corky Thatcher in *Life Goes On* and Theo Cosby in *The Cosby Show*, attempted to "normalize" the presence of Down syndrome and learning disabilities, respectively. More recently, *The Big Bang Theory* has a mainstream character, Sheldon Cooper, with Asperger-like characteristics, who is also featured in a spin-off prequel, *Young Sheldon*, about his childhood. The reality TV show *Little People, Big World* provided viewers with insights into the world of a family with achondroplasia/short stature, and ran for ten seasons.

And while disability visibility is slowly on the rise, "normalizing" portrayals have been few and far between. Finally, it is noteworthy that disabled actors rarely get to portray characters with disabilities, yet actors without disabilities are frequently given accolades for their portrayals of characters with disabilities. Some notable exceptions to this situation have been R.J. Mitte, an actor with cerebral palsy who played Walter Jr. in the popular series *Breaking Bad*, and Michael J. Fox, who played Louis Canning, an unscrupulous lawyer with Parkinson's, in *The Good Wife*—a character who often played "the disability card" to achieve his desired ends (Safran, 1998).

Charities

In the public imagination, disabilities have long been associated with charity, bolstered by long-running cultural institutions such as the Jerry Lewis Telethon, the March of Dimes, Easter Seals, and United Cerebral Palsy. Poster children for these and other charities called attention to the vulnerability of infants, children, and youth—portraying them as perpetually sick. In doing so, they neglected to depict many more adults with various disabilities who struggle to gain increased access to society. In a relentless focus on the cause of the disability, high-profile charities serve to negate its effect (Russell, 1998). In worst case scenarios, high-profile charities conveyed the pain, suffering, and victim status of children with disabilities. Moreover, former poster children grew up and began to question the motives and operations of many institutionalized charities that did nothing to highlight the limitations being placed on disabled citizens by society. Ironically, such media coverage appears to reinforce notions of tragedy, despair, and hopelessness rather than to promote accepting children with disabilities for who they are. Many adults with disabilities who watch telethons suspect that the charity's objective is to prevent people like them from being born, rather than to advocate for their place within the wider community (Fleischer & Zames, 2001; Haller, 2010; Shapiro, 1994).

Humor

"Did you hear the one about the cripple/dyslexic/blind guy...?" While people laugh, such jokes reinforce stereotypes about individuals with disabilities. Jokes about wheelchair users, dyslexics, blindness, deafness, people with cerebral palsy, and so on, focus upon what that specific person cannot do. This element is elevated above all others and negates consideration of people with disabilities as complex and capable. Such joking goes largely unnoticed in television sitcom talk shows, and mainstream late-night comedy programs, constantly reinforcing ability as a source of humor at the expense of the disabled.

Language

The language of disability is often unnoticed in daily conversations. Consider, for example, the following questions: "Are you blind?", "Are you deaf'?", "Are you retarded?", "Are you crazy?" Or throwaway lines said with humorous intent to denote a personal failing, such as "I'm bipolar," "It's my ADD" (Attention Deficit Disorder), "It's my OCD" (Obsessive Compulsive Disorder). Or the phrases: "a dumb question," "a lame answer blind spot," "being shortsighted," and "the blind leading the blind"; or name-calling, such as "moron," "cretin," "lunatic," and "imbecile." The commonality among all of these expressions is that disability-related language reinforces the connection between disability, inability, negativity, undesirability, abnormality, and inferiority. The pervasiveness of such language is most likely because people do not consider disability issues to be on a par with those of race, ethnicity, gender, and sexual orientation. Disability still remains a repository of bad images and associations, a concept that people continue to fear and look down upon. Although we do not wish to be language police, we cannot but find interesting (and troubling) how socially acceptable it is to denigrate people with disabilities—to the point that people do not recognize that they are doing it.

Spotlight on Disability Culture

Like other self-identified minority groups, such as women, LGBTQ people, and African-Americans, people with disabilities have to reconcile who they are with often contradictory messages received on many fronts. Similar to other grass-roots movements, the ability rights movement foregrounded the rights of people with disabilities to determine their own lives—where they live, work, and socialize—and how they are represented. The phenomenon known as disability culture evolved as a counter-assertion to the overwhelmingly inaccurate depictions of disability. One premise of the movement is the mantra "Nothing about us without us," a direct statement as to the importance of representation and the unacceptability of being spoken for (Charlton, 2000). Cheryl Marie Wade (1992) describes disability culture as "coming at you from the inside out" (p. 17), and advocates for the sharing of disability experience as imperative for forging a culture in which people speak only for themselves but also struggle against the existing status quo to create a more desirable and socially just world. Confronting ableism can take many forms, including challenging pervasive stereotypes by taking action; speaking out against misrepresentation within television shows, films, telethons, and other forms of media; and creating accurate representations of people with disabilities, as in the documentaries *Vital Signs: Crip Culture Talks Back* (1995) and *When Billy Broke His Head ... and Other Tales of Wonder* (1995).

A large contribution to disability culture has been made by many first-person narratives that vividly describe living with a disability. These works offer insights that significantly contrast with the lists of disability categories and characteristics found in traditional education textbooks (see Box 2.4).

Box 2.4 A Selection of First-Person Narratives

Like documentary films, first-person narratives offer readers ways to examine issues of disability from the point of view of people with disabilities. The following are a selection of recommendations that we encourage students to read. Perhaps you can read several of them as a class and compare observations and understandings ... or simply pick one and "enjoy the read" as you explore one person's experiential understandings of disability.

The Short Bus: A Journey beyond Normal (2008), **by Jonathan Mooney**

A man with dyslexia who self-identifies as having ADHD buys a yellow school bus, a symbol of school segregation within his own history, and travels around the U.S. meeting people with disabilities to share their life stories.

My Body Politic: A Memoir (2007), **by Simi Linton**

The life story of an author, activist, and educator who has argued passionately that disability is a status to be "claimed," a form of human diversity, and a valuable position from which to understand how society is currently configured—as well as how to critique it with a view to changing it for the better.

Look Me in the Eye: My Life with Asperger's (2009), **by John Elder Robison**

A funny and informative autobiography of writer Augusten Burroughs' brother, describing his own life as a creative misfit, oddball, and outsider before the term Asperger's became widely known.

Thinking in Pictures: And Other Reports from My Life with Autism (2006), **by Temple Grandin**

A highly respected scientist who has designed over one-third of all livestock-handling facilities in the U.S., Grandin conveys how the way she perceives the world influences her successful inventions.

Waist-high in the World: A Life among the Nondisabled (1997), **by Nancy Mairs**

With scalpel-like precision, the author humorously dissects the world and how it turns, illuminating the absurdities of taken-for-granted physical configurations, and the social beliefs and behaviors that maintain them.

Sight Unseen (1999), **by Georgina Kleege**

This is a collection of masterfully written essays that explores living with blindness in a world of negative associations and commonplace fears, replacing myths and stereotypes with acute observations and insights.

Past Due: A Story of Disability, Pregnancy and Birth (1990), **by Anne Finger**

An eloquent book in which a writer disabled by polio meditates on the complex issues of disability and reproductive rights through her own narrative of pregnancy and childbirth.

Twitch and Shout: A Touretter's Tale (1998), **by Lowell Handler**

A tale of a photojournalist who seeks to understand his condition, known as Tourette syndrome, through meeting others with the same label.

Exile and Pride: Disability, Queerness, and Liberation (2015), **by Eli Clare**

A truly unique text in which the author braids many aspects of life (being working class, rural, disabled, transgendered) to convey how all aspects interact with, and inform, one another.

The Cancer Journals (1980), **by Audre Lorde**

Poet Audre Lorde powerfully narrates how a diagnosis of cancer influences her life and understanding of what it means to be human.

Learning Disabilities and Life Stories (2000), **edited by Pano Rodis, Andrew Garrod, and Mary Lynn Boscardin**

Thirteen college students, variously labeled as learning disabled, ADHD, and/or behavior disordered, tell their own insightful stories of how they negotiated the demands of K-12 schooling to get to college.

A Healing Family: A Candid Account of Life with a Disabled Son (1995), **by Kenzaburo Oe**

Representing a subgenre of parents' narratives describing lives shared with children who have disabilities, the Nobel Prize winner describes his rejection of doctors' advice to let his newborn die and the productive life his son subsequently enjoyed as a musical composer.

Ugly (2013), **by Robert Hoge**

The story of an Australian boy who was born with a large tumor in the middle of his face and short, twisted legs that resulted in many painful operations. Confronting the low expectations of many adults, teasing, and bullying, Hoge shares his even-handed and insightful views of life.

d/Deaf and d/Dumb: A Portrait of a Deaf Kid as a Young Superhero (2011), **by Joseph Valente**

The author's tale is one of navigating "between worlds" of the hearing and d/Deaf, the empowered and the disempowered, the included and excluded.

White on Black: A Boy's Story (2006), **by Ruben Gallego**

Born with cerebral palsy in Moscow and separated from his family as a baby, Gallego narrates his life in state hospitals, orphanages, and old-age homes, and his ultimate reunion with his mother.

From a historical perspective, there is a renewed interest in disabled people who lived in previous eras, including those who perished in Nazi death camps, circus performers, freak show artists, and those institutionalized for part or all of their lives. In addition, heroes have also been claimed within disability culture, including Helen Keller for her pioneering socialist activism against poverty; Ed Roberts for insisting on his right to attend college at Berkeley thereby igniting the Independent Living Movement; and Irving Zola, prolific writer and disability activist who founded the *Disability Studies Quarterly*. Activist work is an integral part of disability culture. For example, the Not Dead Yet group consistently protest against the notion of "assisted suicide" proffered by Dr. Jack Kevorkian, and the euthanasia of children with severe disabilities as advocated by Dr. Peter Singer of Princeton University.

In sum, disability culture celebrates the lives of people with disabilities in self-propelled movement from the margins of society to center stage. Reclaiming words such as "cripple," disability culture (also known as Crip Culture) provides a vital counterforce to what initially appears as overwhelming negativity, counter-asserting disability as an ordinary part of human diversity. The influence of disability culture appears far and wide, surfacing in mainstream culture in unexpected ways (think of Nemo's "gimpy fin").

A Brief History of Disability in American Public Schools

During the nineteenth century, several institutions opened to provide an education to students with particular disabilities. These included the first school in the United States for deaf students, in Hartford, Connecticut (1817), and the National Deaf-Mute College (1864), which eventually became known as Gallaudet University. However, when attendance at public school became compulsory at the start of the twentieth century, there were very few programs for children with disabilities. Students who had what are now thought of as "mild" disabilities, such as struggles in learning, behavioral problems, or certain physical disabilities, usually received an education. Most children who had "moderate," "severe," or "multiple" disabilities did not receive a public education, as school districts had the power to label them uneducable (Giordano, 2007). Many did not attend school, and some were placed in institutions. Special classes evolved as large numbers of students filled public schools and were sorted into tracks that represented above, at, and below average academic skills. Many of the lower-track classes were filled with poor, immigrant children for whom English was a second language (Franklin, 1987; also see Chapter 1).

In 1954, the landmark *Brown v. Board of Education* ruling declared that separate and unequal education facilities for African-Americans were illegal. As students became integrated, the increased use of tracking systems served as a legitimate mechanism to preserve a high degree of racial segregation (Ferri & Connor, 2006). The civil rights movement broadened its focus to embrace other citizens, including the disabled. What we have come to know as special education commenced during the 1960s and 1970s, when, using a civil rights framework, parents initiated court cases in which they strongly advocated for the right of their children with moderate, severe, and multiple disabilities to receive a free and appropriate public education. The following is a brief summary of federal laws that influenced how special education developed and expanded.

Section 504 of the Vocational and Rehabilitation Act of 1973

This legislation ensured the protection of civil rights for individuals with disabilities in programs that receive federal funding, including schools. In addition, students who do not fall under a federally defined disability are included under Section 504, which allows them to receive necessary supports in school. For example, the category of Attention Deficit Hyperactivity Disorder (ADHD) falls under this law, as do health-related issues such as asthma, diabetes, and so on.

P.L. 94–142, Education for the Handicapped Act (EHA) of 1975

P.L. 94–142 established federal guidelines for the provision of special education services to students with disabilities via an Individual Education Plan (IEP); defined 11 specific disability categories, procedures for identification of disabilities, related services, and due process; and ensured the rights of parents who disagreed with educational personnel. P.L. 99–457. The Infants and Toddlers with Disabilities Education Act of 1986, extended the rights of P.L. 94–142 for children with disabilities from birth to age five; required the development of an Individualized Family Service Plan (IFSP); and urged states to develop early-intervention childhood programs.

P.L. 101–476, Individuals with Disabilities Education Act of 1990

This legislation reauthorized P.L. 94–142 and changed its name to reflect "individuals" first; incorporated usage of the term disability and disuse of the word handicap; expanded disability categories to include traumatic brain injury and autism; expressed an increased obligation to linguistically and culturally diverse students with disabilities; and provided a focus on transitional services for high school students as part of their IEP.

P.L. 105–07, Individuals with Disabilities Education Act Amendments of 1997

These amendments reauthorized P.L. 101–476 and expanded provisions to include the following: general education teachers to be part of the IEP team when generating goals for each student with a disability; students with disabilities to be assessed using the same district and state assessments as non-disabled learners or to be provided with an alternative assessment; an increased emphasis on family participation, and the option of mediation services if they disagree with professional decisions; and the requirement of states to collect and analyze data on overrepresentation of students of color in special education (although this has been temporarily halted by the current federal administration under Secretary of Education, Betsy DeVos).

P.L. 108–446, Individuals with Disabilities Education Improvement Act of 2004

This Act permitted the use of IDEA funding for pre-referral services for students identified as "at risk" of receiving special education services who were not classified as disabled; mandated school districts to execute pre-referral systems to address overrepresentation of students of color; prohibited school districts from requiring students to take medications; raised the age of transition requirements from 14 to 16; expanded the use of mediation services to resolve differences in opinion between parents and professionals; and added Tourette syndrome to the disability category of "Other Health Impaired."

An approach called Response to Intervention (RtI) was introduced within the 2004 reauthorization. Although it was not specified as part of the law, it was included along with regulatory notes as a method that could be used to identify students with learning disabilities. In brief, it signified an attempted shift to a proactive model (identifying students earlier) from a reactive model (identifying students after prolonged periods of struggle). Under IDEIA, schools have an affirmative duty to "find" children with disabilities. The process of RtI is one of matching research-approved teaching methodologies to reading at all three phases. If whole-class teaching (Tier 1) is not working, the student can be referred for Tier 2 intervention that involves small-group instruction. Similarly, if that is not successful, then a student can be referred to testing for special education services and individualized support (Tier 3).

Featured Voice of Meric Gulum Weinkle

"Everyone can learn something about everything!"

What I love most about teaching at my elementary school is that it is not just students who are in the integrated collaborative teaching (ICT) classes who have their individual needs addressed. As a community of teachers, we meet the varying educational needs of *all* kids in every general education classroom in our school.

In my classroom, for example, I follow the tenets of Response to Intervention (RtI), which has three tiers of instruction. With Tier 1 in mind, I make supports available for everyone and children make their *own choices* about the supports that they need (e.g., graphic templates, pre-made graphic organizers, boxes drawn on paper). In the beginning of the school year, I might need to encourage some children to take advantage of supports. But before long, everyone catches on to what they need in order to learn most efficiently. It is both differentiation by choice and differentiation by readiness.

For example, I offer supports at the beginning of a unit so that they are embedded within lessons. We all have things that are trickier for us. Everyone has something to work on! I have students who are not labeled (as having a disability) who also need things like visual supports, behavior modification, a system to take breaks, or strategies to organize their work. Some parents have told me that no teacher has ever offered their children modification before. The parents are appreciative, as are their children. For example, my student, Leila, told me recently, "I love how you are understanding about how things can be hard. I can take breaks and do it little by little."

Jamal, a student who needs visual support to remind him of his academic goals, uses a Goal Bot. Each body part of the Goal Bot is labeled with a different goal. When he meets a goal, he colors in the body part and checks it off his goals list. Visual supports also work well with Stevie, a student with behavioral challenges who loves to play chess. His goals are listed on a drawn chessboard. He colors in a row when he achieves a behavioral goal. These kinds of supports are framed as academic tools. Our classroom community understands that everyone has their own pace and their own strengths and goals.

Lastly, I would like to share my advice for facilitating RtI within a successful inclusive classroom:

1. Acknowledge that all students have a knack for some things and some things are harder—no matter what the degree. Variation is simply something to expect in a classroom.
2. Don't be afraid to make and offer tools of support at the beginning of a unit. Predict and embed them from the start. Be proactive and fill in the gaps as the unit progresses
3. Remember that every child can find an access point to a lesson or respond to an access point that you have created.
4. Acknowledge that everyone can learn something about everything! How long it takes or how much might vary, but kids can figure it out with your support. It is like a self-fulfilling prophecy to succeed. Here is how we understand learning in my class: "It was hard, but now I'm okay!"
5. Stress that everyone has their own path and abilities.
6. Go with the flow and be open to the students in front of you!

Special Education: A Place or a Service?

Originating within P.L. 94–142 of 1975, and still present today, is the concept of least restrictive environment (LRE), defined as follows:

> (i)To the maximum extent appropriate, children with disabilities, including children in public or private institutions or care facilities, are (i) educated with children who are not disabled; and (ii) Special classes, separate schooling, or other removal of children with disabilities from the regular educational environment occurs only when the nature or severity of the disability is such that education in regular classes with the use of supplementary aids and services cannot be achieved satisfactorily.[4]

This means that each student must be individually evaluated and, as a result of that evaluation, placed on a continuum including general education classes, separate classes, separate schools, home, or hospital setting for part or all of the day. Although P.L. 94–142 can be viewed as mostly successful in providing students with disabilities access to public education, the preponderance of decisions that place students in separate facilities created a largely segregated system, often referred to as "parallel."

The mechanism of LRE has been interpreted as a legal and valid option (placing a student with a disability in a general education classroom). To disability advocates and activists, LRE is a loophole that allows educational institutions to maintain the non-integration of children with disabilities into schools, symbolizing people in society at large (Linton, 1998).

To other scholars, researchers, and parents, LRE is viewed as a necessary protection guaranteeing flexibility and individualization of placement for students who are often overlooked by teachers and/or overwhelmed within general education classrooms. By all accounts, it can be argued that there has always been friction between the required considerations of both an "appropriate education" and the concept of LRE. The vast growth in the number of students labeled disabled has caused concern among educators, parents, and the federal government. The "subjective" categories, those that are related to academic performance and student behavior, include learning disabilities, speech and language disorders, and emotional/behavioral disabilities. Special education professionals who evaluate students identify these "unseen" disabilities, thus sustaining a system in which students are identified as having deficits in need of intervention and remediation, and traditionally placed in segregated settings for all, most, or some of the school day. The popular slogan in the 1990s, "Special Education Is a Service, Not a Place," reflects how commonplace segregated settings had become for special education students.

Regular Education Initiative

One early attempt to counter the separatist tendencies of special education was the Regular Education Initiative (REI). Developed in the mid-to-late 1980s by Madeline Will, Assistant Secretary to the U.S. Department of Education in charge of special education and rehabilitation programs, the REI sought collaboration between general and special educators. One main goal was to include students with mild to moderate disabilities because schools had inadvertently created obstacles to their successful education with non-disabled peers. These obstacles included the provision of financial incentives to local education authorities when students with disabilities were placed in more restrictive environments, the exclusion of students with disabilities from local and state assessments, and federal data in national reports that omitted statistics on students with disabilities in segregated settings—meaning that these were children who the government literally did not count. Such barriers contradicted the spirit of the original legislation, making it easy to see why three out of four students received their education in segregated classes and/or pull-out programs (Gartner & Lipsky, 1987).

The Growth of Inclusion

Over the years, the debate about where to best educate students with disabilities continued to intensify. Mainstreaming, initiated in the original passage of P.L. 94–142, assumed that only students who approximated "normal" could benefit from a general education classroom. In other words, a student with a disability would be mainstreamed into a general education classroom provided that she or he could negotiate the academic and social demands just like students without disabilities and without assistance. In contrast, inclusion assumed that a student with a disability could benefit academically and/or socially from being in the general education classroom, even if her or his goals were different from those of non-disabled students. It is important to point out that the two terms, "mainstreaming' and "inclusion," are frequently used interchangeably, but they differ significantly in terms of definition and philosophy.[5]

The Individuals with Disabilities Education Act of 1990 furthered the public's general awareness of people with disabilities and the need to continue increasing access to all aspects of society. The concept of full inclusion grew, becoming one of the hottest topics (or hottest potatoes) in education. It was characterized in various ways, including the attendance of students with disabilities in their home-based schools, a natural proportion of disabled and non-disabled students together, age-appropriate placements, no segregated classes, special education support provided in an integrated learning environment and a zero-reject policy (Sailor, 1991). Other proponents went further, stating that inclusion should be considered not simply a service placement, but instead a way of life, a way of life together, based on a belief that each individual is valued and does belong (Villa & Thousand, 1995).

Most professional organizations and child advocacy groups issued official position statements in response to the widespread influence of and controversy surrounding inclusion. Several organizations supported full inclusion (Association for People with Severe Handicaps; United Cerebral Palsy Association). Others supported a moderate stance of fully supported inclusion for most children (National Parent Network on Disabilities). Still others sought to maintain the current continuum of services (Council for Exceptional Children; Council for Learning Disabilities). The Learning Disabilities Association (LDA) declared that placement of *all* children with disabilities in the regular classroom is as great a violation of IDEA as is the placement of *all* children in separate classrooms on the basis or type of their disability (Lipsky & Gartner, 1997). It became clear that professional groups varied considerably in their support of inclusion, frequently clashing as the idea became more influential.

Around the same time, national concern emerged in the media about the financial cost of special education, and the poor academic and social outcomes of students within the system. A prominent article in *U.S. News & World Report* expressed alarm at the overrepresentation of minority students in special education classes: commenting that "nearly 40 years after *Brown v. Board of Education*, the Supreme Court's landmark school desegregation ruling, Americans continue to pay for and send their children to classrooms that are often separate and unequal" (Shapiro, Loweb, Bowermaster, Wright, Headden, & Toch, 1993). In 1996, *The Merrow Report*, broadcast on television, posed the provocative question, "What's So Special About Special Education?" featuring critics who talked of dead ends for many children in classrooms serving as "welfare annexes." While detractors of inclusion were given equal airtime, what remained at the end of the day were sobering points made about racial segregation. Finally, documenting successful inclusion for the world, the film *Educating Peter* (Goodwin & Wurzburg, 1992) won an Academy Award for Best Achievement in Documentary (Short Subject) for capturing the efforts and triumphs of a ten-year-old boy with Down syndrome included in his local school. Through the 1990s and continuing throughout the 2000s, the number of inclusive classrooms continued to grow.

Backlash and Apathy toward Inclusion

The growth of any social change is accompanied by challenges. Many districts, schools, and classrooms moved successfully to inclusive models of education. Others managed to create and sustain imperfect-but-viable models, considered "works in progress." However, others attempted inclusion using irresponsible models without sufficient support, which could only result in failure. Such failures were then summarily cited as a reason for not providing inclusive classes. In New York City, for example, a model known as Integrated Co-Teaching (ICT) consists of a general and special educator working together to instruct all students. This model can work very effectively or be disastrous, depending on various factors. For example, a best-case scenario in middle school would feature two teachers who have worked together for several years and maintain adequate shared planning time, ongoing professional development, a limit of co-teaching one or two content areas, classes that have 15 to 20 percent of students with disabilities, and a special education partner who works with only one other general educator during different periods. On the other hand, a worst-case high school scenario would involve a general educator and a special educator who do not know each other (the latter working with three other general educators within a total of three content areas), all teachers without scheduled common planning time or professional development, all teaching classes in which 40 percent of students have disabilities and the remaining students are considered "at risk" of academic failure. As you can see, if it is to succeed, inclusion requires careful, ongoing planning that reflects responsible choices made by administrators, teachers, and parents.

Many educators do not believe in inclusive practices for a variety of reasons. Some general educator teachers express concern about not having the training, resources, and/ or support to provide individualized, specialized instruction to students with disabilities. Given the current emphasis on increasing standardized scores on mandated statewide examinations, teachers can feel pressured to "teach to the middle' or teach to the neediest students to the neglect of more independent students. Other educators view inclusion as a cost-cutting measure that places more (and unreasonable) responsibility on already overburdened classroom teachers.

Special educators sometimes fear a diminished sense of importance when working with general educators who predominantly teach the entire class. They are also concerned with being "spread too thin" when serving a group of children integrated throughout several classes, preferring the separate system in which they taught an entire group of students with disabilities. In addition, some parents who struggled to obtain specialized instruction for their children (particularly those labeled learning disabled) believe that general education cannot afford the degree of specificity needed. Likewise, many parents of students labeled gifted and talented have also resisted inclusive practices, as they, too, believe their hard-won services in separate settings are better for their children than learning in a heterogeneous classroom. Other concerns come from the Deaf community, who prefer to utilize sign language among one another than have an isolated student working through an interpreter within the hearing community.

Unintended Consequences of Special Education

Of course, there is much food for thought in all the points raised in the preceding section. However, we seek to challenge the notion that the field of special education, as it is currently configured and operationalized, has sufficiently succeeded in helping the majority of those students it seeks to help. We acknowledge that the field of special education has achieved many goals, including a guaranteed public education for all citizens and an increased number of people with disabilities within the workforce (Andrews et al., 2000). Nonetheless, special education has given rise to serious unintended consequences.

One major consequence is how special education pathologizes children, bestowing labels such as "disorder," "dysfunction," and "deficit," based on "standard deviation." In brief, the basic conceptualization of disability is one of human difference that deviates from what is considered "normal." This idea is so deeply entrenched in special education that its major proponents are unable to see it and the potential damage it causes (Kauffman & Hallahan, 1995). Thomas Skrtic (1991) outlined the grounding assumptions of special education into which new teachers are unwittingly acculturated as follows:

1. Disabilities are pathological conditions that students have.
2. Differential diagnosis is objective and useful.
3. Special education is a rationally conceived and coordinated system of services that benefits diagnosed students.
4. Progress results from incremental technological improvements in diagnosis and instructional interventions.

In contrast to the grounding assumptions of special education, the tenets of Disability Studies in Education (DSE) promote research, policy, and/or action that

1. Contextualizes disability within political and social spheres.
2. Privileges the interest, agendas, and voices of people labeled with disabilities/disabled people.
3. Promotes social justice, equitable and inclusive educational opportunities and full and meaningful access to all aspects of society for people labeled with disability/disabled people.
4. Assumes competence and rejects deficit models of disability.

(Connor, Gabel, Gallagher, & Morton, 2008, p. 448)

As you can see, beliefs about the nature of disability and the purpose of education vary widely. Of particular importance is how belief systems serve as the framework for people's personal and professional actions. Many people with disabilities believe experiences in special education were not in their best interest (Connor, 2006; Rodis, Garrod, & Boscardin, 2001), while others believe they were (Keefe, Moore, & Duff, 2006). We believe that the experience of students with disabilities can vary greatly. When special education programs are well staffed and well run, students are supported academically. Yet, because of unquestioned acculturation into deficit models of thinking, special education teachers still view "their children as broken, waiting to be (remediated) in a location away from their peers, rather than accepting them *as is* (Brantlinger, 2006). Most important, our own experiences have shown us that special education services are ideals that few programs can live up to. Some of our observations about segregated classrooms include:

- Deficit-based teacher perceptions of students.
- Lack of "research-based" instructional strategies.
- Minimal evidence of differentiated instruction.
- Repetitive and rote instruction that leads to student boredom and disengagement.
- Little evidence of individualized attention in classes of 12, 15, or 18 students.
- Oversubscribed special education classes (more students on the register than legally stipulated).
- Removal from academic instruction to attend "pull-out services" such as speech and language therapy, occupational therapy, physical therapy, counseling.
- Little or no use of the IEPs (largely due to missing, inadequate, incorrect, outdated, or computer-generated information).
- High levels of student absenteeism, particularly in the upper grade levels.
- An overrepresentation of males.
- An overrepresentation of African-Americans, Latinos, and Indigenous peoples.
- Placement of students with varying disabilities in the same classroom (e.g., students labeled LD are often placed in classes with students labeled with behavioral/emotional disabilities as if their "special needs" are interchangeable).
- Lack of student knowledge about disability and the absence of self-advocacy.

Unofficially, many segregated classes in special education are viewed as "dumping grounds" for students whose differences make them not "fit" into general classrooms. Moreover, there has always been a shortage of qualified teachers who work in special education, particularly in urban areas (Kincheloe, 2007), adding to the bleakness of the general picture.

Dropout Rates

Statistics on the dropout rate of students with disabilities vary dramatically according to source. Overall, the federal government estimates that 29 percent of youth with disabilities leave school before graduating. Students labeled emotionally disturbed have the highest dropout rate (53 percent), followed by those with learning disabilities (27 percent), speech and language impairments (26 percent), and intellectual/cognitive disabilities (25 percent).[6] These statistics contrast sharply with the 16 percent dropout rate of non-disabled students.[7] Several other sources cite much higher numbers of students with disabilities dropping out, approximately one-half (Hehir, 2005).

High School Diplomas

High school diplomas serve as society's reward for making it through school. Yet because they are largely tied to high-stakes written exit exams, they are unattainable for many students with disabilities. For example, less than one-third of students with a specific learning disability graduate with a standard diploma.[8] Students who do not obtain a standard high school diploma recognize the system of gatekeeping as a competition they have lost. At best, they will receive the consolation prize of an alternative diploma; at worst, they can drop out without any documentation of their efforts. Options for alternative "special' diplomas vary from state to state and include a certificate of completion/attendance, a certificate of achievement, an IEP/special education diploma, or an occupational diploma.

Transitioning out of high school can be extremely difficult. In some states, such as New York, high school students who do not pass mandatory final state examinations graduate with an IEP diploma that cannot be used for college or governmental positions such as serving in the armed forces. Unfortunately, students are therefore left with very few realistic or exciting career options.

Limited Employment Opportunities

As the majority of individuals with disabilities either drop out or gain an alternative diploma of limited use, existing employment opportunities tend to be unskilled. Referred to as the "Six Fs," they describe a highly circumscribed world that revolves around food (franchise-based fast service, food preparation); flowers (arranging, selling); folding (retail clothing stores); filth (cleaning, collecting); fetching (e.g., filling supermarket shelves, waiting on tables, being caregivers); and filing (minor clerical tasks). Although many of these positions can be seen as "dead end," some individuals do "work their way up" to managerial positions. However, most of these jobs remain low paying, with little job security and few, if any, benefits (Moxley & Finch, 2003).

The School-to-Prison Pipeline

The term "least restrictive environment" unwittingly conveys a sense of confinement not unlike incarceration. The U.S. is number one in the world for both the number and the percentage of its citizens in jail, exceeding much more populated China and India by far.[9] Of the 2.3 million incarcerated, the number of inmates with disabilities ranges from 40 to 65 percent, the largest group being those with literacy problems, whether officially labeled LD or not.[10] African-Americans are particularly affected, with one in nine men aged 20 to 34 serving time.[11] Several pieces of research have called attention to what has been termed the "School-to-Prison Pipeline," focusing attention on how some school policies drive out students before they are able to obtain the necessary skills to break the cycle of poverty.[12] Students without safety nets can too easily move from school to prison, almost as if the institutions dovetailed in this way (Walden & Losen, 2003). The National Association for the Advancement of Colored People has identified resource-deprived public education systems as the entry point into the pipeline, through systematic practices that vary by race, including special education labeling, school suspensions, grade retention, representation in special education classes, and restrictive placements.[13]

The Problem of Overrepresentation

Special education classes contain a disproportionate number of black and Latino students identified as disabled and placed in segregated settings. Evidence to support these claims has been found in city, state, and federal data (Losen & Orfield, 2002). On a national level, studies reveal that black males are more than twice as likely as white males to be identified as (a) mentally retarded (MR) in 38 states, (b) emotionally disturbed (ED) in 29 states, and (c) LD in 8 states (ibid.). In analyzing these data, Thomas Parrish concluded that, in general, whites are "only placed in more restrictive self-contained classes when they need intensive services" (cited in Macrine, 2010, p. 83). Minority students, however, "may be more likely to be placed in these settings whether they require intensive services or not" (ibid.). Other researchers have noticed similar patterns and conclude that such over-labeling results in segregation, signifying "unwarranted isolation" from the mainstream. Several researchers have concluded that increased time in the general education classrooms is largely attributable to the student's race (Fierros & Conroy, 2002). Furthermore, research indicates that, in addition to overrepresentation in the MR and ED categories, black and Latino students have been overrepresented in the category of LD for several decades, although not to the same degree (Parrish, 2002). Most recently, and quite disturbingly, key figures in special education have embraced research claiming that children of color are underrepresented in disability categories and advocate for increased identification (Morgan, Farkas, Hillemeier, & Maczuga, 2017; Morgan et al., 2015, 2018), despite half a century of research providing evidence to the contrary (Losen & Orfield, 2002; Skiba, Artiles, Kozleski, Losen,& Harry, 2016), dividing the field in terms of how research on race and disability should be perceived, conducted, and interpreted (Blanchett & Sealey, 2016; Collins, Connor, Ferri, Gallagher, & Samson, 2016; Ford & Russo, 2016; Harry & Fenton, 2016).

College Students with Disabilities

Students with disabilities constitute approximately 10 percent of all students attending college, a significant rise from the 2.6 percent in 1978 (Thomas, 2000). Although this denotes movement in the right direction, there are complicating factors that continue to impinge upon student success. As compared to non-disabled students, students with disabilities are more likely to attend two-year colleges; to have poorer attendance rates; are less academically prepared for college; are more likely to take remedial courses than advanced classes; and are more likely to drop out in their first year. Students with learning disabilities are the largest subgroup, and, historically, they are often the least academically prepared (Gregg, 2007; Henderson, 1999). All in all, the completion of college for students with disabilities is still comparatively more difficult than for their non-disabled peers (Vickerman & Blundell, 2010).

We've Come a Long Way, Baby … Or Have We?

Returning to the question posed at the beginning of this chapter ("Why can't I remember going to school with kids with disabilities or having a teacher with a disability?"), we assume that your school experience was different from our own. It should have been for the generation who followed ours. Schools are microcosms of society, and, as we have shown, society is configured to prevent access to and acceptance of a diverse body of people known as disabled. We are heartened by changes that have occurred in schools and society in general within the past few decades. At the same time, we ask educators who already negotiate many competing agendas to consider disability on a par with issues of social equality associated with gender, race, ethnicity, class, and sexual orientation. We believe that, when they do so, they will be actively attempting to dismantle the status of second-class citizenry, allowing children with disabilities to gain greater access to classrooms that, in turn, help them prepare for the world. In regard to teachers with disabilities, they have become a greater presence in schools, creating organizations such as the Capably Disabled of the United Federation of Teachers, a group that self-advocates as well as educates. So, as the old saying goes, while we have come a long way, there is still a long way to go…

Questions to Consider

1. In your own school experiences, who are the students with disabilities that you remember? Who are the teachers with disabilities that you remember? What do you recall about their inclusion in all school activities?
2. What do you already know of disability history? What are the sources of information?
3. Reflect upon members of your own family with disabilities. What are their opinions about the inclusion of students with disabilities in schools? What do they think about accessibility issues in society in general?
4. Do you think that disability should be considered along with race, ethnicity, gender, and sexuality in creating a school where "real" community exists?
5. Think about people with disabilities that you have seen in films and television programs, read about in books and newspapers. What were some of the first examples that you remember? What are some recent examples you recall? How were they represented? What messages did these representations send out about disability?
6. In what ways can it be argued that charities hurt and/or help people with disabilities? Who benefits from charitable organizations and in what ways do they benefit?
7. How might disability culture be defined? What is its purpose? How might you describe disability culture to another person?
8. What are some benefits and drawbacks of disability-related laws?
9. In your opinion, should inclusion be a civil right? Explain your answer, sharing examples and details.
10. Which examples of disability-related language do you use unconsciously? Do you think it is important to change some aspects of your own language? Explain your answer.
11. Despite sustained, long-term critiques, special education has largely remained constant over time. Why do you think this is so?
12. What is the relationship between special education and overrepresentation?
13. In what ways does access to schools for children and adolescents with disabilities parallel access to college for young people with disabilities?

Notes

1 All names have been changed to pseudonyms.
2 See www.bfi.org.uk/education/teaching/disability/thinking/stereotype.
3 See www.mediaanddisability.org/portrayal.htm.
4 See http://idea.ed.gov/download/finalregulations.html.
5 Inclusion means all students have a right to be educated with their non-disabled peers while receiving special education services. Hence, any student with a disability can be included. Mainstreaming means a student approximates the academic levels and behaviors of general education peers and can survive for part of the school day in general education classes without any special education support. Mainstreamed students, therefore, "earn" the right to be in a less restrictive environment because of their abilities.
6 See http:/inces.ed.gov/pubs2007/dropout/ListOfTables.asp#Table13.
7 See https://nces.ed.gov/programs/coe/indicator_coi.asp.
8 See U.S. Department of Education, Adult Literacy in America Survey, at http:// ed.gov/naal/nalsproducts.asp.
9 See www.washingtonpost.com/wp-dyn/content/story/2008/02/28/. ST2008022803016.html.
10 See www.ldanatl.org/.
11 See www.nsf.gov/statistics/nsf)3312/c2/c2s1.htm.
12 Ibid.
13 National Association for the Advancement of Colored People (see https://tbinternet.ohchr.org/Treaties/CERD/Shared%20Documents/USA/INT_CERD_NGO_USA_17809_E.pdf).

References

Andrews, J. E., Carnine, D. W., Coutinho, M. J., Edgar, E. B., Forness, S. R., Fuchs, L. S., Jordan, D., … & Wong, J. (2000). Bridging the special education divide. *Remedial and Special Education, 21*(5), 258–67.

Ayala, E. C. (1999). "Poor little things" and "brave little souls": The portrayal of individuals with disabilities in children's literature. *Reading Research and Instruction, 39*(1), 103–16.

Baynton, D. C. (2016). *Defectives in the Land: Disability and immigration in the age of eugenics.* Chicago, IL: University of Chicago Press.

Blanchett, A. & Sealey, M. (2016). "We won't be silenced": Senior scholars in special education respond to deficit derived claims that 'minorities' [students of color] are disproportionately underrepresented in special education. *Multiple Voices, 16*(1), 1–3.

Blaser, A. (2006). Awareness days: Some alternatives to simulation exercises. Retrieved from www.raggededgemagazine.com/0903/0903ft1.html

Brantlinger, E. (Ed.). (2006). *Who benefits from special education? Remediating (fixing) other people's children.* Mahwah, NJ: Lawrence Erlbaum.

Burch, S. & Rembis, M. (Eds.). (2014). *Disability histories.* Champaign, IL: University of Ilinois Press.

Charlton, J. I. (2000). *Nothing about us without us: Disability oppression and empowerment.* Berkeley, CA: University of California Press.

Childress, K. D. (2003). Genetics, disability, and ethics: Could applied technologies lead to a new eugenics? *Journal of Women and Religion, 20*, 157–78.

Clare, E. (2015). *Exile and pride: Disability, queerness, and liberation.* Durham, NC: Duke University Press.

Collins, K., Connor, D. J., Ferri, B. A., Gallagher, D., & Samson, J. (2016). Dangerous assumptions and unspoken limitations: A disability studies in education response to Morgan, Farkas, Hillemeir, Mattison, Maczuga, Li, and Cook (2015). *Multiple Voices, 16*(1), 4–16.

Connor, D. J. (2006). Michael's story: "I get into so much trouble just by walking": Narrative knowing and life at the intersections of learning disability, race, and class. *Equity & Excellence in Education, 39*(2), 154–65.

Connor, D. J., Gabel, S. L., Gallagher, D., & Morton, M. (2008). Disability studies and inclusive education: Implications for theory, research, and practice: Guest editor's introduction. *International Journal of Inclusive Education, 12*(5–6), 441–57.

Dickens, C. (1843). *A Christmas carol.* London: Chapman & Hall.

Elder Robison, J. (2009). *Look me in the eye: My life with Asperger's.* London: Ebury Press.

Ferri, B. A. & Connor, D. J. (2006). *Reading resistance: Discourses of exclusion in desegregation and inclusion debates.* New York, NY: Peter Lang.

Fierros, E. G. & Conroy, J. W. (2002). Double jeopardy: An exploration of restrictiveness and race in special education. In D. J. Losen. & G. Orfield, G. (Eds.), *Racial inequities in special education* (pp. 39–70). Cambridge, MA: Harvard Education Press.

Finger, A. (1990). *Past due: A story of disability, pregnancy and birth.* London: Women's Press.

Fleischer, D. & Zames, F. (2001). *The disability rights movement: From charity to confrontation.* Philadelphia, PA: Temple University Press.

Ford, D.Y. & Russo, C. (2016). Historical and legal overview of special education overrepresentation: Access denied. *Multiple Voices, 16*(1), 50–7.

Franklin, B. M. (1987). The first crusade for learning disabilities: The movement for the education of backward children. In T. Popkewitz (Ed.), *The formation of the school subject-matter: The struggle for creating an American institution* (pp. 190–209). London: Falmer Press.

Gallego, R. (2006). *White on black: A boy's story.* London: John Murray.

Garland-Thomson, R. (1996). *Freakery: Cultural spectacles of the extraordinary body.* New York, NY: New York University Press.

Garland-Thomson, R. (1997). *Extraordinary bodies: Figuring physical disability in American culture and literature.* New York, NY: Columbia University Press.

Garland-Thomson, R. (2009). *Staring: How we look.* Oxford: Oxford University Press.

Gartner, A. & Lipsky, D. K. (1987). Beyond special education: Toward a quality system for all students. *Harvard Education Review, 57*(4), 367–95.

Giordano, G. (2007). *American special education: A history of early political advocacy.* New York, NY: Peter Lang.

Golfus, B. (1995). *When Billy broke his head … and other tales of wonder.* Boston, MA: Fanlight Productions.

Goodwin, T. C. & Wurzburg, G. (1992). *Educating Peter.* Retrieved from www.kanopy.com/product/educating-peter

Grandin, T. (2006). *Thinking in pictures: and other reports from my life with autism.* London: Bloomsbury.

Gregg, N. (2007). Underserved and unprepared: Postsecondary learning disabilities. *Learning Disabilities Research & Practice, 22*(4), 219–28.

Grossberg, M. (2011). From feeble-minded to mentally retarded: Child protection and the changing place of dis/abled children in the mid-twentieth century United States. *Pedagogica Historica,* 47, 729–47.

Grue, L. (2010). Eugenics and euthanasia—then and now. *Scandinavian Journal of Disability Research,* 12, 33–45.

Haller, B. (2010). *Representing disability in an ableist world.* Louisville, KY: Advocado Press.

Handler, L. (1998). *Twitch and shout: A Touretter's tale.* Boston, MA: Dutton Adult.

Harry, B. & Fenton, P. (2016). Risk in schooling: The contribution of qualitative research to our understanding of the representation of minorities in special education. *Multiple Voices,* 16(1), 17–28.

Hehir, T. (2005). *New directions in special education: Eliminating ableism in policy and practice.* Cambridge, MA: Harvard Education Press.

Henderson, C. (1999). College freshmen with disabilities, 1999: A biennial statistic profile – statistical year 1998. Washington, DC: American Council on Education.

Hoge, R. (2013) *Ugly.* New York, NY: Penguin/Random House.

Kauffman, J. M. & Hallahan, D. P. (Eds.). (1995). *The illusion of full inclusion: A comprehensive critique of a current special education bandwagon.* Austin, TX: ProEd.

Keefe, E. B., Moore, V. M., & Duff, F. R. (2006). *Listening to the experts: Students with disabilities speak out.* Baltimore, MD: Paul H. Brookes.

Kincheloe, J. L. (2007). Why a book on urban education? In S. R. Steinberg & J. L. Kincheloe (Eds.), *19 urban questions: Teaching in the city* (pp. 1–27). New York, NY: Peter Lang.

Kleege, G. (1999). *Sight unseen.* New Haven, CT: Yale University Press.

Linton, S. (1998). *Claiming disability.* New York, NY: New York University Press.

Linton, S. (2007). *My body politic: A memoir.* Ann Arbor, MI: University of Michigan Press.

Linton, S. & von Tippelskirch, C. (Dir.). (2014). *Invitation to dance.* New York: Metuffer Films.

Lipsky, D. K. & Gartner, A. (1997). *Inclusion and school reform. Transforming America's classrooms.* Baltimore, MD: Paul H. Brookes.

Longmore, P. K. (2003). *Why I burned my book and other essays on disability.* Philadelphia, PA: Temple University Press.

Lorde, A. (1980). *The cancer journals.* San Francisco, CA: Aunt Lute Books.

Losen, D. J. & Orfield, G. (Eds). (2002). *Racial inequality in special education.* Cambridge, MA: Harvard Education Press.

Lozoff, B. (2002). *The wonderful life of a fly who couldn't fly.* Charlottesville, VA: Hampton Roads.

Macrine, S. L. (2010). Barriers to inclusion of culturally and linguistically diverse students. *Peace Studies Journal, 3*(1), 76–90.

Mairs, N. (1997). *Waist-high in the world: A life among the nondisabled.* Boston, MA: Beacon Press.

Mitchell, D. T. & Snyder, S. L. (1995). *Vital signs: Crip culture talks back.* Boston, MA: Fanlight Productions.

Mooney, J. (2008). *Short bus: A journey beyond normal.* New York, NY: Holt McDougal.

Mooney, J. & Cole, D. (2000). *Learning outside the lines: Two Ivy League students with learning disabilities and ADHD give you the tools for academic success and educational revolution.* London: Touchstone.

Morgan, P. L., Farkas, G., Hillemeier, M. M., Maczuga, S., Li, H., & Cook, M. (2015). Are minority children disproportionately represented in early intervention and early childhood special education? *Educational Researcher, 41*(9), 339–51.

Morgan, P. L., Farkas, G., Hillemeier, M. M., & Maczuga, S. (2017). Replicated evidence of racial and ethnic disparities in disability identification in U.S. schools. *Educational Researcher, 46*(6), 305–22.

Morgan, P. L., Farkas, G., Cook, M., Strassfeld, N. M., Hillemeier, M. M., Pun, W. H., Wang, Y., & Schussler, D. (2018). Are Hispanic, Asian, Native American, or language-minority children overrepresented in special education? *Exceptional Children, 84*(3), 261–79.

Moxley, D. & Finch, J. (Eds.). (2003). *Sourcebook of rehabilitation and mental health practice.* New York, NY: Plenum Press.

O'Brien, G. (2011). Anchors on the ship of progress and weeds in the human garden: Objectivist rhetoric in American eugenic writings. *Disability Studies Quarterly, 31*(3). Retrieved from http://dsq-sds.org/article/view/1668/1603

O'Brien, G. & Bundy, M. E. (2009). Reaching beyond "the moron": Eugenic control of secondary disability groups. *Journal of Sociology & Social Welfare, 36*(4),153–72.

Oe, K. (1995). *A healing family: A candid account of life with a disabled son.* Tokyo: Kodansha International Online.

Parr, T. (2001). *It's okay to be different.* New York, NY: Machete Book Group.

Parrish, T. (2002). Racial disparities in the identification, funding, and provision of special education. In D. J. Losen & G. Orfield (Eds.), *Racial inequality in special education* (pp. 15–37). Cambridge, MA: Harvard Education Press.

Rembis, M., Kudlick, C. J., & Nielson, K. (Eds.). (2018). *The Oxford handbook of disability history.* New York: Oxford University Press.

Richards, P. L. (2009). Disability history online. *OAH Magazine of History, 23*(3), 45–8.

Rodis, P., Garrod, A., & Boscardin, M. L. (Eds.). (2001). *Learning disabilities and life stories.* Needham Heights, MA: Allyn & Bacon.

Russell, M. (1998). *Beyond ramps: Disability at the end of the social contract.* Monroe, ME: Common Courage.

Safran, S. P. (1998). The first century of disability portrayal in film: An analysis of the literature. *Journal of Special Education, 31*(4), 467–79.

Sailor, W. (1991). Special education in the restructured school. *Remedial and Special Education, 12*(6), 8–22.

Sandell, R., Dodd, J., & Garland-Thomson, R. (Eds.). (2010). *Re-Presenting Disability: Activism and Agency in the Museum.* New York, NY: Routledge.

Schweik, S. M. (2010). *The ugly laws: Disability in public.* New York, NY: New York University Press.

Serres, M. de. (2014). *The fly who couldn't fly.* Reading: Dolman Scott Ltd.

Shapiro, J. P. (1994). *No pity: People with disabilities forging a new civil rights movement.* New York, NY: Random House.

Shapiro, J., Loweb, P., Bowermaster, D., Wright, A., Headden, S., & Toch, T. (1993, December 13). Separate and unequal. *U.S. News & World Report,* pp. 46–60.

Skiba, R. J., Artiles, A. J., Kozleski, E. B., Losen, D. J., & Harry, E. G. (2016). Risks and consequences of oversimplifying educational inequities: A response to Morgan et al. (2015). *Educational Researcher, 45*(3), 221–5.

Skrtic, T. M. (1991). *Behind special education: A critical analysis of professional culture and school organization.* Denver, CO: Love Publishing.

Snyder, S. L., Brueggemann, B. J., & Garland-Thomson, R. (Eds.). (2002). *Disability studies: Enabling the humanities.* New York, NY: Modern Language Association of America.

Stiker, H. J. (1999). *A history of disability.* Ann Arbor, MI: Love Publishing.

Thomas, S. B. (2000). College students and disability law. *Journal of Special Education, 33*(4), 248–57.

Valente, J. M. (2011). *d/Deaf and d/Dumb: A portrait of a deaf kid as a young superhero.* New York, NY: Peter Lang.

Vickerman, P. & Blundell, M. (2010). Hearing the voices of disabled students in higher education. *Disability & Society, 25*(1),21–32.

Villa, R. A. & Thousand, J. (1995). *Creating an inclusive school*. Alexandria, VA: Council for Supervision and Curriculum Development.

Wade, C. M. (1992). Disability culture rap. *Ragged Edge Magazine*. Retrieved from http://courses.washington.edu/intro2ds/Readings/Wade_Disability_Culture_Rap.pdf

Walden, J. & Losen, D. J. (Eds.). (2003). *Deconstructing the school-to-prison pipeline: New directions for youth development*. Malden, MA: Blackwell Online Publishing.

Williams, T. (1944). *The glass menagerie*. New York, NY: Random House.

3 Examining Beliefs and Expanding Notions of Normalcy

"What if I don't feel ready to teach those kids?"

Cartoon # 3 Don't be afraid of the water

Since the implementation of P.L. 94–142 (now known as IDEIA), the field of special education has convinced a generation of classroom teachers that they are not "special" enough (meaning patient, qualified, knowledgeable, and gifted) to teach children with disabilities. Even the general public believes that special educators are a breed apart from others. All we have to do is enter a room of strangers, strike up a "cocktail party" conversation, and wait to be asked what we do for a living. As soon as "I am a special education teacher" leaves our lips, we are transformed in the eyes of our audience, who lightly gasp and murmur, "Why, you must be a *very* special person yourself." Amid a circle of nodding heads, there is always one who goes on to confess what the others are thinking, "You know, I could *never* do what you do. I am glad there are people in the world like you."

Let's unpack the assumptions at work in this exchange. What is unspoken is the belief that disability is a most unfortunate life circumstance—so unfortunate (and far removed from "ordinary" life experience) that this audience cannot imagine life other than one disencumbered with disability. It is further implied that a *very* special person is needed—preferably one with the zeal and sacrificial nature of a missionary—to work with disabled children, who present formidable and presumably undesirable challenges. Perhaps most troubling is the gratitude expressed toward people who *choose* to work with disabled children so that others (meaning themselves) may be spared from having to engage with disability at all.

In the previous chapter, we explored the origins of disability stereotypes within popular culture. Given that public school is a particular culture, where might ideas about disability originate in an educational context? For example, what might account for the willingness of general education teachers to believe that only special educators can and should teach children with disabilities?

Disability Perspectives

Prior to the implementation of P.L. 94–142 within public schools, the medical community (e.g., family doctors, neurologists, psychologists, psychiatrists, neurologists, ophthalmologists, audiologists, physical therapists, speech/language pathologists, occupational therapists) functioned as the primary source of information, treatment, and support for parents of children with disabilities. It is rather unsurprising, then, that the framing of disability within P.L. 94–142 and the subsequent reauthorizations of IDEIA reflect this historical relationship between medicine and disability.

The Medical Model of Disability

Anyone who has visited a doctor's office in America is familiar with the medical model. A patient presents with symptoms. The doctor performs a medical examination to confirm or rule out a diagnosis based upon the patient's symptoms. Once a diagnosis is confirmed, the doctor prescribes a curative course of medical treatment to restore the body to health. The patient is asked to return for a follow-up appointment to evaluate the effectiveness of the treatment.

Now let's look at the assessment, eligibility, and placement procedures delineated under IDEIA. The patient (student) presents with symptoms (educational problems). The scientific expert (school psychologist) performs an examination (psycho-educational assessment) in order to confirm or rule out a diagnosis (disability). Once a diagnosis (disability) is identified, a prescription (Individual Education Plan, or IEP) is written, with recommendations for a course of treatment (special education placement and individualized instruction) intended to cure (remediate) the patient (student). A follow-up appointment (annual IEP review) is scheduled to evaluate the effectiveness of the treatment plan (special education services). The medical model's presence within special education practice is unmistakable.

For more than 40 years now, special education has relied upon the medical model as its framework for understanding and responding to disability. Viewed through a medical model lens, disability is conceptualized as a pathological condition intrinsic to the individual. Thus, it is a naturalized practice within special education to position the individual student as the unit-of-analysis. For example, under the evaluation procedures set forth by IDEIA, a school psychologist administers an individual and "scientifically based" assessment battery to determine if a student meets the criteria for one or more of 13 disability categories (see Chapter 4). Following testing, special education committee members (school professionals and parents) review results and, in turn, determine student eligibility and placement in regard to special education services. Lastly, an IEP is developed to target and remediate the student's identified cognitive, academic, and/or behavioral deficits.

Now that you are reading our third chapter, you might anticipate that we are about to invite you to look beyond the existing state of affairs to examine the underbelly of our agreed-upon educational response to children with disabilities. Again, we are not suggesting that non-disabled people are orchestrating some kind of sinister plot—à la comic book action flick—to ensure their superior position in the world. However, it is worth reminding ourselves that public schools are highly politicized spaces (see Chapter 1) populated by people who bring along their values, cultures, ethnicities, languages, beliefs, histories, and behaviors. It is also worth remembering that we can legislate policy, but we cannot legislate attitude. We need only look at the unintended consequences of special education discussed in Chapter 2 (e.g., social and academic stigma, persisting overrepresentation of students of color in segregated classrooms, inaccessibility to general education curriculum) to recognize the significance of attitude upon student outcomes.

Having relied upon the medical model of disability for more than four decades, public school personnel generally regard special education's grounding framework as natural and unproblematic. It is, after all, the way we *do* things. Our professional language is rife with phrases to describe the pathology of students with disabilities—"significant discrepancy between ability and achievement," "visual and auditory processing deficits," "delayed visual-motor development," "immature speech," "low risk-taking behavior," "poor inhibitory control," "inattentive behaviors," "language impairment," "erratic performance," "atypical gait," "tactile defensiveness," and so on and so forth. Consider for a moment how you might conceptualize a child described in a report with *all* of the aforementioned phrases. Hold that picture in your mind. Are you looking at a child in all of his or her humanity—or as the sum of his or her deficits? What were your immediate thoughts about this child's academic potential and your ability to teach him or her? Did the language of pathology influence your viewpoint in any significant way? When we conceptualize difference as deficit, it engenders a particular way of thinking about and responding to children with disabilities. The more we focus upon the individual, the more it seems the individual is determined by his or her disability status. Perhaps, as disability studies scholar Simi Linton (1998) contends, "We are deficient in language to describe it any other way than as a 'problem'" (p. 141).

The Social Construction of Disability

Let's return for a moment to the example of Teacher A and Teacher B, described at the end of Chapter 1. To recap, Teacher A evaluates if a new student with a learning disability will fit into her classroom (as well as her teaching repertoire), while Teacher B considers what a new student with a learning disability needs in order to succeed in his classroom and engages knowledgeable others (special education staff and parents) to help achieve this goal. We can expect a different outcome for the student depending upon which context he enters. The biological fact of the student's disability remains constant. What shifts is the *response* to disability. We do not dispute the biological differences inherent to disability. Nor is it our intention to diminish the positive contributions of science in the lives of persons with disabilities. We wish to emphasize, however, that the *meaning* that societies attribute to disability shifts across both time and culture. Less than 50 years ago, for example, it was considered right and natural in the United States for a person with severe disabilities to spend his or her lifetime within an institution (Nielsen, 2012). In contrast, it is commonplace in today's culture for persons with severe disabilities to reside in group homes within their communities. Have the disabilities once deemed severe enough to warrant institutionalization disappeared? Absolutely not. What *has* disappeared is American society's wholesale *response* to severe disabilities—the practice of institutionalization. And, as we continue to point out, it is society's agreed-upon response to disability that determines particular outcomes for persons with disabilities.

In recent years, people with disabilities, disability studies scholars, and disability advocates have distinguished impairment from disability in the following way. An *impairment* refers to "variations that exist in human behavior, appearance, functioning, sensory acuity, and cognitive processing" (Linton, 1998, p. 2). In contrast, a *disability* is the product of social, political, economic, and cultural practices (Corker & Shakespeare, 2002). In other words, there is more at work than an individual's inherent biological difference. For example, a wheelchair user may have an impairment that requires moving through the world in a way other than walking; however, should the wheelchair user wish to enter a building that is accessible *only* to people who walk, she is now disabled by the context. In this way, disability can be understood as a social construction.

Constructing Disability in Public Schools

As we explained earlier in this chapter, public education relies upon the medical model as its framework for understanding and responding to disability. So, it is unsurprising that special education practice incorporates the language and methods of science. It follows, then, that students with disabilities will be conceptualized within the language of pathology in ways that produce particular consequences.

As disability moved from the purview of medicine into public education, the scientific language used to describe disability entered the school context. The language drawn upon in psycho-educational evaluations differs significantly from the way in which teachers talk about children who struggle to learn. Think about the elevated status that American society affords to science and scientists. The language of pathology is *culturally* positioned as a powerful discourse. For example, within special education committee meetings, scientific language routinely carries greater status than the language of both teachers and parents (Valle, 2009; Valle & Aponte, 2002). The educational needs of children, described in scientific and psychological terms, sound alien to general education teachers unfamiliar with such terminology—leading them to believe that they possess neither the knowledge nor the skills to address such seemingly complex issues. Thus, special education teachers (and an array of support service providers) become positioned as *the* trained professionals to work with *those* children. And an educational myth begins to take shape—that there are two types of children, able and disabled, who require different kinds of instruction delivered by differently trained teachers working in parallel systems of public education. And for the last four decades, this myth has circulated among a generation of teachers who have come to regard it as truth. Certainly, there are children whose severity of disability *may* require special instruction outside of the general education classroom. However, it has become more and more naturalized to construct struggling learners as *belonging* in special education—a stance increasingly challenged by proponents of inclusive educational practices who contend that all children are far more alike than not, and that general education teachers, in fact, already possess a rich repertoire upon which to draw in teaching everyone.

We realize that you may be asking yourself, why *not* teach children with disabilities in smaller classes using specialized instructional materials and strategies? That must be a good thing, especially in this Age of Standards and Accountability, right? Why *should* general education teachers include children with disabilities in their classrooms when special classrooms and teachers are available? Well, the answer to that question has to do with "all that *other* stuff" we talked about in Chapter 1, which has everything to do with the unintended consequences of special education discussed in Chapter 2. In other words, we must consider how the medical model of disability functions within both public education and American culture.

As established earlier in this chapter, the medical model centers the individual as the unit-of-analysis. Working within the conceptualization of disability as inherent to the individual, an "objective expert" (school psychologist) administers a one-on-one standardized assessment battery that can include an IQ (intelligence quotient) test (e.g., Wechsler Intelligence Scale for Children®—WISC®-V [Psychological Corporation, 2014]; Stanford–Binet Intelligence Scales, 5th edition [Roid, 2003]; Woodcock–Johnson IV Tests of Cognitive Abilities [Schrank, Mather, & McGrew, 2014a]); achievement tests (e.g., Wechsler Individual Achievement Test®—WIAT®-IV [Psychological Corporation, 2014]; Woodcock–Johnson IV Tests of Achievement [Schrank, Mather, & McGrew, 2014b]; Peabody Individual Achievement Test—PIAT-R/NU [Markwardt, 2009]); and behavioral measures (e.g., Vineland Adaptive Behavior Scales, 3rd edition [Sparrow, Cicchetti, & Saulnier, 2016]; Conners Comprehensive Behavior Rating Scales, third edition [Connors, 2008]). Results of the evaluation form the basis of a treatment plan intended to remediate the individual's deficits. This appears to be a reasonable approach. What could be the problem?

For starters, let's consider some assumptions embedded within our naturalized practices. Special education spins around the notion of normal/abnormal. In order for "abnormal" to exist, there necessarily must be a concept of "normal." In other words, the parameters of "normal" must be defined in order to determine what is "abnormal" by comparison. And here is where "all that *other* stuff" comes into play again. *Who* decides what constitutes "normal" and "abnormal" across the range of human behavior? Is it right and natural to conceptualize human ability as distributed along a "normal curve"? Does strict adherence to scientific and objective standardization (with regard to test environments, procedures, and measurement tools) yield the most accurate representation of human ability? What might be the consequences of our agreed-upon methods for determining and responding to disability within American public schools?

The Reign of Normal

When, where, and how did the concept of *normal* originate in the first place? Have you ever wondered, or is the concept so natural that you have never even thought about it?

The Origins of Normal

We can trace the word *normal* to the mid-1840s, when it first appeared within the English lexicon as part of the vocabulary generated by the emerging discipline of statistics. The new field had been conceived in Europe as a way to amass data about industrial production and public health; however, Adolphe Quetelet, a French statistician, thought to apply statistical usage to physical attributes (e.g., height and weight), thereby constructing an abstraction of "the ideal man"—the first framework within which to compare human beings as either "normal" or "not normal" (Davis, 2016).

In the second half of the nineteenth century, Sir Francis Galton, scientist, explorer, statistician, and half-cousin of Charles Darwin, extended Quetelet's work to include a "normal curve of distribution" and quartile divisions for ranking human traits as average, inferior, or superior (Hanson, 1993). (It is worth noting that Galton's notion of the "normal curve of distribution" is used in *current-day* assessment and eligibility criteria for special education services.) Galton, along with other European statisticians, promoted the statistical study of human traits as part of a popular ideology of the day known as eugenics. Eugenicists sought to enhance positive traits of a population by keeping its weakest members from mixing with more desirable members (Connor & Valle, 2015; Thomas & Loxley, 2001); in other words, the human race could be improved through the practice of controlled breeding. Galton advanced the idea that intelligence is an inheritable trait distributed *unequally* among human beings according to class and race, and urged intelligent people to marry one another to offset the increasing birth rate of the undesirable lower classes (Connor & Valle, 2015; Hanson, 1993). We begin to see how science—a particular discourse of truth that gained momentum well beyond the late nineteenth century—began to function in such a way as to support the dominant culture's socially constructed ideas about race, class, and intelligence.

It appears, then, that science enabled the rationalization for assigning value to human beings along a hierarchy of inherited traits. Let's consider a few examples. Early in the twentieth century, eugenicists contributed to the passage of the Immigration Act of 1924 by testifying that inherent undesirable traits of southern and eastern Europeans posed a significant health threat to the American population (Baynton, 2016). Around the same time, American legislators, drawing upon the eugenics literature, passed state laws to prohibit marriages among the mentally ill and mentally disabled, forcing sterilization as a preventive measure against transmission to subsequent generations (Stern, 2015). And, most sobering of all, the eugenics movement figured heavily in Adolf Hitler's construction of the Final Solution—providing him with scientific justification for eradicating so-called genetic defects in order to create the Master Race. It is worth noting that Hitler first targeted the mentally and physically disabled, whom he referred to as "useless eaters," before turning his attention to the persecution and extermination of gypsies, homosexuals, and Jews (Valencia, 1997). Who could have anticipated that the development of statistical data analysis would contribute to the unimaginable horrors of the Holocaust?

And so, our point is this. We must be vigilant about both intended *and* unintended consequences of scientific practices. In the case of eugenics, its proponents meant to lessen human suffering through selective breeding, a scientific means for eradicating disease and disability in order to create stronger and healthier families. Yet, as history was to reveal, things are not so simple. *Who* decides what inheritable traits are more or less desirable (which ultimately defines *which* people are more or less valued), for what purpose, and for whose benefit? These questions sustain relevance as we consider the "rise of normal" within American public schools.

The Rise of Normal within Public Schools

The intelligence test is a ubiquitous feature within public schools. Sitting center stage in the process for determining eligibility for special education services, the IQ test is the standard against which other measurements are compared (e.g., discrepancies between IQ and achievement scores are thought to hold significance in regard to identifying certain disabilities). The intelligence test requires that we believe in its efficacy in order for the institution of special education—as we have chosen to conceive it—to operate smoothly. Although IQ testing has always had its critics, there has been little actual resistance to our reliance upon IQ scores as part of the assessment required for determining eligibility and placement in special education.

So how did intelligence testing become a naturalized practice within public education? Let's return to the early twentieth century. With eugenicists steadily advancing the notion of inheritable intelligence, it is unsurprising that the field of psychometrics emerged to provide a means by which to measure intellectual capacity. By 1905, Alfred Binet, a French psychologist, had constructed the first intelligence test at the behest of the French ministry of education to identify students in need of educational assistance. (It is noteworthy that French law extended public education to *all* students, including those considered "mentally handicapped.") Foreseeing the potential for over-reliance on a single IQ score, Binet publicly expressed caveats about its use (Thomas & Loxley, 2001). Despite Binet's concerns about widespread use of his intelligence test, demand for the test immediately grew, particularly in the United States. By 1916, Lewis Terman, a psychologist at Stanford University, had modified, expanded, and renamed the test the Stanford–Binet, thereby popularizing its use in the United States (Hanson, 1993).

Science reigned supreme as the Discourse of Truth in the early twentieth century. Remember those social efficiency proponents (see Chapter 1) who drew upon "scientific rationality and technology" to increase the efficiency of public schooling? The emerging field of psychometrics supplied just the "scientific tools" needed to differentiate education according to students' predicted vocational potential. Thus, IQ testing became the means by which to sort individuals into performance levels (e.g., below normal, normal, above normal), thereby maximizing efficiency by offering students *only* the education needed for their predetermined places in society. Given that IQ tests emerged out of the tradition of science, their legitimacy was not called into question, nor was the practice of separating students according to IQ scores (Dudley-Marling, 2010). What naturalizes such practices is their association with the methods of natural science.

If we think about the historical relationship between science and disability as well as the long-established tradition of IQ testing within public schools, it is rather predictable that the IQ test is chosen as a primary assessment tool for special education's eligibility and placement procedures. It is worth noting again that our reliance upon IQ testing has contributed to a well-documented and persisting overrepresentation of children of color in segregated special education settings (see Chapter 2). In the name of meeting the educational needs of children with disabilities, might we have inadvertently re-inscribed notions advanced by the eugenicists—that is, that culturally dominant students of middle to upper social class *belong* in mainstream public education and represent the ideal ("normality") to which others are compared and sorted? And we pose our question again for your consideration—who benefits from this conceptualization and practice?

Featured Voice of Jonathan Mooney

Dear Normal,

You suck.

I know this might sound harsh, and I'm sorry/not sorry to be the one who has to break this to you, but it's time that you heard the truth. You've misled so many people—teachers, children, all of us really—into thinking that there's a "normal" mind and body that we all should have, and you have caused a lot of pain. I know this pain personally because you and I didn't get along right off the bat. I was the kid in school who had such a hard time sitting still that I spent most of the day chilling out with the janitor in the hallway; spent a lot of time hiding in the bathroom to escape reading out loud with tears streaming down my face; and eventually left school for a year in sixth grade. I was diagnosed with multiple language-based learning disabilities and attention deficit disorder. When the educational psychologist broke the news to my mom and me, it was like someone had died. Tissues on the table. Hushed tones. Mirrors covered. Sitting Shiva for the death of my normality. When we left the shrink's office I asked my mom, "Am I normal?" I had crossed that invisible line between the normal and the not normal, the one we all know is there, but aren't quite sure where, or who drew it, and how or why.

Whatever normal was, I wasn't.

But Normal, what are you? Where did you come from and why do you have the power you do in our lives, in our institutions, in our world? How did you become like air—invisible, essential, all around us? Look up normal in any English dictionary and the first definition is "usual, regular, common, typical." How did *this* become something to be aspired to and have the cultural force it has? And force it has. When I walked out of that shrink's office with my mom, I knew that whatever normal was, I wasn't, but it was what I wanted to be.

When I think back on my school experience, I realize it wasn't the ADD or the dyslexia that disabled me. I'm not naïve about the bad stuff that comes with my brain. I struggle with executive functioning and organization; I have explored the feasibility of stapling my car keys to my forehead; and I spell at a third-grade level. But guess what? Good things come with this brain. Research shows that learning and attention differences correlate with enhanced problem-solving abilities, creativity, and entrepreneurship. What disabled me were limitations not in myself, but within the environment. The passive learning experience where kids sit at a desk most of the day; a narrow definition of intelligence conflated with reading and other right brain skills; and a medicalization of differences that reduced my brain to a set of deficits and ignored the strengths that go hand in hand with many brain differences. Normal, you were the problem, not my differences.

I'm far from being alone in thinking you, Normal, are a pain in the ass. We've become infatuated with you in our lives and we worship you without thinking, or knowing, in casual conversation to judge peoples' actions and behaviors; to draw our own lines of who is in and out; to sharpen our individuality and cleave the "others" from our head. We aspire to be like you in all your ambiguity, because of your ambiguity. Canadian philosopher Ian Hacking summed it up when he wrote, "The normal whispers in your ear that what is normal is also right." You are a force, like gravity, holding us in place, sorting the fragments and detritus of the lives, our world, into fixed and knowable categories so we don't get way from ourselves.

Your everywhereness is part of your power—of *your* normality. You name the word; shape the world; then justify the world you have shaped with a shrug of neutrality—*hey, it's just the way it is*. This is normal.

But here is the thing, Normal, you have a history and it is not a history of discovery, but a history of invention. You were born in the mid-1840s with the rise of standardization, industrialization, and statistics. I didn't do too well in my AP statistics class (okay, I didn't even take it!) but I do know that averages are, by definition, abstractions. A statistical norm doesn't exist in the world—it is an aggregation of multiple differences on a curve. The normal or average birth rate for women in America: 2.5. Haven't seen many half-babies in my life. Before you came on the scene we had *the ideal* which, by definition, doesn't exist in the world. The ideal is something to aspire to, to emulate, but never something to impose or mandate. You represent a fundamental shift in human power dynamics. Normal isn't something to just emulate. It is something to be. And as something to be, it is something to enforce. You've been responsible for a great number of social injustices. Because of you, whole groups of people have been labeled as abnormal or sick and their subjugation justified as "treatment." In the nineteenth century, black folks who were enslaved and ran away to escape this injustice were diagnosed with "slave running away sickness." Up until the mid-twentieth century, women were diagnosed by doctors and psychiatrists as suffering from hysteria—a diagnosis used to justify their disenfranchisement. Homosexuality was listed in the American Psychiatric Association's *Diagnostic and Statistical Manual of Mental Disorders* as a personality disorder until the 1970s.

Oh yeah—one more—let's not forget the eugenics movement. In the early twentieth century, a bunch of folks—scientists, geneticists, doctors, and social workers—were so enamored by you that they decided to rid the world of "defectives." Not my word—theirs. Drawing on the new science of genetics, these folks believed that they could "perfect" the human race through forced sterilization and other "interventions." If that sounds a little Third Reich to you—that's because it was. The group first targeted by Nazis were people with "cognitive and physical deficits" in a little-known state-sanctioned eugenics program called Aktion T4. Nazi scientists traveled to the United States to learn the best practices in eugenics. It was, after all, Oliver Wendell Holmes, the chief justice of our Supreme Court, who ruled in *Buck v. Bell* that state-mandated sterilization of defectives against their will was legal.

So, Normal, your time's up. You got to go. The only normal people are people you don't know very well. The moment you get to know another human being—*really* know them, see them not how they should be, but as they actually are—it is not their normality that matters, but their differences, eccentricities, fallibilities, strengths, and weaknesses that constitute their humanity.

Every human being has a right to be different.

Sincerely,

Jonathan Mooney

Disability in Context

Imagine the following scenario. You are teaching in your classroom as you do each day. There is a knock at the door. A stranger enters and asks you to come with her. When you ask what this is about, she smiles and explains that she needs to find out how best to help you teach. Although you are not aware that you need any help in the classroom, you intuit that this encounter has been pre-arranged by someone and is not up for negotiation. Your students stare as you are led from the classroom. On your way down the hallway, you note that all the other teachers remain in their classrooms as usual. The stranger takes you to a small windowless room. She explains that you will be answering questions and that you should do your best. She cautions that there will be some questions that she cannot repeat and some questions that you must answer under a time limit. She takes out a stopwatch. Lastly, you are reminded not to ask whether your answers are correct. The questioning begins. You wonder why the questions do not seem to have much to do with teaching. At the end of two hours, the stranger thanks you for your hard work and accompanies you back to your classroom.

Weeks pass. You are too embarrassed to ask if any other teacher has met with the stranger. You finally put the encounter out of your mind. Then one day the principal calls you into his office. He opens a file that contains paperwork regarding your teaching performance, including a report written by the stranger, in which she explains how well you answered questions compared to same-age teachers working in other parts of the United States. Numeric scores sum up her discussion. In addition to this report, the file contains observations of your teaching (conducted unbeknownst to you) and teacher performance checklists filled out by your principal and your supervisor. The principal explains that your assessment results indicate that you would benefit from teaching fewer students in a smaller classroom with closer supervision. You are moved to the new classroom the following day. You hear the unspoken message. You are less competent than the teachers who remain in their classrooms.

We acknowledge a bit of hyperbole in making our point. However, given that school personnel typically regard special education practices as natural and largely unproblematic, we hope to challenge you to reflect more deeply upon what is considered business as usual. The scenario just described sounds absurd when applied to assessing teacher performance. Yet we expect students (and their parents) to accept this process—without question—as legitimate and beneficial.

Special education assessment is grounded in methods of science. Standardized tests compare an individual's performance to a normative sample; thus, examiners must follow a strict procedure (e.g., using exact words when prompting and only under prescribed circumstances, presenting tasks in a pre-determined order, placing blocks and puzzle pieces in front of the examinee in a specified way). Environmental conditions are likewise standardized. Testing must take place in a de-contextualized setting free from visual and auditory distraction. Moreover, examiners are required to maintain an objective stance to minimize unintended influences upon the testing conditions. Any violation of these procedures invalidates results.

The assessment procedures outlined under IDEIA require us to regard such methods of science as "right and good" and beyond reproach. We are asked to believe that (1) standardized methods yield accurate measures of behavior and cognition; (2) objectivity, de-contextualization, and standardization control for undue influences upon test performance; and (3) deviation from these procedures invalidates truth as conceived by the test author. It is assumed that the "practice of science" *itself* is bias-free and a non-contributory factor within the assessment context. Yet how might the very *practice of standardization* influence test performance as well as the construction of disability?

Context Matters

Not unlike our hyperbolic teacher performance illustration, we might consider what an unnatural social situation it is for a child (who typically is caught unawares) to accompany an unfamiliar adult (who offers minimal explanation) to a small room where timed and untimed questions (of the adult's choosing) are presented for the duration of at least two hours. What is a matter of routine practice to the adult may be experienced by a child as something akin to being "taken in" for police interrogation. In both cases, "the authority" possesses knowledge to which "the subject" is not privy; thus, heightened anxiety on the part of "the subject" might be anticipated and acknowledged as an undue influence upon performance. Yet it is not. Other than the occasional case of a child's extreme resistance to testing, assessments are typically considered to be valid measures of performance. Special education's reliance upon methods of natural science neglects an essential truth—that "human beings are not, like the objects of natural science, things which do not understand themselves" (Joynson, 1974, p. 2). What might children have to tell us about themselves? What aspects of children do we *not* consider, and does that matter? Is it possible that our agreed-upon assessment procedures construct ability/disability in some ways and not others? To engage you in thinking about these questions with us, we introduce two persons with disabilities, Paul and Madelyn, for you to consider within the *context* of their respective real-life stories.

Genius of Invention

Jan's husband, Paul, has a congenital sensorineural hearing impairment. He easily moves through the world with two hearing aids and a lifetime's worth of acquired compensatory strategies. What began as a mild hearing loss during childhood is now a moderate to severe hearing loss at midlife. Although there are a few tones within the speaking range that he cannot hear at all, Paul's hearing loss is not readily discernible to others. He considers his hearing loss as one of many traits that make him who he is—a contributing trait no different in scale than, for example, his Italian-American heritage.

Having attended elementary school during the 1960s (before the advent of P.L. 94–142), Paul's hearing loss drew attention only during the routine vision and hearing screenings administered by school nurses. Each year, he took a letter home indicating a failed hearing screening. And each year, his parents disregarded the letter. Within the context of a large and lively Italian-American household, Paul's hearing loss was simply a matter of accommodation. Rather than "fix" Paul's ears, everyone watched television with the volume turned up a little louder. Instead of asking Paul to approximate normal hearing behavior, family members adjusted *their* manner of interaction (e.g., using touch to get his attention, facing him when speaking, repeating speech as needed). No more attention was given to these accommodations than those made for any other family member's needs. And, in turn, he figured out how to compensate for his hearing difference in ways that worked for him and others.

Paul earned a college degree without the benefit of academic accommodations or sound amplification. By young adulthood, however, his hearing had worsened. At the time of our marriage in 1980, Paul was fitted with a single hearing aid for the first time. Given the shifting nature of his hearing loss over time, each new stage brought another opportunity for problem solving—not unlike other life challenges we faced together. Increasing technological advances offered a range of solutions at every phase—most of which we could not have imagined years earlier.

We keep a thickening file of annual audiograms that traces the degenerative path of Paul's hearing. At his yearly examination, he sits in a soundproof booth and repeats single words spoken to him through a headset. He takes the same test each year so that comparisons can be drawn. Based upon the results, the audiologist calibrates his hearing aids or recommends new hearing aids.

I always go with Paul to his audiology appointments. And each year, the extent of hearing loss revealed by the examination stuns me. I began to wonder if I might be in denial about the progression of his hearing loss because he never seems to me as impaired as results indicate. Paul dreads these sessions because of his own inability to reconcile the audiograms with the way he sees himself. For years, it never occurred to us to question the *nature* of the examination.

Certainly, the technology of sound amplification has had a positive impact upon Paul's daily life. In fact, I initially attributed Paul's successful negotiation of the "hearing world" solely to the technology in his ears—until we took our first trip abroad. Having convinced him that we could rely upon my high school French, I eagerly took up the task of translation as soon as we touched European soil. In the time it took for me to translate the first sign, Paul figured out where to go and what to do. I stared at him. He grinned back. "You know what? I can't hear in English. And I can't hear in French. It really doesn't matter where I am, now does it?" And so, I trailed behind my tour guide who moved competently and confidently through the world as he does every day—relying upon ingenious ways of his own invention to cull meaning from visual context.

Because of that trip, I came to understand the discrepancy between my perceptions of Paul "in the world" and the audiogram results. The enclosed environment of the audiology booth strips Paul of all sensory input other than auditory stimuli presented through a headset. It is a pure measure of auditory acuity. What the examination does not measure is Paul's "hearing behavior" within the context of daily life. His *actual* level of functioning in the world, even without hearing aids, is stronger than would be expected given the level of pathology documented on the audiogram. In other words, Paul's disability can be constructed differently depending upon whether we focus upon his auditory acuity as measured within a clinical context to calibrate his hearing aids or upon his "hearing behavior" as performed within the context of everyday life.

If we return to our discussion of special education assessment practices, we can see how a focus upon uncovering pathology (disability) as a condition within-the-individual might yield a different construction than an evaluation that acknowledges the individual-in-context. If context matters—which we believe it does—what might we be missing by evaluating children using de-contextualized, standardized, and objective methods of science? Is it possible that children appear less able when asked to perform under conditions that remove everyday contextual cues? Could reliance upon methods of science account for discrepancies parents report between depictions of their child within psycho-educational reports and their perceptions of their child-in-context? How might educational ideas and practices about what constitutes normal/abnormal (and the accompanying values assigned to children on either side of this imposed dichotomy) extend into our communities and larger culture? We invite you to consider these questions as you read on to Madelyn's story.

Madelyn's Village

Madelyn is a newly-turned nine year old (an important distinction in Kid World) with deep brown eyes and an impish grin. She wears her light brown hair in a jaunty ponytail that swishes from side to side as she walks. I spent a recent warm and breezy Saturday with Madelyn. We shared a lazy afternoon playing cards on the back porch, munching on chips and dip, pouring endless refills of soda, and shaking pinky fingers to swear secrecy about Madelyn's whispered opinions about the cutest boys in the fourth grade.

But all is not as it seems. Madelyn is the daughter of a friend of mine who participated in a pilot study I conducted a few years ago on mothers and special education. Currently, Madelyn's mother is challenging the school district's change in her daughter's disability status from "language impaired" to "mentally impaired" and asked for my consultative assistance.

Madelyn's story belongs to the discourse of school in America that has naturalized ways of talking about the characteristics of *individual* children. In its adoption of the necessary dichotomy of success/failure put forth by school in America, Madelyn's public school has enveloped her within the discourse of child development, norms, tests, grade levels, and achievement and labeled her deficient on all counts. Her immediate world is a white middle-class family with college-educated parents and four academically gifted older siblings. The family lives in a wealthy bedroom community of New York City, whose mostly white and Asian-American inhabitants are successful (in American terms), as are their offspring. This is a community comprised of persons at the top of the competition game in America. Madelyn does not fit neatly within any of these worlds. Given that her cultural, socioeconomic, and ethnic background is a good match for success in school, there can be only one explanation for the unexpected failure in her young life. She *is* "mentally impaired," and what a tragedy it is for her and her family. Madelyn *is* a failure as defined for nine-year-old children in America.

I had not seen Madelyn in a few years. She is, however, quite close to a mutual friend, Kate, who frequently spends time in the family's home. I arrange to visit Kate on a day when she had agreed to babysit Madelyn. I anticipated that my presence in this scenario would be more natural than an artificially arranged time with Madelyn. To my surprise, this was not to be. As soon as I arrive, Kate makes quick introductions between Madelyn and myself and breezes out to attend a wedding—abruptly leaving Madelyn and me to ourselves. We barely turn to one another when a neighbor comes onto the porch. Out of nowhere, Kate's cousin materializes to urgently shoo him away. I hear her whisper to him, "She's here to work with Madelyn." And so, it seems that Madelyn and I are unable to escape the discourse of school. Others behave around us in accordance with the labels school has given us. Madelyn is the Failing Child and I am the Benevolent Special Educator. The school discourse has followed us into the community.

On a beautiful Saturday afternoon, a nine-year-old (supposedly "mentally impaired") girl confronts an unusual social situation. An unfamiliar overgrown playmate is dumped inexplicably into her world. Through some sense of intuition, Madelyn recognizes and accepts the responsibility that has been thrust upon her and dutifully interacts with me. She is engaging and embracing. I wonder how many other nine-year-old children would have done the same.

As we play a card game, Kate's cousin reappears, watches for a moment, and asks aloud, "Is this to test her cognitive skills?" I grimace and state the obvious—we are playing a game. Immediately I recognize my lie. I am complicit in constructing Madelyn in terms of success and failure. Like those who search for evidence of What Madelyn Cannot Do, I, under the guise of play, search for evidence of What Madelyn *Can* Do. I am likewise guilty of participating in the endless gazing upon and documenting of Madelyn.

Kate returns and asks, "How did she do?" I flatly reply that Madelyn and I had a fun time together. She goes on to describe her concerns about Madelyn's conversational skills, recounting a series of questions she asked Madelyn earlier in the day on which she received little elaboration—the boring kinds of questions that adults ask children when they are not really interested in hearing what they have to say. Any nine year old might have responded in monosyllables. Yet this behavior is registered and documented as deficient because that is what Madelyn is *expected* to be—and the behavior is catalogued as additional evidence of Madelyn's failure. This exchange supports Varenne and McDermott's (1998) critique of American public schools in which they point out that "the child is made to occupy the foreground for comparison to other children. It may take a whole village to raise a child, but in America, at the most sacred of times when lives are in balance, the child stands alone for the village to judge" (p. 107). And Madelyn's village sets comparisons at the highest competitive point.

Later, we gather on the front porch. The neighbor fumbles for a lighter. Madelyn watches him. She asks me discreetly to remind her of his name. She politely steps up to him, addresses him by name, and asks that he please not smoke around us. This massive young man, a bouncer by profession, smiles around the cigarette poised in his mouth for lighting and continues his smoker's ritual. Madelyn stands firm and politely repeats her request. He stares at her momentarily, then moves off the porch. Satisfied, Madelyn resettles herself back into her chair.

It is worth noting that Madelyn scored below her age level on the Vineland Adaptive Behavior Scales—one of the social behavior measures that contributed to her newly acquired label of "mentally impaired." Had the previous scenario been a test of social competence, how many nine year olds could have negotiated it as successfully as Madelyn? Is this but one example of the "fleeting moments of success that no one notices… the things kids can do that nonetheless disappear in the normal tellings of their lives" (Varenne & McDermott, 1998, p.107)?

Now let's return to the questions we asked you to consider while reading Madelyn's story. How well do you think a typical special education assessment might reflect the *essence* of Madelyn? Is it possible that Madelyn could appear less able when asked to perform in a de-contextualized and standardized environment? How might reliance upon methods of science account for a discrepancy between the way Madelyn's mother understands her child-in-context and the scientific test results that point to acquired "mental impairment" since her last assessment? In what ways could you see ideas and values regarding "normal" and "abnormal" circulating beyond school and into Madelyn's community? And what does this mean for Madelyn's young life?

The Individual Model: Disability Narratives

Having presented explanations of the medical model of disability and the social model of disability for your consideration, we must point out that neither of these frameworks includes the individual and embodied experience of disability. Where is knowledge told by people with disabilities? What perspectives do people with disabilities have to tell us about negotiating a world designed for the able-bodied? What is the impact of temporarily able-bodied people (meaning that anyone can acquire a disability through accident or health issues and everyone who lives long enough will develop infirmities of old age) speaking and writing for and about people with disabilities?

In the inclusion courses that we teach, disability narratives are an important aspect of the curriculum. In fact, our students engage with disability narratives before exposure to two major medical model sources for defining disability—the 13 categories of disability identified within IDEIA (see Chapter 4) and the diagnostic criteria for "mental disorders" (including ADHD, autism, and specific learning disorder) in the *Diagnostic and Statistical Manual of Mental Disorders* (*DSM-5*; American Psychiatric Association, 2013) used by healthcare professionals in the United States and much of the world. As teacher educators, we find that juxtaposing autobiographical narratives with other disability models gives rise to rich and textured classroom conversations about the nature of disability.

First-person narratives "frame our understandings of raw, unorganized experience, giving it coherent meaning and making it accessible to us through story" (Garland-Thomson, 2007, p. 121). In contrast to acritical renderings of disability that underlie special education practice, disability narratives offer stories of lived experiences, most of which include personal commentaries about schooling. Narratives are necessarily told within a particular context and, as such, reveal much about the society and culture within which the storyteller lives (Smith & Sparkes, 2008).

Disability narratives are especially relevant if you have not had a personal experience with disability (your own or a relative or friend with a disability). Unless disability impacts our lives in some way, most of us move through life giving it little to no thought. We are not suggesting that lack of attention to disability is a moral failing, but rather is the result of living in a world that actively privileges able-bodied people. For example, you enjoy able-bodied privilege if you regularly *do not* have to think about whether:

• The place where you are meeting your friends is wheelchair accessible
• The elevator is working in the subway or even has an elevator
• A theater or conference center provides augmented listening devices or audio-transcription
• A street has an audible crossing signal
• The house or apartment building where your friend lives has front steps
• The restroom in the restaurant is upstairs or downstairs
• The doctor, police officer, waiter, sales clerk or anyone knows American sign language
• The restaurant has a braille menu
• The taxi you hail is accessible or will stop for you as a wheelchair user
• The printed material you need is also available in large type font
• The play you want to see has sudden loud sounds or strobe lights

The above list is a mere sampling of able-bodied privilege. Once you gain awareness, you will wonder how you never noticed it before. It is, quite simply, everywhere.

With the rise of inclusion, every general education classroom has students with and without disabilities. Acknowledging and understanding able-bodied privilege is imperative for working in integrated spaces. If you are an able-bodied teacher, how might your privileges impact the ways in which you understand students with disabilities? In what ways might your classroom context and practice privilege students without disabilities?

Try jumpstarting your thinking by engaging with authors of disability narratives who have much to teach us. We promise that you will be drawn into compelling stories that will significantly enhance your understanding of disability experience—especially when compared to lists of diagnostic criteria. If you are like most of our students, you will discover more about your similarities to the authors than differences. For your convenience, we have organized a list of narratives by disability category in Box 3.1.

Box 3.1 Disability Narratives

Attention Deficit Hyperactivity Disorder

Jergen, R. (2004). *The little monster: Growing up with ADHD*. Lanham, MD: Rowman& Littlefield.
Taylor, B. (2008). *ADHD & me: What I learned from lighting fires at the dinner table*. Oakland, CA: New Harbinger Publications.

Autism/Asperger syndrome

Grandin, T. (2006). *Thinking in pictures, expanded edition: My life with autism.* New York, NY: Vintage Books.

Higashida, N. (2016). *The reason I jump: The inner voice of a thirteen-year-old boy.* New York, NY: Random House.

Prahlad, A. (2017). *Secret life of a black Aspie.* Fairbanks, AK: University of Alaska Press.

Robison, J. E. (2007). *Look me in the eye: My life with Asperger's.* New York, NY: Random House.

Tammet, D. (2007). *Born on a blue day: Inside the extraordinary mind of an autistic savant.* New York, NY: Simon & Schuster.

Willey, L. H. (1999). *Pretending to be normal: Living with Asperger's syndrome.* London: Jessica Kingsley.

Deafness/hearing impairment

Brueggemann, B. (1999). *Lend me your ear: Rhetorical constructions of deafness.* Washington, DC: Gallaudet University Press.

Galloway, T. (2009). *Mean little deaf queer.* Boston, MA: Beacon Press.

Kisor, H. (2010). *What's that pig outdoors? A memoir.* Urbana, IL: University of Illinois Press.

Laborit, E. (2000). *The cry of the gull.* Washington, DC: Gallaudet University Press.

Vasishta, M. (2006). *Deaf in Delhi.* Washington, DC: Gallaudet University Press.

Down syndrome and developmental disabilities

Austin, P. (2014). *Beautiful eyes.* New York, NY: W.W. Norton and Co. (Parent memoir)

Kingsley, J. & Levitz, M. (1994). *Count us in: Growing up with Down syndrome.* New York, NY: Harcourt Brace & Co.

Simon, R. (2002). *Riding the bus with my sister.* New York, NY: Houghton-Mifflin. (Sibling memoir)

Learning disabilities

Abeel, S. (2004). *My thirteenth winter: A memoir.* New York, NY: Scholastic Press.

Mooney, J. (2008). *Short bus: A journey beyond normal.* New York, NY: Holt McDougal.

Schultz, P. (2012). *My dyslexia.* New York, NY: W.W. Norton.

Villasenor, V. (2005). *Burro genius: A memoir.* New York, NY: Harper Collins.

Physical disabilities

Bauby, J. D. (1998). *The diving bell and the butterfly: A memoir of life in death.* New York, NY: Random House.

Burcaw, S. (2014). *Laughing at my nightmare.* New York, NY: Roaring Brook Press.

Fries, K. (2003). *Body, remember: A memoir.* Madison, WI: University of Wisconsin Press.

Grealy, L. (2003). *Autobiography of a face.* New York, NY: Harper Collins.

Johnson, H. M. (2005). *Too late to die young: Nearly true tales from a life*. New York, NY: Henry Holt & Co.

Linton, S. (2007). *My body politic: A memoir*. Ann Arbor, MI: University of Michigan Press.

Long, M. S. (1999). *If your dreams are big enough, the facts don't count*. Wallace, CA: Massey-Reyner.

Mairs, N. (1996). *Waist-high in the world: A life among the nondisabled*. Boston, MA: Beacon Press.

Mee, C. L. (1999). *A nearly normal life*. Boston, MA: Little, Brown.

Rapp, E. (2006). *Poster child: A memoir*. St. Martin's Press.

Sanford, M. (2006). *Waking: A memoir of trauma and transcendence*. Emmaus, PA: Rodale.

Tourette's syndrome

Cohen, B. (2005). *Front of the class: How Tourette syndrome made me the teacher I never had*. New York, NY: St. Martin's Press.

Wilensky, A. (2000). *Passing for normal*. New York, NY: Broadway.

Visual impairment

Kleege, G. (1999). *Sight unseen*. New Haven, CT: Yale University Press.

Kuusisto, S. (1999). *Planet of the blind*. New York, NY: Delta.

While we recommend any of the disability titles on this list, we wish to point out that most of the books are written by white, educated, heterosexual, middle- to upper-class authors—reflecting the general privilege of this demographic. Just as the experience of a disability is specific to an individual (even those with the same disability), so is the intersection of disability with multiple identities. In other words, identity markers such as race, class, gender, ethnicity, and sexual orientation—along with the privileges and oppressions that each marker holds for an individual—influence the disability experience. We recognize that most disability narratives "privilege white bodies, demonstrating the need to seek out narratives that can address the politics of race and disability" (Ferri, 2011, p. 2275). The Autism Women's Network has made a significant contribution toward the goal of bringing diverse voices of people with disabilities to the fore in their recent publication, *All the Weight of Our Dreams: On Living Racialized Autism* (Brown, Ashkenazy, & Onaiwu, 2017), a volume that includes poetry, essays, short fiction, photography, and artwork by 61 writers and artists who represent people of color with autism.

Social media is a teeming public platform for disability. There are many information websites for people with disabilities (e.g., https://themighty.com/, www.disabilityscoop.com/, and http://disabilityhorizons.com/); parents of children with disabilities (e.g., www.parentcenterhub.org/, https://exceptionallives.org, and www.p2pusa.org/); and teachers of students with disabilities (e.g., www.teachervision.com, www.cast.org, and www.theinclusiveclass.com).

A wide range of websites address disability topics, such as disability organizations (e.g., www.disabled-world.com/disability/foundations/us-organizations.php); assistive technology (e.g., www.ctdinstitute.org, www.thetechadvocate.org, and www.understood.org);

adaptive clothing (e.g., www.target.com/c/adaptive-clothing/-/N-ksyrz, https://usa.tommy.com/en/tommy-adaptive, and https://abldenim.com/); and disability law (e.g., www.pacer.org/parent/section504, www.parentcenterhub.org/idea, and www.wrightslaw.com).

The internet is a democratic medium for diverse disability voices. We recommend that you check out "The 8 Most Powerful TED Talks on Disability" at https://101mobility.com/blog/8-most-powerful-ted-talks-on-disability/), and, on YouTube: Sue Austin, "Deep Sea Diving … in a Wheelchair"; Caroline Casey, "Looking Past Limits"; Rosie King, "How Autism Freed Me to Be Myself"; Aimee Mullins, "The Opportunity of Adversity"; Keith Nolan, "Deaf in the Military"; Janine Shepherd, "A Broken Body Isn't a Broken Person"; Stella Young, "I'm Not Your Inspiration, Thank You Very Much"; and Maysoon Zayid, "I got 99 Problems … Palsy is Just One."

Disability bloggers have a strong presence on social media and offer individual perspectives on disability experience. The following is a sample of disability blogs to get you started: http://cripperella.blogspot.ca/, www.dominickevans.com/, http://disabilitythinking.blogspot.ca/, http://wordsiwheelby.com/, www.autistichoya.com/, http://feministsonar.com/, http://nonspeakingautistics peaking.blogspot.ca), http://kriphopnation.com, and https://learnfromautistics.com).

Our "Blog" on Temporary Disability

After a lifetime of working as special educators and professors/researchers in disability studies, we both (ironically) experienced temporary disability last year. Drawing on the current practice of "blogging," we offer our individual perspectives on how temporary disability led us to rethink what we thought we already knew.

As referenced elsewhere in this chapter, I (Jan) have lived life alongside my husband whose congenital hearing impairment has shifted from mild to severe over the years. I thought I understood his disability…until I experienced a sudden hearing loss of my own. On a weekend trip to a college reunion, I flew with a head and chest cold. After landing, I noticed that my hearing was severely muffled. When home remedies did not "pop" my ears, I visited an urgent care center. I was diagnosed with an ear infection and bronchitis. Antibiotics did wonders for the bronchitis, but not for my hearing. After the return flight home, I could hear close to nothing. A visit to an ear, nose, and throat doctor confirmed that I did not have an ear infection; rather, my Eustachian tubes had collapsed. I was assured that my hearing would return, although it was impossible to predict how long it might take.

What I learned during what turned out to be a full month is that no one anywhere expected me to show up. Not a single context in my everyday life was prepared for someone with severe hearing loss. The abrupt disruption of my able-bodied privilege resulted in immediate lack of access to the world I had always known. Perhaps most disconcerting was the impact of my hearing loss on my ability to teach. Communication is the heart of teaching and I could not hear my students. Suddenly a case study in my own course on inclusion, my students rallied with brilliant ideas for how we could communicate. I cannot say the same for my colleagues. I began every meeting with a reminder that I could not hear and a few simple suggestions for accessibility; yet, without exception, it was forgotten after a few minutes of interaction. It is noteworthy that my colleagues are caring and thoughtful people who showed genuine concern for my situation. But when my temporary disability required *doing* something, there was almost immediate default to able-bodied privilege with little to no recognition of its exclusionary impact.

I was exhausted by hearing loss. Like an observer behind a glass wall, I could *see* life unfolding around me but could not figure out how to participate. People who know me well remarked that I seemed withdrawn. Two weeks into the experience, my husband remembered he had an old pair of hearing aids. He put them into my ears. I burst into tears at hearing *sound*—albeit tinny. Wearing ill-fitting hearing aids, I managed to teach for another two weeks and lead a large professional development workshop for teachers. I do not think that I could have done so otherwise.

My hearing returned as suddenly as it left. What has not left is the memory of living in a world no longer meant for me and entering the world my husband inhabits each day. This "crossing over" was meaningful for both of us. In a strange way, we kind of miss it. I am acutely aware that my temporary disability is *my* experience and not his. Paul lives his life with a lifetime of experiences, acquired "hearing strategies", and the benefit of hearing technology. I knew that my hearing would return. He knows his hearing will worsen. As close as this experience placed me to Paul's everyday life, I know, now more than ever, that I cannot fully know his world because of the able-bodied privileges within which I live my own life.

A short while ago, I (David) experienced a temporary disability. In brief, my kneecap became irritated by something within it, likely ripped cartilage. A visit to the doctor put my mind at rest as he told me I could continue to do everything I usually did, including swimming several times a week for exercise, as long as I did not "overdo" stress on the knee by walking excessively, running, or dancing—and it would very likely self-heal. He gave me a shot of Cortisone directly into the knee to remove my awareness of pain. Alas, things did not go as well as he predicted and I found my ability to walk was being compromised. The knee swelled. I forced myself (the stoic upbringing, what can I say?) to go to a dissertation proposal defense at Fordham University, as I did not wish to add any stress to the doctoral student who was presenting. And yet, I knew I could not manage the steps to the subway, so needed to take the bus. In getting on and off the bus I experienced a spike of anxiety, feeling I was now much slower than "normal," and New Yorkers are not known for their patience. Once off the bus, I experienced significant pain and wondered if I was inadvertently exacerbating the original irritation by going about my daily basis. I still had to walk two blocks to the university and found myself stopping periodically, holding onto a fence, and willing myself to continue. People looked at me, aware that all was not well, yet whatever it was did not evoke a response from them other than mild curiosity.

As soon as I arrived at the proposal defense meeting I told them I was in pain and it was easier to stand and/or pace very slowly, rather than sit stationary in a chair. The student and other committee members were understanding, and we adapted to me being vertical and in motion. It was then that I realized I was in a form of denial and needed help. Once the student "pass" was agreed upon, I called for an appointment and the doctor agreed to see me within a couple of hours. When I approached the bus to get home, dragging my leg, the driver closed the doors abruptly. So I banged on the window with my hand and, unable to ignore me, he begrudgingly opened them. I found myself saying, unexpectedly, "I have difficulty walking," as if it justified my challenging his original decision and explained my assertive gesture of banging.

To cut a long story short, I took a taxi to the doctors, but was by then in excruciating pain as I could not bend my leg; I had to enter the car as best I could using three malleable limbs. Once there, the doctor drew a pint of amber-colored fluid from my knee, gave me strong painkillers, told me to stay put in the apartment and to cancel my flight to the UK to spend Christmas with my folks. The doctor also gave me his personal cell number in case things got worse and he needed to facilitate emergency surgery. The following few days proved challenging as I could not place any weight at all on the knee, and I invented ways to side-shuffle to the rest room on one foot and two hands on the wall. As the days passed, the body healed, and my flight home was rescheduled for early January.

I am mindful not to dwell too much on pain in this story, because pain is… painful. I don't want to equate it with disability, although it can't be taken out of the equation altogether in this case. Drugs and rest, and then physiotherapy, literally got me back on my feet again. On reflecting on this experience, I asked myself what did I observe, experience, learn? How did society respond to me in a disabling condition, and how did I respond to the challenges society posed? I realized that my travel options were restricted as very few subway stations have elevators (and as a friend who uses a wheelchair informs me, those that have them are not necessarily working). Getting on and off buses as a slower person seemed as if I was inconveniencing others, including the driver. Not moving at a "normal" pace in the street and stopping to rest meant I was given "looks" that I could not quite discern. I'd like to think of them as a form of veiled concern, but I didn't know for sure. The confined space of the taxi actually caused me greater pain as I had to lift and slightly bend my inflated knee (not without a string of expletives). In sum, the everyday modes of travel all became difficult. To add insult to injury (literally), the airline would not accept my doctor's letter and with Scrooge-like indifference to Christmas told me I'd have to pay a steep change of ticket fee. I heard businesses are often not empathetic to disabling conditions, but now I knew personally. Issues of lack of access (to transport) and accommodation (needed to change original plans) were duly noted. On the bright side, I found out how inventive we can be with our bodies when we need something, such as my one-foot shuffle trip to the loo, or balancing on furniture in the kitchen to make a meal, or using a prosthesis such as a cane to "lean on," as needed, so we can participate in the world.

In closing, I weighed the pros and cons of including this narrative as I don't wish to trivialize, minimize, or misrepresent disability in general through my temporary experience. It did strike me that I have had a number of colleagues in similar situations such as having a leg or arm in a cast, and they wanted to speak about their experience as it gave them an entirely different perspective on how the world is configured in ways small and large, from public transport to the shape of door handles. In attempting to reconcile my own thoughts about the topic of temporary or permanent disability, I see it as a way to: think differently; rise to existing challenges; create new ways of doing things; remind us that we're all interdependent, and melt the sacred myth of individualism.

Expanding Notions of Diversity

We recognize that it is unsettling to trouble what appears natural and right. Here you are, a new teacher, focused upon *getting* it right, and we ask you to think about *if* it is right. We imagine that survival takes up most of your energy. And now we remind you that teaching is also a *social* responsibility requiring careful thought and action. Young lives are at stake. The responsibility of it all can—and should—seem overwhelming. It is tempting to believe that "all that *other* stuff" will take care of itself somehow. Besides, it feels good to receive praise for carrying out your prescribed duties well and without question. Why complicate an inherently complicated job with concerns about ethics?

From our vantage point as veteran special educators, we regard the passage of P.L. 94–142 as a *major* advancement for persons with disabilities in this country. The spirit of the law reflects the hopes and dreams of persons with disabilities and their advocates. Special education law guarantees the right to a free and appropriate public education for *all* children. Thus, it is not our intention to dismiss the many positive contributions of this law. We do not doubt the "right and good" intentions of those who work hard to uphold the procedures and practices that support our agreed-upon response to disability in public schools. What does concern us, however, is that a far greater amount of time, energy, and money is devoted to maintaining the current system than is spent on recognizing, reflecting upon, and responding to the *consequences* of those procedures and practices in the lives of children with disabilities and their families.

It is easier to believe that the current system is unproblematic than to name and respond to challenges. The former does not require action, while the latter does. Reflecting upon ourselves is, quite frankly, hard work. For example, let's consider the question posed in our chapter title: *"What if I don't feel ready to teach those kids?"* We might understand the question as concern about not having proper training to teach children with disabilities. In fact, a teacher who poses such a question may truly believe that lack of training is her biggest concern. However, "I don't feel ready" may also reflect a variety of *unexamined* attitudes, fears, and beliefs, such as:

- I don't want to teach those kids.
- I am afraid to teach those kids.
- It is not my job to teach those kids.
- I don't believe those kids belong in my classroom.
- I don't know how to work with those kids.
- I think those kids differ significantly from kids without disabilities.
- I believe that those kids need special teachers because they learn differently.
- I don't think that I can handle those kids *and* do my job.
- I have way too many responsibilities to take on teaching those kids.
- I don't think I have the patience to work with those kids.
- I don't know why I am expected to teach those kids.
- I am afraid that I *can't* teach those kids.
- I don't understand special education paperwork and I don't want to.
- I think that only experienced teachers should teach those kids.
- I believe that those kids unfairly take time from other kids.
- I am afraid those kids will make me look like I don't know what I'm doing.

Do any of these statements ring true to you? If you acknowledge having had any of these thoughts, pat yourself on the back. You are on your way to reflection. It is not our intention to pass judgment on teachers (new or experienced) who agree with any of the above statements. In fact, we hope that our first three chapters help clarify *why* such ideas circulate among teachers. To honestly examine and reflect upon our beliefs, values, attitudes, and fears is to take the first step toward creating inclusive communities. So far, we have focused a great deal upon explaining both how "we got here from there" and how the medical model constructs disability. It is our hope that such discussions provide new space within which to (re)consider naturalized ideas about children with *and* without disabilities.

As teacher educators, we ask our students to rethink the "myth of homogeneity" that drives the unending pursuit of new methods for sorting children according to their sameness. We routinely hear teachers lament about the number of students who fall outside of defined "grade level" performance. Year after year, teachers express disappointment that a "grade level" class has yet to materialize in their teaching career. And it never will. We have *constructed* notions about "grade level" in the same way that we have constructed notions about normal and abnormal. In fact, it appears that the institution of special education has reinforced the notion of "grade level" by providing a *place* to send the children *not* on "grade level." If we properly sort out those children who qualify for special education (i.e., those children deemed outside the range of "normal"), surely then we will have "grade level" classrooms. And yet it does not happen—despite all the ways we devise to determine who belongs and who does not belong. So perhaps the problem lies within our expectations. To believe that homogeneity exists (presumably out there somewhere, in someone else's classroom) is to be forever disappointed and to miss the point of teaching. Somehow it seems that special education's conceptualization of normal/abnormal has influenced teachers to see students as either "belonging" or "not belonging." Woe be to the child deemed as "not belonging" in special education (i.e., test results indicate ineligibility for services) whose teacher sees him or her as "not belonging" in general education either. We must step back and ask ourselves what a free and appropriate public education for *all* children really means.

We might begin by reframing our expectations. Why is it that we continue to be surprised by the diversity inherent among students in any given classroom? Why not anticipate *diversity* rather than homogeneity? Every class community is a unique mosaic of variation. Children come to us with all kinds of multiple and intersecting forms of diversity (e.g., ethnicity, socioeconomic class, family configuration, religion, culture, race, linguistic tradition, background knowledge, gender, life experience, and ability). In other words, children come to school bearing all of what makes them human.

Inclusive communities acknowledge and draw upon all manner of human variation. Unlike traditional special education that serves only those students deemed "eligible" because of an identified disability, inclusive practices address the academic and social needs of *all* students. Diversity *is* the heart of inclusion. So, let's move on to the next chapter for a discussion about the nature of inclusive practices.

Questions to Consider

1. What do you see as the consequences of the medical model of disability within public schools?
2. How is disability constructed within public schools?
3. Should we include students with disabilities in general education classes? Why or why not?
4. Can you see vestiges of eugenics within special education today? Explain.
5. Who benefits from a medical model of disability within public schools and why?
6. How might standardized testing methods influence test performance as well as the construction of disability?
7. How much influence do you think that *context* has upon the way in which we perceive disability? Give examples to support your position.
8. What unexamined attitudes, fears, or beliefs might you have about students with disabilities? What do you think is the origin of those ideas?
9. In what ways has special education reinforced expectations for homogeneous classrooms?

References

American Psychiatric Association. (2013). *Diagnostic and statistical manual of mental disorders* 5th ed.). Arlington, VA: Author.

Baynton, D. (2016). *Defectives in the land: Disability and immigration in the age of eugenics.* Chicago, IL: University of Chigaco Press.

Brown, L. X. Z., Ashkenazy, E., & Onaiwu, M. (Eds.). (2017). *All the weight of our dreams: On living racialized autism.* Lincoln, NE: Dragonbee Press.

Connor, D. J. & Valle, J. W. (2015). A socio-cultural reframing of science and dis/ability in education: Past problems, current concerns, and future possibilities. *Journal of Cultural Studies of Science Education, 10*(2), 1103–12.

Conners, C. K. (2008). *Conners Comprehensive Behavior Rating Scales* (3rd ed.). New York, NY: Pearson.

Corker, M. & Shakespeare, T. (2002). *Disability/postmodernity: Embodying disability theory.* New York, NY: Continuum.

Davis, L. J. (2016). Constructing normalcy. In L. J. Davis (Ed.), *Disability studies reader* (5th ed., pp. 9–28). New York, NY: Routledge.

Dudley-Marling, C. (2010). *The myth of the normal curve.* New York, NY: Peter Lang.

Ferri, B. (2011). *Disability life writing and the politics of knowing.* Retrieved from www.academia.edu/651432/Disability_Life_Writing_and_the_Politics_of_Knowing

Garland-Thomson, R. (2007). *Extraordinary bodies: Figuring physical disability in American culture and literature.* New York, NY: Columbia University Press.

Hanson, F. A. (1993). *Testing, testing: Social consequences of the examined life.* Berkeley, CA: University of California Press.

Joynson, R. B (1974). *Psychology and common sense.* London: Routledge.

Linton, S. (1998). *Claiming disability.* New York, NY: New York University Press.

Markwardt, F. C. (2009). *Peabody Individual Achievement Test—PIAT-R/NU.* New York, NY: Pearson.

Nielsen, K. (2012). *A disability history of the United States.* Boston, MA: Beacon Press.

Psychological Corporation. (2014). *Wechsler Individual Achievement Test®—WIAT®-IV.* New York, NY: Author.

Roid, G. H. (2003). *Stanford–Binet Intelligence Scales* (5th ed.). Rolling Meadows, IL: Riverside Publishing.

Schrank, F. A., Mather, N., & McGrew, K. S. (2014a). *Woodcock–Johnson IV Tests of Cognitive Abilities.* Rolling Meadows, IL: Riverside Publishing.

Schrank, F. A., Mather, N., & McGrew, K. S. (2014b). *Woodcock–Johnson IV Tests of Achievement.* Rolling Meadows, IL: Riverside Publishing.

Smith, B. & Sparkes, A. C. (2008). Narrative and its potential for contribution to disability studies. *Disability & Society, 23*(1), 17–28.

Sparrow, S., Cicchetti, D. V., & Saulnier, C. A. (2016). *Vineland Adaptive Behavior Scales* (3rd ed.). New York, NY: Pearson.

Stern, A. M. (2015). *Eugenic nation: Faults and frontiers of better breeding in modern America.* Oakland, CA: University of California Press.

Thomas, G. & Loxley, A. (2001). *Deconstructing special education and constructing inclusion.* Philadelphia, PA: Open University Press.

Valencia, R. R. (1997). *The evolution of deficit thinking: Educational thought and practice.* Portland, OR: Psychology Press.

Valencia, R. R. (2010). *Dismantling contemporary deficit thinking: Educational thought and practice.* London: Routledge.

Valle, J. (2009). *What mothers say about special education: From the 1960s to the present.* London: Palgrave Macmillan.

Valle, J. & Aponte, E. (2002). IDEA: A Bakhtinian perspective on parent and professional discourse. *Journal of Learning Disabilities, 35*(5), 469–79.

Varenne, H. & McDermott, R. (1998). *Successful failure: The school America builds.* Boulder, CO: Westview Press.

4 Practicing Educational Equity in a Democracy

"What if I'm still not sure about inclusion?"

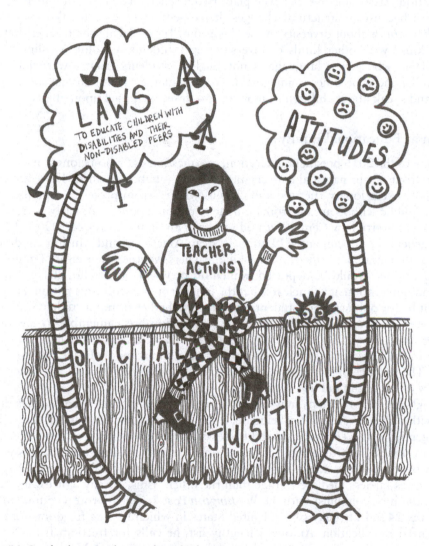

Cartoon #4 On the fence in the Garden of Education

As is routine for the first class of my education courses, I (Jan) ask students to introduce themselves to one another and talk a bit about their current teaching positions and/or past teaching experiences. Recently, a first-year teacher—with a mere few days under her belt—described her new assignment as a second-grade bilingual special education teacher co-teaching in an inclusive classroom with a general education teacher. Reflecting for a moment on the past few days, she wondered aloud about her preparation for this model of inclusion. Her face clouded. Then she said, "My co-teacher told me how glad she is to have me in her classroom because she does not like to work with slow kids. That's not *right*, is it?" A few days into her career, this young teacher knows what her experienced colleague does not. This is *not* inclusion. And it is *not* right.

We can pass laws. We can move children out of segregated classrooms and into general education classrooms. We can even place two teachers in a classroom. Inclusion does not happen because of structural changes. It happens when a shift takes place in the way teachers *think* about diversity in the classroom. Try replacing the teacher's reference to "slow kids" with other kinds of diversity (e.g., students of color, Muslim students, girls, students whose first language is not English, students from low socioeconomic backgrounds) and it becomes unimaginable. Yet it remains natural among some teachers to think and speak about children as more or less desirable based upon ability.

Inclusion as Educational Equity

In the wake of the 2016 presidential election, the question of "who belongs" in America is at the forefront of our national conversation. We are a nation divided. There are citizens who support exclusionary rhetoric and citizens who resist in protest. As pointed out in Chapter 1, public schools are far from immune to national politics. As early as April 2016, the Southern Poverty Law Center released results of an online survey of 2000 K-12 public school teachers that documented "Latino, African American, and Muslim children, and children of immigrants, terrified…and asking teachers whether their entire families (even American citizens) would be deported, walled off or worse" (Costello, 2016). Now well into this administration, it is unclear what the long-term impact of this national conversation might be for public school students; however, "whether or not a student is a member of a targeted group, all students witnessing it in action are vulnerable to the stresses" (Sword & Zimbardo, 2018). As public school teachers, we cannot control the intrusion of politics into public schools, but we can promote equitable and inclusive classroom communities. The practice of inclusion is perhaps more relevant now than at any other time in the history of American public education.

Although American citizens may not be in agreement about what constitutes discrimination within the current political climate, federal law ensures individual rights in regard to race, gender, class, ethnicity, disability, sexual orientation, religion, and age. Shared cultural awareness regarding various "isms" (e.g., sexism, racism, ageism, classism) has increased over recent decades—with the notable exception of ableism (see Chapter 2), which receives far less media coverage than the other "isms," if any. For example, Dana Milbank, an op-ed columnist with the *Washington Post*, recently wrote a column in observance of the 242nd birthday of the United States in which he lists freedoms that, in his opinion, need rededication. Among a lengthy list, he calls for freedom from "constant attacks on women, immigrants, people of color, gay people and Muslims; freedom to work and live without discrimination, harassment, and violence because of your gender, race, or religion" (July 3, 2018). Did you notice the omission of disability? In response to Milbank's column, Christine DeZinno Bruno, a disabled actor/arts inclusion consultant and disability rights activist, responded online:

Yes, BUT once again, disabled people are NOWHERE to be found in this call to action for ALL Americans. The press consistently ignores us. Disabled people seem to be fighting a solitary battle for not only our freedoms, but our lives.

(July 4, 2018)

We would go so far as to say that the average American may never have heard of ableism. If ableism (i.e., discriminatory practices toward people with disabilities, unearned privileges of persons without disabilities, environments designed with the non-disabled in mind) has yet to take hold in our national consciousness, it is reasonable to expect some unacknowledged ableist thinking and practices within our public schools.

What Inclusion Is Not

A few years ago, I visited an elementary school with a good reputation as an inclusive community. In fact, the school had been one of the first in its district to implement inclusion. A co-teaching model is in place at each grade level in the school. In other words, a pair of teachers (general education teacher and special education teacher) co-teach a class comprised of students with and without disabilities.

In moving among the co-taught classrooms in this school, I observed the primary model of instruction to be "alternative teaching" (see Chapter 8 for a discussion of the six models of co-teaching)—that is, a general education teacher working with students generally on grade level and a special education teacher working with a smaller group comprised mostly of students with IEPs. Although the groups worked on a common subject area (e.g., math, reading), the content and tasks presented to each group were qualitatively different. Subsequent conversations with several teachers confirmed my observations. They explained that it worked better for the special education teacher to teach the students with disabilities in order to most effectively address the educational needs outlined on their IEPs. And, conversely, the general education teacher was better able to meet the needs of the general education students without the distraction of "inclusion kids" upon the pace of instruction. One teacher proudly showed me a portable wall that her husband recently built for the classroom. She explained that the "inclusion kids" sometimes wanted to see and hear what the other students were doing, so the wall is used (as needed) to reduce distraction.

I could not help but be reminded of my own school experience of "segregation within integration" during the early 1970s (see Chapter 1). As we continue to point out, we can pass laws that mandate structural changes, but we cannot legislate attitudes. In the example just described, the placement of disabled bodies into general education classrooms represents adherence to a mandated structural change, but its implementation recreates segregation. This is *not* inclusion. And yet these no doubt well-intentioned teachers believe not only that it *is* inclusion but also that their classroom model meets the needs of all children. What is missing is a fundamental understanding of inclusion as *educational equity*.

Throughout its history, American public education has earned a reputation for latching onto the latest trend while developing acute amnesia about its previously touted ideas. In our present historical moment, it seems we believe that if we *call* something inclusion, then it *is* inclusion. Let me offer another real-life example. Some years ago, I engaged in advocacy work with a family who wanted their son, Brock, to be included in general education rather than remain in a segregated classroom for students with physical disabilities. Brock, an astute adolescent with a wit far beyond his years, challenged the rationale for his segregated placement by asking, "Why would anyone think that I only want to be with other students in wheelchairs? Why would *anybody* want to be only with people just like themselves? Do they think that I am only with disabled people when I am not in school? Who lives like that?"

Brock has cerebral palsy. He moves through the world in a motorized chair. He has some involuntary movements of his body and face. His speech differs in pace and clarity. Based upon his embodiment in the world, people routinely assume that he is cognitively impaired. In fact, school personnel considered Brock "too disabled" for general education despite his above-grade-level academic achievement. Following intense negotiations between the family and school personnel, Brock finally was "included" in an eighth-grade general education class with special education support services.

Although the fact of Brock's disability remained constant, the *meaning* others attributed to his disability proved variable. Within the general education context, Brock was expected to perform like his non-disabled peers to justify his presence. It is worth noting that school personnel referred to Brock's integration into general education as inclusion. In actuality, Brock's integration reflected the tradition of mainstreaming, as described in Chapter 2. Apparently, inclusion was understood to be an updated term for mainstreaming rather than a significantly different philosophical orientation. The general education teacher conceptualized Brock's disability (i.e., his way of being in the world) as a fact that need not be acknowledged if he *really* belonged in the classroom. (Translation: We will allow you into our able-bodied world if you can manage to act like one of us and not require us to think or do anything differently for you.) The teacher's choice to "not see" Brock's disability is akin to proclaiming "color-blindness"—a naïve attempt to prove a lack of prejudice that instead reveals a lack of understanding and acknowledgment of complex historical and contemporary issues. On the other hand, the school's physical therapist (operating out of a medicalized perspective of disability) conceptualized Brock as the sum of his pathology. For example, she recommended that Brock remain seated in his wheelchair during class. Although Brock explained that he routinely moves from his wheelchair to sit in chairs, the therapist insisted upon the "enhanced stability" that the wheelchair provided. (Brock always sat in a chair when I talked with him. I observed him shifting himself from the wheelchair to a chair many times.) In his negotiation of the world as a person with cerebral palsy, Brock regarded his wheelchair as a means to move from place to place—not as the only seat available to him. Despite Brock's efforts to assert his way of being in the world (a way that happened to approximate "normal seated behavior"—supporting his teacher's expectation that he be like everyone else), the therapist insisted upon medicalizing his condition based upon her understanding of how to best "treat" persons with cerebral palsy.

A class field trip to a local history museum revealed the extent of Brock's positioning as an outsider in this "inclusive" context. Arrangements were made for students to ride a school bus to and from the museum. It did not occur to the teacher that Brock would be unable to travel on a bus without handicapped accessibility—until his mother called. The conversation ended with Brock's mother offering to drive him to the museum in their accessible family van. It did not occur to the teacher to suggest that other students ride in the van with Brock. The small museum consisted of two rooms—a large room on the ground floor and a smaller room on an upper level. There was no elevator to the second level. It did not occur to the teacher to inquire beforehand about wheelchair accessibility in the museum. Lunch at a fast-food restaurant delighted the students—especially the balcony area to which everyone scrambled to eat. It did not occur to the teacher that Brock could not access the balcony until she noticed him eating with his mother downstairs.

It is tempting to judge this teacher's actions (or lack of action) harshly, yet the truth is that such ableist thinking is pervasive in our culture. And schools, as we continue to point out, embody the culture in which we live. Ours is a society designed for the able-bodied (see Chapter 3). Accessibility is often an afterthought and mostly thought about when mandated. Accommodating *everyone* strikes some able-bodied persons as pandering to the unreasonable demands of a few. After all, don't we live in a country where the majority rules? Why should able-bodied people be inconvenienced by the needs of the disabled? Here in New York City, for example, it is not uncommon for some passengers to show visible irritation at the delay caused by a wheelchair user boarding a city bus (see Chapter 3).

So, let's consider what Brock's peers might have learned about disability based upon his "inclusion" in their classroom:

- The world is meant for us, not others.
- Persons with disabilities can be with us, but we do not have to be with them.
- The needs of persons with disabilities are secondary to our needs.
- Disability is not something we talk about, especially not to the person with a disability.
- We do not have anything in common with persons with disabilities.
- Persons with disabilities do not have feelings or opinions. They are not like real people to be friends with.
- People with disabilities cause problems for everyone else.
- People with disabilities cause problems.
- It is not our responsibility to engage people with disabilities. They have issues that are beyond us.
- It really does not work for people with disabilities to be with us.
- People with disabilities take up too much of our time.
- We have nothing to learn from people with disabilities.
- People with disabilities make us uncomfortable. We do not know how to talk to them.
- We do not know why people with disabilities have to be in our class.

If public schools prepare our nation's children to become the citizens of tomorrow, what might that future look like for persons with disabilities? The practice of ability-based segregation teaches our future citizens that it is "right and natural" to live in a society meant for some but not others—in fact, it is the *privilege* of able-bodied citizens to consider equity only in terms of themselves. To leave ability-based segregation in public schools unchallenged guarantees a future in which persons with disabilities can expect a second-class status. And ableism will continue within the social structures that support its reproduction.

Inclusion: A Matter of Social Justice

Our inclusion of Brock's experience is not meant to be a characterization of all teachers. Nor do we mean to diminish or dismiss the work of teachers who endeavor every day to include all children. Rather, we wish to bring to your attention the naturalized attitudes and responses toward disability that *can* persist within public schools and challenge you to think about the impact of our practices upon the lives of students with disabilities. We need only look to the past to identify other examples of naturalized attitudes and behaviors that seem unimaginable by today's standards. For example, the popular AMC television series, *Mad Men* (2007–2015), depicted America of the not-so-distant past (early 1960s) in which African Americans and women shared second-class status. What seemed unproblematic then is considered unequivocally racist and sexist now. It took the civil rights movement and women's liberation movement to awaken our collective consciousness to these social injustices. Likewise, inclusive practices challenge us to recognize and address the social injustices of ableism.

In Chapter 2, we presented documentation of negative outcomes for special education students nationwide (e.g., rising dropout rates, underemployment, and unemployment). How might students with disabilities describe their experiences in the system created for their benefit? What do they have to tell us? In more recent decades, narratives told by special education students have begun to appear within the literature—largely through the work of disability studies scholars (e.g., Connor, 2008; Keefe, Moore, & Duff, 2006; Reid & Button, 1995; Rodis, Garrod, & Boscardin, 2001).

A View from the Inside

Our own scholarship reflects this narrative trend. In one such study, we (along with three other colleagues) interviewed four special education teachers who identify as learning disabled (LD) themselves. We were interested to learn how these teachers negotiated cultural discourses of disability to develop their own understanding of LD (Ferri, Connor, Solis, Valle, & Volpitta, 2004). Through individual interviews, participants shared their experiences as students—and later as special education teachers—with LD. It is worth noting that all four teachers chose to enter the field of special education so that students like themselves might have a more positive school experience than their own. Common to each of the four narratives is reliance upon metaphor as a means of descriptive storytelling. As an artist, I (David) was struck by these vivid verbal images and subsequently (re)presented them in the form of visual mosaics (Figures 4.1–4.4). Let's take a look at what each participant's mosaic reveals about special education from the inside.

Jeff, initially classified as LD during his elementary school years, bitterly described the "never-ending testing" as a "demoralizing experience." He likened his experience of testing (see Chapter 3) to that of a laboratory rat forced to run mazes. Once publicly marked and set apart as LD, Jeff struggled to resist assumptions of deficit held by teachers and peers. Describing himself as a "self-hating LD person" during his school years, Jeff shared numerous instances in which he felt positioned as a victim by authoritative others (e.g., teachers, evaluators, administrators) who presumed to act in his best interest. In an effort to preserve his self-esteem, Jeff chose to see himself as a "rare species" whose learning disability had been identified mistakenly as the deficit-laden type that plagued *other* students with LD. Had it not been for the support of his family, Jeff suspects he would have dropped out of school.

Patrick learned of his LD diagnosis as a third grader. Having been told that he was "not like other boys and girls," Patrick initially thought of himself as having a disease in need of treatment. (It is of interest that Patrick' understanding of disability as a child mirrored the medical model.) Bearing the newly acquired label of LD, Patrick was advised that he would need to "learn differently and work harder" to keep pace with his peers. And indeed, Patrick consistently trailed behind speedier competitors in the race of public schooling. As a special education student who received LD services outside of his general education classroom, Patrick recalled the daily embarrassment of having to "run the gauntlet of my peers" on the way out of the classroom—his disability status exposed to all. In the silence that accompanies such public rituals of schooling, Patrick learned the shame of disability—so shameful that others spoke of it only in whispers.

Having emigrated at age 12 from the Dominican Republic to the United States, Mia struggled through her secondary school years with learning challenges considered typical for second-language learners. It was not until her second attempt at college that Mia was diagnosed as dyslexic. Inspired by Patricia Polacco's book about her own dyslexia (*Thank*

Figure 4.1 Jeff

Figure 4.2 Patrick

Figure 4.3 Mia

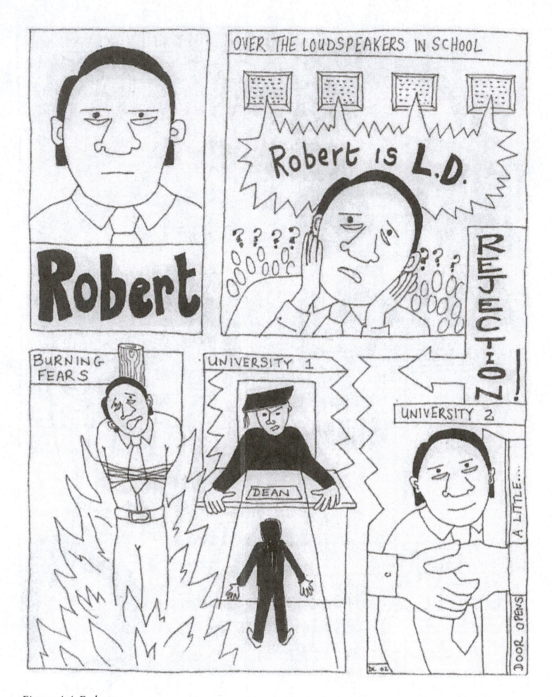

Figure 4.4 Robert

You, Mr. Falker, 1998), Mia chooses to speak openly to her special education students about her own LD in hopes of serving as a role model. From her perspective as a special education teacher, Mia observes that segregation leads others (e.g., students, teachers, parents) to stigmatize students with disabilities ("they think you have five heads") as outsiders who belong elsewhere ("they think special ed is a closet [where] they're retarded, or they're crazy, or stupid"). Concerned about what she sees as the negative effects of labeling, Mia breaks the silences surrounding disability and encourages students to see themselves as "different, not disabled."

Robert, the oldest participant, attended public school before the advent of P.L. 94–142. He was not identified as LD until college, although he had sensed that "something was wrong" throughout his school career. Having been diagnosed as an adult, Robert has possessed choice (unlike Jeff and Patrick) about disclosing his LD. As a special education teacher and a part-time staff developer, Robert is privy to the negative attitudes that some general education colleagues have toward students with disabilities. He sees public school as a hostile context and that disclosure would subject him to the same prejudices that befall his students with LD. He imagines how announcing his own LD ("via the loudspeaker") would result in him being "scorned, burned at the stake" by colleagues who, he believes, would no longer respect him. Robert's fears originate in his prior experiences with disability disclosure at the university level—demeaned in one context and supported in the other—instilling within him deep feelings of vulnerability to the perceptions of others. By distancing himself from his students, Robert unwittingly shares rather than resists the shame of disability.

Ethical Practice

While we acknowledge that these participant mosaics do not represent the experiences of all special education students and special education teachers with disabilities, it is worth noting that our interview content does support other first-person narratives about special education documented within a growing body of literature. Likewise, our observations as veteran special educators confirm that unintended consequences do exist for those presumed to benefit from special education practice.

As discussed in Chapter 2, parents of children with disabilities and their advocates built upon the momentum of the civil rights movement to claim "equal protection under the law" for a class of people (students with disabilities) whose civil rights were violated by systematic exclusion from public education. If we think about inclusion in terms of civil rights, does any teacher have the right to exclude a student on the basis of ability? After all, we cannot exclude a student from general education on the basis of race, class, gender, religion, linguistic heritage, culture, or sexual orientation. Moreover, if we choose not to acknowledge unintended consequences of special education and proceed with business as usual, are we not as complicit in the ongoing marginalization of people with disabilities by our *inaction* as those who actively exclude?

The decision to create a parallel system of special education—a decision made with the best of intentions— resulted in a "separate but unequal" education for many students with disabilities (see Chapter 2). If we continue to rely upon segregated special education placements, the right of students with disabilities to access the same educational opportunities as students without disabilities remains unrealized. We acknowledge that it may not be possible to include every student with disabilities all the time; however, we contend that schools still have a way to go, in general, toward embracing students with disabilities as belonging in general education. When we frame inclusion as a matter of social justice and educational equity, the debate around whether or not to include students with disabilities is resolved. The question posed in this chapter—"*What if I'm still not sure about inclusion?*"—becomes "What can I do to include *all* students?" It is not a question of *if* we should practice inclusion but *how* to do it well.

Inclusion Envisioned

Throughout one academic school year, I (Jan) visited a New York City elementary classroom every week to study how two fourth-grade co-teachers (general and special education) enacted inclusion. Walk with me into this classroom. Feel the palpable energy emanating from students and teachers working together. Look around. Evidence of learning-in-progress is everywhere—student projects, original writings, posters that document student thinking—not a tidy teacher-generated bulletin board in sight. This classroom belongs to the children who work here. Everywhere small groups engage thoughtfully with one another. Over there is the Help Wanted bulletin board where students post notes about their current challenges (e.g., spelling, typing, research, proofreading, organization, computer skills) and classmates respond with services they can offer. Both teachers circulate around the classroom, asking children to share their thinking aloud. Notice the class constitution that students created and signed on the first day of school. There are framed photographs of students engaged in various projects and class activities—much like family photos that adorn a home. In this inclusive classroom context, children understand learning to be a collaborative rather than a competitive endeavor. Smiles abound. The joy of learning is contagious. Everyone belongs. And, as usual, I am reluctant to leave.

Each week during that academic year, I had the pleasure to observe moment-to-moment exchanges among students and teachers as they learned to think and work in new ways, dispel misconceptions about one another, negotiate and renegotiate what works best for their learning community, struggle through challenges that diversity can present, and come to understand themselves and others more deeply. Inclusion does not just happen. It is enacted daily by people learning to live and work together meaningfully.

What Inclusion Is

Framed as an issue of social justice and educational equity, inclusion is a school-wide belief system in which diversity is viewed as a rich resource for everyone rather than a problem to overcome. Note that we refer to *diversity* rather than disability. Inclusive education is often understood to be about children with disabilities being in general education without having to earn the right to be there. Inclusion certainly addresses the right of students with disabilities to access general education curriculum alongside non-disabled peers, but it is an educational philosophy that extends beyond disability to affirm the diversity within all children. In other words, teachers of inclusive classrooms acknowledge, respect, and draw upon the strengths of all manner of diversity in a classroom community.

Inclusion means that we help all children to learn and participate in meaningful ways. Thus, the inclusive classroom is a nurturing learning community where everyone belongs and everyone benefits. It is an educational context within which children cultivate friendship, collaborate rather than compete, and deepen their appreciation for diversity. In its deepest sense, inclusion is a model of democracy at work that holds relevance for all of us. Think back for a moment to Madelyn (Chapter 3), as well as Brock, Jeff, and Patrick. Imagine each of them embraced within the inclusive context just described. How might inclusive practices have produced different consequences in their lives? If the teachers, administrators, evaluators, and students around them had been working out of an inclusive philosophy and context, how might their school experiences have been different?

Featured Voice of María Cioe Peña

Complicating Notions of Inclusion

It would be dishonest to say that I have always been a champion for inclusion. Rather, my relationship with inclusion has been a cyclical one and as such my support for it has ebbed and flowed. In the following essay, I will guide you through the experiences that have led to this realization.

My first introduction to inclusion was during my practicum year when I was placed in an inclusive elementary school in Brooklyn, NY. At the time, this school was unusual because each class was comprised of children with and without disabilities. In addition, it was also racially and culturally diverse—at least more so than most other schools in the community, which meant that there was also some socioeconomic inclusion as well. The school was situated in a wealthy district so, although the building itself was older, the services provided within the school were many—a computer lab equipped with the latest technology; theater, music, and video electives; afterschool cooking classes; and a classroom assistant for each class funded exclusively by parent donations. Within this school the integration of students seemed pretty evident. Students of varied backgrounds and ability levels were learning alongside each other, or so it seemed. The reality was that, within this grade in particular, students were grouped with similarly-performing peers and taught by one teacher at a time. In some instances, that was one of the homeroom teachers; in other instances, it was a teacher from the grade. For example, in the mornings all the students would fall into their respective "math group," comprised of children across the grade who had performed similarly. One teacher directed each group. During reading the class would split into two groups: "middle to high performing" would be with the general education teacher, "low performing" with the special education teacher, and those who were considered particularly low would work with the class paraprofessional. Similarly, I was only allowed to teach two lessons to the whole group—the minimum requirement for my course—and spent most of my time teaching to the "small(est) group." While this was the best way to make use of the teachers and ensure that all students were getting what they needed, it also meant that the two students who had the most severe cognitive disabilities in the class were more often than not segregated from their peers. This was not only a metacognitive segregation but a physical one as well since these students were often removed from the class for small-group work. From this experience, I walked away with the impression that inclusion as a pedagogical tool worked well for students with high-performing disabilities. Yes, there were students with disabilities in the "middle to high performing" groups but those students had disabilities that did not interfere with their cognitive ability as much as with their ability to perform as typically developing students.

After a couple of months observing/practicing at this school, and just a few days before graduation, I landed my first job as a public school teacher. For the next six years, I worked as a bilingual special education teacher in the same elementary school my sister had attended—a rarity in NYC where most teachers do not work in the neighborhoods they live in, much less the neighborhood they grew up in. For the first three years I taught in a self-contained bilingual bridge class, which meant that all of the students in my class spoke Spanish as their home language, had a disability label and were in grades 3–5. There were students with high incidence disabilities such as speech and language impairment and learning disability but there were also students with multiple health impairments and intellectual impairment. There were students who were emergent bilinguals at different stages of development and one student who was selectively mute. The room, which had previously served as a storage room, was never intended to be a classroom so it was devoid of a sink, closets or bookcases like all the other rooms in the school. There were many needs and many bodies within one very small room. In addition to 12 students there were 6 adults (myself and 5 paraprofessionals) who called this classroom home. While the amenities were few, this class and school community felt integrated in ways that the other school had not. While I was the only "teacher" in the classroom, it was in the middle of the "third-grade" floor. Across the hall was a third-grade bilingual class, next door was the monolingual 3–5 self-contained class and on the other side was a monolingual third grade. This class was both a chore and a delight to work with. I was part of the third-grade planning team and the special education planning team. As such, my students were exposed to the same curriculum as their typically developing peers with the added bonus of doing so in both the school language and their home language. I was not aware of it then but I would later learn that bilingual[1] special education is considered a specialized setting in NYC. As such, not all schools offered the program option and so students who were designated for a bilingual setting would be bussed from district to district in order to access this type of program or they would be given an alternate placement paraprofessional until a setting could be procured.

After three years, the monolingual special education and bilingual special education classes were disbanded. This was the result of the implementation of a special education reform titled Shared Pathways to Success (SPtS). The goal of SPtS was to allow students to attend their community schools. No longer would students be bussed across the city in order to find a setting that met their needs; instead, each school was being required to meet the needs of its learners. The primary goal of this reform was not just integration of students into community schools; it was a push for inclusion. Up until now, two children within the same family—one with dis/abilities and one without—would be relegated to different school districts, different schedules, and different social circles. SPtS was a way to eradicate this very tangible type of segregation. Not only were students with disabilities kept out of their community schools, they were also in many ways shut out of their communities. Viewed in this way, SPtS seems like a worthy cause. However, these motivations did not take into account what would happen to culturally and linguistically minoritized children with disabilities. While SPtS resulted in a boon of inclusive classes—most of which looked like the class I had taught students in—there were no bilingual inclusive classes created to replace the bilingual self-contained classes. So much of the focus was placed on the inclusion of children with disabilities into typically developing classes that there was no accounting for the ways in which these types of inclusion could result in new forms of exclusion. So while, yes, SPtS eradicated the need for students to be bussed across the city in order to attend a school that could meet their needs, the conveniences of community integration often resulted in linguistic and familial alienation for these children at home and for their families at school.

I recall the experience of my former student, Angel. Angel lived in a district outside of the one in which I taught so his mornings tended to be long. He woke up early and would have spent upwards of an hour riding the bus to and from my school in order to access the bilingual program that his IEP demanded. After SPtS, Angel was able to participate in his local community school—a mere 15-minute walk from home. However, he was no longer enrolled in a bilingual program. Initially this was viewed as an indication of his English fluency, but it was also an indication of the compromises that emergent bilingual students labeled with disabilities and their families were asked to make. Angel stopped developing his biliteracy, his expressive bilingualism diminished and slowly he began to eradicate his use of Spanish both at school and at home. This forced monolingualism not only placed a strain on his relationship with his mother but also his mother's relationship with the school. While previously she had been able to communicate with all of Angel's teachers and service providers, the reality was that after SPtS she needed a translator to mitigate even the smallest and most basic home–school communication. The way I saw it, inclusion was to blame. This mother had been pushed out of her child's school, his academic experiences and in many ways his life because of a desire to "include" children with dis/abilities. For me, these children had not been included as much as they had been excluded. Ultimately, it was this observation that motivated me to attend graduate school. I was intent on proving that inclusion was not appropriate for all learners. First, I learned that it wasn't appropriate for learners with low incidence disabilities. After this experience, I learned that it wasn't appropriate for bilingual children.

It wasn't until graduate school that I was able to understand that the two aforementioned experiences were not representative of inclusion. Instead they represented poor, albeit well-meaning, implementations of an idea. I also learned that the spaces least likely to be inclusive are the ones that are named as such. Inclusive education is not defined by the class with multiple teachers teaching multiple lessons at the same time. Inclusive education is the two years I spent teaching a general education bilingual class—a class that had no special title, yet the range of students' ability was varied; a class with no student to student ratio or quota, but still a class where some students had individual education plans; a class where the special education teacher and the general education teacher were one and the same, yet there were a myriad of service providers who pushed into the class to support all learners who were struggling with an idea or a concept. During those two years, inclusion was defined by the setting that made students feel completely included with all of their gifts, all of their needs, in all of their languages. Inclusive education should not be defined by the classrooms students inhabit but rather by the ways in which those classrooms reflect and continue to support the ways in which a child is included in their home and within their community. Placing a multilingual child in a monolingual inclusive class is not inclusive. It may appear as though it is inclusive but it is just an illusion. Stripping a child of their ability to hold onto and develop their multilingualism strips them of their linguistic freedom. In many ways, stripping a multilingual child of their multilingualism adds a new type of disability: linguistic mutism to their life, further alienating them from society at large.

Inclusion should not look like a class composed of students with and without dis/ability labels. Inclusion should look like the dinner table that a child sits at: a table where no one has a label; a table where a child can speak to their mother and father in Spanish and their sibling in English; a table devoid of groupings on the basis of performance. Inclusive education should be a transcendent space curated by teachers, families and administrators. Inclusive education should be a pedagogical space that most allows a child to be their truest and most complete self—alongside others who are doing the same. Just like special education is a service not a place, inclusive education is a practice not a program.

Disabilities in the Classroom

Although we just described inclusion in terms of diversity rather than disability per se, we recognize that new teachers are not always familiar with—or may not remember from prior coursework—the 13 categories of disability as defined under IDEIA. Thus, we include them for your information and reference. In that these categories focus upon disability as pathology, we wish to clarify our position that children with disabilities are more similar than dissimilar to children without disabilities. Moreover, it is important to keep in mind that children do not always fit neatly within categories. For example, a child with a communication disorder might manifest characteristics of a child who bears the label of an emotional/behavior disorder, a child labeled as developmentally and cognitively delayed might display characteristics associated with dyslexia, a gifted child might reflect some Asperger-like characteristics, a child labeled with an emotional/behavior disorder may have learning disabilities, or a child with language impairments might appear developmentally and cognitively delayed. Labeling is a messy business. With these caveats in mind, the 13 categories defined within IDEIA are as follows:

(1) (i) **Autism** means a developmental disability significantly affecting verbal and nonverbal communication and social interaction, generally evident before age 3, that adversely affects a child's educational performance. Other characteristics often associated with autism are engagement in repetitive activities and stereotyped movements, resistance to environmental change or change in daily routines, and unusual responses to sensory experiences. The term does not apply if a child's educational performance is adversely affected primarily because the child has an emotional disturbance, as defined in paragraph (b)(4) of this section.

(ii) A child who manifests the characteristics of "autism" after age 3 could be diagnosed as having "autism" if the criteria in paragraph (c)(1)(i) of this section are satisfied.

(2) **Deaf-blindness** means concomitant hearing and visual impairments, the combination of which causes such severe communication and other developmental and educational needs that they cannot be accommodated in special education programs solely for children with deafness or children with blindness.

(3) **Deafness** means a hearing impairment that is so severe that the child is impaired in processing linguistic information through hearing, with or without amplification, that adversely affects a child's educational performance.

(4) **Emotional disturbance** is defined as follows:

(i) The term means a condition exhibiting one or more of the following characteristics over a long period of time and to a marked degree that adversely affects a child's educational performance:

(a) An inability to learn that cannot be explained by intellectual, sensory, or health factors.

(b) An inability to build or maintain satisfactory interpersonal relationships with peers and teachers.

(c) Inappropriate types of behavior or feelings under normal circumstances.

(d) A general pervasive mood of unhappiness or depression.

(e) A tendency to develop physical symptoms or fears associated with personal or school problems.

(ii) The term includes schizophrenia. The term does not apply to children who are socially maladjusted, unless it is determined that they have an emotional disturbance.

(5) **Hearing impairment** means an impairment in hearing, whether permanent or fluctuating, that adversely affects a child's educational performance but that is not included under the definition of deafness in this section.

(6) **Mental retardation** means significantly subaverage general intellectual functioning, existing concurrently with deficits in adaptive behavior and manifested during the developmental period, that adversely affects a child's educational performance.

(7) **Multiple disabilities** means concomitant impairments (such as mental retardation–blindness, mental retardation–orthopedic impairment, etc.), the combination of which causes such severe educational needs that they cannot be accommodated in special education programs solely for one of the impairments. The term does not include deaf-blindness.

(8) **Orthopedic impairment** means a severe orthopedic impairment that adversely affects a child's educational performance. The term includes impairments caused by congenital anomaly (e.g., clubfoot, absence of some member, etc.), impairments caused by disease (e.g., poliomyelitis, bone tuberculosis, etc.), and impairments from other causes (e.g., cerebral palsy, amputations, and fractures or burns that cause contractures).

(9) **Other health impairment** means having limited strength, vitality, or alertness, including a heightened alertness to environmental stimuli, that results in limited alertness with respect to the educational environment, that:

  (i) Is due to chronic or acute health problems such as asthma, attention deficit disorder or attention deficit hyperactivity disorder, diabetes, epilepsy, a heart condition, hemophilia, lead poisoning, leukemia, nephritis, rheumatic fever, and sickle cell anemia; and

  (ii) Adversely affects a child's educational performance.

(10) **Specific learning disability** is defined as follows:

  (i) **General.** The term means a disorder in one or more of the basic psychological processes involved in understanding or in using language, spoken or written, that may manifest itself in an imperfect ability to listen, think, speak, read, write, spell, or to do mathematical calculations, including conditions such as perceptual disabilities, brain injury, minimal brain dysfunction, dyslexia, and developmental aphasia.

  (ii) **Disorders not included.** The term does not include learning problems that are primarily the result of visual, hearing, or motor disabilities; of mental retardation; of emotional disturbance; or of environmental, cultural, or economic disadvantage.

(11) **Speech or language impairment** means a communication disorder, such as stuttering, impaired articulation, a language impairment, or a voice impairment, that adversely affects a child's educational performance.

(12) **Traumatic brain injury** means an acquired injury to the brain caused by an external physical force, resulting in total or partial functional disability or psychosocial impairment, or both, that adversely affects a child's educational performance. The term applies to open or closed head injuries resulting in impairments in one or more areas, such as cognition; language; memory; attention; reasoning; abstract thinking; judgment; problem-solving; sensory, perceptual, and motor abilities; psychosocial behavior; physical functions; information processing; and speech. The term does not apply to brain injuries that are congenital or degenerative, or to brain injuries induced by birth trauma.

(13) **Visual impairment including blindness** means an impairment in vision that, even with correction, adversely affects a child's educational performance. The term includes both partial sight and blindness.

(https://sites.ed.gov/idea)

It is of interest that IDEIA defines specific criteria for each of the 13 disability categories, but not much in the way of how disabilities might manifest within a classroom context. Of the 13 categories, the disabilities most likely to present within general education classrooms (referred to as "high incidence" disabilities) are learning disabilities, speech/language impairments, and mild emotional/behavioral disabilities. In our experience as special educators, students labeled with "high incidence" disabilities may experience a few, some, or many of the academic challenges listed below:

Challenges in reading

> Phonemic awareness
> Phonology
> Word recognition/decoding skills
> Automaticity/fluency
> Syllabication
> Reading comprehension
> Text strategies
> Reading stamina/attention

Challenges in written language

> Spelling (related to phonemic awareness and phonology)
> Handwriting fluency and accuracy
> Punctuation and capitalization
> Basic grammar (e.g., use of tenses, noun/verb agreement, irregular verb constructions)
> Sentence construction and elaboration
> Organization of thought
> Text planning and revision
> Spatial orientation on paper
> Writing stamina

Challenges in oral language

> Word retrieval/fluency in expression
> Organization of verbal expression
> Quality of oral language relative to age
> Basic grammar
> Understanding figures of speech/metaphors/jokes
> Vocabulary
> Pragmatic language (e.g., conversational skills, understanding nonverbal communication cues)

Challenges in mathematics

> Directional aspects (e.g., up–down in addition, left–right in regrouping)
> Retention of math facts and new information
> Number sense and place value
> Clock time
> Spatial orientation on paper
> Number lines
> Algorithms
> Multi-step word problems

It is worth noting that such academic challenges are also common to students who struggle academically but do not have a disability label—supporting our contention that students with disabilities are more alike than different from children without disabilities.

Diversifying the View Inside

Let's pause for a moment and reflect upon IDEIA's 13 categories of disability. As you read the definitions, did you notice how deficit language is used to describe disability? Words such as *adversely, unusual, deficit, disorder, sub-average, limited, imperfect, maladaptive, impairment, inappropriate* construct disability as a pathological condition that falls outside the range of an established "normal." Know that if *you* claim a "normal" identity, you do so on the backs of people labeled "abnormal." There is no "normal" without "abnormal." "Normal" only holds meaning in opposition to what is constructed as *not* "normal."

The assumption within IDEIA is that disability is a biological fact located within individual bodies and minds. The context within which those bodies and minds live and learn is of no consequence within this particular conceptualization of disability. As discussed elsewhere (see Chapters 1 and 3), we are not disputing the biological differences of disability. However, we do argue that an individual's *experience* of disability is influenced by his or her social location (e.g., race, class, ethnicity, gender, sexual orientation). In other words, within the context of lived experience, disability is not a singular identity but, rather, intersects with an individual's multiple identities.

Think back to Chapter 2 to our discussion of the overrepresentation of students of color in special education—a fact that has persisted for decades. As we stated previously, if you are black *and* male, you are more likely to be labeled mentally retarded, emotionally and/or behaviorally disturbed, or learning disabled than if you are white *and* male (Losen & Orfield, 2002). On the other hand, it seems that autism diagnoses may be missed or delayed among children of color in comparison to white children (Mandell et al., 2009). It is worth noting that the current prevalence of "autism spectrum disorder" diagnoses (generally considered a more "desirable" disability label than intellectual disability or conduct disorder) among white children is reminiscent of a similar pattern that existed for LD diagnoses in the late twentieth century (see Chapter 1). Moreover, Mandell and associates (2007) found that black children were over two and a half times less likely to receive an autism diagnosis on their first specialty visit compared to white children. Among black children who did not receive an autism diagnosis on their first specialty visit, they were five times more likely to receive an adjustment disorder diagnosis and almost two and a half times more likely to receive a conduct disorder diagnosis, compared to white children (Hannon, 2017, p. 155). And when black children *are* diagnosed with autism, nearly half of those children are also diagnosed with an intellectual disability compared to 25 percent of white children diagnosed with autism (Centers for Disease Control and Prevention, 2014).

Once again, it seems that "all that *other* stuff" (see Chapter 1) is at work. We share these data with you to raise your awareness about how racism and ableism intersect to marginalize some groups of students and not others. In fact, a new theoretical framework called Disability Critical Race Studies (Dis/Crit) looks at ways in which racism and ableism work together to create societal and educational barriers (Annamma, Connor, & Ferri, 2013). As a teacher, you will be asked to contribute to conversations and decisions about students who struggle in school. Keep in mind that disability has become naturalized within public schools in a *particular* way—so commonplace that it typically goes unchallenged in the everyday work of schools. And many educators seem unable to see disability in any other way. We hope that you will consider what you have read here as you advocate for the students in your care.

Inclusion in Action

Let's return for a moment to the medical model of disability. If disability is conceptualized in terms of deficits, it follows that our instructional methods will be remedial in nature in an effort to "fix" what is wrong. It is little wonder that remediation became the focus of special education instruction. And given the scientific grounding of special education, it is rather predictable that remediation would become synonymous with behaviorist approaches to instruction. If we "treat" the pathology successfully, we can return to general education students with disabilities who have been "fixed." Thus, the teacher-directed, skills-based instruction associated with behaviorism became institutionalized as "best practice" for students in special education.

By the 1990s, however, the taken-as-shared assumptions that undergirded special education instruction began to receive increasing criticism (Brantlinger, 1997; Heshusius, 1994; Poplin, 1988; Varenne & McDermott, 1998). Moreover, a growing number of scholars, most of whom grounded their work in Piagetian and Vygotskian theories of learning, asserted that behaviorist instructional practices actually *construct* students with disabilities as passive and dependent learners (Dudley-Marling, 2004; Englert, 1992; Englert, Mariage, Garmon, & Tarrant, 1998; Reid & Valle, 2005). Could it be that conceptualizing students with disabilities in terms of their deficits inadvertently positions them to become less capable learners? How deeply invested in a deficit orientation to disability might general and special educators be?

In the previously referenced classroom where I observed for the course of an academic year, the co-teachers shared instances in which their colleagues questioned if students with disabilities could benefit from general education instruction. For example, the speech/language therapist expressed doubt that students with learning disabilities could gain anything valuable by participating in the class Read Aloud, recommending instead that they attend pull-out language instruction during that time. Likewise, some co-teachers on other grade levels challenged their decision not to "pull aside" students with disabilities as an instructional group within the classroom. Despite such critiques from colleagues, these co-teachers held fast to their conviction of the necessity of fully including students with disabilities within their learning community.

Let's take a look at some transcripts that illustrate the kind of instruction that takes place within this diverse and inclusive classroom. To demonstrate the participation of students with disabilities, I identify within the transcripts which contributions are made by students with disability labels.

Transcript 1

The teacher begins by modeling a Think Aloud strategy for the class.

Teacher: The poem is *The Blue Between*. I am going to model reading this poem. Then, you will talk to a partner about what I am doing in my brain. *The Blue Between*. In poetry, titles are super important. "*Everyone watches the clouds.*" A lot of people watch clouds. "*Naming creatures they've seen.*" People lie on their backs in the park and see clouds that look like a car, a giraffe—not like a car in the sky, but people see things in the clouds. "*I see the blue between.*" Instead of looking at the clouds, she [the poet] is looking at the sky inbetween. It is different than what other people are doing. Turn to a partner. What did you notice me doing?

As the children engage in discussion, the teacher circulates, listens in, and facilitates conversations as needed.

Teacher:	I listened to a couple of people talking. Jamal noticed that I took notes. Raymond noticed that I stopped to talk to myself. Let's go back to the first four lines.
Serena (LD):	She sees animals in the clouds.
Teacher:	Anyone want to add on to what Serena said?
Gary:	She is looking at the cloudless part. The blue surrounded by the clouds.
Harriet (LD):	I agree.
Teacher:	Does she actually see a blue woman in the sky?
Children:	Nooooo!

By this point in the lesson, the teacher has made a number of moves that reflect her belief that *all* children are active meaning-makers. She chooses a "think-aloud" strategy to introduce the class to poetry interpretation (rather than direct instruction), reflecting trust in the children to draw their own conclusions about what they hear and read. She regards each child as a valuable, contributing member to the knowledge they construct as a classroom community. Serena, a student labeled LD, enters the dialogue by offering a valid, yet concrete, idea about the poem. Her contribution is embraced in the community conversation and acknowledged by the teacher as a point worth adding on to. Harriet, another student labeled LD, participates by noting her agreement with a peer's contribution. This is significant in that Harriet, who typically needs time to formulate verbal expression, easily enters the discussion by listening to a peer's well-crafted response and evaluating if it fits with her own not yet verbalized understanding of the poem.

Transcript 2

Teacher: Read the next few lines with your partners.

The teacher moves from the front and listens among the children. She cues for one remaining minute, then regroups the children.

Teacher:	I saw some people sketching a picture. Zachary was helping Howie by drawing out what it might look like. That is a good way to help your partner.
Frank:	There is a lot of distance between the clouds because of the giraffe. It is stretched.
Andy:	It is not a stormy day. It had to be a sunny day to see the blue.
Jamie:	The dolphins need a big space because it is a pod. A lot of them!
Andy:	There are lots of clouds.
Jamal:	The cargo ships are like clouds full of rain.
Teacher:	Everybody listen. He just said something really smart.
Jamal:	I looked at the word "cargo." I know cargo ships hold something and the clouds hold something.
Susan:	A boy twirling his clouds around and then blue fingertips. Since it is thin, the clouds are closer together.

In this section of transcript, the teacher supports children working together to construct meaning. It is particularly noteworthy that she acknowledges the spontaneously generated drawing strategy used by Zachary and Howie (who has an Asperger's label), not to highlight how a non-disabled student helps a student with a disability, but to illustrate an effective way in which *all* partners might work together to help one another.

Transcript 3

Teacher:	The last stanza, I will read it to you and then I want you to talk to your partner about what you think it means.

The teacher reads the last stanza. The children engage with one another in discussion. The teacher moves among the children to listen to their conversations.

Serena (LD):	Because she was looking at spaces in between, she sees something different than people looking at the clouds.
Jamie:	We noticed that the first and third stanzas are similar. They repeat.
Sharon:	It's kind of like Jabberwocky. It ends with what it started with.
Iris (CP/LD):	We imagined the clouds separating.
Teacher:	This is something you can do with any kind of text. With poems, it is easy to do this. Look at each word and infer from the clues the writers give you. It is like being a detective.

Here, Serena (LD) offers a second and more sophisticated idea than her first response. Although she did not contribute to the previous discussion (Transcript 2), she is listening, constructing ideas, and benefiting in a way that enables her to contribute an important thought reflecting a higher level of abstraction (Transcript 3). Her level of participation is particularly noteworthy in that, after several years of traditional special education instruction, Serena began the school year with little understanding of how to engage in group conversation and hardly any confidence in her ability to do so.

In the next transcript, the teacher is engaging students in a reading workshop about *Fly Away Home* by Eve Bunting, a story about a homeless father and son who are living in an airport. Each student has a copy of the story to read silently. They read the story in short sections, then stop to engage in conversation about the story. The teacher rereads parts aloud from a copy displayed on the smartboard to ensure that all students have access to the story.

Transcript 4

Teacher:	How does "Dad and I sleep sitting up" fit into what we just read? Talk to a partner.

The children engage with one another. The teacher notices that Jon (LD) is not talking to anyone. She encourages him to join a conversation.

Teacher:	Raise your hand if you have an idea.
Angie:	So, it *seems* like they are about to get on a plane. They don't want to get caught.
Teacher:	How many people agree or want to add on?
Jamal:	They want to look like they are napping, waiting for a plane.
Randy (LD):	They don't want to look like *her* [referring to a homeless woman in the airport pushing a cart of belongings].
Jamie:	It might be a map of the airport [referring to a notebook the father carries].
Sharon:	Or a schedule. To keep track.

The teacher asks the children to read the next section.

Teacher: If you have an idea, jot it in the margin or underline an idea.

The children read to themselves.

Teacher: Turn to your neighbor. How does this fit in?

The children engage in conversation. The teacher directs their attention to a particular section.

Teacher: What does this part mean?
Lisa: *Everything's* moving, even the escalator. But *they* stay.
Teacher: Can anyone repeat what Lisa said?

Students continue to build upon one another's thoughts about the story.

Randy (LD):   I agree with Lisa and Kenny [referring to statements just made by his peers].

Using text evidence to support his opinion, Randy spontaneously reads aloud from the text, "Sitting together will get you noticed."

Randy (LD):   I'm thinking that they [the homeless people who inhabit the airport] don't sit together because they don't want to get caught.
Teacher: Nice thinking, Randy. You connected back to the earlier idea of not wanting to get caught. Did everyone hear Randy's connection?

In this section of transcript, Randy, a student labeled LD, actively contributes to the discussion. Randy, a struggling reader who had been constructed by previous special education teachers as benefiting from drill and practice, demonstrates his capacity to engage intelligently with a text considered to be significantly "above his reading level." Like Serena, Randy began the school year without having learned the language for engaging in conversation about a text. In this transcript, he tracks the conversation, adds appropriate remarks, uses conversational turn-taking strategies, and offers text evidence to support his own interpretation. Given the opportunity to participate, Randy demonstrates just how capable he is.

In this last section of transcript, the teacher generates conversation around a part in the story where a bird becomes trapped in the airport.

Transcript 5

Teacher: Why is *that* there? Turn to a neighbor and discuss.

The children talk with one another. The teacher engages Jon (LD) in conversation.

Teacher: Okay, we have one minute to see if we can figure this out. Why is there a bird here?
Sharon: I think the bird is like a symbol. *Fly Away Home* is the name of the story, so I think it is a symbol.
Teacher: So, you are saying something similar to what Jon (LD) was saying.

Jon (LD):   They want to go free like the bird.

Lisa: He knew what it was like. So even if he couldn't be free, he wanted the bird to be free.

Teacher: How many people felt like they were doing some good digging?

Throughout the reading workshop, Jon (LD), another struggling reader, appears reluctant to engage in conversation. In a previous section of the transcript, the teacher facilitates Jon's entry into a peer conversation. Here, she decides to talk to him individually to get a better feel for his engagement with the text. While the group discussion ensues, the teacher opens a space for Jon to *choose* to contribute. He does so confidently, stating that, "They want to go free like the bird." Sharon's and Lisa's verbalizations about the meaning of the bird might be considered more developed and textured; nonetheless, Jon's more simply expressed interpretation reveals that he, too, grasps the meaning of symbolism, demonstrating his capability for thinking abstractly.

These transcripts show us how inclusion is enacted moment to moment in the interactions that take place among teachers and students. In a classroom where *all* students are respected as competent and active learners—regardless of skill level—there is space for everyone to learn and grow. Remember, it is not about whether to include students with disabilities within the general education classroom, but *how* to do so effectively. In the next four chapters, we share specific strategies for making inclusion happen.

Questions to Consider

1.   What evidence of ableism do you see in your school and community?
2.   Why do you think that Americans are less aware of ableism than of racism, sexism, and classism? In what ways does ableism intersect with racism, sexism, and classism?
3.   If we leave ableist practices unchallenged within our schools, what might the future look like for persons with disabilities?
4.   Do you believe that inclusion is an issue of civil rights? Why or why not? Give examples to support your position.
5.   How is special education represented in the four mosaics? Did the mosaics influence your thinking in any way? Explain.
6.   Do you agree that special education has resulted in a "separate but unequal" education for many students with disabilities? Why or why not?
7.   What is the argument for conceptualizing inclusion in terms of diversity rather than disability? How does your school conceptualize inclusion?
8.   How has traditional special education instruction (grounded in behaviorism) constructed students with disabilities as passive and dependent learners?
9.   In what ways is inclusion a matter of social justice and educational equity? Explain.

Note

1   There are several types of bilingual education models in practice in the United States. *Transitional bilingual education* is where the students begin the year by taking 90 percent of classes in the home language and 10 percent in the target language (the school language), with the goal of meeting a target of 50/50 by the end of the year. *Dual-language classes* are those that are comprised of 50 percent of students who speak English in the home and 50 percent who speak a language other than English in the home. These students are then being dually immersed in language learning

depending on their home language. However, the class I taught was a *bilingual class*. As such, students all came from households with a shared home language and, following a roller-coaster model, received instruction 50 percent of the day in the home language and 50 percent of the day in the target language.

References

Annamma, S. D., Connor, D., & Ferri, B. (2013). Disability critical race studies (DisCrit): Theorizing at the intersections of race and disability. *Race Ethnicity and Education, 16*(1), 1–31.

Brantlinger, E. (1997). Using ideology: Cases of non-recognition of the politics of research and practice in special education. *Review of Educational Research, 67*, 425–60.

Bruno, C. D. (2018, July 4). Do better, #Washington Post. Facebook.com.

Centers for Disease Control and Prevention. (2014). *Autism spectrum disorder: Key findings.* Retrieved from www.cdc.gov/ncbddd/autism/data/html

Connor, D. J. (2008). *Urban narratives: Portraits in progress.* New York, NY: Peter Lang.

Costello, M. (2016). *The Trump effect: The impact of the presidential campaign in our nation's schools.* Montgomery, AL: Southern Poverty Law Center.

Dudley-Marling, C. (2004). The social construction of learning disabilities. *Journal of Learning Disabilities, 37*(6), 534–49

Englert, C. S. (1992). Writing instruction from a sociocultural perspective: The holistic, dialogic, and social enterprise of writing. *Journal of Learning Disabilities, 28*(3), 153–72.

Englert, C. S., Mariage, M. T., Garmon, A., & Tarrant, K. L. (1998). Accelerating reading progress in early literacy project classrooms: Three exploratory studies. *Remedial and Special Education, 19*(3), 142–59.

Ferri, B. A., Connor, D. J., Solis, S., Valle, J., & Volpitta, D. (2005). Teachers with LD: Ongoing negotiations with discourses of disability. *Journal of Learning Disabilities, 38*(1), 62–78.

Hannon, M. (2017). Acknowledging intersectionality: An autoethnography of a Black school counselor educator and father of a student with autism. *Journal of Negro Education, 86*(2), 154–62.

Heshusius, L. (1994). Freeing ourselves from objectivity: Managing subjectivity or turning toward a participatory mode of consciousness? *Educational Researcher, 23*, 15–22.

Individuals with Disabilities Education Act (IDEA). (1990). P.L. 101–476 20, U.S.C #1400 et seq.; Amendments of 1997, 2004. Retrieved from http://uscode.house.gov/view.xhtml?path=/prelim@title20/chapter33&edition=prelim

Keefe, E. B., Moore, V. M., & Duff, F. R. (2006). *Listening to the experts: Students with disabilities speak out.* Baltimore, MD: Paul H. Brookes.

Losen, D. J., & Orfield, G. (2002) (Eds). *Racial inequality in special education.* Cambridge, MA: Harvard Education Press.

Mandell, D. S., Ittenbach, R. F., Levy, S. E., & Pinto-Martin, J. (2007). Disparities in diagnoses received prior to a diagnosis of autism spectrum disorder. *Journal of Autism and Developmental Disorders, 37*, 795–802.

Mandell, D. S., Wiggins, L. D., Carpenter, L. A., Daniels, J., DiGuiseppi, C., Durkin, M. S., Giarelli, E., & Morrier, M.J. (2009). Racial/ethnic disparities in the identification of children with autism spectrum disorders. *American Journal of Public Health, 99*, 493–98.

Mariage, T., Paxton-Buursma, T., & Bouck, E. (2004). Interanimation: Repositioning possibilities in educational contexts. *Journal of Learning Disabilities, 37*(6),

Milbank, D. (2018, July 3). The fight against Trump is a battle for freedom. *Washington Post.* Retrieved from www.washingtonpost.com/opinions/the-fight-against-trump-is-a-battle-for-freedom/2018/07/03

Polacco, P. (1998). *Thank you, Mr. Falker.* New York, NY: Philomel Books.

Poplin, M. S. (1988). The reductionist fallacy in learning disabilities: Replicating the past by reproducing the present. *Journal of Learning Disabilities, 21*, 389–400.

Reid, D. K. & Button, L. J. (1995). Anna's story: Narratives of personal experience about being labeled learning disabled. *Journal of Learning Disabilities, 28*(10), 602–14.

Reid, D. K. & Valle, J. W. (2005). A constructivist perspective from the emerging field of disability studies. In C. T. Fosnot (Ed.), *Constructivism: Theory, perspectives, and practice* (2nd ed., Chapter 9). New York, NY: Teachers College Press.

Rodis, P., Garrod, A., & Boscardin, M. L. (2001). *Learning disabilities and life stories*. Needham Heights, MA: Allyn & Bacon.

Sword, K. M. & Zimbardo, P. (2018). The Trump effect. *Psychology Today*. Retrieved from www.psychologytoday.com/gb/comment/973370

Valle, J., Solis, S., Volpitta, D., & Connor, D. J. (2004). The disability closet: Teachers with LD evaluate risks and benefits of coming out. *Equity and Excellence in Education, 37*(1), 4–17.

Varenne, H. & McDermott, R. (1998). *Successful failure: The school America builds*. Boulder, CO: Westview Press.

Part II

How Practice Deepens Knowledge

5 Selecting Approaches and Tools of Inclusive Teaching

"How do I figure out what to teach in an inclusive classroom?"

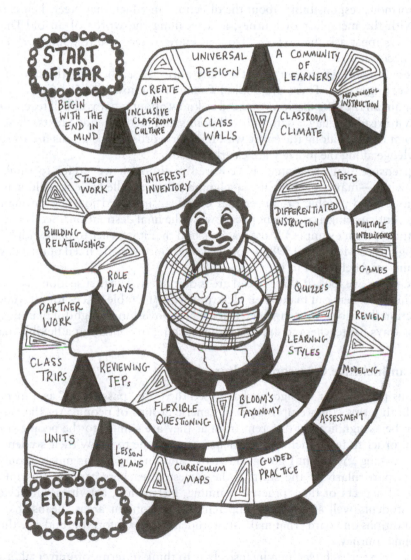

Cartoon #5 The world is your oyster

In many respects, a teacher is like the captain of a ship who needs to get from one port of call to a final destination far away. As the captain, she is responsible for the wellbeing of all passengers for the duration of the journey. Once the ship leaves the dockside and sails off into the ocean, she must negotiate two worlds. The first is within her control—overseeing conditions onboard; the second is not within her control—responding to the external elements of sun, wind, clouds, and rain. Her job is to transport the passengers safely, navigating an outside world that can change from glorious to tempestuous and back again in the blink of an eye. At the same time, the comfort of all passengers within the environment is of great importance. As they sail across the seas, becoming familiar with each part of the journey, passengers learn more about each other, themselves, and the world.

Okay, this is a little hokey, we admit. Our point, however, is not. Every day teachers face an enormous responsibility about the directions in which they steer their classrooms. Keeping with the metaphor of journey, and recalling the words of an old Diana Ross song, teachers must ask themselves, "Do you know where you're going to?" Decisions, decisions, decisions…

But, there is good news: you're not exactly adrift at sea holding the fate of children in your sweating hands. There are guides! Commonly known as The Curriculum, these guides contain all the information you need to know about what you will teach. Often laid out in easy-to-read language, with bulleted points and recommended texts, these "official guides" point teachers along the entire way. In other words, expectations for accruing content knowledge along the journey are clearly stated.

To help ensure that all content is "covered"—although we prefer to think of it as "engaged with"—many teachers use a planning device called a curriculum map. This device is a detailed graphic organizer that charts an intended journey through content knowledge, anticipating a consistent pace toward the final destination. (See Table 5.4, later in this chapter, for an example.) Most teachers find that it is easier to plan with "the end in mind" (Wiggins & McTighe, 1998). In other words, once you are fixed upon a destination, a curriculum map helps you to get there.

In this chapter, we look at three broad areas of interest. The first section discusses many ways in which teachers can make their classrooms comfortable places for all students. The second section describes ways in which teachers can invest in thoughtful planning. Finally, we suggest ways for teachers to approach the teaching of content in a flexible manner.

Creating an Inclusive Classroom Culture

Up until this point in our voyage, we have used the term "passengers" as a metaphor for students. Both terms conjure up images of generic groups of people. Yet the truth is that people can be as significantly different from as they are similar to the people sitting next to them. In order to teach inclusively, teachers must come to know their students as individuals. By asking "Who am I going to teach?" and finding out as much about students as possible, particularly at the start of the semester, teachers can use this information to inform all aspects of their practice-planning, instruction, activities, and evaluations. Knowing students well and being competent across content areas means that teachers create "conditions on board" that make sure students feel comfortable and safe throughout their learning journey.

One way to approach teaching inclusively is to think in terms of universal design. Not surprisingly, the concept of universal design translates to the notion "created with all people in mind." The original use of the concept hails from architecture and arose during the 1960s with the requirement to create new buildings accessible to citizens with mobility limitations. However, Ron Mace, the leader of the universal design movement, discovered that rethinking how buildings were traditionally configured actually benefited all users. So, while universal design was originally intended to incorporate people with disabilities, the flexibility it provides benefits everyone. For example, corner curb cuts for wheelchair users help people pushing strollers, rolling luggage, or wheeling large or heavy items.

The idea of creating accessible environments from inception, rather than retrofitting existing designs, is very powerful when applied to classroom instruction. Used within education, universal design helps teachers plan curriculum and lessons accessible to all students from the outset. The Council for Exceptional Children supports the idea of universal design applied to learning in the classroom, as follows:

> In terms of learning, universal design means the design of instructional materials and activities that makes the learning goals achievable by individuals with wide differences in their abilities to see, hear, speak, move, read, write, understand English, attend, organize, engage, and remember. Universal design for learning is achieved by means of flexible curricular materials and activities that provide alternatives for students with differing abilities. These alternatives are built into the instructional design and operating systems of educational materials—they are not added on after the fact.
>
> (Burgstahler, 2006, p. 1)

Experienced teachers who are new to this concept often express mixed feelings. Many say, "I didn't know I could use those options at the same time!" and feel they have greater flexibility within instruction to reach and teach a diverse body of students. In contrast, others say, "This is too much work! I can't do three separate lessons! I don't have time!" To the former group, we say "Yes, you're right. It makes teaching respectful of all students, and challenges us to think in nontraditional ways." To the latter group, we say, "It's not about three separate lessons. But it may be about providing an assortment of opportunities to engage in the same content." In other words, it is not more work *per se*, but is a different way of thinking about how we plan and teach.

Principles of Universal Design for Learning (UDL)

At the Center for Universal Design at North Carolina State University, a group of architects, engineers, product designers, and environmental design researchers met to develop guidelines for creating environments that are accessible to all people.[1] The group suggested seven principles, listed below. Underneath each principle are some examples of how they can be applied to instruction, popularly known as universal design for learning (UDL).

1. *Equitable use*: The design is useful to all people.

Application to instruction: Instruction is designed to be useful and accessible to people with diverse abilities. The same means can be provided for all students, and, when it is not possible, an equivalent must be provided.

- Books on tape can be given to or recorded for students who are dyslexic.
- A class web page must be accessible to everybody. For blind or dyslexic students, text-to-speech software can be employed.
- Films, documentaries, and educational television programs should have closed captions for deaf and hard-of-hearing students.

2. *Flexibility of use*: The design accommodates a broad array of individual abilities and preferences.

Application to instruction: Instruction is designed to accommodate a wide variety of individual abilities. The instructor must provide choice in methods used.

- Information can be accessed through a variety of sources, such as books, documents, the Internet, or interviews. Choices for a class project may include a presentation or a written paper.
- Culminating work can be reflected in a portfolio or through taking a test.
- The format of tests can be varied (e.g., short written response, multiple choice, creative application, problem solving, illustrations and labeling).

3. *Simple and intuitive*: The design is straightforward and easy to understand, regardless of a user's knowledge, experience, language skills, or current concentration level.

Application to instruction: Instruction is designed in a straightforward and easy-to-understand manner, regardless of student knowledge, experience, language skills, or current concentration level.

- Clear instructions can be provided for all tasks.
- Instructions that have been given in writing can be repeated orally.
- Materials, such as classroom texts and activities, should be straightforward to follow.
- Expected outcomes need to be clearly stated (e.g., through the use of rubrics).
- Multiple accessible methods (e.g., collaborative learning, hands-on activities) should be offered.
- Teacher and/or peer support may be available throughout tasks and assignments.

4. *Perceptible information*: The design communicates necessary information to the user, regardless of ambient conditions or the user's sensory abilities.

Application to instruction: Instruction is designed so that necessary information is successfully communicated to the student, regardless of where the student is or his or her sensory abilities.

- Digital copies can be available as well as hard copies.
- Large print can be available for students with visual impairments.
- Students can audiotape the class.
- All media should have closed captioning.

5. *Tolerance for error*: The design minimizes hazards and the adverse consequences of accidental or unintended actions.

Application to instruction: The instructor anticipates variation in individual student learning pace and prerequisite skills.

- Additional accommodations can be provided for skill building, in class or outside (online, with another support teacher, in partnership with parents, etc.).
- Students can hand in assignments in segments for feedback.
- Rate, volume, and complexity of specific tasks can be modified (Levine & Reed, 1999).

6. *Low physical effort*: The design can be used efficiently and comfortably, and with a minimum of fatigue.

Application to instruction: Instruction is designed to minimize nonessential physical effort to allow maximum attention to learning. (This principle does not apply when physical effort is integral to essential requirements or fundamental nature of the course.)

- A word processor can be used for an exam.
- The classroom should be configured to allow for mobility of students using wheelchairs.
- Texts can be provided in digital or auditory format.

7. *Size and space for approach and use*: Appropriate size and space are provided for approach, reach, manipulation, and use, regardless of the user's body size, posture, or mobility.

Application to instruction: Instruction is designed with consideration for appropriate size and space for approach, reach, manipulation, and use, regardless of a student's body size, posture, mobility, and communication needs.

- Equipment can be adjustable.
- Work surfaces can be at different levels.
- Handles on doors and cabinets increase accessibility for all.
- All-in-one chair/desks for left- and right-handed students need to be available. Seating arrangements should be flexible, according to type of instruction (e.g., semicircle, circle, arena style, rows, horseshoe, tables).

Scholars at the University of Connecticut added the following two concepts to the list of UDL principles.

8. *A community of learners*: The instructional environment promotes interaction and communication among students and between students and faculty.

- Learning can occur as a whole class, in groups, in pairs, and one-on-one with the teacher.
- Everyone knows everyone else's name.
- The skills and talents of every student are recognized. Discussion is deliberately fostered among students.

9. *Instructional climate*: Instruction is designed to be welcoming and inclusive. High expectations are espoused for all students.

- The teacher models the creation of a welcoming and inclusive environment with respect for diversity.
- Diversity is supported by statements in the syllabus, at the start of the semester, and in ongoing relevant ways throughout the semester.
- Specific feedback to individuals is ongoing.
- High expectations are conveyed (e.g., communicating with students who have excessive absences or inconsistent test scores).

As can be seen, UDL is about taking a proactive stance toward instructing students with diverse abilities, rather than a reactive stance by making time-consuming changes to retrofit classrooms and curricula. You might start by thinking about your class as a broad array of individual learners rather than a single "average" user. It is also important to mention that disability is just one of many characteristics that an individual person might have. The concept of "universal" applies to variation among all of us (e.g., racial and ethnic backgrounds, gender, social class, nationality status, language, culture, sexual orientation). Finally, employing these principles does not preclude the need for specific accommodations for students with disabilities as they arise (e.g., collaborating with sign language interpreters working with students who are deaf).

Featured Voice of Louis Olander

UDL and Rethinking Disability

Universal design for learning (UDL) can be a great set of tools in inclusive classrooms. Instead of providing individual "special" accommodations, UDL emphasizes supports that can be made available to all students in a classroom, especially by way of allowing students to choose supports for themselves and giving them opportunities to reflect on whether those supports are actually helpful to them. It is based on the premise that curricula itself can often be inadvertently disabling to many students, shifting the location outside of what is initially understood to be "lacking within" children, and towards inaccessible teaching practices.

For example, traditional approaches to differentiation might involve grouping students into low-, medium-, and high-level groups for a math activity. In this example, the "low" group would likely have the least complex problems and the "high" group would likely have the hardest ones. At its worst, this can be difficult to implement and leads to in-class tracking systems, especially when determinations about who gets to be in the "high," "medium," and "low" groups can be based on problematic assessments of student ability.

In contrast, a more universally designed approach could allow all students to have access to all of the same problems at varying levels. Students choose the problems appropriately challenging for them. In order to ensure that students are actually challenging themselves, teachers must structure ongoing opportunities for engagement, such as teacher–student conferences or reflective journals that allow students to not only learn math facts but also gain an awareness of their own learning needs and develop strategies that support them.

In the same way, supports can be made available to all students in a classroom and not just those with documented "needs." Closed-captioning of videos and having texts read aloud help many students, not just those with low hearing or vision. Likewise, providing speech-to-text software could be an essential support for some students, a merely helpful support to others, and be entirely unnecessary to a few, but all would have such software, often available as a plugin through existing platforms, available.

Importantly, UDL-aligned teaching pays attention to the relationships between long-term emotional patterns in learning environments (affect) and learning. It is difficult to disagree with the idea that students need to be free from threats and distractions in order to learn. Therefore teachers should pay particular attention to the ways in which their own practices may become either threatening and/or serve as a distraction to learning.

That said, UDL does have limitations. It does not yet account for student cultural differences beyond supporting their interests or generally promoting making content relevant. Teachers employing UDL-aligned teaching still need to remain responsive to student cultural norms and find ways to enable students to see themselves and their communities in positive and culturally sustaining ways in their classes and schools.

Similarly, UDL has not had strong applications for supporting the needs of emerging bilingual learners who are often viewed as English-deficient instead of as budding language experts. Even outside of UDL, teachers can still recognize their students' diverse language talents and invite them to share their home languages through the curricula. This may sometimes require teachers to reposition *themselves* as language learners. Most importantly, many important UDL-aligned supports are already part of most teachers' practice. In fact, one of the most promising ways in which teachers can improve access is to think about the things that they already do that support students, in iterations by making sure that new supports are well aligned to their students' needs in meaningful ways.

Assistive Technology in the Inclusive Classroom

Technology is everywhere. It influences our everyday lives—how we bank, date, consume news, communicate, work, purchase, and on and on. And it is increasingly present within our schools. High technology devices, now more portable and affordable, assist teachers to effectively implement UDL, in that many proactive strategies (e.g., accommodations and adaptations) are (or can be) built into such devices (Nepo, 2017). Technology benefits both students with and without disabilities in the inclusive classroom.

Let's return to the origins of assistive technology as it relates to IDEIA. The 1980s ushered in a new age of technology. As the potential to assist persons with disabilities through technology became increasingly evident during this decade, the United States Congress passed the Technology-Related Assistance Act of 1988 (P.L. 100–407) to obtain funding for technology-related services for people with disabilities. The definition used for *assistive technology device* within this law later became incorporated verbatim into the 1990 reauthorization of IDEA—"any item, piece of equipment or product system, whether acquired commercially or off the shelf, or customized, that is used to increase, maintain, or improve functional capabilities of individuals with disabilities" (20 U.S.C. 1401 (1)). IDEA's *assistive technology services* have to do with choosing, obtaining, and helping students with disabilities to use assistive technology devices as well as providing customization as needed. It is worth noting that the inclusion of assistive technology within IDEA arose out of a larger disability rights movement that resulted in the passage of the Americans with Disabilities Act of 1990 (Peterson-Karlan, 2015). Amendments to IDEA (1997) shifted requirements from giving assistive technology devices and/or services to a student *only* if necessary to achieve FAPE (free and appropriate public education) to requiring the IEP team to consider assistive technology devices and/or services regardless of a student's category. In other words, the IEP team "must not only consider the students' needs of assistive technology but also provide support for their access to the system" (Nepo, 2017, p. 212).

Under the current iteration of IDEIA (2004), assistive technology (AT) is warranted if results of an AT evaluation deem it necessary in order for a student to access curriculum, participate in class, and show what he or she knows and can do. The use of a technology device is not restricted to use in school if also needed at home for study; however, the device is owned by the school and remains there after a student moves on to another school. If the IEP team determines a student's need for AT, the school must fund the device and cannot require parents to use private or public insurance (Musgrove, 2018).

For students with disabilities in inclusive classroom settings, AT can support literacy (e.g., reading comprehension, text strategies, written composition) (Anderson-Inman & Horney, 2007; Peterson-Karlan, 2011; Peterson-Karlan, Hourcade, & Parette, 2008), listening (Rekkedal, 2014); (Zanin & Rance, 2016); executive functioning (Kulman, 2014); mobility (Oien, Fallang, & Ostensjo, 2016), as well as augment communication through technology (Brumberg, Pitt, Mantie-Kozlowski, & Burnison, 2018; Walker, Lyon, Loman, & Sennott, 2018). Below is a sample of the kinds of AT that could be used in an inclusive classroom (Lorah, Parnell, Whitby, & Hantula, 2015; Neese, 2015; Peterson-Karlan, 2015).

Literacy (Reading and Writing)

Text-to-speech (TTS) technology is helpful for students with print disabilities (e.g., blindness, dyslexia, or any other visual impairment) and can also be used to support students with disabilities such as autism, attention deficit hyperactivity disorder (ADHD), or developmental disability. TTS technology scans text and reads it aloud, thereby enabling students to read and listen simultaneously. It also has the capacity to make audio files from text files.

Intel Reader, a mobile, hand-held TTS device, is comparable to a paperback book in size and weight. Its high-resolution camera scans printed text that is changed into digital text and read aloud. A variety of voices are available. It comes with a stand (Intel Portable Capture Station) that makes scanning easier. As text is read aloud, words are highlighted. The device can be paused for spelling words aloud.

Kurzweil 3000, a TTS software program that offers a multisensory approach, is available for Windows and Macintosh. In addition to routine text-to-speech features, it provides support in 18 languages and dialects, magnifies print text, and includes picture dictionary graphics for more than 40,000 words. Reference tools are also available for test-taking, written composition, and note-taking.

Audiobooks, read by human voices in contrast to computer-generated voices as is the case for TTS, are available on iPad and iPhone (iTunes App Store), Kindle Fire (Amazon App Store), and Android (Google Play Store). Two good examples of children's audiobook apps for the iPhone and iPad are *Audiobook Pop!* and *Epic!* The International Children's Digital Library (ICDL) has thousands of books in more than 60 languages that can be accessed online (http://en.childrens library.org/) and on iPads and iPhones.

There are numerous assistive technology tools for students who struggle with handwriting as well as written expression (organization and mechanics). For example, keyboards and touchscreens replace pen and pencil challenges as students enter letters and words by typing or touching the screen. Using speech-to-text technology (dictation software), students speak what they wish to write and it appears on a screen. For students who use a keyboard, word prediction software is useful for suggesting correct spellings of words and generating words to complete sentences. Most computers have built-in spell-check and grammar check; however, there is more sophisticated proofreading software available for students with learning disabilities in written expression, such as those described below (Neese, 2015).

Ginger (www.gingersoftware.com), available for Windows and Macintosh systems as well as iOS and Android mobile devices, works well for students with dyslexia or other writing challenges because its spelling and grammar check analyzes context when searching for errors and suggesting replacements. Other features include word prediction and sentence rephrasing tools, built-in TTS for reading aloud what is typed, and individualized practice based on error patterns.

Ghotit (www.ghotit.com), described on its website as "assistive technology that gets you," offers software and mobile apps "designed by dyslexics for dyslexics." This software is sensitive to the user's error patterns and personalizes suggestions for rewriting. It includes word prediction, contextual review, TTS technology, and an integrated dictionary. According to its website, "Ghotit solutions are offered as: Real Writer & Reader for Windows; Real Writer & Reader for Mac; Dyslexia App for Android; Dyslexia App for iPhone and Dyslexia App for iPad."

For students who have difficulty visualizing components of a composition, *Draft-Builder*, available for Windows and Macintosh, is a writing tool that organizes the writing process into three steps. A graphic template provides an organizational system into which the user can enter text. A drag and drop feature allows the user to move text to create a rough draft. Additional features include a talking spell-checker and a bibliography tool.

Listening

In an inclusive classroom, you may have students who need assistive technology for listening—because of hearing impairment, challenges in auditory processing (e.g., difficulty recognizing subtle differences in the sounds of words, high distractibility to background noise, mishearing oral directions), or problems paying attention to auditory information. Below are examples of AT that provide support for students with hearing impairment, central auditory processing disorder (CAPD), and attention deficit hyperactivity disorder (ADHD).

FM Systems, a personal listening device, is comprised of a microphone, transmitter, and receiver that rely on radio broadcasting technology. The teacher speaks into a microphone and sound is transmitted to a receiver that the student wears, thereby reducing the sound distance between teacher and student. This technology is useful for students with hearing impairment, CAPD, and ADHD.

Sound Field Systems, specialized speaker systems for the classroom, distributes the teacher's voice evenly throughout the classroom so that everyone can hear well. This type of AT may be helpful to students with hearing loss, attentional challenges, language delays, CAPD, and developmental delays.

Noise-canceling headphones are useful to students who are sensitive to noise or background distractions. These headphones block out extraneous noise and can be used with a white noise app (e.g., rain, rushing water).

Executive Functioning

Students with various disabilities may struggle with executive functioning skills that underlie most classroom tasks and assignments. Executive functioning refers to the neurologically-based capacity to think flexibly and self-regulate. Classroom examples of executive functioning include: paying attention, starting and completing tasks, planning ahead, prioritizing, organizing, remembering information needed to complete a goal, managing time, note-taking, and self-monitoring. There are many apps to support both children and adults in these areas. Below are a few that have received strong teacher ratings (Holderman, 2014).

My Video Schedule is an app designed to support students with time management and motivation. Teachers can use the photo and video modeling feature of scheduled activities to assist students. There is also a reward system built into the app.

Time Timer is designed to support students who have difficulty estimating and visualizing time. The app features customizable timers that represent time through colorful visuals that help concretize the passage of time. The app can be used to help students judge the amount of time remaining to complete a task, waiting for a period of time, and/or managing transitions.

MindMeister (www.mindmeister.com) is a website that offers a variety of mind-mapping templates designed to organize thought. The site also includes templates for making To Do lists and documenting brainstorming ideas.

Notability features tools to make note-taking easier, more efficient, and interactive. For example, a student can take a page of notes and "type, write, draw, highlight, record audio, cut, paste, and even insert multimedia content captured from websites."

Mobility

For students with challenges in mobility and fine motor skills, assistive technology offers options for operating a computer or mobile device through Sip-and-Puff Systems. Basically, a switch device, the student can navigate a computer screen, for example, by controlling the device by mouth—clicking on icons or letters by using either a sip or a puff (Neese, 2015).

Origin Instruments, a company that specializes in sip-and-puff systems, advertises on its website (www.orin.com/access/sip_puff) that, "If you can use a drinking straw, you can use our Sip/Puff switch." The mouthpiece is positioned by either a headset or a "flexible shaft with a universal clamp," enabling navigation of a computer screen through sip or puff. The second-generation Sip/Puff Breeze can be used with an iPad, iPhone, and iPod Touch.

Jouse3, compatible with Windows, Macintosh, Linux, and Unix as well as Android and iOS mobile devices, is a sip-and-puff device that is not worn by the user but instead is affixed to a desktop. The student controls the device by using any part of the mouth, cheek, chin, or tongue.

Communication

Assistive technology in the form of augmentative and alternative communication (AAC) meets the needs of students challenged by conventional language expression and/or comprehension. Students who use AAC may have autism, cerebral palsy, intellectual disability, or traumatic brain injury. With the advent of increased technology, the number of "speech-generating devices" (SGDs) has exploded, ranging from simple single-message devices to high tech computer-based systems. Even portable handheld tablet-based computers (e.g., iPad, Galaxy) or portable multimedia players (e.g., iPod) can be transformed into speech-generated devices by downloading a range of apps.

Dynavox (www.tobiidynavox.com/en-us/products/devices) offers an iOS-based speech tablet with iPad specifically designed for augmentive alternative communication users. It is highly durable and features extra loud speakers.

Go Talk 20-Plus (www.attainmentcompany.com/gotalk-200) is a handheld AAC device that supports users with "little to no speech throughout their daily lives." It has a 100-message capacity in five levels, five core buttons for frequently used words across the levels, and 20 programmable buttons "to personalize each level with pictures and vocal recordings."

Any iPad, Galaxy, or iPod can be turned into an AAC device by simply downloading relatively low-cost communication apps. Moreover, the everydayness of smartphones and tablets has gone a long way to reducing stigma associated with communication devices. Students who communicate non-verbally join the ranks of users who likewise enjoy alternative communication technology. Below is a sample of ACC apps that come highly recommended.

TouchChat HD—AAC with WordPower enables a user to navigate through "page sets" to locate messages that are spoken with a built-in voice. Users select a voice among many choices, in both English and Spanish. This version is loaded with WordPower, a series of AAC vocabularies created by Nancy Inman. Provided page sets can be customized to create new page sets. TouchChat is compatible with iPhone, iPod, and iPad. It is now also available in Hebrew, Arabic, and Canadian French.

Dynavox Compass, designed by "a team of leading clinicians," provides customizable communication pages based on the user's age, interests, communication level, and prior experience with communication apps. This app is compatible with Common Core vocabulary and offers practice to build literacy and language skills. Users access the app by using direct touch, keyboard, and/or switch scanning. Dynavox Compass is available only through the App Store for iOS devices.

Avaz, a picture and text-based communication app, meets not only the needs of the user but also the parent. Avaz promises to "grow with your child" with its three levels of "graded, research-based vocabulary." The app is customized to add words and phrases particular to your family. It also provides ideas for parents to converse with their child in multiple ways and to "think like a therapist." Progress is represented through easy-to-read graphs and charts. Avaz is available for download through the App Store.

The Big Picture: From Principles to Practice

Now that you have the basics of UDL and ideas for using assistive technology to support UDL, let's think about how to create an inclusive classroom culture for diverse students. Box 5.1 contains an overview of what to consider in universal design.[2]

While this may look like a step-by-step plan, we acknowledge that teaching and learning are rarely as straightforward. In many ways, universal design is a useful framework (even an "ideal") that helps us to think through "the big picture" of classroom teaching. We urge you to contemplate both the theory of universal design and its promise for classroom practice. In the section titled "Environment," we discuss practical concerns about how to teach in an inclusive classroom that address many of the areas listed earlier.

The following classroom aspects fall somewhere within the nine principles of UDL, and all are integral to establishing and maintaining "the big picture." While they are interconnected pieces of the same puzzle, we believe each merits foregrounding to temporarily highlight its relevant issues.

Box 5.1 The Process of Universal Design

1. Become familiar with the course, goals, and content.
2. Define the group of students who will be in the class. Identify potential diversity within the group with respect to gender, age, size, ethnicity, race, native language, learning styles, and abilities to see, hear, move, manipulate objects, and learn.
3. Apply universal design methods.
4. Apply universal design processes.
5. Apply universal design process assessments.
6. Monitor effectiveness of instruction by gathering feedback from student participation, and learn to make modifications based on this feedback.

Environment

Perhaps we are stating the obvious when we say classrooms should always look inviting. Students and teachers spend a lot of time in classrooms, so they should be as cheerful and pleasant as possible—places where everyone likes to be. This does not mean that the walls should be festooned with "inspirational" images, such as the *You Can Make It If You Really Try* poster featuring an adorable kitten hanging below a tree branch with one claw. However, we do recommend that you consider the following issues.

Classroom Space

Although it may initially seem a secondary concern to some educators, we cannot emphasize enough the importance of how classroom space is utilized. There are many options in configuring desks, chairs, closets, and other furniture. Regardless of grade, we believe that even if a teacher has a preferred way of arranging furniture, it should be movable and reconfigured to suit the objectives of a specific lesson. For example, students should be afforded the opportunity to work individually, in pairs, in small groups, and as a whole class. Spatial arrangements of classroom furniture should be taken into account so that all students may move freely around the classroom.

In addition to the fluidity of classroom seating arrangements, there can be "permanent" areas within a classroom that offer students consistency of experience. For example, centers can be established as places where students are expected to perform specific tasks. At a computer center, students can use word processors or do Internet research. At a class store, students can buy hypothetical items and check their change. At a pet center, students can feed, observe, measure, and draw a live turtle.

Classroom Walls

Walls can be used to inform children about one another by displaying student work. A rule of thumb: display student work prominently! There should be at least one example from every student, whether it is the formation of a single letter, a five-paragraph essay, original artwork, how a particular mathematical problem was solved, a report about a country, or illustrations of a food web. Works should include samples that indicate varying levels of success. In other words, do not just post the work of students who earned 10/10 or a grade of A+; instead, incorporate a variety of response levels, explaining what is valuable about each. It is also equally valid to display work without grades.

Children's interests can also be displayed on walls. Student profiles, statements, biographies, likes/dislikes, photographs, self-portraits, "Wanted Posters," and so on, can motivate students to read and analyze information about one another, helping them to make connections within their unique learning community.

Important concepts should also be represented on walls, either permanently (as in a multiplication chart) or temporarily (as in a weekly vocabulary list). Teachers always have the option of moving temporarily displayed concepts to permanent displays such as Word Walls, where accumulated content-specific terms are kept within reach of students (flowers: petal, stamen, pistil, stalk, leaves, roots, soil). Such vocabulary clusters might be teacher-generated or made from commercially available materials.

The physical features of the classroom just described should reflect the sense of community among the individuals who work there. Building relationships with and among students is a vital part of teaching. It should be an early objective of all teachers. After all, how well you can teach your students is intricately linked to how well you know their abilities and personalities.

As the Song Goes: "Getting to Know You, Getting to Know All About You"

During the first few sessions of class, students need an opportunity to transition into a new environment and get to know who you are. As a teacher, you can introduce yourself and require the same of students. The following are activities that can be used to promote sharing information about all class members:

- Have students complete a simple formula of stating two or three things (e.g., My name is …; Something I like is …; My hobby is …).
- Read a list of statements to students and have them stand up if the statement relates to them (e.g., "I was born in this city," "I have more than two siblings," "It takes me more than 30 minutes to get to school," "I prefer the color blue to the color red," etc.). Students can be invited to comment upon the statement or ask questions of their peers.
- Have students draw a picture of themselves and describe three things (or people) who are important to them. Each student can then share with the person next to her or him who can then, in turn, introduce her or his "new classmate" to the large group.
- Have students form two circles, one within the other. The students in the inner circle should face out; those in the outer circle should face in. Each person should be facing another. The teacher can then provide a topic (Do you have any pets? What's your favorite TV show? What's your favorite subject in school?) and ask students to converse. After a minute, have the outer circle move one place clockwise and then provide a new topic.

Interests, Learning Preferences, and Points of Academic Entry

In terms of coming to know students' interests, learning preferences, and points of academic entry, teachers can do the following:

- Provide interest inventories (Reif & Heimburge, 1996).
- Give a detailed checklist asking students for self-analysis in terms of reading, writing, attention, and so on (Levine, 1994).
- Have students self-evaluate in various areas, chart their self-scores, and discuss areas in which they are good and areas in which they need to improve. These charts can be revisited during the semester to chart growth in various areas.
- Ask students to "divide up" their multiple intelligences (see "Tool 3" later in this chapter for a more detailed explanation) and create a pie chart of eight slices that reflects how they view themselves.
- Create a time capsule in an envelope for each student containing a variety of items, such as biographical information, academic goals, and predictions for the upcoming year.

Knowledge about Disabilities

In terms of assessing students' knowledge of disabilities, teachers can use the following approaches:

- Use an attitude assessment and begin open-ended statements, such as "People in wheelchairs make me feel…" or "People born with disabilities…," etc. (Shapiro, 1999).

- Use a sample probe on disabilities, including questions like this: "Is a person with a disability usually ill? Yes/No/Not Sure (Barnes, Berrigan, & Biklen, 1978).
- Use observation to assess how students with and without disabilities are interacting with one another (Salend, 2011).

All the foregoing activities help teachers learn about their students while actively promoting a sense of community. In encouraging students to share and listen to one another by using the technique of "round robin," each has the opportunity to come to know his or her peers in greater depth. Furthermore, by creating opportunities for students to regularly share in pairs or small groups, teachers encourage social interactions that make for a dynamic classroom.

Building and Maintaining Relationships

Building relationships with students occurs overtime. However, when students recognize that a teacher prepares lessons by respectfully taking into consideration individual levels of knowledge, likes/dislikes, interests, abilities, and areas of need in order to provide an interesting, engaging, challenging lesson that helps students progress, then a mutual sense of respect develops. Teachers dedicate much of their time, energy, and effort toward providing quality instruction, continually reflecting upon how well students "got it." By consistently providing quality instruction and being fair in decisions, teachers can build a strong sense of rapport with their students. However, do you ever wonder what responsibilities teachers have in building relationships, even friendships, among students?

While recognizing that friendships cannot be forced, a teacher can facilitate them within a friendly classroom. For example, students are more likely to converse with one another if they have the opportunity to interact within classroom situations created by the teacher. There is potentially great social as well as academic benefit in having students work together in pairs, triads, small groups, and large groups.

Working in pairs, students can:

- First think as individuals, then pair off to share.
- Compare and explain answers.
- Brainstorm topics.
- Problem solve.
- Debate point and counterpoint.

Working in triads, students can:

- Take roles (question poser, note taker, reporter).
- Debate issues, taking three perspectives on any issue (e.g., as three branches of government).
- Role play situations.
- Problem solve.
- Create a project, poster, or booklet. Take turns in reading a text.

Working in small groups, students can:

- Practice and rotate roles (reader, highlighter, definer, solver, checker).
- Practice specific skills, such as organization, time management, listening.

- Share original thoughts, responses, suggestions.
- Split up and inform another group of their findings.
- All contribute in some shape or form.
- Use opportunities to reflect and self-evaluate cooperative behaviors (Vernon, Deshler, & Schumaker, 1999).

Working as a whole class, students can:

- Share original information with everyone.
- Continue adding onto one another's ideas.

By requiring students to work together sometimes and making it an option to work together at other times, they experience a wide variety of opportunities to access all members of the class community.

Here are additional ideas for facilitating friendships in the classroom:

- Create long-term or ongoing projects, such as classroom newspapers, plays, planting school gardens, organizing a sponsored event, etc.
- Explicitly teach the concept of friendship within the curriculum (Shapiro, 1999).
- Teach social skills instruction that includes role plays. Model social interactions, good behaviors, appropriate use of language.
- Organize class trips.
- Form a committee/group to problem-solve issues around friendship and inclusion (Salend, 2011).

Informal Assessment

Standardized tests often yield a score or ranking for a child. For example, a percentile reveals how well a child scored in comparison to her peers (77th percentile means she scored better than 77 percent of her fellow test takers). Or, a continuum between 4 and 1 (from high to low) broadly shows the current standard of a student. However, neither of these scores provides sufficient information about a student's specific areas of need. Teachers are, however, able to gather information about their students throughout the entire year using a variety of means. (See Chapter 7 for discussion of multiple forms of assessment, such as portfolio assessment, think-aloud techniques, student journals and logs, error analysis, student self-evaluation, student interviews, cooperative group testing, teacher-made tests, quizzes, informal observations, dynamic assessment, rubrics, curriculum-based measurement, authentic/performance assessment, and analyzing student work samples.)

Students with Individual Education Plans (IEPs)

All teachers need to know which students in their classrooms have an "official" disability classification in order to understand their particular needs. The Individual Education Plan (IEP) of a student with disabilities contains a wide variety of information, including:

- Present levels of the student's academic performance.
- Measurable annual academic and/or social goals of the student, and necessary steps to achieve them.
- Special education services being received by the student (type, duration, frequency).

- Any related services being received by the student (e.g., counseling, speech and language therapy, occupational therapy, etc.).
- A statement rationalizing why the student is not receiving his education in a general education classroom. Testing accommodations for the student.
- Any assistive technology needs of the student. Assessments made by school-related staff (psychologists, teachers).

IEPs are intended to inform teachers about their students, listing specific goals that should be factored into planning, instruction, and evaluation. It is important to note that IEPs vary enormously in clarity, accuracy, and appropriateness. While some are close to perfect documents that function as a rich description of who the student is, and what and how the student needs to learn, others appear as a disconnected compilation of reports, required forms, checklists, and computer-generated goals. In other words, the degree of helpful information in an IEP varies enormously.

With the recent reauthorization of the Individuals with Disabilities Education Improvement Act (IDEIA), the goals and objectives within IEPs have become aligned with the general education curriculum. This means that a general educator is required to attend each annual IEP meeting to ensure that the content of the curriculum is considered in any plans being developed. Unfortunately, the importance of IEP meetings can become minimized in the hectic context of everyday school routines.

Three Useful Tools for Teaching

The good news about being in the world of teaching is that there are many useful tools to help educators plan effectively. We have found three tools to be extremely useful, both in our days as fledgling teachers and in our current college classes. Bloom's taxonomy, an awareness of learning styles, and an understanding of multiple intelligences can all be used for honing your teaching skills.

Tool 1: Bloom's Taxonomy

Over half a century ago, Benjamin Bloom led a group of educational psychologists in clarifying the levels of behavior they believed were required for the learning process. The classification system came to be known as Bloom's taxonomy, and consists of six levels, from the simple to the complex (Bloom, 1984). Studies have shown that the majority of questions asked in classrooms and on tests are on the lower levels of cognition and revolve around students' recall of information without their necessarily understanding it (ibid.). Since then, research on how the brain works has emphasized how higher levels of cognition are achieved by requiring students to answer higher-level questions and partake in activities that require more than recollection and application (Wolfe, 2001). However, all individuals benefit from thinking through all levels, and each can be embedded into classroom activities and questions.

Flexible Questioning

Broadly speaking, questions can be categorized into two types, those using the lower-order thinking skills, or LOTS (knowledge, comprehension, application), and those using the higher-order thinking skills, or HOTS (analysis, synthesis, evaluation). Each serves a purpose, with the LOTS serving to connect students to specific knowledge, and

Table 5.1 Using Bloom's taxonomy for questioning

Level	Types of questions	Useful verbs
Knowledge	Who...? When...? Where...? How much...? How many...? Define... Count... List... Name... Describe... State... Recite...	Arrange, use, cite, choose, list, tell, match, select, label, group, find, locate, name, offer, omit, pick, quote, sort, show, say, reset, repeat, spell, touch, write, identify, point to...
Comprehension	State in your own words... State in one word... What does this mean? Is this the same...? Indicate... Explain what is happening... What part doesn't fit? Read the graph or table... Translate... Outline... What exceptions are there...? Which is more probable? Summarize...	Convert, render, construe, reword, change, translate, expand, explain, infer, restate, retell, define, spell out, outline, offer, submit, advance, propose, project, alter, vary, moderate, account for...
Application	Predict ... Select... Tell what would happen... Show in a graph or table... Give an example... Which...? Judge the effects... How much change would there be... Identify results of...	Solve, classify, explain, try, use, employ, utilize, manipulate, solve, modify, make use of, compute, show, relate...
Analysis	What is the function of...? What assumptions...? What is the premise...? State the point of view of...What is the relationship between...? What is the main idea...? What is the subordinate idea...? What conclusion can be drawn? What ideas apply...? What is fact and opinion in...? What does the author assume?	Break down, uncover, examine, divide, deduce, look into, dissect, test for, relate, outline, infer, illustrate, diagram, distinguish, categorize, analyze, select, separate, classify, contrast, compare, discriminate...
Synthesis	Create... Design ... Plan... Formulate a theory... How would you test...? Propose an alternative... Choreograph... Choose... Develop... Imagine... Make up... Solve the following... Compose...	Create, combine, build, compile, produce, develop, reorganize, reorder, structure, make, compose, construct, generate, evolve, make up, form, formulate, conceive, originate, constitute...
Evaluation	What is more important...? Evaluate... Appraise... Defend... Criticize... Judge...	Decide, rate, prioritize, appraise, rank, weigh, accept, reject, grade, classify, settle, criticize, award, arbitrate, referee, determine...

Source: Composed from a variety of sources, including J. Maynar, unpublished list, Pomana, CA: G. Disenberg and G. Stevens, unpublished handout given at SETRC/Albany Meeting.

the HOTS requiring a more questioning and creative approach to understanding information. See Table 5.1.

Flexible Activities

In addition, Bloom's taxonomy is useful to apply when choosing or designing classroom activities. In scanning Table 5.2, it becomes apparent how different forms of engagement within the classroom can be employed to make the classroom environment a challenging place for all students.

Table 5.2 Using Bloom's taxonomy for activities

Level	Purpose	Expectations for learner	Activities
Knowledge	Knowing specifics Using facts	Remember an idea or fact in the same form learned	—Question and answer sessions —Worksheets —Workbooks —Programmed instruction —Games and puzzles —Information search —Reading assignments —Drill and practice —Finding definitions —Memory games or quizzes
Comprehension	Being able to interpret, extrapolate, translate	—Communicate an idea in a new or different form —Communicate in relation to one's own experience —See relationships among things —Project the effect of things	—Debate —Make predictions or estimations —Suppose —Do small-group projects —Dramatize —Give examples —Do peer teaching
Application	Being able to practice what has been taught	Use learned material in new situations —Apply rules, laws, methods, frameworks, theories	—Solve mathematical problems —Construct charts and graphs —Demonstrate correct use of a method or procedure —Predict how a character would act in a certain situation
Analysis	Being able to understand at a deeper level than comprehension or application, as it requires understanding of both content and structural form of material	Break things apart and examine pieces of information —See the relationship between the parts and recognize organizational principles involved	—Distinguish between facts and inferences —Recognize unstated assumptions —Analyze the structure of writing —Analyze a work of art or piece of music

Synthesis	—Communicate in a unique way —Develop a plan or proposed set of operations —Develop a set of abstract relations (make a hypothesis)	—Think creatively —Make original things —Take existing things and reconfigure them in a new way	Produce an original plan —Define a problem —Identify goals and objectives —Create an original product —Show how an idea or product can be changed —Find new combinations —Write a well-organized theme —Give a well-organized speech
Evaluation	Judge in terms of internal standards —Judge in terms of external criteria	—Think creatively —Make original things —Take existing things and reconfigure them in a new way —Make judgments about things based on either external or internal criteria, conditions —Accept or reject things based on standards	—Generate criteria for evaluation —Evaluate peer projects and presentations —Evaluate data, given criteria to apply —Self-evaluate ideas and products

Tool 2: Learning Styles

The term "learning styles" is used to understand and capitalize upon the many ways in which students learn. The idea that students possess different learning styles originated with Dunn and Dunn (1972) almost half a century ago. Some of these factors are environmental, others are developmental, and learning styles can change according to time, place, and context. However, these ideas are useful to bear in mind for planning instruction. Below are five major lenses through which to view a learner, along with the considerations each perspective offers.

Environmental Lens

Comfort and receptivity toward learning are significantly influenced by the individual's surroundings. For example, consider these questions:

- Is the lighting bright, dull, somewhere in between?
- Is the temperature cool, warm, somewhere in between?
- Does the individual have the ability to regulate the temperature?
- Is the seat soft, hard, somewhere in between? Can the individual move?
- Is the atmosphere quiet, noisy, somewhere in between? Is music playing? If so, which types are favored and which avoided?

Sociological Lens

This perspective focuses on ways in which individuals learn in association with others. For example, consider these questions:

- Does the person prefer to work alone or with peers?
- Does the individual like to be mentored or to mentor?

Physiological Lens

This view takes into consideration people's mental and physical body rhythms. For example, consider these questions:

- When is the best time to learn in terms of energy—morning, noon, afternoon, evening, night?
- When is the best time to learn in relation to eating—before, during, after?
- To what degree must a person be moving his body to learn? How well can an individual learn by sitting still? Moving a little? Moving a lot?

Psychological Lens

This element considers different ways in which people process information and then respond to it. For example, consider these questions:

- Are the people reflective or impulsive?
- Are they holistic or atomistic?
- Do they see and work from the whole to the parts, or from the parts to the whole?

Emotional Lens

This perspective considers how comfortable individuals are in managing their work. For example, consider these questions:

- Do individuals prefer to complete one task at a time?
- Do individuals prefer to have several tasks in progress simultaneously?

These five lenses and the issues they raise have far-reaching implications for teachers. While all of these styles cannot be provided simultaneously, teachers can incorporate choices and options in their classes that allow students to become aware of their learning styles and how to best use them for learning.

Another conceptualization of learning styles comes from the traditional view in special education that students should be taught through multisensory approaches: visual, auditory, and kinesthetic-tactile ways (VAKT) (Fernald, 1943).

Visual Learners

Visual learners process and understand information primarily through seeing it. This learning style corresponds to diagrams, charts, photographs, and/or illustrations that help students create a strong mental image of what is being taught. In addition, visual learners benefit from seeing a teacher's facial expressions, hand gestures, and body movements to process and understand information presented.

Auditory Learners

Auditory learners process information primarily through listening and speaking. This can take the form of listening to the teacher, conversing with others, and/or discussing concepts/issues/themes with classmates. Written information in texts, worksheets, or handouts is often insufficient to satisfactorily engage auditory learners, who need to process through active conversation.

Kinesthetic-Tactile Learners

These learners understand information and concepts better when they have a physical connection, that is, something to touch. These learners like to explore by actively moving and manipulating materials (e.g., counters, models, games, art materials). Learning may be inhibited without such materials and opportunities.

Teachers should plan with a view to incorporating all three elements into their classrooms by simply asking themselves questions like this: What visual supports will I use to help reach my objectives for the lesson? What spoken instructions will I give, when will I give them, and how will I give them? What kind of manipulatives will I use to help students process the skills/concepts that I'm teaching?

Finally, many educational researchers have long noted how learning styles are influenced by cultural differences according to race, ethnicity, and social class (Grant & Sleeter, 1986; Ladson-Billings, 2009; Paris & Alim, 2017). In other words, social interactions and expectations within all subcultures can significantly influence the receptivity and comfort levels of all learners.

Tool 3: Multiple Intelligences

For a long time, intelligence was thought to be fixed, innate, and quantifiable, known as an intelligence quotient (IQ). However, this view has been undermined by Howard Gardner's (1984) theory of multiple intelligences, in which he posits that every individual has varying types of intelligences. In outlining the various intelligences, Gardner claims that everybody has all eight (with more yet to be recognized), but they vary greatly among us. Each intelligence is listed in Table 5.3, along with the abilities associated with it, examples of people who exemplify each "type," and classroom activities that promote the growth of each area. While discussing this theory alone could take up our entire book, we still believe that introducing you to this idea will immediately allow you to see ways in which it is useful to consider for everyday classroom practice.

Investing in Thoughtful Planning

In terms of planning, teachers must ask themselves a series of questions, including these: What will I teach? Why will I teach it? How will I teach it? When will it be taught? How will I know that it has been taught? Furthermore, when co-teaching, these questions must be discussed with a partner in pedagogy (see Chapter 8). We believe that time must be spent in thoughtful preparation and understanding the interconnectedness of long-, medium-, and short-term planning. Broadly stated, long-term planning involves the general course of study; medium-term planning focuses on the unit of study; and short-term planning is the immediate lesson of study.

Backwards Planning

While acknowledging that different educators have a range of approaches to planning, we are advocates of "backwards planning," or starting from the outset with the big picture in mind (Wiggins & McTighe, 1998). In brief, by planning with the end in mind, educators are able to state their intended outcomes and then plot their course toward them.

Stage 1: Identify Desired Outcomes/Results

Which goals are the desired outcomes of student learning stated in the curriculum? What are some objectives in order to reach those goals? What are the "enduring understandings" for students that are taking this course of study? The notion of enduring understandings is valuable, as it helps focus the teacher on foregrounding big ideas that are integral to the discipline and of lifelong value, not merely items on a checklist to "cover the curriculum." These ideas serve to engage students, they must have significance in the world beyond the classroom, and they may be abstract or often misconstrued ideas. By answering key questions, students are able to deepen their understanding of concepts. These are examples of key questions:

- What is the meaning of being fully human?
- What is the relationship between conflict and change?
- How does the environment shape animal behavior?
- How do civilizations define themselves versus how others define them?
- What is the connection between exploration and progress?

Table 5.3 Gardner's multiple intelligences

Intelligence	The ability to...	Examples of famous people	Activities to develop this skill
Verbal-linguistic	—Be sensitive to the nuances of language —Use words effectively —Understand other people's use of words —Create poetry and prose —Write speeches —Use formal and informal conversation	William Shakespeare, playwright and poet; Martin Luther King, Jr. civil rights leader; Amy Tan, novelist; Toni Morrison, novelist	—Writing journals —Reading aloud —Storytelling —Giving speeches —Making presentations —Debating —Creating publications —Dramatizing —Role playing
Visual-spatial	—Visual patterns, designs, and shapes in concrete form —Discern space —Know directionality —Understand one's position in space —Interpret and create one's visual experiences	Antoni Gaudi, artist and architect; Frank Lloyd Wright, architect; Frida Kahlo, artist; Tim Burton, director	—Completing puzzles —Drawing —Using graphic organizers —Making models —Charting or graphing —Making visual analogies —Visualizing and describing
Logical-mathematical	—Understanding through patterns —Know and use symbolic representations —Apply reasoning —Solve numerical problems	Marie Curie, scientist; Albert Einstein, scientist; Stephen Hawking, scientist	—Using money —Measuring —Collecting and analyzing data —Problem solving —Classifying
Bodily-kinesthetic	—Use gross motor skills, making the body compete in sports (e.g., football, gymnastics) or in an aesthetic capacity (e.g., dance, performance) —Use fine motor skills to complete intricate tasks —Work skillfully with objects	Alvin Ailey, dancer; Greg Louganis, swimmer; Venus Williams, tennis player; David Beckham, soccer player	—Dancing —Participating in hand-on activities —Experimenting —Dramatizing explanations —Creating tableaux —Playing games —Doing activities involving body movement

(continued)

Table 5.3 (Cont.)

Intelligence	The ability to…	Examples of famous people	Activities to develop this skill
Musical	—Perceive, analyze, perform, and create music —Recognize and appreciate different forms of music —Perceive rhythm, pitch, melody, harmony	Stevie Wonder, singer, songwriter; Aaron Copeland, composer; Annie Lennox, singer, songwriter; Philip Glass, composer	—Rapping —Playing instruments —Creating rhythm —Writing lyrics —Singing —Performing
Intrapersonal	—Analyze and know one's own feelings, emotions, and strengths in relation to those of other people —Act upon that understanding	Dalai Lama, religious leader; David Sedaris, author	—Reading independently —Personalizing projects —Personalizing responses —Conferencing —Developing personal goals
Interpersonal	—Observe and understand the perspectives, feelings, and emotions of other people, and act accordingly —Socialize well with others —Work well with people	Oprah Winfrey, entrepreneur, actress, businesswoman; Ellen DeGeneres, comedian; John Stewart, talk show host	—Learning cooperatively —Studying in groups —Editing with peers —Tutoring younger children —Mediating conflict —Teaching peers
Naturalist	—Understand, explain, and act in relation to what is encountered in nature	Jacques Cousteau, ocean conservationist; Jane Goodall, primatologist; Al Gore, environmental activist	—Collecting —Classifying —Identifying

Stage 2: Determine What Represents Acceptable Evidence of Student Competency

What type of evidence will reveal that goals have been achieved? How will a teacher and students know that key questions have been answered? The student should be able to perform a task-contextualized within real-world application, which reveals his or her knowledge and skills. Evidence can be measured through formal criterion-referenced assessment (e.g., tests, quizzes, cues), informal assessment (e.g., conversations, observations), and student self-assessments.

Stage 3: Plan Instruction and Learning Experiences

In what order should content be presented? What kinds of activities will engage students to process the information presented? Teachers plot a sequence of content-specific concepts, and then connect them to activities that promote student engagement with material.

Balancing the Time to Plan: Having Your Cake and Eating It, Too

Once a course of study has been set, it is helpful to break it down into instructional units. For example, a 20-week course might be divided into six or seven units ranging from one to six weeks each. In turn, within each unit, there are a series of sequential lessons. It may be useful to think of a cake (the course) that is divided up into different sized slices (the units), and within each slice there are bites of cake (lessons). Plotting the course of study into a graphic organizer helps teachers get a sense of the big picture as well as its components. Some people refer to such organizers as "pacing calendars," as they help teachers manage and organize the timing and sequence of a curriculum. Other people prefer to use a curriculum map, which is a more detailed organizer that literally serves as a semester-long (or year-long) map to get from A to B, and includes essential questions, content, skills, activities, and assessment. See Table 5.4.

Designing a Differentiated Curriculum

Inclusive education requires that teachers create and maintain flexible classrooms. Instruction is geared to match students at all different levels of achievement. This means that instruction is creative, malleable, and designed to meet a variety of students "where they are" in terms of content and skills while facilitating their growth toward "the next step." Differentiated instruction is one of the most creative and vital ideas to grow within education over the last decade. It asks teachers to create classrooms that fit student needs rather than creating students to fit classroom needs. Differentiated instruction is also highly compatible with inclusive education. According to Carol Ann Tomlinson (2001), features of a differentiated classroom include the following:

- Student differences are studied as a basis for planning.
- Assessment is ongoing and diagnostic to understand how to make instruction more responsive to learner need.
- The focus on multiple forms of intelligence is evident.
- Excellence is defined in large measure by individual growth from a starting point.
- Students are frequently guided in making interest-based learning choices. Many learning profile options are provided. Many instructional arrangements are used.
- Student readiness, interest, and learning profiles shape instruction.
- Essential skills are used to make sense of and understand key concepts and principles.

Table 5.4 Curriculum map, ninth-grade English

	Content	Skills	Assessment	Standards
September	—Autobiography Introduction —Chapter 2: Interview —Chapter 3: Research culture —Introduction to literature circles	—format styles —keywords/ vocabulary —grammar —drafting —reading comprehension/ application —group-work skills	—grammar and vocabulary quizzes —group projects —finished drafts	*Ela—Read books *Elc—Information *E2a—Info report *E3b—Group meetings *E4a—Grammar *E4b—Revision *E5A—Literature response *E5b—Produce genre *E6a—Critique pub doc
October	—Chapter 4: Narrative of a meaningful memory —Chapter 5: Debating public education —Chapter 6: Neighborhood tour —Autobiography literature circles	—format styles —keywords/ vocabulary —grammar —drafting —reading comprehension/ application —group-work skills	—grammar and vocabulary quizzes —group projects —finished drafts	*E1a—Read books *E1c—Information *E2a—Info report *E2c—Narrative account *E2e—Personal essay *E3b—Group meetings *E4a—Grammar *E4b—Revision *E5a—Literature response *E5b—Produce genre
November	—Chapter 7: Letter —Chapter 8: Freewrite —Autobiography literature circles	—format styles —keywords/ vocabulary —grammar —drafting —reading comprehension/ application —group-work skills	—grammar and vocabulary quizzes —group projects —finished drafts	*E1a—Read books *E1c—Information *E2c—Narrative account *E3b—Group meetings *E4a—Grammar *E4b—Revision *E5a—Literature response *E5b—Produce genre

Month	Content/Topics	Skills	Assessments	Standards
December	—Chapter 10: Obituary or award speech —Autobiography literature circles —Student-led lessons	—format styles —keywords/ vocabulary —grammar —drafting —reading comprehension/ application —group-work skills —finishing book reflection theme/ character development	—grammar and vocabulary quizzes —group projects —finished drafts —literature circle final project	*E1a—Read books *E1c—Information *E2b—Literature response *E2f—Reflect essay *E3b—Group meetings *E4a—Grammar *E4b—Revision *E5a—Literature response *E5b—Produce genre
January	—Chapter 1: Introduction —Oral presentation	—reflection and understanding theme —compilation and final drafting —speaking skills —understanding evaluation	—completed written autobiography —unit test —oral report and visual poster	*E1a—Read books *E1c—Information *E2f—Reflect essay *E3a—Teacher conference *E3b—Group meetings *E3c—Individual presentation *E3e—Analyze public speaking *E4a—Grammar *E4b—Revision *E5a—Literature response *E5b—Produce genre *E7b—Produce functional document
February	—History of revolutions —Background on Charles Dickens —Introduction to *A Tale of Two Cities*: setting, plot, subplot, point of view —Character study groups (T2C)	—understanding historical connections in literature —author influences in literature —vocabulary building —group-work skills —understanding multiple story lines —reading comprehension; understanding the basics of a novel	—grammar in context —character group projects —reading and vocabulary quizzes	*E1a—Read books *E1c—Information *E2b—Literature response *E3b—Group meetings *E3d—Inform judgments *E4a—Grammar *E5a—Literature response

(continued)

Table 5.4 (Cont.)

	Content	Skills	Assessment	Standards
March	—Conclusion of *A Tale of Two Cities*: theme, character development, plot development, symbolism —Analyzing history (revolution) —Character study groups —Five-paragraph essay writing —Reflective project and presentations —Introduction to short stories —Exploring short story necessities	—understanding historical connections in literature —vocabulary building —group-work skills —reading comprehension: connecting multiple plots, developing larger themes, understanding symbols —developing a thesis and essay scaffolding —using primary sources —drafting/revising —student presentations —short story: characters, plot, setting, themes, point of view, devices, genre	—grammar in context —character group projects —reading and vocabulary quizzes —soundtrack/letter/symbol project —Essay: is the novel one of love or hate? —Short story critiques	*E1a—Read books *E1c—Information *E2b—Literature response *E2f—Reflective essay *E3b—Group meetings *E3c—Individual presentations *E3d—Informed judgments *E4a—Grammar *E4b—Revision *E5a—Literature response *E5b—Produce genre
April	—Exploring short story additions —Introduction to Shakespeare and Elizabethan play writing —Introduction to *Romeo and Juliet*: how to read a play, back history, character introductions, plot development, setting —Acting groups (*R & J*) —Analyzing play versions	—short story: devices, structure, genre —understanding historical connections in literature —play terminology —reading comprehension; character relationships —understanding directors' interpretations	—original short story —grammar in context —reading and vocabulary quizzes —acting performances —movie version quizzes	*E1a—Read books *E1c—Information *E2b—Literature response *E3b—Group meetings *E3d—Inform judgments *E4a—Grammar *E5a—Literature response *E5b—Produce genre

May	—Conclusion of *Romeo and Juliet*; character development, foils, major themes, subplots, understanding endings —Acting groups (*R&J*) —Analyzing play versions (*R&J*) —Refining five—paragraph essay —Revising the play	—understanding historical connections in literature —vocabulary —reading —group acting —reading comprehension; connecting multiple plots, developing larger themes, understanding character reactions —understanding directors' interpretations —rewriting plays —developing a thesis and essay scaffolding —recognizing and using literary terms and devices	—grammar in context —reading and vocabulary quizzes —acting performances —movie version quizzes —changing endings; cause and effect scene project —Essay: Do Romeo and Juliet die because of fate or because of their choices?	*E1a—Read books *E1c—Information *E2b—Literature response *E2f—Reflective essay *E3b—Group meetings *E3d—Inform judgments *E4a—Grammar *E4b—Revision *E5a—Literature response *E5b—Produce genre
June	—Introduction to poetry: form, devices, themes, genres —Developing your own poetry: style, voice, and forms —Poetry reflection and talking back to poems —Global history heritage poem —Ninth-grade literary magazine	—reading comprehension; poetry styles and forms —writing poetry; finding your voice —responding to poetry —speaking skills practice —analyzing historical poetry —using historical information in poetry	—Individual poems —Heritage poem (for Global History Portfolio) —Ninth-grade literary magazine submission	*E1a—Read books *E1c—Information *E3d—Inform judgments *E3e—Analyze public speaking *E4b—Revision *E5a—Literature response *E5b—Produce genre *E7b—Produce functional documents

Source: Fran Bittman, high school teacher, New York City and Greenwich, Connecticut.

- Multi-option assessments are frequently used.
- Time is used flexibly and in accordance with human need.
- Multiple materials are provided.
- Multiple perspectives on ideas and events are routinely sought.
- The teacher facilitates students' skills to enable them to become more self-reliant learners.
- Students help other students and the teacher solve problems.
- Students work with the teacher to establish both whole-class and individual learning goals.
- Students are assessed in multiple ways.

Planning for an inclusive classroom means that teachers are aware of the benefits associated with the tenets listed above. One way in which to ensure that planning is "sliced" into units and lessons that reflect differentiated instruction is to use planning pyramids.

Using Planning Pyramids

We acknowledge that units can be planned in many ways and in different formats. Experienced teachers tend to customize the task to their own style and preferred format, taking ideas from here and there. So far in this chapter we have shared units created in a "backwards design" format, but we would also like to introduce the reader to pyramid planning (Schumm, Vaughn, & Leavell, 1994). The basic premise of the pyramid design is to help teachers plan for a range of expected outcomes for students in their classes by making them think in terms of what *all*, *most*, and *some* students will be able to do. The intention of thinking along these lines is not to predetermine the level that any student may reach, but rather to establish what core knowledge and skills are expected of all students, and to acknowledge that, in the learning process, some will gain more than others. The pyramid plan can be used at any level on the K-12 spectrum. Note that planning does not have to be physically mapped in the shape of a triangle; the triangle can act as a "mental" device to remind teachers to plan on multiple levels. See Figures 5.1 and 5.2 for examples of this device.

As an aside, the information contained in unit plans (pyramid or otherwise) can be shared with students in the form of a calendar that clearly shows expectations in terms of pace and assignments. See Table 5.5 for an example of this. In addition, pyramid plans can be used in lesson format too, as shown in Figures 5.3 and 5.4.

Pulling it All Together

This chapter is focused on the value of creating a classroom culture of inclusivity that benefits all students. We hope that the principles of universal design for learning (UDL) will help you to consider all students in planning and delivering instruction. Broken down into nine components, it may appear complex at first. However, its foundation rests on one simple point: the teacher has great influence in providing meaningful instruction for students, whatever their academic levels and needs. As a new teacher, you cannot possibly incorporate everything at once that we have called to your attention. Instead, we encourage you to gravitate to suggestions that you like in this chapter, those that make immediate sense to you, and those you believe are within your current reach. We understand that new teachers must consciously plan and refine their thinking and work and that

Unit Title: Grade 2 Addition and Subtraction Facts

Materials/resources:

Math notebooks, math workbooks, large class number grid, individual number grids, number line, individual whiteboards, markers, counters, scrap paper, extension addition/subtraction worksheets, dominoes, overhead projector, transparency of a fact table, transparency of a domino showing double facts, numbers written on construction paper with Fun-Tac on back, base 10-blocks.

Instructional strategies and adaptations:

The use of individual number grids to help students count
The use of counters to show addition and subtraction visually
The restating of addition and subtraction problems
Individual whiteboards to draw specific attention and subtraction equations

Team teaching options:

1. Small-group instruction to complete a number story using the words and/or pictures.

2. One teacher can stay on the carpet and work with students who want to do another example before beginning their classwork while the other teacher circulates.

3. While one teacher is teaching the mini-lesson, the other teacher circulates checking on student progress.

4. Teachers take a small group and shows them the "Beat the Calculator" game.

5. One teacher holds up pieces of paper (or other visual aids) to help demonstrate doubles facts while one teacher is reciting and writing doubles facts on the board.

6. One teacher can move numbers posted on cardboard paper to show the turn-around facts while the other teacher discusses them with the class during the Math Message.

7. Teachers can take groups of four to five students at a time and show the −0 and −1 facts using base 10-blocks.

Evaluation/products:

Informational assessment of Math Message answers
Student-created addition and subtraction number stories (with pictures)
Informal assessments of classwork, recorded in teacher's data notebook
End-of-unit formal assessment

Some students will learn to:

(a) create a subtraction number story; (b) create their own + number stories; (c) write their own + story using doubles; (d) understand why turn-around facts can't be used in subtraction; (e) use base 10 blocks to show −0 and −1 facts.

Most students will learn to:

(a) write an addition number story; (b) use a calculator to solve + stories; (c) write and solve vertical and horizontal number models; (d) recite the 5–10 double facts; (e) write 10 single-digit turn-around facts; (f) write turn-around facts using two-digit numbers; (g) use −0 and −1 facts with double-digit numbers; (h) create their own −0 and −1 facts in horizontal and vertical form.

All students will learn to:

(a) understand what a "unit" in a number story is; (b) pictorially show an addition number story; (c) write an additional number model; (d) identify patterns in +0 and +1 addition problems; (e) show a pictorial representation for an addition number problem; (f) add +0 and +1 facts using a calculator; (g) the definition of the word "sum"; (h) use the 1–5 doubles facts; (i) use the +/−facts table; (j) recognize double patterns on dominoes; (k) demonstrate an understanding of single-digit turn-around numbers; (l) list 5 single-digit turn-around facts; (m) understand the meaning of a turn-around fact; (n) use the addition fact table to answer turn-around addition problems; (o) write a simple subtraction number story; (p) use −0 and −1 facts with numbers 1–10; (q) create an example of a −0 and a −1 fact using numbers 1–10.

Figure 5.1 Planning pyramid unit: Addition and subtraction, elementary level
Source: Rob Van Voorst, elementary school teacher, Pennsylvania.

Unit Title: *Rome and Juliet* (approximately 4 weeks)

Essential questions:
How can writing be transported to the stage?
Does fate or our own choices control our lives?

Materials/resources:
• "Split texts" (one side Elizabethan English, the other in contemporary language).
• Films: *Shakespeare in Love, Romeo & Juliet* (Zeffirelli), *Romeo + Juliet* (Luhrmann)
• Selected handouts with interesting information and illustrations about: Elizabeth I and England, Elizabethan theater, The Globe, Shakespeare's life and work, etc.
• Pacing calendar shared with students (see Table 5.5).

Instructional strategies and adaptations:
• Individual, paired, small-group, and large-group reading (silent and dramatic)
• Text analysis
• Anticipation guides
• Graphic organizers (cause and effect, comparison of characters and themes, etc.)

Team teaching options:
1. Each day determined individually
2. Teachers take turns to introduce the lesson, then switch as planned/needed
3. When one teacher is "frontal" the other moves to assist students individually
4. Split grading of assignments
5. Daily "check in"

Evaluation/Products:
• Rewritten scenes
• Individual projects (menu of options)
• Character analysis including evaluation of all character actions and interpretation of quotations
• Weekly quizzes and tests
• Formal essay (in components, then assembled) answering the Essential questions

Some students will learn to:
(a) write a short play
(b) compare and contrast R & J with another Shakespeare play

Most students will learn to:
(a) explain major themes in detail
(b) articulate and evaluate different viewpoints
(c) stage an unwritten scene
(d) compare and contrast cinematic interpretations of R & J
(e) develop a philosophical essay about "fate"/choice in the lives of R & J

All students will learn to:
(a) make historical connections to literature; (b) define terminology used in plays; (c) describe character relationships and explain ways in which they help understand the text; (d) understand director's interpretations; (e) understand historical connections in literature; (f) use new vocabulary; (g) act within a group; (h) connect multiple plots, develop large themes, and understand character reactions; (i) rewrite plays by creating a "missing" scene; (j) develop a thesis statement and scaffold an essay; (k) recognize and use literary terms and devices

Figure 5.2 Planning pyramid unit: *Romeo and Juliet*, secondary level

Source: Fran Bittman, high school teacher in New York City and Greenwich, Connecticut, and David Connor.

Table 5.5 Calendar for Romeo and Juliet

	Monday	Tuesday	Wednesday	Thursday/Friday
April 24–28	—Introduction to Shakespeare —Elizabethan England —*Shakespeare in Love*	—Globe Theatre —*Shakespeare in Love*	ACT I —Unit introduction —Scene I —Plot analysis	ACT I —Scenes 2–3 —Character relationship analysis
May 1–5	ACT I —Scenes 4–5 Performance groups	ACT II —Scenes 1–2 —Plot analysis	ACT II —Scenes 2–3 —Performance pairs	ACT II —Movie quiz Acts I and II
May 8–12	ACT II —Scenes 4–6 —Characters/relationship analysis —Plot additions	ACT III —**Big quiz** Acts I and II —Scene I —Performance groups	ACT III —Scenes 2–3 —Character analysis —Performance groups	ACT III —Scenes 4–5 —Character relationships —Partner acting
May 15–19	ACT IV —Scenes 1–2 —Plot analysis (subtext)	ACT IV —Scenes 3–4 —Character analysis	ACT IV —Scene 5 Character analysis	ACT IV —**Big quiz Acts III and IV** —Movie quiz, Acts III and IV
May 22–26	ACT V —Scenes 1–2 —Scenes project Intro	ACT V —Scene 3 —Essay intro	ACT V —Essay body —Performance groups	ACT V —**Scene proposal due** —Essay conclusion —Movie endings
May 29–June 2	No school	—**Essay draft due** —Scene project work time	—Love vs. hate debate trial —Scene project work time	—**Projects due/Presentations** —Essay review —Prequel/sequel —Book form

Source: Sarah Bickens, high school teacher, New York City.

Date: **Class: Grade 2**   **Unit: Addition and Subtraction**

Lesson objective: Students will make up, represent, and solve number stories.

Materials:	**Evaluation:**
Calculators, math notebooks, math workbooks, extension sheets.	Assessment of math message work and individual conferencing.

In-class assignments:	**Homework assignments:**
Math message, Math workbook, pages 20–21	Math homework book, page 242

Team teaching options: (1) Teachers can take students into two small groups and complete a number story using words and/or pictures. (2) One teacher can stay on the carpet and work with students who want to do another example before beginning their classwork while the other teacher circulates.

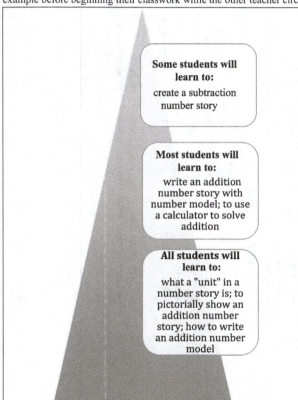

Some students will learn to:

create a subtraction number story

Most students will learn to:

write an addition number story with number model; to use a calculator to solve addition

All students will learn to:

what a "unit" in a number story is; to pictorially show an addition number story; how to write an addition number model

Agenda:
1. The children will complete the following math message in their math notebooks: 5 children are skating, and 8 children are playing ball. How many children in all?
2. The teacher will introduce what a "unit" is and review the correct answer with the class.
3. The teacher will model creating an addition number story using words and pictures and solve it with the class (including the number model).
4. Students will create their own addition number stories in words or pictures, using similar units, in their math notebooks.
5. Students will share their number story with a partner.
6. Students will return to their seats and complete pages 20–21 in their math workbooks.
7. Extension activity: A worksheet that contains addition number stories using larger numbers. Students will have access to calculators.
8. Students will return to the carpet to review answers to workbook pages and extension sheets.

Figure 5.3 Planning pyramid lesson: Elementary level
Source: Rob Van Voorst, elementary school teacher, Pennsylvania.

Date: **Class: Grade 9**   **Unit: Poetry**

Lesson objective: Students will be able to (a) define a poetry slam, emphasizing the focus on social issues, (b) interpret and inform poetry written by selected slam poets, (c) create and perform their own slam poetry.

Materials:	**Evaluation:**
Video clip of poetry slam in New York, information sheet on poetry slams, two sets of poems by slam poets	Performance and written poem

In-class assignments:	**Homework assignments:**
"Practice poem" and own poem	Extend/refine original poem

Team teaching options: Fluid. Fran leads until video clip. David does all warm ups and exercises. Both circulate and help students. Fran manages the first performance. David manages the second performance. Key: (F) Fran and (D) David

Some students will learn to:

use a refrain in their poetry

Most students will learn to:

perform their own poetry integrating emotion, projection, and gesture

All students will learn:

define poetry slam; list issues of social relevance; express emotion, utilize voice projection and perform using gestures; perform poetry of others; create and perform their own slam poetry

Agenda:
Desks are arranged in a U-shape, with a large space in the middle.
1. Do now: Make a list of 5 social issues that you feel strongly about. List on board (F/D).
2. Who has heard about poetry slam? What do you know? (F/D)
3. Background information: discuss sheet with short description of poetry slams (F/D).
4. Video clip: selections from a poetry slam. Students list the social issues.
5. Performance cue: Students leave desks and stand up in a circle for a series of *"warm up" performance exercises,* round-robin or choral, including: (i) breathing, (ii) clapping, (iii) using varied emotions with the same phrase [3 rounds]: *"I love you," "Are you talking to me?"* and *"You think I have an attitude?"* [D/F]. Discuss emotion, projection, gesture.
6. Distribute two poems, allowing students a choice. Students practice alone or in pairs (D/F).
7. Students volunteer to perform using all three skills (emotion, projection, gesture) (F/D).
8. Students write a poem using one of the social issues listed on the board (D/F).
9. Class ends with student performance of their own poems (D/F).

Figure 5.4 Planning pyramid lesson: Secondary level

Source: Fran Bittman, high school teacher in New York City and Greenwich, Connecticut, and David Connor.

takes time in contrast to more seasoned teachers who are able to plan more easily and quickly, given their base of accrued experiences. We hope that our deliberate inclusion of a wide variety of practical applications facilitates your planning. In Chapter 6, we move from considerations for planning to considerations for teaching in the inclusive classroom.

Questions to Consider

1. Why is creating a classroom community so important for teacher(s) and students?
2. In what ways can Bloom's taxonomy be used in every lesson?
3. What are some readily identifiable ways in which teachers can use the principles of universal design for instruction?
4. In terms of multiple intelligence theory, what intelligences do you self-identify as your own strengths and areas of need?
5. In contemplating learning styles, what kind of environment maximizes your own learning?
6. In your own experience as a student (in elementary, middle, high, undergraduate, or graduate school), describe a number of times where you worked alone, with a partner, and in groups. How did you feel about it at the time? How do you feel now about the prospect of making these decisions?
7. Describe a way that you might teach anything (for those of you who need a topic picked for you, try these: rhyming, rectangles, the Roman Empire, or igneous rocks), in visual, auditory, and tactile ways.
8. What are some of the benefits to planning an overview of what is to be taught during the semester?
9. Which aspects of planning appeal to you most? Why?
10. If you could create your ideal classroom, what might it look like?

Notes

1 www.nchpad.org/Directories/Organizations/2558/Center~for~Universal~Design~~~North~Carolina~State~University
2 Modified from Burgstahler (2006).

References

Anderson-Inman, L. & Horney, M. A. (2007). Supported eText: Assistive technology through text transformations. *Reading Research Quarterly, 42*(1), 153–60.

Barnes, E., Berrigan, C., & Biklen, D. (1978). *What's the difference? Teaching positive attitudes toward people with disabilities.* Syracuse, NY: Human Policy.

Bloom, B. S. (1984). *Taxonomy of educational objectives.* Boston, MA: Allyn & Bacon.

Brumberg, J. S., Pitt, K. M., Mantie-Kozlowski, A., & Burnison, J. D. (2018). Brain–computer interfaces for augmentative and alternative communication: A tutorial. *American Journal of Speech-Language Pathology, 27,* 1–12.

Burgstahler, S. (2006). *Equal access: Universal design of instruction.* Seattle, WA: DO-IT, University of Washington.

Dunn, R. & Dunn, K. (1972). *Practical approaches to individualizing instruction.* Englewood Cliffs, NJ: Prentice Hall.

Fernald, G. M. (1943). *Remedial techniques in basic school subjects.* New York, NY: McGraw-Hill.

Gardner, H. (1984). *Frames of mind: The theory of multiple intelligences*. New York, NY: Basic Books.

Grant, C. & Sleeter, C. (1986). Race, class, and gender in educational research: An argument for integrative analysis. *Review of Educational Research, 56*(2), 195–211.

Holderman, E. (2014, July 27). 9 best apps and sites to improve executive function. Retrieved from www.commonsense. org/education/blog/9-best-apps-and-sites-to-improve-executive-function

Individuals with Disabilities Education Act (IDEA) (1990). P.L. 101–476 20, U.S.C # 1400 et seq.; Amendments of 1997, 2004. Retrieved from http://uscode.house.gov/view.xhtml?path=/prelim@title20/chapter33&edition=prelim

Kulman, R. (2014 May 16). 5 must have apps for improving executive functioning in children. Retrieved from www.beyond booksmart/executive-functioning-strategies-blog/5-great-apps-for-improving-executive-functioning-in-children

Ladson-Billings, G. (2009). *The dreamkeepers: Successful teachers of African American children*. San Francisco, CA: Wiley.

Levine, M. (1994). *Educational care*. Cambridge, MA: Educators Publishing Service.

Levine, M. & Reed, M. (1999). *Developmental variation and learning disorders*. Cambridge, MA: Educators Publishing Service.

Lorah, E. R., Parnell, A., Whitby, P. S., & Hantula, D. (2015). A systematic review of tablet computers and portable media players as speech generating devices for individuals with autism spectrum disorder. *Journal of Autism Developmental Disorders, 45*, 3792–804.

Musgrove, M. (2018). Who pays for assistive technology? Parents or schools? Retrieved from www.understood.org/en/school-learning/assistive-technology/assistive-technologies-basics/who-pays-for-assistive-technology-parents-or-schools

Neese, B. (2015). 5 assistive technology tools that are making a difference. Retrieved from https://online.alvernia.edu/5-assistive-technology-tools-that-are-making-a-difference/

Nepo, K. (2017). The use of technology to improve education. *Child Youth Care, 46*, 207–21.

Oien, I., Fallang, B., & Ostensjo, S. (2016). Everyday use of assistive technology devices in school settings. *Disability and Rehabilitation: Assistive Technology, 11*(8), 630–5.

Paris, D. & Alim, H. S. (Eds.). (2017). *Culturally sustaining pedagogies: Teaching and learning for justice in a changing world*. New York, NY: Teachers College Press.

Peterson-Karlan, G. R. (2015). Assistive technology instruction within a continuously evolving technology environment. *Quarterly Review of Distance Education, 16*(2), 1–22.

Peterson-Karlan, G. R. (2011). Technology to support writing by students with learning and academic disabilities: Recent trends and findings. *Assistive Technology Outcomes and Benefits, 7*(1), 39–62.

Peterson-Karlan, G. R., Hourcade, J. J., & Parette, P. (2008). A review of assistive technology and writing skills for students with physical and educational disabilities. *Physical Disabilities: Education and Related Services, 26*(2), 13–32.

Rekkedal, A. M. (2014). Teachers' use of assistive listening devices in inclusive schools. *Scandinavian Journal of Disability Research, 16*(4), 297–315.

Reif, S. F. & Heimburge, J. A. (1996). *How to reach and teach all students in the inclusive classroom*. New York, NY: Center for Applied Research in Education.

Salend, S. (2011). *Creating inclusive classrooms: Effective and reflective practices for all students* (7th ed.). Upper Saddle River, NJ: Pearson.

Schumm, J. S., Vaughn, S., & Leavell, A. G. (1994). Pyramid planning: A framework for planning diverse students' needs during content area instruction. *Reading Teacher, 47*(8), 608–15.

Shapiro, A. (1999). *Everybody belongs: Changing negative attitudes toward classmates with disabilities*. New York, NY: Routledge.

Tomlinson, C. A. (2001). *How to differentiate instruction in mixed ability classrooms* (2nd ed.). Alexandria, VA: ACSD.

Vernon, S., Deshler, D. D., & Schumaker, J. B. (1999). *The THINK strategy*. Lawrence, KS: Edge Enterprises, Inc.

Walker, V. L., Lyon, K. J., Loman, S. L., & Sennott, S. (2018). A systematic review of functional communication training (FCT) interventions involving augmentative and alternative communication in school settings. *Augmentative and Alternative Communication, 34*(2), 118–29.

Wiggins, G. & McTighe, J. (1998). *Understanding by design.* Alexandria, VA: ASCD.

Wolfe, P. (2001). *Brain matters: Translating research into classroom practice.* Alexandria, VA: ASCD.

Zanin, J. & Rance, G. (2016). Functional hearing in the classroom: Assistive listening devices for students with hearing impairment in a mainstream school setting. *International Journal of Audiology, 55*(12), 723–9.

6 Creating a Dynamic Classroom Culture
"How can I be sure that I reach everybody?"

Cartoon #6 Everyone reached

"Why is it hard to get children's attention?"
"What happens to kids who aren't motivated to learn?"
"How can I get students more interested in the lesson?"
"What if a group of children is keeping the rest of the class behind?"
"What's fair when differentiating work?"

The questions listed above all fall under the larger umbrella question posed in the subtitle of this chapter. All teachers constantly face the challenge of connecting with students in a meaningful way by introducing new information, building upon established knowledge, having students interact with new knowledge, encouraging creative work, and demonstrating knowledge in some shape or form. Whether classrooms have 5, 20, or 35 students, teachers must try to engage all of them throughout the lesson. Although this may seem a daunting task at first, many teachers are able to maximize student engagement through a variety of approaches and meaningful activities.

In this chapter, we focus on the many ways in which a teacher can reach students. Although lessons may vary in type and length, it is useful to conceptualize all of them in terms of having a beginning, a middle, and an end. We describe ways in which teachers can (1) begin a lesson, (2) facilitate student engagement in a variety of ways, and (3) bring a lesson to closure. Our suggestions are based upon our own teaching experiences, the wisdom of teachers with whom we have worked, and research-based teaching practices.

There is no doubt that teaching is a complex process between teachers and students. In Figure 6.1, we attempt to make visible the dynamic process involved in facilitating knowledge construction in the classroom.

Throughout this chapter, we focus upon the architecture of a lesson and its interlocking components. We begin by introducing eight basic elements of a lesson. Each element is described and applied to five content topics across the curriculum. In other words, you will be able to see how each element works within the sample topics selected for this chapter:

1.   The seven continents
2.   Different types of triangles
3.   *Romeo and Juliet*
4.   The growth of seeds
5.   Abstract art

At the end of the chapter, we integrate the eight elements to illustrate a complete lesson plan for each of the five content topics.

The Art of Lesson Planning

We believe lesson planning to be an exercise in crafting an interactive, engaging environment in which students learn and demonstrate knowledge about what the teacher has predetermined and what has not been predetermined. Lesson planning can be a complex process that takes time. However, with experience, teachers can and do refine their planning and teaching skills.

Eight Basic Elements of a Lesson

Lesson planning can be one of the more overwhelming aspects of being a first-year teacher. It is helpful to think about lessons in terms of the following eight components:

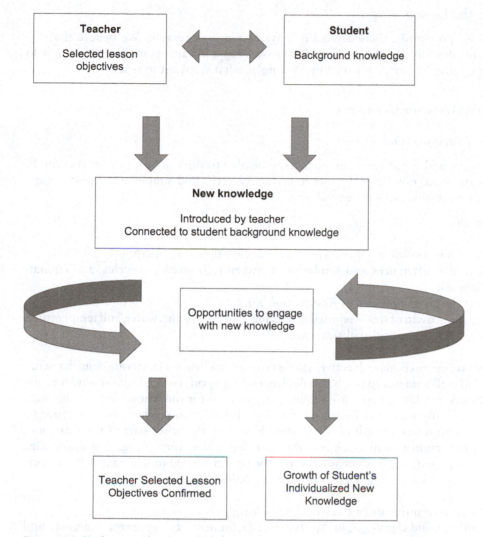

Figure 6.1 Student–teacher knowledge connections

1. Generate objectives (always instructional, possibly social and behavioral).
2. Provide opportunities for applications of recent skills and/or demonstration of recent knowledge.
3. Pose engaging questions to discover a student's background knowledge.
4. Explicitly introduce what is expected of students during a lesson.
5. Provide opportunities for clear explanations of content material and multiple opportunities for students to engage with it.
6. Check in with students throughout the lesson to ascertain the degree to which students are understanding the targeted content.
7. Provide opportunities for students to demonstrate their knowledge and abilities, whether short-term (question, quiz, exercise, problem-solving) or long-term (test, project, portfolio).
8. Culminate the lesson by reviewing what was learned (targeted information) and what was realized (student connections).

Beginning the Lesson

As mentioned previously, there are many ways to plan instruction. We believe that the eight elements described in the previous section serve as a broad, yet manageable, guide to developing quality lessons. Let's start by looking at what we want to teach.

Element One: Generate Objectives

Generate Instructional Objectives

A lesson begins with what we want students to be able to do as a result of instruction. In writing instructional objectives, be sure to use active verbs and simple sentence structure. Examples of clear objectives are as follows:

Students will:

- *List* the seven continents of the world and *identify* them on a map.
- *Compare* the differences and similarities between right-angle, isosceles, and equilateral triangles.
- *Describe* the characteristics of *Romeo and Juliet*.
- *Analyze* the growth of seeds exposed to varying degrees of light, water, and temperature.
- *Create* an original work of abstract art.

In selecting an instructional objective, teachers in an inclusive classroom consider what they would like all students to be able to do. Depending upon the needs of the students, the objective can be modified, while still retaining it as a goal for the whole class. In this way, teachers begin with a clear vision of their intended destination, which is what students should be able to do as a result of instruction. However, the other part of the classroom equation is the students you teach and the knowledge that they bring. The knowledge students begin to generate in class as a result of being introduced to new material connects to their prior knowledge base. Here are some examples:

1. *List* the seven continents of the world and *identify* them on a map.
   Possible knowledge brought by students: Definition of a country; examples and non-examples of countries (California, Africa); countries visited; countries where their families or ancestors are from, etc.
   Possible collective knowledge made in the lesson: Definition of continent; comparison of continent and country; recognition of where specific animals come from (tigers in Asia); geography (rainforests in Africa, Asia, Central and South America).
   Possible individual student connections within the lesson: Continents that are the biggest to smallest, the closest to farthest away.

2. *Compare* the differences and similarities between right-angle, isosceles, and equilateral triangles.
   Possible knowledge brought by students: Triangles are polygons with three sides; they are easily drawn; the shape of certain intersections; they are almost the shape of a slice of pizza.
   Possible collective knowledge made in the lesson: Different triangles all share certain attributes (e.g., contain 180 degrees, have three sides, can vary in size).
   Possible individual student connections within the lesson: Bermuda Triangle; "tri" means three like tricycle, triple, triathlon....

3. *Describe* the characteristics of Romeo and Juliet.

   Possible knowledge brought by students: Shakespeare is the author; the theme is love; there are several movie versions; the story is set in Italy.

   Possible collective knowledge made in the lesson: Both characters are young; Juliet is trusting; Romeo is overwhelmed by love; both feel a sense of loyalty toward their families—but a greater attraction to one another.

   Possible individual student connections within the lesson: Love can transcend social divisions; young people in former times also experienced strong emotions; families can greatly influence their members in terms of choosing a partner.

4. *Analyze* growth of seeds exposed to varying degrees of light, water, and temperature.

   Possible knowledge brought by students: Plants and trees grow from seeds; seeds can be found in the fruit of many plants, such as oranges, apples, and tomatoes.

   Possible collective knowledge made in the lesson: The growth of seeds is subject to certain environmental conditions, including light, water, and temperature.

   Possible individual student connections within the lesson: Different types of trees; which trees grow where; which trees grow all year round; why trees in the rainforests are so tall.

5. *Create* an original work of abstract art.

   Possible knowledge brought by students: Colors; shapes; definition of abstract; recognition of abstract works.

   Possible collective knowledge made in the lesson: Recognition of certain artists, such as Jackson Pollock or Piet Mondrian; techniques to begin, experiment with, and develop an original piece of abstract art.

   Possible individual student connections within the lesson: Recollecting images in life reminiscent of abstract paintings (e.g., colors in a sunset, floor tiles, clothing designs with patterns of color, or aerial views of the landscape).

Thus, we begin with the premise of a teacher defining a desired instructional objective, followed by the importance of recognizing and accepting the knowledge students bring. The instructional objective is the foundation of a lesson, anchoring all decisions about practice that follow. However, building upon the foundation involves structuring questions, activities, and opportunities for students to engage in the process of learning. Within this structure, students understand what a teacher is guiding them to learn and, at the same time, generate their own knowledge about how it connects to a world beyond the classroom.

Generate Social Objectives

Although we have foregrounded instructional objectives as the anchor of each lesson, teachers may also define social objectives when and where appropriate. Social objectives can be incorporated to address the explicit teaching of social skills. For example, cooperative grouping is an excellent method to promote student learning, yet a large part of its success lies in the interactions among participants. Students might not come to class with prerequisite skills for this approach to learning, and therefore may need to be taught each step of the process. Integrating social objectives can be done on a short-term basis or throughout the year. For example, you might have objectives for cooperative workgroups, such as the following:

Students will:

- Take turns speaking.
- Adhere to assigned work roles.
- Practice complimenting each other.
- Share responsibility for the task assigned.
- Evaluate themselves as individuals and group members.

As with instructional objectives, teachers must have a device to evaluate these, whether it be direct teacher observation, large-group debriefing at the end of class, or individual/small-group self-evaluations in writing.

Generate Behavioral Objectives

Behavioral objectives can be created for the entire class to ensure that learning time is maximized, and classrooms are managed in an expeditious manner, respectful of all who participate in them. In addition, behavioral objectives can be developed for an individual student, customized to change behavior(s) that may interfere with his or her own learning and/or that of others. Behavioral objectives can be thought of as increasing a desired behavior or decreasing an undesirable action. Once teachers are able to articulate what they would like to occur, they must also provide support for the students to change behaviors. Examples for a whole class may include these:

The class will:

- Generate two original questions based upon their independent reading (increasing desired behavior).
  Possible support(s): Teacher models how to generate original questions, as large group "practice time" to elicit student examples or provides sentence starters.
- Store their materials and clean the desks before the next class enters (increasing desired behavior).
  Possible support(s): Teacher models, asks students to complete in increments (i.e., one side of the room first, the other side of the room next).
- Raise their hands to speak during whole-class work (increasing desired behavior).
  Possible support(s): Kinesthetic reminder (teacher raises hand); verbal reminder ("Hands, please"); recognition that students have something to contribute, and teacher is delighted, but it must follow the protocol of raising hands.

Examples of behavioral objectives for individual students:

- David will self-monitor for concentration (decreasing undesirable behavior: daydreaming).
  Possible support(s): Teacher-generated checklist for David to mark every five minutes; teacher "checks in" with him throughout class.
- Santiago will refrain from touching other students (decreasing undesirable behavior: overstepping spatial boundaries).
  Possible support(s): Reminder at start of class; seating placement with students who can remind Santiago; partnership with a paraprofessional; praise.
- Jan will reduce the number of times she shouts out in class (decreasing undesirable behavior: interrupting class).

Possible support(s): At the start of class, review the objective with Jan; planned ignoring if she shouts out; discreet nonverbal reminders (finger to lips); review at end of class; reward with praise; send a positive note home to parent.

Before a lesson begins, students are usually required to be seated, ready to pay attention. How to get students to do this varies among teachers and is often influenced by factors such as age, grade, readiness, and whether they have been in the classroom for a lesson that precedes the current one (much of elementary school) or have just entered the classroom (most of high school). Either way, teachers must help students transition to a new lesson by presenting a brief orientation activity.

Element Two: Provide Opportunities for Applications of Recent Skills and/or Demonstration of Recent Knowledge

Begin by exploring what students already know and what they can already do. You can probe by giving instructions orally, on the board, at individual desks, or on group tables. Examples are as follows:

1. *List* the seven continents of the world and identify them on a map.
   Focusing activity: In a couple of sentences, describe the difference between a continent and a country.
2. *Compare* the differences and similarities between right-angle, isosceles, and equilateral triangles.
   Focusing activity: On a sheet of paper, match the six triangles to their similar shapes.
3. *Describe* the characteristics of Romeo and Juliet.
   Focusing activity: List five characteristics (not physical) that make you who you are. For example, "I am… honest, quick tempered, optimistic, etc.)."
4. *Analyze* the growth of seeds exposed to varying degrees of light, water, and temperature.
   Focusing activity: Categorize these named seeds (e.g., corn, grass, peas, roses, cabbage, etc.) into plants we eat and plants we do not eat.
5. *Create* an original work of abstract art.
   Focusing activity: Choose your favorite from these three works of abstract art (show posters/projections of Kandinsky, Rothko, and Delaney) and briefly write what exactly distinguishes it from other works of art, incorporating comments about color, shape, tone, and pattern.

Of course, there are many ways to start a lesson, but this approach ensures that students transition into the content area, are actively engaged, and are given a task related to what has been taught in the previous lesson (reigniting knowledge). This approach also helps students experience continuity in content as well as gain multiple opportunities to apply related skills.

Element Three: Pose Engaging Questions to Discover Students' Background Knowledge

Once students are settled and have finished their brief starting assignment, the teacher can then see how well (or, perhaps, not well) they are doing with the task at hand. Such structure allows the teacher to see what students remember and how well they apply knowledge, and even to determine their level of interest. Gauging these things benefits the teacher, as she can then use this information in decisions as she proceeds with the rest of the lesson.

A review of information previously taught can also be very useful. This can be in the form of questions that are general and open-ended, or highly specific:

1. *List* the seven continents of the world.
    General post-focusing question: Who will start off and remind us what we remember about countries from yesterday's class?
    Specific post-focusing question: Is Africa a country or a continent?
2. *Compare* the differences and similarities between right-angle, isosceles, and equilateral triangles.
    General post-focusing question: How many different types of triangles did you see within the 12 examples?
    Specific post-focusing question: What great works of architecture are based on a triangular design?
3. *Describe* the characteristics of Romeo and Juliet.
    General post-focusing question: What is the most important characteristic that you would seek in an ideal partner?
    Specific post-focus question: How would you prioritize the traits you listed?
4. *Analyze* the growth of seeds exposed to varying degrees of light, water, and temperature.
    General post-focusing question: Think for a moment and be ready to tell your partner what we have already learned about how water and temperature can influence the growth of seeds into plants.
    Specific post-focusing question: Using your categorization, which are the plants that we eat and which don't we eat?
5. *Create* an original work of abstract art.
    General post-focusing question: Which do you think is the most important quality of abstract work: size, tone, color, shape, or pattern?
    Specific post-focusing question: Which do you think is most important in the abstract work you chose: size, tone, color, shape, or pattern?

As you can see, the line of questioning is always related to what students have been doing but can also be either general and open-ended (inviting all kinds of student responses) or highly specific (guided response). In essence, the teacher is attempting to connect with all students by tapping into their current levels of knowledge. By reviewing what has been taught, the teacher reignites their connections to the subject matter at hand.

Once students have responded, indicating their piqued interest and captured attention, you can then begin to establish what students already know, thus meeting them at their collective knowledge base. This serves as a "check in," and means the teacher does not make assumptions about preexisting student knowledge. It is often useful to chart responses in the form of a semantic map. Some examples of prompting students to reveal what they know are given below:

1. *List* the seven continents of the world and *identify* them on a map.
    Options to elicit background information: Where have you heard the term "continent" mentioned before? What are some distant places in the world that you have seen on television and in movies? Who has heard of Antarctica? If you could go anywhere in the world, where would you go and why? What are the names of some bodies of water (seas, oceans, lakes) that separate land masses?

2. *Compare* the differences and similarities between right-angle, isosceles, and equilateral triangles.

    Options to elicit background information: Tell me what you know already about triangles. How many types of triangles do you know?

3. *Describe* the characteristics of Romeo and Juliet.

    Options to elicit background information: Let's recap on what we know about Romeo and Juliet. What have been some of their actions—and what might the actions tell us about them? What have been some of their words—and what might these words tell us about Romeo and Juliet?

4. *Analyze* the growth of seeds exposed to varying degrees of light, water, and temperature.

    Options to elicit background information: Tell me the names of all the different types of trees that you know, and where they can be found.

5. *Create* an original work of abstract art.

    Options to elicit background information: What are the things that artists might take into consideration when they are planning an abstract work? From what sources might they get some ideas?

Opening up students to one another's knowledge by encouraging them to share and participate is a respectful way to teach and communicate the value of all student contributions. It also allows the teacher to spiral information previously taught, helping students make connections.

Element Four: Explicitly Introduce What Is Expected of Students During a Lesson

Teachers have the option of sharing the objective of the lesson with students either before or after establishing their background knowledge. Students should be informed of the clear expectations placed upon them. In other words, they are told what they should be able to do by the end of the lesson as defined by the instructional objective:

- "Today we are going to learn the names and locations of the seven continents of the world."
- "By the end of the lesson we will be able to tell the differences and similarities between three types of triangles."
- "The focus of today is to explore the characters of Romeo and Juliet, and to describe what makes them who they are—their characteristics."
- "Our job today will be to study variations in seeds that have been exposed to different conditions, including amounts of light, water, and temperature."
- "Today our goal is to create an original piece of art that is abstract."

While this seems both an obvious and a simple step, it is often omitted or overlooked. To include it is to be clear and direct, helping children focus on what they are to learn.

Facilitating Meaningful Engagement

In this section, we call attention to the importance of planning for meaningful student engagement. We emphasize the word "meaningful" to point out that, while many of the strategies featured in this section promote student engagement, "activities' can easily slip into an aimless "fun time," "busy work," or "ground already covered." All activities should clearly support the learning objectives. This point is too important to forget, so… we repeat: *all activities should clearly support the learning objectives*. It is also a perfect example of how backwards planning is used. Once the end result is envisioned and identified, then everything planned for class—big and small—should be geared toward that goal.

Element Five: Provide Opportunities for Clear Explanations of Content Material and Multiple Opportunities for Students to Engage with It

Teachers must provide clear explanations of content material that is to be covered before providing instructions about how students are to engage with it. For teachers who are swimming in a sea of information, it is useful for them to determine the core concepts within the curriculum (e.g., continent as division of land mass, types and properties of polygons, literary characterization, conditions for plant life on the earth, abstract and figurative art). These concepts must be taught clearly, keeping in mind multiple intelligences and learning styles, as well as student readiness and preferences. Oftentimes, large-group instruction is the best method by which to teach everyone the core concepts. Once students have grasped what is being taught and connected their existing knowledge to it, they are able to interact in numerous ways. (See Box 6.1 for a fuller explanation.)

Box 6.1 Teaching Different Things in Different Ways to Different Students

As we alluded to earlier in this book (see Chapter 3, for example), inclusive practices often challenge many fundamental and traditional assumptions of education. One of these assumptions is that all children should be working on approximately the same content, at the same rate; be evaluated in the same way; and be expected to produce similar results to one another. In an inclusive class, the teachers consider the needs of each student. Oftentimes, accommodations are explicitly stated on the child's Individual Education Plan (IEP; see Box 6.3). However, teachers have autonomy in making informed decisions about what, when, and how to teach students differently. Of course, ongoing differentiation may call unwanted attention to certain students, and this should be avoided. Nevertheless, decisions really depend upon the specific context of a classroom situation.

Why?

- Not all students learn in the same way or at the same rate.
- Students with multiple and severe needs may require curriculum modification throughout the year.

When?

- Differentiation does not need to occur all of the time during a class. There are times when whole-group instruction can reach all students, small-group instruction can incorporate all students, and individualized instruction can be used when and where appropriate.
- At any time during the lesson.

How?

- If possible, in consultation with a team teacher or paraprofessional.
- Using different levels of questions ("What colors did the artist use?", "What might these colors symbolize?", and "Which artists were influenced by Pollock, and in what ways?")

- Changing the rate, volume, or complexity of what is being asked of the student. Examples are as follows:

    Rate: Change the time, requiring some students to complete 5, 10, or 15 problems. Alternatively, all students can "go as far as they can go." The objective is to see whether students can actually do the work, not necessarily how fast they can go.

    Volume: Reduce or increase the number of concepts being taught. Some students may be able to compare only two different triangles, not three or more.

    Complexity: In describing the characteristics of Romeo and Juliet, some students may begin to understand the concept of characteristics by first listing physical characteristics. Others already familiar with psychological characteristics can speculate upon how these influence Romeo and Juliet's interactions with one another, and with other characters.

- It is important to remember that the *content matter* should be the same for all students. For example, when studying a particular continent, a class could be divided into groups that have materials of different levels—yet they are all studying an aspect of that continent.

- Reading materials can also vary. For example, a teacher can have four versions of *Romeo and Juliet*. The first is a "standard" text. The second is a modern-day language text. The third is a bilingual text (one page in English, the other in, say, Spanish). The fourth is an abridged version with illustrations, even in comic strip form. The teacher can assign various texts to specific students, or students can pick themselves.

Because teachers have already emphasized from the first day that they teach in a classroom that acknowledges and accepts human difference, students understand that it is *fair* to give different students different things to do. In seeing this as integral to everyday classroom culture, all students learn how to work with difference, instead of marginalizing it or attempting to eradicate it. One great resource for elementary school is the book *It's Okay to Be Different*, by Todd Parr (2001). The colorful text lists, "It's okay to have an imaginary friend… it's okay to use a wheelchair… it's okay to have two moms…" and teachers can add, "it's okay to have different work in class" when teaching about individual differences and how they influence needs.

Below are some possibilities for individual work and working together in various formats.

Individual work:

- Pick a continent and list everything you know about it.
- Create three patterns using (a) one, (b) two, and (c) three types of triangle.
- Expand on three characteristics of your ideal partner, giving details.
- Make a prediction of the growth of five plants, based upon the information presented.
- Use seven straight or curved lines to create an idea for an abstract design.

Work in pairs:

- Using the graphic organizer with your partner, write what you would like to know about each continent.
- Decide who will be Partner A and who will be Partner B. Now look at an isosceles triangle and a right-angle triangle and Partner A must explain what these have in common and partner B must explain the differences between them.
- Fill out this T-chart on Romeo's physical characteristics on one side, and some of his corresponding actions on the other (we will discuss what these actions may tell us about his personality).

Work in triads:

- Read about China and discuss the information before deciding upon the three most important points to share with the class.
- Each of you take notes on one of the following—the importance of (a) light, (b) water, or (c) temperature—with a view to presenting your information to the others. Together, rank them in order of importance.
- Create a series of abstract drawings that are related in some way (pattern, color, texture). Each person can make a separate drawing, or you can collectively work on them and rotate.

Work in groups of four:

- In your group, create a chart of visual images to help all class members remember the name of the continent the teacher assigns to you.
- Record side lengths and angle measurements of the 16 numbered triangles placed in an envelope.
- Write a short "missing scene" involving four characters in the play talking about what they think of Romeo.

Work in large groups:

- Contrast China and Russia.
- Create a two-team quiz on the effects of light and water, before we consider temperature.
- Prepare notes and comments for a debate on "Which is the most important form of art in the twentieth century: abstract or figurative?"

Work as a whole class:

- Any of the above activities can have a "share out," allowing the teacher an opportunity to engage the whole class in student-generated thoughts and knowledge.
- Review important points/information so far.
- Brainstorm about the best way to explain ways in which the environment influences plant growth.

In the suggestions that follow, we elaborate upon popular methods that have proven successful in many K-12 classrooms. Bear in mind that these methods can be customized to correspond to a particular grade and/or a level of current academic performance.

Although we have chosen to categorize them according to use with individual students, they can all be adapted for use with pairs, small groups, and large groups.

Individual Students

Graphic organizers are visual supports that show relationships between key concepts and other important related ideas. They can be used at all stages in the learning process: pre-teaching information, organizing information as students engage with it, and post-teaching information to clarify relationships. Examples include structures that compare and contrast, show the order of events, relate components to one another, show hierarchical relationships, and support solutions to problems.

Concept mapping is a means of graphically organizing a concept and its subcomponents. The main idea (such as India) is often placed at the center, and various related subconcepts (e.g., population, history, food, religion) spiral from it. In addition, sub-subconcepts can be attached (e.g., population = largest in world, relatively young, differences in languages).

Brainstorming occurs as students share their own connections to a set topic. For example, when given "The Rainforest," they can either personally list and/or orally share related ideas, such as "Africa," "tall trees," "monkeys," etc. Teachers can accept all suggestions and create a web of connections on the board.

Readers' theater allows students to read their own work or a selected piece (poem, scene, newspaper article), to the entire class. Time is earmarked for rehearsal, and all readings should be full of drama and expression.

Quick writes usually take one to six minutes and give all students the chance to record their thoughts about a certain topic. These can be used to tap into prior knowledge about a subject soon to be introduced, or in the middle of learning about a topic (sometimes referred to as "stop and jot"), or at the end of learning. Because students are frequently asked to capture their thoughts on paper, they become increasingly accustomed to formulating and recording their thoughts.

Free writes are similar to quick writes but longer, and often more open-ended, inviting speculative thoughts around a concept such as art, love, the environment, and so on. The flow of ideas is encouraged, thereby inspiring many ideas from which to build a more formalized piece of writing.

Story maps are graphic organizers to help students recall the elements of a story they have read, as well as create a plan for their own writing. The elements include setting, characters, problem, rising action, climax, solution, and lesson learned.

Story boards are another form of graphic organizer consisting of blank squares, one after another. In each box, students pencil in a drawing, state an idea, or record both. The outcome is a sequential plan for creating a new narrative, or recalling one presented by the teacher.

Drawing can be used for students of any age, and often helps them memorize content information. For example, drawing and labeling illustrations about the effects of light, water, and temperature on plants will help some students remember. Drawing multiple types of triangles, drawing figures of Romeo and Juliet, or carving up and shading the world map into continents encourages meaningful participation and serves to help students focus upon, and discuss, the targeted content area.

Interactive journals promote individualized conversation, usually in writing, between teacher and student. Students can select topics of importance, topics can be teacher generated, or both. Journals can be incorporated into any content area class and can be used at any point in the lesson, including the start ("Write about plants in the apartments of people you know," "Describe what 'true love' means to you") or the end ("Record what you learned about triangles today" or "Free-write on the idea of abstract art").

Double-entry journals are designed to promote personalized interaction with a text. Each journal page is folded in half lengthwise. While reading a text, students can write a question, list words, note a phrase, and so on, in the left-hand column. After reading, the student returns to the right-hand column to respond to information selected, such as making personal connections to a phrase, defining unfamiliar words or new vocabulary, or answering a self-imposed question. Students have the option of sharing in pairs or with the large group.

Plus/minus/interesting is an approach used to connect students to a text before they start reading. The main idea can be stated, summarized, or quoted, and students are asked to analyze and comment upon the issue (the pluses, the minuses, and general comments). For example, "The population of the world uses more trees than ever" may yield responses such as these: PLUS—Nearly everyone has furniture in their homes, and fuel to keep them warm; MINUS—Trees are not growing fast enough to be replaced, areas of the earth are changing rapidly, and animals are losing their natural habitat; INTERESTING—What could happen if there's not enough wood to go around? What can we use for furniture and fuel instead of wood?

Question–answer–relationships is a method that requires students to analyze types of questions, their answers, and the relationship to the text (Raphael, 1994). Question types are either in the text ("right there" or "think and look") or in the author's head ("the author and reader" or "the reader alone"). This approach is worthwhile, if somewhat time consuming at first, as it promotes understanding of the interactive nature of reader and text. For example, Romeo and Juliet could be considered this way:

- Where does the story take place? ("right there")
- How do we know that Juliet's love for Romeo developed very quickly? ("think and look")
- What would you do if your parents forbade you to see a person you loved? ("the author and reader")
- Why do people fall in (and out of) love? ("the reader alone")

Timelines are graphic organizers that help students plot incidents that happened sequentially, as in the life of a person, such as Christopher Columbus, or the events of a period in history, such as fifteenth-century European Colonialism.

Student Pairs

Think–pair–share is a multi-step, yet simple, approach to encourage the participation of all students in responding to a question posed by the teacher. First, each student is asked to compose his or her thoughts and/or briefly write them down. Second, each student is paired with a peer to share thoughts between them. Third, once everyone has shared in pairs, they are encouraged to share with the whole group. Teachers can use this method with any content area, and it is an appropriate device for posing higher-order, open-ended questions.

Pantomime asks students to silently act out a story or a scene from a story that is read aloud by another student or the teacher. This can be a story in the traditional sense, such as *Romeo and Juliet*, or it can be a content-related story, such as a story of three scientists who decide to experiment with the conditions needed for optimal plant growth or about what could be seen by a traveler if she visited the seven continents of the world.

Role play requires students to "try on" another character or point of view and engage in dialogue with a partner. It can be used to engage all students with the targeted content, such as having one student play the role of a television interviewer talking with the other student in the role of Romeo; having two painters (one abstract, one figurative) explaining their art to one another; or having scientists debating the most important conditions for plant growth.

Buddy reading provides the opportunity for students to read together in pairs. They can take turns to read and then pose questions or discuss what has been read. It is also possible for students less proficient in reading to be paired with more proficient readers who model fluency.

Read aloud/think aloud provides practice of the seven habits of good readers (see Box 6.2). For example, when reading a passage about a particular continent or how plants grow, students can "think out loud" to a partner, explicitly calling attention to how they are determining what is important in the passage.

Reciprocal teaching (four types of questions) is a framework that encourages students to "interrogate the text" by using four strategies, either separately or in combination (Ahmadi & Gilajani, 2014). These strategies are as follows: questioning, summarizing, clarifying, and predicting. When one student reads a chunk of the text, the other student can ask questions like these: How did the abstract movement start? (questioning); Briefly explain the qualities of abstract art (summarizing); What is "Sotheby's"? (clarifying); According to the rise in interest in abstract paintings, what do you think will happen to their prices? (predicting). Note that reciprocal teaching can be used in many ways, and that each component must be explicitly taught and practiced many times before students feel confident enough to use it independently.

Box 6.2 Using the Seven Habits of Good Readers

Most of our formal education comes through the medium of reading the written word. Broadly speaking, until the third grade, students are learning to read. After the third grade, they are *reading to learn*. Although content-area teachers oftentimes do not think of themselves as reading teachers, those who do incorporate explicit reading strategies into their teaching actively support *all* students. Regardless of content area, reading is an interactive process between the reader's thoughts and the text. Successful readers have internalized specific strategies to help them make meaning from a text. The following list highlights the seven habits of good readers (Harvey & Goudvis, 2000). These can be used by all teachers in all content areas.

1. *Activate background knowledge*
   During pre-reading, ask students what they know and how they know it. The more connections they make about the subject, the more likely this will be to stimulate their interest in a text and create new connections.
2. *Visualize*
   During reading, have students pause to talk about what they see in their mind's eye. How do they describe Juliet's garden? What does the balcony look like? How far above Romeo is it? What kind of clothes is she wearing? What kind is Romeo wearing? What do their faces look like? Who do they remind you of?

3. *Question*

   Questions should be constantly posed in relation to the text: before, during, and after it is read. If they are reading about the continent of Asia, student self-questions may look like the following:

   Pre-reading: Who do I know who is from Asia? What countries are there? What cities have I heard of? What does the scenery look like? What animals live there?

   During reading: [passage on Japanese fishing industry] Will there always be enough fish in nearby seas for the growing population? What might happen there if over-fishing takes place? Which countries would be able to trade which products to give Japan fish?

   Post-reading: How has the tradition of whale fishing clashed with attempts to conserve oceans? How successful have fish farms been? How might the traditional Japanese diet change in the future?

4. *Make inferences*

   A careful reading of the text allows the reader to process information, gather clues about what is happening and why, and, based on that information, speculate on what is to come. For example, in a passage about what makes seeds grow, the reader has already learned that too much or too little light and water will influence the growth of a seed. When the next subheading is "Temperature," the reader may already predict that temperatures that are either too high or too low may inhibit the growth of a plant. What they will be cued in to do is learn more about the exact temperatures that either spur or inhibit growth.

5. *Determine importance*

   There is a lot of information in any text, and readers must learn to differentiate between what is most important in terms of the central meaning of the text. For example, in a text about polygons, students who are currently studying triangles will ascertain that this information is currently the most important to know *for this lesson*, even though they may be equally intrigued by squares and pentagons.

6. *Synthesize*

   Readers combine new information (from the text) with existing knowledge (background information) to form new thoughts. Synthesizing is an ongoing process in which multiple pieces of information—old and new—come together to make an original thought. For example, in reading about conditions needed to make a plant grow, a student may begin to develop ideas about where and when to plant seeds in a home garden.

7. *Monitor for meaning*

   Effective readers also self-monitor what they are reading, asking themselves, "Does this make sense?" If the answer is "no," then the reader resorts to different strategies, such as slowing down, rereading, asking another person, pausing to make connections to background knowledge, and any of the other options listed above.

Explicitly Teaching the Seven Habits of Good Teachers

All of these skills promote greater comprehension of a written text. However, although successful readers have developed these skills, less proficient readers benefit from being taught these skills explicitly. This can be done using the "To, With, and By" method as follows:

To

- The teacher initially explains the value of a strategy.
- The teacher models the strategy out loud to his students, including the mental processes used when reading ("'The sun came up over the hill'… hmm… that must mean the action took place during early morning…").

With

- The teacher and students practice the strategy numerous times together. The teacher slowly decreases the level of support.

By

- Students try the strategy on their own (or with a peer) and receive feedback.
- Each student applies the strategy alone in a simple format.
- Students apply the strategy in different formats and/or with more difficult problems.

Source: Co-created with Ida Benton, veteran teacher, New York City.

Small Groups

Cooperative learning is a broad term that encompasses many forms of group work in which all members rely upon one another to solve problems, create solutions, practice skills, or develop ideas. Students can be grouped in many ways, including by interest, by strength, or at random.

Literature circles provide the opportunity for small groups to read the same book. Teachers may assign the same book to all class members, or each literature circle may select its own text according to interest or reading level. Students must pre-read sections and come prepared to discuss certain aspects of the text. The teacher encourages discussion and offers various prompts. However, students may also establish topics they would like to talk about.

Jigsaw is an approach in which small groups work on learning different aspects of a single topic, then share what they have learned with the whole class. In a class of 28 students, for example, seven groups of four can share different information they learned from teacher-provided texts.

Acting scenarios provide students an opportunity to dramatize important information from each content area. For example, groups could create a television advertisement persuading viewers to visit a specific continent; three types of triangles could come together to see if they can find "common ground" despite their "differences"; Romeo and Juliet could be transported into the twenty-first century, including their speech and interests; a row of plants cultivated by students could demonstrate physical changes according to increased and decreased amounts of light, water, and temperature; four painters could meet to discuss whose work was the most important.

Whole Class

Carousel involves teacher-created "stations" on clusters of desks or the walls of the room. The stations contain materials such as a historical document, text, law, character analysis, or photograph. Each group of students begins at a station and, after completing the task for that station (e.g., discuss the photograph or historical document while taking notes), moves clockwise to the next station following a signal from the teacher. After all stations have been visited by all students, the teacher can debrief with the large group or continue the discussion within small groups.

Carousel graffiti operates on the same premise as "carousel," listed above, except that students are asked to write a response on the document provided (Connor & Lagares, 2007). Writing can be in the form of an original idea, a personal response, or an "agree" or "disagree" statement accompanied by a signature. When all stations have been visited, the teacher can select certain responses, share them with the class, ask a given writer to expand her or his thoughts/reasons, and invite the rest of the class to comment upon what the student thinks.

Anticipation guides prepare students to read by asking them to respond to a series of brief statements about the upcoming content. Students respond to these statements by articulating "agree" or "disagree." For example, "Australia is the largest continent in the world," "Romeo and Juliet were too young to know true love," or "All triangles contain 180 degrees." Student interest is piqued, and the actual responses are "answered" by the content of the subsequent text. Comparing their original responses to information in the text gives students the opportunity to readjust their thinking.

Predictions is a simple yet effective technique that asks students to use all of the information at their "brain tips" (e.g., background knowledge, current information presented, illustrations, observations, class discussions) to make an informed guess about what might happen next. Predictions can be made in relation to all texts, experiments, and discussions.

Know/want to know/learned (KWL) can be used before, during, and/or after a lesson or unit. As a graphic organizer with three columns, KWL begins by asking students what they already know (teachers can obtain this information through a variety of activities, such as brainstorming). From this baseline knowledge, students are asked to generate what they would like to know. Of course, this can be modified as the class proceeds through the lesson or unit. The final column is used toward the end of the lesson or unit to record answers to questions students wanted to know as well as miscellaneous new knowledge.

Classification is used by the teacher, who selects a key concept and asks the class to brainstorm associated words. When all of the words are written down (an option is one per sticky note), students then group them into classifications. For example, the word "polygon" as a key word may evoke 20 or so responses that could be classified into "regular examples," "irregular examples," "angles," and "number of sides." In creating classifications, students develop higher-order thinking skills.

Webs are graphic organizers (also referred to as semantic maps) that clearly show how concepts are related to each other. They can be co-created with a class or organized by the teacher.

Songs can be used to help students practice certain skills (e.g., the pronunciation of vocabulary) as well as promote retention of targeted knowledge. In addition, teachers can map important concepts onto songs familiar to students (e.g., "Happy Birthday," or a hit song by a contemporary singer or group).

Call and response is a dynamic way to interact with a whole class of students. The teacher makes oral statements to the class (e.g., "A country is bigger than a continent") and asks students to respond with a brief answer ("yes/no" or "true/false"). Alternatively, the teacher can ask a specific question (e.g., "How many continents are there?"). This can be used when explicitly teaching any concept and/or during review.

Class cue, individual response is very similar to the choral nature of call and response, operating on the principle that all students can be asked all questions instead of one student in class raising a hand. For example, a math teacher can cue, "Draw an isosceles triangle!" and all students can (or try their best!) to do so using an erasable marker on their own small whiteboards. The teacher can immediately see which students are struggling, and struggling students get to see plentiful examples of what an isosceles triangle looks like.

Element Six: Check In with Students Throughout the Lesson

The foregoing extensive list only skims the surface of how information can be presented and engaged with in classrooms. While methods have been purposefully grouped according to how they can be used with individuals, pairs, small groups, or whole classes, all can be modified and used with various student configurations.

Introducing information, connecting to background knowledge, asking pertinent questions, and providing opportunities for students to meaningfully engage with materials sets teachers up for the next important step: How do we know students are "getting it"? We do this by observing, interacting, asking questions, facilitating conversation, and studying the work that students produce. Below are some examples of ways in which teachers can identify their students' levels of understanding:

- Graphic organizers: How well are they filled out? Are they complete? Are responses appropriate, simple, sophisticated?
- Individual brainstorming: How long is the student list? Which students volunteer to share their answers the most? What are the benefits of quickly walking around to see if everyone is on task and generating connections?
- Quick writes: Who writes most? Who writes least? What is the quality and focus of all students?
- Interactive journals: How well is a student expressing herself? To what degree are students interacting with the content area?
- Timelines: How detailed are they? How informative?
- Pantomime: How accurate is the silent acting in describing the action? In what ways does it enhance or stimulate the conversation on content afterwards?
- Reciprocal teaching: How "staged" (versus how "natural") does it feel when two students are working through a text chunked into manageable sections? What kinds of questions are being asked? What kinds of concepts are being clarified?
- Literature circles: How well are the group "norms" working? What is the quality and relevance of the items they suggest to discuss and debate? How well do they respond to teacher cues?
- Carousel: How well do groups work together and take notes? In what ways do their individualized notes reflect the content being taught?

- Anticipation guides: How much do students know or think they know? In what ways do they "return" to their initial position about a statement, and how might they adjust it?
- Predictions: How many students make realistic predictions? Creative predictions? Outlandish or unlikely predictions? How do their responses inform you about the way they think, and the degree to which they have interacted with content information?
- Class cue, individual response: Who is responding most quickly, slowly, accurately?

Above all, teachers should provide opportunities for students to ask questions in a safe and supportive environment. This can be done one-on-one with the teacher, in a whole-class setting, or as part of a written response. Student questions are the best source of information for understanding where students "are" in understanding what you have taught.

Element Seven: Provide Opportunities for Students to Demonstrate Their Knowledge and Abilities

Most, if not all, of the teaching approaches in this chapter encourage students to show what they know and can do. Opportunities to share knowledge, exchange ideas, and ask questions should be woven throughout every lesson. In this section, we touch upon some ways in which teachers gather knowledge about how students are learning and thinking in their classes.

Short-Term Assessment

The following methods can be used to assess student short-term progress:

- *Teacher questions*: Questions can be "matched" to student level and ability, with some questions being posed to the entire class.
- *Student questions*: When such questions are part of the everyday classroom routine, students develop habits of asking questions in relation to content they are engaging with.
- *Quizzes*: These quick assessments can be of varying length (e.g., true or false, multiple-choice, fill-in-the-blank) and allow teachers to "take the pulse" of what is being remembered.
- *Exercises*: Worksheets can be an important way for students to practice what they have recently learned. However, they are over-utilized by many teachers, so they should be used carefully and with a view to giving students corrective feedback that is helpful.
- *Problem solving*: Real-life application of content that has recently been learned facilitates students' making connections to the real world.

Long-Term Assessment

In the longer term, the following methods of assessment are useful:

- *Tests*: Teacher-made tests should always reflect what has been taught and offer a variety of formats for students to demonstrate knowledge.
- *Projects*: Students can work on a self-selected project (in some cases, guided by the teacher). Time for the project can be scheduled as an ongoing part of class. Final projects should be displayed, exhibited, or presented.

- *Presentations*: Teachers can incorporate presentations resulting from a sustained period of engagement with a topic. Students can present to the class individually, in pairs, or in groups.
- *Portfolios*: Students can gather and organize their work over a period of time. Work samples should reflect evidence of academic growth. Students may have the opportunity to share selected aspects of their portfolio with the class or an audience of staff members and parents.

It is also important to note that required testing accommodations may be listed on a student's IEP or Section 504 Plan (a formal plan that schools develop to give students with disabilities appropriate supports) see Box 6.3.

Box 6.3 Testing Accommodations and Modifications for Students with IEPS or Section 504 Plans

Many students with disabilities are granted accommodations for testing situations. These apply to all tests, be they official state education examinations or in-house informal classroom tests. Oftentimes, accommodations are explicitly stated on the child's IEP and are the legal right of the child. It is important to remember that accommodations are given to students so that they can show what they are capable of doing, without the standardized conditions of tests that are disabling. Generally speaking, accommodations are related to scheduling or time, setting for the administration of assessments, changes in the presentation method, and changes in terms of response method. These may include:

- Time and a half
- Double time
- Alternative location
- Use of scribe
- Large-print copies
- Directions read aloud three times

Although some teachers feel that students may not need the following accommodations, they should always be given if they are stated on the IEP:

- Simplification or explanation of test questions.
- Use of a calculator on a test of computational skills.
- Reading items designed to test the student's reading skills.
- Use of grammar-checking devices in a test of the student's writing skills.

Source: Adapted from New York State Department of Education.

Bringing the Lesson to a Close

Toward the end of a lesson, teachers need to see or hear evidence of what their students have learned. In order to do this, a teacher can employ a variety of strategies that allow her to "wind up" a lesson and check for learning.

Element Eight: Culminate the Lesson by Reviewing What Was Learned (Target Information) and What Was Realized (Student Connections)

Perhaps the easiest way for a teacher to wrap up is to return to the objectives and ask the question: How do I know if students can...

1. *List* the seven continents of the world and identify them on a map?
   Students can...
   • Write them in a list, then point to them on a map.
   • Add another four continents onto a list of three.
   • List them orally.
   • On a blank map, color and name areas that represent the continents.

2. *Compare* the differences and similarities between right angle, isosceles, and equilateral triangles?
   Students can...
   • Articulate similarities and differences in writing.
   • Describe similarities and differences to a partner, and present their information to another pair of students.
   • Complete an organizer that lists similarities and differences.
   • Working in triads, and given triangle shapes, explain ways in which their triangle (right-angle, isosceles, or equilateral) is similar to and different from the others.

3. *Describe* the characteristics of Romeo and Juliet?
   Students can (working in groups of four or five)...
   • Create a poster that summarizes the characteristics of Romeo and Juliet.
   • Debate which characteristics are clear, which are implied, and which are emerging.
   • Individually summarize the characteristics of either Romeo or Juliet in a sentence or two.
   • Create a short personal ad that lists the characteristics of Romeo or Juliet.

4. *Analyze* the growth of seeds exposed to varying degrees of light, water, and temperature?
   Students can...
   • Discuss the results obtained through plotting graphs about the growth of seeds exposed to different levels of light, water, and temperature.
   • Compare and contrast given graphs.
   • Write a brief summary of findings via information presented and personal observation.
   • Make predictions based upon information they have ascertained.

5. *Create* an original work of abstract art?
   Students can...
   • Produce a variety of artwork.
   • Discuss questions about abstract art.
   • Analyze each other's work, articulating connections and speculating upon artist choices.
   • Describe the thinking behind their own work.

From this brief list of possibilities, it is clear that time must be allotted for students to reconnect to the larger issues introduced in class, the connections that students have made, and the application of knowledge. Providing students with multiple opportunities to share both informally (e.g., oral responses, discussions) and formally (e.g., written exercises, lists to be collected) is important, as it holds them accountable for their own learning and encourages reflective thinking.

In a similar manner, teachers can quickly ascertain whether students have met social and behavioral goals by listening and observing. For example, did students take turns speaking, follow their assigned roles, compliment one another's contributions, share responsibility for the task assigned, and evaluate themselves as individuals and group members? Customized sheets can be designed for students to self-evaluate their behavior. In terms of the behavioral goals cited earlier in this chapter, does the teacher have evidence that students (for example) generated two original questions based upon their independent reading; stored their materials and cleaned the desks before the next class entered; or raised their hands before speaking during whole-class work? Examples for individuals may include David's completed checklist, Santiago's decrease in crossing of personal boundaries, and Jan's raising her hand rather than calling out.

Additional strategies that assist in a quick evaluation of student learning that can be generalized to many topics are as follows:

1. *Encourage students to pose questions*: What are they wondering based upon what they have learned? Oftentimes, the depth and complexity of student thinking is simply revealed in their questions. Students could each write a question and pose it to the class, or to their partner, or hand it in for the teacher to answer.
2. *Give students a "Ticket to Leave"*: This can be on a specifically prepared slip or on a sticky note. Everyone must write a response to the teacher's prompt and hand it in before leaving class (the teacher can even stand by the door to collect them). Examples of tickets to leave may be as follows:

Academic

- Which content intrigues you most, and why?
- Tell me something new that you learned about triangles today.
- What are your favorite characteristics of Romeo and Juliet? Why?
- Which of the three factors (light, water, and temperature) is most important in the growth of a plant? Why?
- Finish this sentence: "Abstract art is...."

Social

- On a scale of 1–10, how did your group activities go?
- What were you pleased with during group activities?
- What do you think your group needs to improve upon?

Behavioral

- What worked well for you today?
- What are some examples of how you followed your contract today?
- What were you proud of today?
- What do you still need to work on?
- How did you measure up to your own goals today?

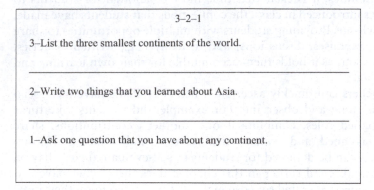

Figure 6.2 An example of a "3–2–1" Ticket to Leave
Note: Tickets to Leave can differ in form and content.

Teachers can create numerous forms of Tickets to Leave, ranging from simple, one-word answers to complex responses in the form of statements, such as making predictions for next class, providing a summary, or offering an original thought. These can be in the form of a "3–2–1," as illustrated in Figure 6.2.

Grading

Grading can be one of the most difficult aspects of teaching. Teachers ask themselves how they can treat students equally and fairly, acknowledging that some students breeze through work effortlessly while others give 100 percent and do not meet the accepted "norms" or standards. The topic of grading does pose "bigger" questions about being fair, including what we teach, how we teach it, and how we understand student differences when deciding upon their grades. The concept of fairness can be slippery at best!

Welch (2000) found it useful to contemplate fairness in three ways: equality, equity, and need. Equality refers to every participant receiving the same reward; everybody is treated in the same way. Equity reflects how reward is proportionate to input. A student who contributed the most or received the highest score is entitled to the greatest reward. Need is based on those having the greatest need receiving the greatest reward. Ramps for wheelchairs and free lunches (and special education services, for that matter) are provided to those who need them. Thus, fairness can be seen as something layered, rather than clear cut. Thinking about fairness in a nuanced way helps guide teachers about ways in which a student can be graded on what she can do, not only as measured against another student but, more importantly, as measured against herself.

Featured Voice of Jody Polleck

"Be a Student of your Students"

Cultural Responsiveness and Culturally Sustaining Pedagogy

"Be a student of your students." This is a mantra I have carried into my classrooms over the last 20 years. It entails spending the majority of my time and effort on getting to know my students' interests, languages, identities, and communities.

Meet Rene: He claims he hates to read yet he loves comedy and has quite the witty sense of humor. During independent reading where students have choice in the texts they engage with, Rene reads the entire collection of *Diary of a Wimpy Kid* in just four months.

Meet Roberto: He has had tremendous problems with attendance and tardiness and is now repeating the ninth grade for the third time. He has his own independent contract in my classroom where he reads only the writings of Latinx authors and recreates their words in the form of digital poems together with images of his own graffiti art combined with the hip hop music he writes in his spare time. While he has limited engagement with our whole class curriculum, for the first time, he has not missed a day of English in a month.

Meet Danielle: Her IEP states that she requires a scribe. Using voice dictation technology, she uses her phone in the hallway to write academic essays on the racism and sexism that Pecola experiences in *The Bluest Eye*. She also sketches the different scenes that speak to her and these are hung on our classroom walls so that other students can experience the text visually through Danielle's lens.

Meet Zhao: He is a recent immigrant from China who is fluent in his first language but is very new to English. He is reading our class text, *The Brief Wondrous Life of Oscar Wao* by Junot Diaz, in Chinese and sits with his partner Bo, who is also from China and helps him to understand the conversations we have as a whole class.

What has helped me to be successful with these students and others over the years is not only getting to know and utilize my students' strengths and assets, but also being flexible enough on a daily basis to meet them where they are. In this way, I can engage each and every one of them through their literary, linguistic, and cultural diversities that only add strength to our classroom community.

While certainly not an easy task, especially my first five years of teaching when my class rosters totaled well over 100 students, I've always made great efforts to spend those first few weeks of school to truly get to know my students. Through use of classroom inventories, parent and guardian surveys, small and whole-class discussions, community-building activities, and simply talking to my students at the door as they enter the room, I have been able to create curricula that students find engaging.

This means relinquishing control and creating a democratic classroom in which students have numerous opportunities for choice and creativity. What does this look like on a practical basis? I offer independent reading where students select books that interest them. When assigning larger essays, students have choice in what they write about. When reading texts as a class, students can read in their first language or a graphic version if available. Opening and closing writing prompts ask students for their thoughts, questions, and ideas, as knowledge should be co-constructed as a classroom community and not dictated by the pedagogue.

Engaging students also means allowing for collaborative learning where students talk to each other and problem solve together on a daily basis. My classroom periods are filled with turn-and-talks, small-group discussions, and Socratic seminars. Students are moving—continually—so as to keep their limbs and brains alert. Most importantly, *they* are doing all the work, and not me.

"Bell to bell, my lovelies," I'd sing to them if their energy levels got low, "We'll be working bell to bell."

> In getting to know my students and using their diversities in my instruction, I am able to not only set high expectations but also provide them with the appropriate academic scaffolding they need. They know that I believe in them, but that I will also help them along the way. Forging these connections is critical as students will go to impossible lengths for themselves, for their families, and for their teachers if they know that we believe in them and that we care.
>
> Just yesterday I ran into Nelson, who I taught over four years ago. I asked him about college, his writing, his curve ball, and his mother. It reminded me of how important it was, despite the time lapse, to still remember these aspects of Nelson's life that most mattered to him. And it reminded me that, while the work of differentiation and cultural relevance can be challenging, it is what keeps students most engaged and allows them the daily and long-term successes that we want them all to experience both when they are with us and when they've moved forward. Being culturally responsive and integrating culturally sustaining practices are not just conceptual, theoretical approaches—they are at the heart of what we do for our students.

Some Final Notes on Lesson Planning

We close with a few last pointers on lesson planning. There are numerous ways to plan and organize lessons; however, we urge you to strive toward developing lesson plans that move beyond scripted templates. We encourage you to think of lesson plans as living documents, crafted by thoughtful and skilled practitioners. Remember, lesson planning is a very personal process. At first, it usually takes time, but once in the rhythm, teachers are able to produce quality plans within reasonable timeframes. Bear these tips in mind:

1. *Allot time to planning and stick to it*: As a rule, the better planned, the better executed.
2. *Start with your objectives*: Everything else must support them.
3. *Understand that conceptualizing the lesson in three parts makes it seem manageable*: Ask yourself: How will I (a) help students transition into the classroom, "warm them up," review old knowledge, connect their own knowledge and backgrounds, and introduce them to something new? (b) In what ways am I providing support and time for them to practice new knowledge and skills? (c) In what ways am I providing opportunities for them to demonstrate, and reflect upon, their knowledge and skills?
4. *Share your objectives with students*: Ensure that they know what they are going to learn.
5. *Plan for everyone*: Be prepared to modify instruction as you go along.
6. *Encourage your own reflective thinking*: Keep a notebook on your thoughts, ideas, experiences, and reactions.
7. *Encourage students to make their own connections but also provide multiple connections yourself*: Weave formerly taught material, purposefully spiraling knowledge in every lesson.
8. *Allow for reviews of what has been previously taught*: Regularly factor in time to stop and assess the learning to date.
9. *Budget time with your co-teacher—and adhere to that time*: Honor the mutual commitment and utilize it well (more information is provided on this issue in Chapter 8).
10. *Remember that it is much better to over-plan than to under-plan*: You have the option of using any "leftovers" from a single lesson next time around.

In this chapter, we have broken down elements of a lesson to show how, at each step, the teacher can engage students in meaningful, interesting, and stimulating ways. Of course, not everyone can be engaged to the maximum extent possible during every minute of every lesson. While we believe that teachers have a responsibility to plan well, it is as important to pay close attention to "in the moment" interactions, deciding how to best move forward in a way that engages students to the maximum extent possible. The teacher who is reflective (thinking about everything that happens in class) and flexible (able to adjust the plan according to student responses and interactions) will reach and teach all students. In other words, the teacher continually encourages students to make knowledge connections throughout every step of the lesson.

In closing this section, we have assembled five examples to show what lessons from various grade levels could look like—a synthesis of all the elements we have spent time discussing. While certainly not perfect (as no teacher is!), these lessons show how each element dovetails with the others to provide a clear path of instruction with adequate support for a variety of learners.

Lesson Plans

Synthesized Components: Lesson on Continents

Grade: 3

Standard:

- Locate places within the local community, state, and nation; locate the Earth's continents in relation to each other and to principal parallels and meridians (adapted from National Geography Standards, 1994).

1. *Generate objectives*: "List the seven continents of the world and identify them on a map."

> *Possible knowledge brought by students*: Definition of a country, examples and non-examples of countries (California, Africa); countries visited; countries where their families or ancestors are from, etc.
>
> *Possible collective knowledge made in the lesson*: Definition of continent; comparison of continent and country; recognition of where specific animals come from (tigers in Asia); geography (rainforests in Africa, Asia, Central and South America).
>
> *Possible individual student connections within the lesson*: Continents that are the biggest to smallest, the closest to farthest away.

- Groupings: Individuals, groups of four, whole class.
- Behavioral objective: David will self-monitor for concentration (decrease daydreaming). Provide a copy of teacher-generated checklist for David to mark every five minutes; "check in" with him throughout class.

2. Provide opportunities for applications of recent skills and/or demonstration of recent knowledge (focusing activity): "In partners, describe the difference between a continent and a country in a sentence or two."

3. Pose engaging questions to discover students' background knowledge:

    General post-focusing question: "Who will start off and remind us of what we learned about countries from yesterday's class?"

    Specific post-focusing question: "Is Africa a country or a continent?"

    To elicit background information: "Where have you heard the word 'continent' used before?" "What are some distant places in the world that you have seen on the TV and in movies?" "If you could go anywhere in the world, where would you go and why?" "Who has heard of Antarctica?"

4. *Explicitly introduce what is expected of students during the lesson*: "Today we are going to learn the names and locations of the seven continents of the world."

5. *Provide opportunities for clear explanations of content material and multiple opportunities for students to engage with it*: As individuals, ask students to "Look at the world map on the wall, pick a continent, and quickly list everything you know about it."

6. Check in with students throughout the lesson to ascertain the degree to which they are understanding the targeted content:

    • Teacher provides each student with a world map on letter-size paper; each table has seven different colored markers or pencils.

    • Teacher uses same map on overhead and explains that the class is going to outline all continents in different colors.

    • Teacher starts off with North America, outlining it in red.

    • Teacher asks students, "What do you already know about North America?" and samples student contributions (made in previous section), mediating answers when necessary.

7. Provide opportunities (short-term and long-term) for students to demonstrate their knowledge and abilities:

    • Repeat for remaining six continents: South America (blue), Europe (purple), Africa (green), Asia (yellow), Australia (orange), Antarctica (brown).

    • In groups of four, teacher distributes seven short documents about animals in each continent

    • Each group reads and discusses the short documents (with focusing questions; can vary in length according to group).

    • Large-group share out, each group describing their continent's animal. As each group presents, students pick an animal to symbolize their group's continent, for example bald eagle (North America), anaconda (South America), tiger (Asia), elephant (Africa), fox (Europe), penguin (Antarctica), kangaroo (Australia). Note that this association serves as a memory device.

8. Culminate the lesson by reviewing what was learned (targeted information) and what was realized (students' own connections):

    • As a whole class, review the location of the seven continents.

    • On a medium-size sticky note, have each student complete a key (legend) using the animals.

    • Place the key on the map.

    • In pairs, have one student list the seven continents of the world, while the other points to them (switch if time).

Synthesized Components: Lesson on Triangles

Grade: 4

Standard:

- Develop relationships among observations to construct descriptions of objects and events so that students can form their own tentative explanations of what they have observed.

1. *Generate objectives*: Compare the differences and similarities between right-angle, isosceles, and equilateral triangles.

> *Possible knowledge brought by students*: Triangles are polygons with three sides; they are easily drawn; the shape of certain intersections; they are almost the shape of a slice of pizza.
>   *Possible knowledge made*: Different triangles all share certain attributes (e.g., they contain 180 degrees; have three sides; can vary in size).
>   *Possible student's own connections*: Bermuda Triangle; "tri" means three, like triple, tricycle, triathlon, etc.

- Groupings: Individuals, pairs, whole class.
- Behavioral objective: Santiago will refrain from touching other students (personal reminder at start of class; placement with Donna and Jamal, students who can remind Santiago; praise at end of class).

2. *Provide opportunities for applications of recent skills and/or demonstration of recent knowledge (focusing activity)*: "On a sheet of paper, draw a line to match the six triangles to their similar shapes (provided, jumbled up).

3. *Pose engaging questions to discover students' background knowledge*:
    General post-focusing question: "How many different types of triangles did you see within the 12 examples?"
    Specific post-focusing question: "What great works of architecture are based on a triangular design? (Clue: found in ancient civilizations)
    To elicit background information: "How many types of triangles do you know?"

4. *Explicitly introduce what is expected of students during a lesson*: "By the end of the lesson we will be able to tell the differences and similarities between three types of triangles: right-angle, isosceles, and equilateral."

5. *Provide opportunities for clear explanations of content material and multiple opportunities for students to engage with it*:
    - Distribute an envelope to each pair of students. The envelope contains three types of colored triangles, five each of right-angled (blue), isosceles (green), and equilateral (yellow) triangles.
    - Ask students to create a pattern using one type of triangle.
    - Ask students to create a pattern using two types of triangles.
    - Ask students to create patterns using three types of triangles.
    - Ask the following questions: "Which triangles do we recognize?" (right and isosceles, already taught); "Which one don't we know much about yet?" (equilateral).
    - Ask students to examine an equilateral triangle and then ask the following questions: "What can you tell me about it?" (3 sides, same length); "Who would like to make a prediction about the angles?"

6. Check in with students throughout the lesson to ascertain the degree to which they are understanding the targeted content: Teacher creates the following chart with three columns; students copy it into their notebooks:

Type of triangle	3 sides	3 angles (= 180 degrees)
Right-angled (with illustration)		
Isosceles (with illustration)		
Equilateral (with illustration)		

- Review of right-angle triangle: In pairs, students write what they know about previously taught right-angles (all three sides can be different, two can be equal; when one angle is 90 degrees, the other two angles equal 90 degrees, etc.).
- Eliciting volunteers, teacher reviews with whole class. Review of isosceles triangle: In pairs, students write what they know about what was previously taught about isosceles triangles (two sides are equal; two angles are equal, etc.) Eliciting volunteers, teacher reviews with whole class.
- Compare to visual of equilateral triangle. Review comments students previously made (observations, predictions). Explicitly teach characteristics of equilateral triangle: 3 sides same length, 3 angles of equal measure.

7. Provide opportunities (short term and long term) for students to demonstrate their knowledge and abilities:
- Students work in pairs. Each partner draws 10 triangles (right-angle, isosceles, or equilateral). Students swap papers and write R, I, or E on each triangle. Students return papers and grade each other's work.
- Teacher can either draw on overhead or present three types of triangle cutouts of construction paper taped to the wall/board. As individuals, students identify 6 to 10 examples (they can use their chart to check).
- Students put away their charts, and then ask each other questions to see if they can all...
   - Describe the characteristics of a right-angle triangle.
   - Describe the characteristics of an isosceles triangle.
   - Describe the characteristics of an equilateral triangle.

8. Culminate the lesson by reviewing what was learned (targeted information) and what was realized (students' own connections):
- Large-group question: "Where do we see these three types of triangles in real life?" (cheese, door wedges, ramps, etc.)
- Quick write: "If your friend in class said to you that he thinks an equilateral triangle is exactly the same as a right-angle triangle, would you agree? If not, how would you explain some similarities and some differences?"

Synthesized Components: Lesson on Romeo and Juliet

Grade: 8

Standard:

- Listen attentively to others and build on others' ideas in conversation with peers and adults.
- Develop information with appropriate supporting material, such as facts, details, illustrative examples or anecdotes, and exclude extraneous material.

1. *Generate objective*: Describe the characteristics of Romeo and Juliet.

> *Possible knowledge brought by students*: Shakespeare is the author; the theme is love; there are several movie versions; the story is set in Italy.
>
> *Possible collective knowledge made in the lesson*: Both characters are young; Juliet is trusting; Romeo is overwhelmed by love; both feel a sense of loyalty toward their families—but a greater attraction to one another, etc.
>
> *Possible student's own connections*: Love can transcend social divisions; young people in former times also experienced strong emotions; families can greatly influence their members in choosing a partner.

- Groupings: Individuals, groups of four, whole class.

2. *Provide opportunities for applications of recent skills and/or demonstration of recent knowledge (focusing activity)*: "List five characteristics (not physical) that make you who you are; for example, 'I am... honest, quick-tempered, optimistic'."

3. Pose engaging questions to discover students' background knowledge:)

   General post-focusing question: "What is the most important characteristic that you would seek in an ideal partner?"

   Specific post-focusing question: "How would you prioritize the traits you listed?"

   To elicit background information: "Let's recap on what we know about Romeo and Juliet. What have been some of their actions—and what might the actions tell us about them? What have been some of their words—and what might these tell us about Romeo and Juliet?"

4. *Explicitly introduce what is expected of students during a lesson*: "The focus of today is to explore the characters of Romeo and Juliet, and to describe what makes them who they are—their characteristics."

5. Provide opportunities for clear explanations of content material and multiple opportunities for students to engage with it:

   - Write a short "missing scene" involving four characters in the play discussing what they think about Romeo or Juliet (including both favorable and unfavorable characteristics). Make sure to base their comments on what Romeo and Juliet have said and done.
   - Teacher models picking a character who has had interactions with Romeo and articulates some of the character's concerns. For example, the nurse-maid notices that Romeo is besotted with Juliet and returns to see her every night.
   - Teacher brainstorms with students about some possible characters.
   - Teacher divides students into groups of four.

6. Check in with students throughout the lesson to ascertain the degree to which they are understanding the targeted content:

   - For five minutes, each student is responsible for writing her own thoughts (texts can be used).
   - Students then share their ideas with each other.
   - Teacher circulates while students are working to assist them as individuals (locating examples, articulating characteristics, etc.) and then as groups (checking examples, all students are contributing, etc.).

7. Provide opportunities (short term and long term) for students to demonstrate their knowledge and abilities:
   - Groups share their responses by performing "in character." This can be at the front of the room or at their tables.
   - At least one group for Romeo and one group for Juliet should share.
8. Culminate the lesson by reviewing what was learned (targeted information) and what was realized (students' own connections):
   - Teacher facilitates discussion about their characteristics: Who agrees? Disagrees? What evidence do we have?
   - Students debate which characteristics are clear, which are implied, and which are emerging.
   - As a culminating activity, the whole class collaborates in filling out a T-chart listing the characteristics of Romeo and Juliet (with examples).

Romeo Characteristics and examples	Juliet Characteristics and examples

Synthesized Components: Lesson on Seeds

Grade: 5

Standard:

- Students carry out their plans for exploring phenomena through direct observation and through the use of simple instruments that permit measurement of quantities (e.g., length, mass, volume, temperature, and time).
- Organize observations and measurements of objects and events through classification and the preparation of simple charts and tables.

1. *Generate objective*: Analyze the growth of seeds exposed to varying degrees of light, water, and temperature (note that this lesson/topic will cover a week).

> *Possible knowledge brought by students*: Plants and trees grow from seeds; seeds can be found in the fruit of many plants, such as oranges, apples, and tomatoes.
>
> *Possible collective knowledge made in the lesson*: The growth of seeds is subject to certain environmental conditions, including light, water, and temperature.
>
> *Possible student's own connections*: Different types of trees; which trees grow where; which trees are all year round; why trees in the rainforests are so tall.

- Groupings: Individuals, pairs, triads, large group.
2. *Provide opportunities for applications of recent skills and/or demonstration of recent knowledge (focusing activity)*: "Categorize these named seeds (e.g., corn, grass, peas, roses, cabbage, etc.) into plants we eat and plants we do not eat."
3. Pose engaging questions to discover students' background knowledge:
   General post-focusing question: "Think for a moment, and be ready to tell your partner what we have already learned about how water and temperature can influence the growth of seeds into plants."

Specific post-focusing question: "Can you describe to a partner, using your categorization, which plants are those that we eat and which are those that we don't eat?"

To elicit background information: "Can you tell me all of the different types of trees and/or plants that you know, and where they can be found?"

4. *Explicitly introduce what is expected of students during a lesson*: "Our job today will be to study variations in seeds that have been exposed to different conditions, including amounts of light, water, and temperature."

5. Provide opportunities for clear explanations of content material and multiple opportunities for students to engage with it:

   - Make a prediction of the growth of five plants based upon the information presented: (1) a plant with moderate light, moderate water, and moderate temperature; (2) a plant with light and water, low temperature; (3) a plant with water and moderate temperature, no light; (4) a plant with light and moderate temperature, no water; (5) a plant with no light, no water, no temperature.
   - Each of you will take notes on the importance of (a) light, (b) water, or (c) temperature, with a view to presenting your information to the others. Together, you will rank their order of importance.

6. Check in with students throughout the lesson to ascertain the degree to which students are understanding the targeted content:

   - Students set up their plant experiment.
   - The teacher circulates, monitors, and provides assistance and clarification when needed.

7. Provide opportunities (short term and long term) for students to demonstrate their knowledge and abilities:

   - Students write predictions about each plant. (Daily conditions to remain constant over seven days)
   - Students chart plant data on a daily basis: general condition, length, etc. (Note: Observing, describing, and measuring plants becomes an integral component of the next four lessons, resulting in final measurement and comparison over one calendar week.)
   - When students plot and update graphs, ask these questions: "What have you noticed so far?" "What is changing?" "What is staying the same?" "How accurate have your predictions been so far?" "Based upon what you have observed, how might you modify them?"

8. Culminate the lesson by reviewing what was learned (targeted information) and what was realized (students' own connections):

[This particular lesson]

   - Orally review what was accomplished today.

[Future lessons]

   - Paraphrase the ongoing results obtained through plotting graphs about the growth of the seeds.
   - Compare and contrast given graphs over time.

[Final lesson]

   - Ask the students: "Based upon your experiences and observations, which of the three factors (light, water, and temperature) is most important in the growth of a plant? Why?"

Synthesized Components: Lesson on Abstract Art

Grade: 10

Standard:

- Create artworks in which students use and evaluate different kinds of media, subjects, themes, symbols, metaphors, and images.

1. *Generate objective*: Create an original work of abstract art.

> *Possible knowledge brought by students*: Colors; shapes; definition or recognition of abstract works.
>
> *Possible collective knowledge made in the lesson*: Recognition of certain artists, such as Jackson Pollock or Piet Mondrian, techniques to begin, experiment with, and develop an original piece of abstract art.
>
> *Possible student's own connections*: Recollecting images in life reminiscent of abstract paintings, e.g., colors in a sunset, floor tiles, clothing designs with patterns of color, or aerial views of the landscape.

- Groupings: Individuals, collaborative triads, large group.
- Behavioral objectives: Jan will reduce the number of times she shouts out in class (review with her at start of class, use of nonverbal reminders, verbal reminders if necessary, and review at end of class).

2. *Provide opportunities for applications of recent skills and/or demonstration of recent knowledge (focusing activity)*: "Choose your favorite from these three works of abstract art (show posters/projections of Kandinsky, Rothko, and Delaney) and briefly write what exactly distinguishes it from the other works, incorporating comments about color, texture, pattern, and tone. Provide a graphic organizer." (See example below.)

Color	Texture
Pattern	Tone

3. *Pose engaging questions to discover students' background knowledge*:
   General post-focusing question: "Which do you think is the most important quality of abstract work: size, tone, color, shape, or pattern?"
   Specific post-focusing question: "Which do you think is the most important in the abstract work you chose: color, texture, pattern, or tone?"
   To elicit background information: "What are the things that artists might take into consideration when they are planning an abstract work? Where might they get some ideas?"
4. *Explicitly introduce what is expected of students during a lesson*: "Today our goal is to create an original piece of art that is abstract."
5. Provide opportunities for clear explanations of content material and multiple opportunities for students to engage with it:
   - Students use seven straight or curved lines to create an idea for an abstract design. (Show some samples.)

- When students have completed the task, they will work in groups of three. Each person will work on his or her abstract design for seven minutes, focusing on one or more aspects of pattern, color, and texture.
- After seven minutes, the drawing will be rotated to the second person.
- After another seven minutes, the drawing will be rotated to the third person.
- After that, the drawing will return to its originator, who can spend five minutes adding any additional contribution.

6. *Check in with students throughout the lesson to ascertain the degree to which they are understanding the targeted content*: Teacher circulates, working with students individually and as a group, giving feedback on their work, answering questions, demonstrating techniques as necessary, making suggestions, etc.

7. Provide opportunities (short term and long term) for students to demonstrate their knowledge and abilities:
   - After all students are satisfied with their work, they place it on a classroom wall. All three pieces should be close together, demonstrating connections of color, texture, pattern, and tone.
   - Students are then invited to move about the room (or optionally, sit) and view all of the paintings.

8. Culminate the lesson by reviewing what was learned (targeted information) and what was realized (students' own connections):
   - Teacher facilitates a conversation: "What do you notice? What connections do you see? How do the paintings make you feel? What can be said about the artists' use of color, tone, and shape? (Opportunity to introduce vocabulary: triptych.)
   - Individual students are asked to describe the thinking behind their own work.
   - Before leaving, students are asked to complete this sentence orally to the large group: "Based on what we have explored today, abstract art is...."

Questions to Consider

1. Broadly speaking, what do you consider to be the most significant elements of lesson planning?
2. Why is it important to connect with students before attempting to teach new information?
3. What are some ways in which to begin lessons? Which do you feel comfortable trying?
4. What are some engaging activities for students working as individuals, in pairs, in small groups, in larger groups, and as a whole class? Which ones were you already familiar with, and which were new to you?
5. As a student, what are the classroom activities that you most benefited from?
6. What are some ways in which you can ascertain the degree to which students are engaging with content?
7. What are some ways to "wrap up" a lesson and consolidate student knowledge?
8. What might be some ways to differentiate the activities suggested?
9. In what ways can you integrate testing accommodations in some of the teaching strategies within this chapter?
10. How would you prioritize the seven habits of good readers? Explain your decisions.

References

Ahmadi, M. R. & Gilajani, A. P. (2014). Reciprocal teaching strategies and their impacts on English reading comprehension. *Theory and Practice in Language Studies, 2*(10), 2053–60.

Connor, D. J. & Lagares, C. (2007). Facing high stakes in high school: 25 successful strategies from an inclusive social studies classroom. *TEACHING Exceptional Children, 40*(2),18–27.

Department of Education. (1994). National Geography Standards. Retrieved from www.research-gate.net/publication/234589183_Geography_for_Life_National_Geography_Standards_1994

Harvey, S. & Goudvis, A. (2000). *Strategies that work: Teaching comprehension to enhance understanding.* Portland, ME: Stenhouse.

Parr, T. (2001). *It's okay to be different.* New York, NY: Machete Book Group.

Raphael, T. (1994). Question–answer strategies for children. *The Reading Teacher, 36*(2), 186–90.

Welch, A. B. (2000). Responding to student concerns about fairness. *Exceptional Children, 33*(2), 36–40.

7 Assessing Student Knowledge and Skills in the Inclusive Classroom

"How do I know they all got it?"

Cartoon #7 Don't gamble... choose carefully

If a teacher teaches something but students have not learned it, has the "it" really been taught? This is a tough one. In some ways, the answer is "yes" and "no," depending upon your perception of what teaching is. If you view teaching as a transmission model whereby the educator provides information and students must learn it regardless of the teacher's style (oftentimes telling, lecturing, worksheets, and so on), then you may conclude that once the teacher has told the students content information her job is done. If the students don't "get it," that is their responsibility. However, as we have seen in previous chapters, effective teaching is not this simple, and teachers must plan ways in which to genuinely engage students.

Maximizing student engagement is part of an interactive model of teaching in which knowledge is constructed among teachers and students. Of course, interactive teaching and learning are not created from scratch; they consist of the content knowledge teachers provide being intertwined with preexisting student knowledge, questions, and ideas, as they engage in activities to stimulate their thinking and apply it in meaningful ways. We believe one of the most important challenges for teachers is to recognize "I know I have taught it," but then to ask themselves, "How can I know to what degree and in what ways it has been learned?"

In this chapter, we examine various ways to assess students, explore the best ways to find out what students can do, and use that information to plan their next level of instruction. In addition, we note the value of pre-, during-, and post-learning assessments. By using formative and summative assessments, teachers can come to know students' understanding and abilities as they progress through the curriculum.

Multiple Purposes of Assessment

First and foremost, we want to emphasize that the purpose of assessment is to know what students can do. In traditional special education, students are primarily seen through a deficit lens that details what they cannot do. Of course, knowing a student's challenges is important in guiding a teacher's decision-making process, but overemphasizing what students are unable to do results in unintended consequences. In other words, a teacher may end up viewing special education students as incapable of learning much and, in turn, these students internalize the low expectations held for them. In contrast, we suggest that teachers view students through a strength-based model that assumes competence.

In operating from a strength-based model, teachers talk with students about the areas in which they excel, emphasizing their talents, gifts, interests, and abilities. As you come to know each student's areas of strength, it becomes possible to capitalize upon these strengths while working on a student's challenges. For example, a child who can memorize intricate rap songs but struggles to recall multiplication tables might learn the tables through rap; a student who is an excellent artist but struggles to write might create the plot of a story through a storyboard.

The assessment of students can take many forms and occur during any part of the learning process: before introducing students to new content; while students are processing information in a lesson; and when they create products to show what they have learned. Assessment can also occur at the end of a unit of study, the end of a semester, or the end of a year. It can take place informally in the form of observations, conversations, and interactions collected by the teacher, or formally using quizzes, tests, and final examinations. It might take place through long-term group work, projects, and class presentations. And it certainly includes local and state standardized examinations. Each type of assessment will be discussed in more depth in the following pages.

In some respects, it is wise to break the idea of assessment down into two broad areas: formative assessment and summative assessment. While these terms sound fancy, they represent ideas that are pretty simple at heart. Formative assessment occurs when teachers take notice of what students say and do daily in the classroom (e.g., how they answer and ask questions, work with others, comment upon what is being taught and learned) and integrate these observations into instructional planning. Formative assessment is an ongoing approach, and it allows teachers to monitor student learning. In contrast, summative assessments occur at the end of a specified period of time (a week, a unit, a semester, a year) to ascertain the growth of a student. The information obtained through summative assessments reveals what a student knows and does not know and is also used for future instructional planning. To maximize effective teaching, both assessment approaches should be used.

Choosing Options for Ongoing Assessment

Before we begin a list describing the many options for assessment… a disclaimer! For some readers, all of the options that teachers have to assess students may seem overwhelming. At first, it may feel like you do not know where to begin. However, as you get more comfortable in the daily routines of classrooms, you will begin to see the benefits of using various assessments for different purposes. Our interest lies in describing creative methods of assessment, both short term and long term, that can be used by teachers in inclusive classrooms.

Informal Observations

Teachers informally assess their students' current levels of knowledge and skills through continual observation. For example, you should ask yourself questions such as these: What are they doing well? What are they struggling with? What do they have partial knowledge of? What do they have a tentative understanding of? What evidence do I see or hear to confirm my initial impression? Many teachers develop ways of ascertaining to what degree each student understands what is being taught. Some prefer to keep some form of notes, from brief to detailed, citing examples ("Jose plotted coordinates on a graph and completed all assigned work," "Maria made a web of places she would like to visit," or "Jongu waited his turn in collaborative grouping"). Many teachers like to carry clipboards upon which to take notes while circulating around the classroom, while others prefer to use record-keeping books. Moreover, observation notes can vary in format; see Figures 7.1 (a–c).

Portfolio Assessment

Student portfolios contain a collection of student work created over a period of time, and demonstrate clear evidence of student learning. They are intended to document the degree of student growth and be seen as a statement of their abilities. By design, portfolios are student centered in that students select work that they feel represents them. Portfolios are highly individualized and can be customized to the needs and ability levels of any student. A good portfolio includes clear goals that students should work toward. Before beginning this kind of assessment, it is helpful for students to see a strong portfolio model to help them visualize what their own final product could look like. Portfolios should be seen not only as a collection of student work but also as an opportunity for students to reflect upon and discuss the progress of their efforts, orally and/or in writing. Some teachers formalize

(a) General observations	
Date:	Notes:
Ayala, Pedro	
Curran, Carmella	
Gorsky, Natasha	
Kashiguro, Ino	
Lewis, Amy	
Leung, Christophe	
Maguire, Katerina	
Samson, Jenita	

(b) Targeted observations, specific feedback, and follow up				
Date:	Strengths:	Areas of need:	Feedback to student:	To look for next time:
Ayala, Pedro				
Curran, Carmella				
Gorsky, Natasha				
Kashiguro, Ino				
Lewis, Amy				
Leung, Christophe				
Maguire, Katerina				
Samson, Jenita				

(c) Writing process observations sheets						
Date:	Prewriting	Planning	First Draft	Revision	Editing	Final piece
Ayala, Pedro						
Curran, Carmella						
Gorsky, Natasha						
Kashiguro, Ino						
Lewis, Amy						
Leung, Christophe						
Maguire, Katerina						
Samson, Jenita						

Note: Teacher can write qualitative notes or use symbols (*, *), letters, or numbers.

Figure 7.1 Samples of teacher record keeping

portfolio assessment by requiring students to present their work to peers, family, and other teachers.

Authentic Assessments and Performance Assessments

Authentic assessments are those that reflect "real-life" tasks that are both meaningful and relevant to students. These are student-centered, activity-based, and product-oriented. In other words, students play an active role in creating something they are interested in that is useful and finite. For example, students might interview a series of adults about their views on immigration or war and then synthesize these views into a presentation (social studies); assemble information and create a brochure to promote neighborhood recycling (science); organize information gathered about peer use of various electronic products into graphs (math); or create a class newspaper (English language arts). Authentic assessment involves backwards planning as teachers ask themselves, "What would I like students to be able to do?" Creating real-life projects gives students experience of using many skills and integrating some new ones. Whether authentic tasks are large or small, teachers often-times use a rubric to convey explicit expectations of what the final product should demonstrate (see more information about rubrics in Figure 7.2). Authentic assessments used in conjunction with rubrics are ways in which teachers can evaluate to what degree their students are meeting state performance standards.

Project-Based Learning

Closely linked to authentic assessment is project-based learning, an approach that contrasts with more traditional short-term, teacher-centered lessons in which knowledge is presented in isolation, decontextualized from the world. A long-term approach that requires the creation of meaningful projects connected to real-world issues, project-based learning provides opportunities for students to develop multiple skills within a particular context. Students are motivated by pursuing their interests with customized guidance from the teacher. This approach also emphasizes working with others, problem solving, taking initiative, and making decisions. In project-based learning, the role of the teacher is multifaceted. For example, there are times when the teacher provides explicit information, models skills, and coordinates whole-group activities and share-outs. At other times, the teacher might guide, coach, provide resources, and co-learn with students. For example, all students may work in groups of four to create a narrative about an "ordinary life" at a specified time in history. After dividing research responsibilities, students can come together to integrate all of the information into a PowerPoint presentation using historical documents to support their tale. In U.S. History, for example, the entire class might consider "ordinary lives" from various eras: a pre-Columbian Indigenous person, a sailor on Columbus's voyages, a female Puritan, an African fisherman enslaved in America, a revolutionary, a plantation owner, an immigrant during the Industrial Revolution, a woman heading West in a wagon train, and so on. Using this approach, students investigate, discuss, create, narrate, and debate life at various times in the U.S.

Using Multiple Intelligences

In Chapter 5, we outlined the benefits of teaching students using a multiple intelligences approach. Similarly, we can draw upon the same approach for assessment. Traditional testing methods unquestionably favor students proficient in linguistic and mathematical skills. Using a multiple intelligences approach validates the efforts and abilities of students

Criterion	1	2	3	4
Group collaboration	Group skills are still in beginning stages, need development.	Group worked well together for part of the time.	Group worked well together.	Group exhibited many supportive skills; excellent rapport.
Making predictions	Predictions rarely accurate, and not based on information provided.	Fairly accurate predictions some of the time, partially based on information provided.	Accurate predictions clearly based on information provided.	Highly accurate predictions based on information provided.
Ongoing observation of plant growth	Discussions and illustrations reflected little accurate observations of plant growth.	Discussions and illustrations reflected some accurate observations of plant growth.	Discussions and illustrations reflected accurate observation of plant growth.	Highly developed discussions and illustrations reflected accurate observations of plant growth.
Charting skills	Graph was largely unclear, difficult to read, and contained many inaccuracies.	Graph was partially clear, was fairly easy to read, and contained some inaccuracies.	Graph was clear, easy to read, and accurate.	Graph was exceptionally clear, well-organized, and accurate.
Conclusion	Group conclusion was mainly inaccurate, with little or no connection to data gathered.	Group conclusion was partially accurate based upon data gathered; in need of further development.	Group conclusion was accurate based upon data gathered.	Group conclusion involved theorizing about data collected, drawing inferences, and making speculations.

Total points:

Specific feedback and pointers for next time:

Figure 7.2 Group rubric for seeds/plants project

who do not excel or who struggle in these areas. In many ways, multiple intelligence theory is linked to authentic assessment, as students have input into what they would like to produce and, in terms of abilities, have the opportunity to "play to their strengths." Once teachers know their students' individual learning profiles, they can provide a variety of ways in which to assess learning: create posters (visual/spatial); self-evaluate and monitor performance (intrapersonal); do a group presentation (interpersonal); take oral exams (linguistic); solve real-life logic problems (math); write and perform a dramatization (body/kinesthetic); rewrite lyrics to a song (musical); describe an endangered animal in depth and outline steps to protect it (naturalist). As you see, most of these examples overlap in their use of more than one intelligence, and they provide innovative ways to assess student work.

Dynamic Assessment

This approach entails: (1) analyzing the principles of the task at hand (and having students perform the task to gauge current levels; (2) teaching students the principles of the task through highly interactive instruction in which students are able to discuss and question what they are learning; and (3) asking students to perform the original task again. Using this three-step model, teachers are able to see student strengths and weaknesses. Instruction can then be tailored to specific needs as the teacher talks to students while they work, asks them questions about their work, and encourages them to ask questions. Within these interactions, teachers ascertain what students are learning, what questions they have, how much time they need, and on what levels they are currently functioning. Ultimately, the goal is to move students to the next level of development. After instruction, a re-test is given to reveal what has been learned and what might still require attention.

Rubrics

Rubrics are helpful devices often used in conjunction with authentic assessment, performance-based assessment, and project-based learning. In brief, a rubric is a grid-like graphic organizer used to assess the level of student performance or progress by evaluating elements within a specific task. For example, a rubric for creating a travel poster to a destination studied in history class might assess the following: design of main image, graphics, use of color, slogan quality, and overall attractiveness. In each of these areas, students may score (4) exemplary, (3) standard, (2) approaching standard, or (1) substandard. Figure 7.2 shows a rubric for assessing a group project on seeds and plants, and Figure 7.3 is a rubric evaluating students' composition of an original scene to add to *Romeo and Juliet*.

By grading each element on a scale of 1–4, students receive specific, honed feedback that informs them (and the teacher) of areas of strength as well as areas of weakness. Rubrics are useful in that they provide students with clear expectations of what a final product should look like. There are many rubrics already available, developed by teachers all over the country (for example, see www.Rubrics4teachers.com), and teachers can develop their own rubrics online (see, for example, www.rubistar.com). However, one of the most effective uses of rubrics is to co-construct them with students. It is also worth noting that some teachers use rubric-type lists that students use to check their work for completeness, accuracy, and quality.

Scene choice — clearly states scene placement — introduces any new characters — good scene choice	__/10
Scene addition format — written in proper play format — stage directions used	__/10
Scene addition content — proper characterization of characters — appropriate topic — adds insight into the play/characters — understandable storyline and dialogue — creative plot	__/45
Conclusion — how this additional scene would affect the play — why this additional scene was chosen	__/10
Follows project requirements — typed or neatly written in blue/black pen — double-spaced — 3 pages solo or 4 pages with partner	__/10
Spelling/grammar	__/15
Extra credit — acting — Shakespearean language — illustration	
Total	__/100

Figure 7.3 Rubric for *Romeo and Juliet* scene project

Logs and Journals

Student logs and journals provide another opportunity to assess students "in the moment," at the end of the lesson, or over time. These can be used across any grades and content areas and give a teacher lots of options for finding out what students think. For example, logs can be used at the start of a lesson ("Describe three things you find interesting about sharks"), during a lesson ("Write down three new pieces of information about sharks that we've learned so far today"), or to close a lesson ("State why a shark cannot stay still and must always swim," plus "Write a question about sharks that you'd like to pose to your classmates"). Teachers can circulate around the room to read student responses and "check the pulse" of what is being learned. Logs and journals can be highly-structured, semi-structured, or open-ended. A highly-structured journal entry, for example, may read as follows:

1. What are coordinates?
2. Describe an example of when they are used in the "real world."
3. What do you find easy about using coordinates?
4. What do you find tricky?
5. Create a short word problem using coordinates.

A semi-structured response might be, "What I've learned about coordinates is...." An unstructured form of journal writing is a "free write" in which students can write about whatever they choose. For example, the teacher could say, "Write down something that you find interesting about coordinates."

Curriculum-Based Measurement

Teachers use this method to find out how students are progressing in core academic areas such as reading, writing, and math. Curriculum-based assessment allows for quick, measurable feedback that can be plotted on a graph. Typically, tests are very brief (a minute or so) and might consist of words to spell in writing and/or orally, a sample of multisyllabic words to read phonetically, or math problems to solve. The brevity of the assessment allows the teacher to rapidly tabulate the number of correct and incorrect responses. Such an assessment has multiple purposes, including giving information about the degree to which the student is learning skills and content; providing a comparison with other students in class; and producing data to use in differentiating instruction.

Error Analysis

Error analysis can be used in any type of assessment. Simply put, teachers analyze students' work with an eye toward looking for patterns of errors, problem areas, undeveloped skills, and ways of approaching the task itself. This approach is concerned with pervasive errors in rule use—not random or careless errors. Once a teacher has ascertained problem areas, several are prioritized (perhaps one to three), and instruction is customized to support the student's needs. Teachers can keep track of student error patterns (along with strengths) in their own records, and explicitly discuss with students the areas being targeted for instruction. Error analysis can be used with students too, including peer feedback, in which fellow class members review each other's work by following specific steps and guidance provided by the teacher. Finally, students can study their own graded quizzes and tests to self-analyze the number and types of errors and to strategize how to avoid repeating the same errors.

"Teacher-Friendly" Assessments/Games

Effective teachers often customize ideas they have read about or seen in other people's classrooms. In addition, many make their own materials, ranging from simple to complex. The following are a few examples from our own experiences and ideas from specific texts containing a wealth of strategies (Kagan & Kagan, 2001; Reif & Heimburge, 1996; Udvari-Solner & Kluth, 2008).

1. *A to Z*: At the end of a unit, students can be given a list (or graphic organizer) with all of the letters of the alphabet in order. Using each letter, students are asked to write associations from the unit taught. For example, when studying the U.S. Civil War, A is for artillery, B is for bayonets, C is for cavalry, D is for dysentery, etc. Note (ironically) that it is *not* a good strategy to think alphabetically as this can take time and cause mental blocks. Rather, it is better to recall as much information as possible, and then put it in the correct place. For instance, a student may recall words/concepts such as retreat, infantry, bombard, Vicksburg, and so on. This method allows students to recollect and reconnect with information, almost as if each part were a piece of a jigsaw. Together, all of the associations help to create a rich picture of student understanding.

2. *Switch*: Students work in partnerships and sit next to, or opposite, each other. When given the signal to start, Partner A begins to tell Partner B as many things as possible that he or she recalls about a topic (tornadoes, polygons, Ancient Greece, war poets, etc.). When the teacher says "Switch," Partner B becomes the speaker and Partner A the listener. Roles may be rotated several times. Depending upon the number of topics reviewed, learning styles, and other factors, students can change partners (to work with "new" students) after each topic has been reviewed.

3. *Matching games/Go Fish*: Teachers create games in which partners try to match concepts learned. For example, 20 cards are placed face down. The partners take turns turning over two cards to find a match. Ideas for cards can be drawn from any instructional area, such as words that begin with the same letter blends (br, bl, fl, fr, and gr); vocabulary words and their definitions; synonyms; antonyms; capital cities and countries; math equations and answers; and so on.

4. *Send a question*: Every student puts his or her name on a piece of paper and folds it in half. In the top half, each student writes a question about something recently discussed in class. The teacher then collects the papers in a bag (or a pile that will be shuffled) and distributes a question to each student that he or she must answer. Each response is then returned to the person who posed the original question. A large class share-out of sample questions and responses can follow. All questions and responses can be posted on a bulletin board for review.

5. *Board games*: With the throw of a dice, what could be an uninteresting, dull, or dreary review is transformed into a challenging competition. Using various generic board game formats in which a student/player can move from one to six spaces (a "board' can be made inexpensively by using a flattened manila folder), students roll dice, draw a question (written on an index card), and give an answer or perform a task before moving forward on the board (e.g., What is the capital of Turkey? What is 5 x 7? Name a four-sided polygon. List three words that include the digraph "ph." Give a sentence using the word "terrified"). Another idea is to ask students to create their own board games about a unit under study. Students can exchange games to play for review. Each game can also be considered as an assessment product.

6. *Vocabulary games*: The explicit teaching of content vocabulary is an oft-neglected aspect of instruction. In order to help students remember vocabulary, teachers need to make explicit the connections among ideas and ask students to use specific ("targeted") words regularly. Try creating card games in which students focus on six to eight words clustered around a central concept, such as transportation, photosynthesis, angles, or commerce. A pack of index cards may feature prompts related to targeted words, such as the following: define the word; give examples of the concept; complete sentences using the targeted word; provide synonyms and antonyms; and identify visual representations. Have students play in groups of three to five to review a small number of words intensely (see Box 7.1).

7. *Top 5/Top 10*: Students work alone, in pairs, or in groups to generate a list of the most important items that reflect recent learning within a content area. The list may be open-ended, such as "The 10 things I learned about the American Civil War" or specific, such as "Five polygons and their features."

8. *Numbered heads together*: In this cooperative learning strategy, the teacher divides students into cooperative groups, giving each group a number. In addition, every student in the group is given a number. A question is posed to the whole class, and then each group discusses possible answers. Once students have had the opportunity to debate, discuss, and reach consensus on an answer, the teacher calls on a

student at random (e.g., "Group 3, student number 4"). This approach helps students review by helping one another and encourages responsibility for group assessment/ performance.

9. *Gallery walk*: While we have discussed a gallery walk to help students process information, it can also be used for purposes of evaluation. Students circulate among documents, writing responses on a worksheet prepared by the teacher or on chart paper that frames the documents (writing their initials next to their comments). In the first instance, the teacher discovers what each student knows and thinks; in the second instance, the teacher can get a "ballpark" idea of students and the class as a whole. In all of these examples, the teacher circulates among students and groups, observing formally (collecting data) or informally (personal noticing), depending on the purpose of assessment.

Box 7.1 Vocabulary Game

The Vocabulary Game©, invented by Kate Garnett of Hunter College, is a low-budget, highly effective way to engage students in practicing the identification and use of vocabulary. With appropriate modifications, it can be used in any content area and at any grade level. The premise is simple: students need time, practice, and reinforcement to learn content-based vocabulary; teachers must select a core concept and a cluster of related vocabulary known as "target" words. Teachers create the pack of cards (index cards are perfect for this), and must demonstrate how to play the game.

1. Contents of a Vocabulary Game pack
   Target cards: Two sets of 6–10 cards (standing out in some way—different color, boxed, etc.). One set is laid face up, the other is dealt to players in a shuffled deck. Each pack should contain 6–10 different target cards.
   Target family cards: A set of cards for each target card, focused on pointing to its meaning. There should be 4–8 example cards for each target family. Target families need to consist of different numbers (to prevent ties when the game is over). Target families can include, when appropriate, illustration cards, example cards, definition cards, synonym cards, antonym cards, etc.

2. How to play
   The objective is to connect and build target word families.
   • Deal out (or lay face up) one of the two sets of target cards. The other is shuffled into the deck.
   • Play round robin, clockwise. Each player picks one card at a time from the pile and must read it out loud so that the other players can hear the words clearly: "The lines on a globe or map that run east to west." Everything must be "out loud" as repeated retrieval and verbal rehearsal are key elements of the game and learning process.
   • If a student's answer is correct, he or she is allowed to take that particular pile. Hence, the game can shift dramatically in one round, as each pile can be won with the correct answer of any question.
   • The winner has the greatest number of cards. Count cards, not piles (counting piles causes too many ties).

Additional options

- For greater structure, use a mat for each player with target words already on it.
- On the back of the mat, list all cards and sentences/clues—in case of dispute.

3. How to make "good" example cards
    - Focus on the word's meaning; almost no other word should fit.
    - Point to the meaning (teach, don't test). Don't be obscure or tricky.
    - Make sentences memorable, so they will "stick." Use references that are personal, emotional, humorous, colloquial, etc.
    - Examples can be in the form of sentences with blanks, e.g., "The _____ of the rose are often bright red." Or use "I", e.g., "I am the part of the rose that is bright red."
    - Keep parts of speech consistent, e.g., "to dream" or "a dream," but not both.
    - Add needed morphological markers (e.g., -ed, -ing, -s) on the sentence cards with blanks, e.g., "The dog walk_ alone down the street."
    - For *illustration* cards—use cut-outs, drawings, clip art, students' artwork. Have an arrow point exactly to the appropriate part, e.g., petal.
    - For *definition* cards—be careful with dictionary definitions. Make your own definition that is helpful.
    - For *synonym* cards—use only when appropriate. Label the word "same as." Do not use words that are more difficult than the target word.
    - For *antonym* cards—use only when appropriate. Label the word "opposite of." Do not use words that are more difficult than the target word.

Example 1

- Big concept: Maps (Grade 2: Social Studies)
- Target words: legend, longitude, latitude, hemisphere, climate, scale
    1. *Legend*
        - Picture of legend
        - Synonym: key
        - What is a legend?
        - The key on a map that explains what symbols stand for.
        - Example: picture of trees = forest
        - To find the symbol that represents a school, look at the _____.
        - To find out what a symbol stands for, you would use the _____.
    2. *Longitude*
        - The lines on a globe or map that run North to South.
        - Define longitude.
        - Picture of a globe with lines of longitude
        - Example: The prime meridian runs along these lines.
        - Antonym: latitude
        - 45 degrees East is an example of a line of _____.
    3. *Latitude*
        - The lines on a globe or map that run East to West.
        - Example: The equator runs along these lines.
        - Define latitude.

- Picture of a globe with lines of latitude.
- Antonym: longitude
- 45 degrees North is an example of a line of _____.
- 55 degrees South is an example of a line of _____.
- The lines of _____ run from East to West.

4. *Hemisphere*
   - Define hemisphere.
   - An area of the world; section of the globe.
   - Example: Eastern and Western.
   - Picture of a globe divided into Northern and Southern hemispheres.
   - The United States is located in the Western _____.
   - New Zealand is located in the Southern _____.

5. *Climate*
   - Define climate.
   - Example: tropical
   - The weather/temperature of an area of the world.
   - Rainy and wet would describe the _____ of an area.

6. *Scale*
   - A map feature that allows us to measure the distance from place to place.
   - A picture of a scale.
   - Define scale.
   - If you wanted to find the distance from New York to Boston, you would use the _____.
   - To find the number of miles from Los Angeles to Denver, you would use the _____.
   - According to the _____, 1 inch may equal 100 miles.

Source: Kristin Fallon, New York City.

Example 2

- Big concept: Birds (Grade 3: Science)
- Target words: beak, nest, feathers, migration, ornithologist, hatch, preening, wings
  1. *Beak*
     - The hard, sometimes pointed part of a bird's mouth.
     - A hummingbird uses its long _____ to get inside a flower and slurp nectar.
     - Toucans have a very long, thick, and brightly colored _____ that helps them pluck fruit from a tree.
     - These birds all have _____ (s) that help them eat the food they love.
     - What is a beak?
     - The _____ of a bird can be used for eating and drinking, as well as for collecting nesting materials, preening, feeding its babies, and attacking enemies.
  2. *Nest*
     - The home that birds build in order to lay eggs and raise their babies.
     - Sometimes the male and the female work together to build their _____.
     - What is a nest?

- The _____ of a peregrine falcon is usually built on the edge of a rocky cliff.
- Some birds use yarn, dried weeds, hair, and grass clippings to build their _____.
- Adult birds must stay close to their _____ in order to protect their eggs and/or babies.
- I saw four little blue eggs in a _____.

3. *Feathers*
   - A light soft part that covers a bird's body.
   - All birds grow _____ which makes them different from all other animals.
   - _____ help birds fly and also protect their skin.
   - The _____ of a parrot can be very colorful.
   - What are feathers?
   - While walking in Crotona Park I found a blue and black striped _____. It came from a blue jay.

4. *Migration*
   - When birds fly to a new location in the spring and in the fall, usually to get away from the cold winter.
   - The Arctic tern's _____, from Northern Maine to the South Pole, is nearly 10,000 miles altogether.
   - What is migration?
   - Birds use the sun to help them find their way during _____.
   - My dad and I bring our binoculars to the beach in the fall so we can see rare birds during their _____.
   - Birds know that it is time for _____ when the days become shorter in the fall or longer in the spring.

5. *Ornithologist*
   - A scientist who studies birds.
   - The _____ gave a special bird tour for people to learn more about the birds in their parks.
   - What is an ornithologist?
   - I love birds so much; I want to know all about them! I want to be an _____.
   - The _____ was studying the different songs of warblers.
   - I was acting like an _____ when I studied the habits of starlings in my neighborhood.

6. *Hatch*
   - When an egg opens and a baby comes out.
   - The mother robin sits on her nest and waits for her eggs to _____.
   - It takes about two weeks for a robin's eggs to _____.
   - What does "to hatch" mean?
   - When we visited the farm we watched the chickens' eggs _____. The chicks were so small.
   - When goose eggs _____, the babies are called goslings.

7. *Preening*
   - When birds pick at their feathers, pulling them, nibbling them, and fluffing them up, this is called _____.
   - When birds clean their feathers, it is called _____.

- Many birds spread oil on their feathers when they are _____. This helps the feathers to stay water-repellent in bad weather.
- Tejuan's parakeet was _____ its feathers by picking at them and fluffing them up.
- I saw a duck _____ its feathers on the side of the pond.
- What is preening?

8. *Wings*
   - The parts of the bird's body that are mostly used for flying.
   - A bird's _____ are similar to our arms.
   - Penguins have _____ but they use them for swimming instead of flying.
   - The _____ of an albatross can be 12 feet across!
   - A hummingbird flaps its _____ so fast that you cannot see them.
   - What do you call these? (picture)

Source: Jody Buckles, New York City.

Teacher-Made Tests

At first, new teachers may take a lot of time creating their own tests. All tests should have clear directions and be readable and uncluttered. Children should not think they are being tricked into giving the wrong answer, but rather should be given a fair chance to share what they know and can do. Preparation and/or practice in class in advance of a test sets the stage for students' feeling confident about the test format and content. The following is a list of fairly common formats for in-class teacher tests, along with some pros and cons:

1. *True/false*: Creating a series of statements and having students choose true or false is a quick way to assess. While seemingly simple, the true/false format may be confusing for some students if the teacher introduces a degree of ambivalence ("Sometimes a rattlesnake may..."), or if the question is long, is awkwardly phrased, or contains contradictory information ("Rattlesnakes that live in Arizona often come out at night near towns and go into garbage containers, but they are not always dangerous").

2. *Matching items*: Another relatively quick way to assess students is to present two columns of information and ask students to make connections between items in each column. Connections might be definitions ("Arizona" and "Southwestern state"), examples ("reptile" and "rattlesnake"), or attributions ("cold-blooded" and "reptiles"). Students either draw a line to connect the items or list a number in the first column with a corresponding letter from the second column. To make the task manageable for students, no more than seven to ten pairings should be listed.

3. *Cloze*: A cloze test is a text with key words or phrases missing. For example, a paragraph about content studies could be given with several items represented by.... A word bank is provided at the top of the page or beside the paragraph (if there are numerous words in the word bank). Students must insert the word they think best "fits" in the blank.

4. *Multiple choice*: Multiple-choice questions are a staple of the current educational landscape. Unsurprisingly, some teachers (and surprisingly, some students) love them; others dislike them immensely. While time-efficient in terms of grading, multiple-choice questions do not allow for depth or complexity of response, and they give the wrong impression that all knowledge is organized in bite-size information and exists free from context. If multiple-choice tests are to be used, teachers should generate

short, clear questions and provide three or four potential answers of roughly equal length. In addition, they should avoid double negatives ("Select which is not the least valuable…") and combinations ("a and b," "b and c," "a and c," or "all of the above").

5. *Short answer*: Responding to questions in short answers allays student fears of writing at length. Short-answer responses also give students the opportunity to show what they know in a focused way, using their own words. Short answers range from a sentence or two to a paragraph or two. Although demanding in terms of time, this format allows the teacher to see a student's personalized connections and ability to express targeted content knowledge in writing.

6. *Essay*: As grade levels increase, so does the expected amount of writing. Essays are typical in many, if not most, content areas. A good essay requires planning and organization, so time should be built in for this purpose. Many students benefit from frequent essay-writing practice, including how to analyze questions, brainstorm ideas, use a graphic organizer to plot ideas, create a strong introduction, provide topic/supporting/concluding sentences and transitions within paragraphs, and effectively conclude. Essay writing does not have to occur in "test" conditions, but can be approached in a variety of ways, using other methodologies such as peer editing, rubrics for essay writing, and inclusion in a portfolio.

7. *Drawing and illustrating*: Drawing is used a lot in the early grades to show what students know and understand, whether it involves personal experiences (e.g., family, friends, pets, homes, parks) or content learned (e.g., boats, planes, flags, seasons). We argue that drawing can be part of assessment at all grade levels. Students can be asked to draw, sketch, illustrate, and label whatever they are studying: a Shakespearean stage, the best use of farmland, a storyboard for an original narrative, or aspects of public safety. For many students, drawing helps them to better conceptualize, organize, and communicate knowledge. This can be said for all content areas, mathematics in particular.

8. *Mixed formats*: In order to accommodate different learning styles and encompass all levels of learning, any of the foregoing suggestions can be combined in a test. For example, an end-of-unit exam could contain five true-or-false questions, five mix-and-match, some cloze responses, a short-answer section, a drawing, and a short essay. Students can be encouraged to begin the test in any order, thus encouraging them to first "access" the test according to their strengths.

9. *Co-constructed tests*: Student apprehension is lessened when they work with the teacher to input what is "on the test." Working in groups, students can analyze lists, lecture notes, or familiar topics to generate "teacher-like" questions. These can be shared with the whole class and used as is or reshaped by the teacher with necessary modifications. Students can also engage in some decision making about the format of the test. These collaborative approaches positively influence student motivation to study for and take tests.

In sum, these are a selection of some common ways in which to use teacher-made assessments in the classroom. If you recall Bloom's taxonomy, each one of these options falls upon the continuum between lower- and higher-order thinking skills. For example, true/false, cloze, and multiple-choice items tend to require less recall because more matching information is provided, offering few opportunities for original or creative thinking. On the other hand, written answers of various lengths, drawings with explanations, and essays that require problem solving encourage original, higher-order thinking. It is important to note that each option has a place, but we must always caution against the traditional overuse of tasks that involve lower-order thinking.

Some Issues Raised by Standardized Testing

The emphasis on standardized testing in recent years has raised many issues of concern for students with and without disabilities. In previous decades, assessment policies did not include students with disabilities (Hehir, 2005). However, since the passage of federal legislation (No Child Left Behind [NCLB], 2001), students with disabilities have been "counted" in local, regional, state, and federal data. Although this change has given access to a more rigorous academic education for many students, it has also resulted in some problems. One of the major difficulties for students with disabilities is the increased emphasis on standardized "high-stakes" tests that, beginning in elementary school, occur at different grade levels for various content areas. Under the drive for increased accountability for student performance, NCLB mandated that schools conduct yearly statewide assessments in reading and mathematics from third to eighth grade. In addition, fourth- and eighth-graders must take national assessments in reading and mathematics under the National Assessment of Educational Progress (NAEP). States are also required to establish standards and gauge student progress in science and history. Student scores are tabulated and published publicly in the form of a school report card. If annual yearly progress (AYP)—largely determined by test scores—is not achieved over a consecutive two-year period, the school is determined to be "in need of improvement," and students may transfer to higher-performing schools. After the third year of not making adequate progress, a school must use 20 percent of its Title I[1] federal monies to provide supplemental educational services.

Norm-Referenced Testing

Many standardized examinations are norm referenced, meaning that the performance of an individual student is compared to the performance of all other students. Grade levels are "normed" according to expectations of what is deemed "normal" for students of the same age. Of course, norms are constructed by the society in which we live, and they change considerably over time to match the demands of society. Norm-referenced tests rank students according to who did better and worse than them. It is worth noting that norm-referenced tests are constructed in such a way that a certain percentage of students are required to fail.

Criterion-Referenced Testing

As its name suggests, this type of assessment uses specified criteria to determine what a student has and has not learned. Most teacher-made tests are criterion based, but some criterion-based examinations are also high-stakes tests. For example, high-stakes content-specific tests include exit examinations in high school, as well as professional examinations, such as state tests required for teacher certification.

Dilemmas: Issues, Tensions, Contradictions, Paradoxes, and Choices

No Child Left Behind (NCLB) was a controversial law that garnered critiques from a variety of sources, including disability rights advocates (Bejoian & Reid, 2005). Standardized examinations (the same test, the same way, the same time) can be counterproductive for learners who have needs not covered under legal accommodations. In a testing culture, teachers often gravitate toward the middle of the class in order to "teach to the test." (A brief digression of note: each state self-governs its standardized testing, making it possible for any state to construct easier tests to enhance scores.) Given the diversity of learners in any classroom, the narrowing down of methods to teach a highly prescribed curriculum inhibits creative, dynamic teaching.

Most importantly, aspects of NCLB appeared to clash with tenets of the Individuals with Disabilities Education Improvement Act of 2004. For example, students who failed to meet the relatively new criteria for promotion established by many local educational authorities were "held back" a grade level, even though research consistently shows that retaining students increases their likelihood of dropping out before completing high school (Jimerson, Ferguson, Whipple, Anderson, & Dalton, 2002).[2] The requirements of NCLB created a labyrinth-like system that was confusing for parents and teachers. For example, on state examinations in New York, students are classified on a continuum of 4 (high) through 1 (low). The following information appeared on the New York City Department of Education website[3]:

> **General Education Students.** Students in grades 3, 5, and 7 will be promoted in June, if they score Level 2 or higher on both the State English Language Arts (ELA) and Mathematics tests this year. For all students who score Level 1 on either the ELA or Math test (or both), an appeal process provides for an automatic, mandatory review of student work.
>
> **Special Education Students.** Students with "standard promotion criteria" listed on page 9 of their Individualized Education Plan (IEP) are subject to the third-, fifth-, and seventh-grade promotion criteria above. Students with "modified promotion criteria" on their IEP will be promoted on the basis of those modified criteria.

Criteria vary according to each grade. For example, for fourth-, sixth-, and eighth-graders, the following information applies[4]:

> In deciding whether students in this age group should be promoted, a school must look at three criteria: whether, in the teacher's view, the student meets the standards for his grade; whether the student passes state tests in math and language arts; and whether the student had an attendance rate of at least 90 percent during the school year—in other words, did not miss more than 18 days of school. For an 8th grader who hopes to go on to high school, there is an additional consideration: whether he has passed classes in the major subject areas—English, math, social studies, and science.
>
> If a child falls short on at least two criteria, he should be held over. All students who receive hold over letters, however, are supposed to be given a second chance and attend summer school. A student should not be held over if he fails to meet only one of the criteria.

Students with disabilities (particularly, by definition, those with learning disabilities) often significantly underperform on standardized assessments, thus placing them at greater risk of being held back despite their documented disability. While there is a clause in the IEP indicating either "modified promotion criteria" or "standard promotion criteria," many parents and teachers are confused and/or positioned on either side of the issue.

Another unanticipated, rarely articulated, but fairly obvious "side effect" of high stakes testing is that many principals do not want low-scoring students, many of whom are students with disabilities, in their schools. Unfortunately, the reason for their undesirability is tied directly to the principal's job security. If scores go down or do not improve, the principal can be removed. In many respects, it has been suggested that low-performing students are being slowly pushed out of schools long before twelfth-grade exit examinations, particularly if they are students of color, and/or English Language Learners, and/or from a lower socioeconomic background.[5]

The curriculum itself has suffered, as requirements for robust instruction in math and English (and arguably, science) now eclipse the provision of a balanced education including social studies, art, music, second languages, and physical education. These content areas often provide a counterbalance to the "set" curriculum, encouraging creativity, individual connections, and personal growth for all students, but especially for those who may not excel in English and math. The "one size fits all" approach of standardized curricula and testing is a direct challenge to the human variation inherent among all students, but particularly to those who have been labeled disabled. Indeed, the "individualized" component of the IEP is under constant strain, as the expectations and demands of the state may be in direct conflict with the ways in which a student best learns and demonstrates knowledge. Recent changes in regulations indicate that a very small number of students with severe disabilities, approximately 1 percent, are entitled to alternative assessments.

Legal Testing Accommodations for Students with Disabilities

Although students with disabilities are required to participate in standardized testing, they may also be eligible for testing accommodations. Any accommodations must be documented with a student's IEP or 504 Plan. In order to obtain accommodations, the strengths and weaknesses of a student are considered by an IEP or 504 team. The core group, consisting of the parent(s), the student, teachers, the school psychologist, and a social worker (subject to local policies and the availability of personnel), must reach consensus. Testing accommodations and modifications should not "automatically" be matched with a disability, as each student should be considered as an individual. Some common testing accommodations include extended time, alternative location, having a test reader, having a large-print or Braille version of the test, twice-read instructions, and the use of sound amplifiers. In addition to having these accommodations on standardized tests, students are also entitled to such accommodations for all in-class testing situations. Modifications may include a change in the constructs within the test, such as using a calculator in an assessment on computation or having a scribe to assist with a written assessment.

Featured Voice of Diane Berman

The Impact of High Stakes Testing for One Family

Changing States of Mind

Some think that residing in a good school district will guarantee an optimal education for their child. That may be true for the child who is wired to learn like we expect, but it is far from the case for those of us with kids who learn in their own unique ways. When looked at through the narrow perspective of common society, these students appear to be children who cannot or will not learn. Each school district has its own philosophy as to how to educate these children. This philosophy has overt as well as subtle ramifications. The differences, as they ripple through time, can have huge consequences for the lives of these students. My husband and I have relocated twice to optimize our son's education. Our son Benny has changed schools four times as we searched for the right fit at the right time. We have had great success in this way, but for most families this type of movement is not feasible. I will describe here what we were looking for in the hopes that someone may hear how simple and rewarding it was to educate Benny. As an educator with 28 years of experience, I know that all that we searched for could have been found in one place. Despite scary disability-related labels, the most important ingredients for his success were opportunity and attitude. Those can be found anywhere.

Benny displayed delays from birth. He failed to suck well, roll over, walk or talk on time. He refused to string beads or stack cups on command. He was labeled over and over for the first few years of his life. He was segregated in school, placed in a class for kids with developmental disabilities, and even there he failed to function. My son flunked out of two special education kindergarten classrooms in a top district in New York City. Teachers threatened to accuse my husband and me of neglect when we refused to allow placement, in their city-wide district exclusively for children with disabilities, into a class of six kids with multiple and severe disabilities.

Instead, after a lot of research, we relocated to a nearby suburb, also a top-performing district, into the arms of a wacky and wonderful principal who literally promised me on bended knee to include Benny. That elementary school was incredible. Benny proved to everyone that he could learn. Little by little, his devastating delays in speech and social skills began to melt away, and his talents emerged. Why? He made friends. Benny's friends gave him motivation to speak. He learned to read and write and academic doors began to open for him. David Connor and I sought to capture exactly what happened there, and describe one school's successful approach to inclusive education, eventually writing a book titled, *A Child, a Family, a School, a Community: A Tale of Inclusive Education* (2017). After all, once Benny was given access to the general education curriculum, he showed us all that he could learn. Although Benny still needed academic supports for his slow processing speed, focusing challenges, and speech delay, creative teachers found ways to keep him engaged and to help him connect to peers.

When middle school came along the pressure of the mandated New York State Regents Examinations began to permeate the classes. Differentiated projects fell to the wayside and were replaced by lengthy packets designed to groom the students for the 40-page tests that lay in wait at the end of the year. Benny surprised us by passing Algebra and Geometry the first time, but not by much. To achieve this feat, he had to fill in all electives and even lunch with special classes designed to help him pass these tests. He failed Earth Science twice, despite having a fondness for and inclination to science. Even though he was basically happy and by all measures functioning well in school, alarm bells began to sound again in my head. I felt he needed a chance to find his interests and academic strengths and I knew that was impossible in a system governed by tests as linear and rigid as the Regents Examinations. While his teachers appreciated him, I felt they were consistently underestimating his abilities. On his Transition Plan/IEP, when Benny told them he wanted to drive a bus, they questioned his ability to focus enough for that job, measuring his ability to focus by his behavior in classes where he was being trained to take a test he did not care about. Meanwhile, their work was focused mainly on preparing him to pass the Regents Examinations. Despite my gut feeling that in the end he could earn a coveted Regents Diploma, I wanted more for him.

I wanted a chance for him to soar. I wanted him to be able to take electives in Music, Art, and Technology. As an educator I knew that high school provided possibly one last chance to experiment and discover skills and interests. I wanted Benny to really find some areas in which he excelled. I knew they existed. I wanted him to strive for more than passing Regents Examinations. It may seem absurd to some people that a family will relocate for these reasons, but having seen the impact of a school on Benny once before, I was ready to try again. While deeply grateful to the district that included him and pushed him to reach the level of his peers, we now needed some more flexibility. I therefore applied for a series of jobs as a math teacher and crossed out ones in states that had state-dictated mandated exams as a requirement for graduation. In the end I accepted a position at a career and tech center, where I would have more freedom as well. My school is in Vermont, and I chose it because I felt both of my children would benefit from a more creative approach in their education. I was also eager to teach in a system that let me spread my wings.

Vermont has adopted proficiency-based grading. This is a system that naturally sets the tone for differentiated instruction for all students in every subject. This differentiation is a fact of life for all students, not just the ones who present with a disability. We placed Benny in tenth grade in a local high school and once again he made spectacular progress. Without the pressure of these tests, Benny found he had ability in Science and Math. Because he was not continually pulled to special classes he was able to take electives in Music and Technology. Benny made more friends in his first year in Vermont than in all the other years combined. For the very first time in his life he was invited out to lunch a few times with a group of friends. As nice as the children were to him in New York, he was never included beyond the school walls. I wonder if part of it had to do with the fact that, even while included, he was separated by virtue of having to have so many extra classes. In the last year he even had to give up lunch. It is in those times when kids are taking elective classes that bonds form. I was so grateful that Benny had access to the regular curriculum in New York that I failed to recognize the subtle ways in which he was excluded from the other equally important arenas for exploration and connection. Currently, we have only completed one year and, as a parent, I still worry about the future. I hope Benny can sustain his success and find a field in which he can excel. I think we are closer now to those goals than we have ever been.

We received a letter a week ago saying that Benny was going to get an award at the school's awards night. This was not new to us. Benny always won some award, but always the award for trying his best or showing most improvement. We relish those beyond measure. This night turned out to be different, though. This time Benny was called for the "Scientific Thinker Award for Outstanding Academic Accomplishment in Chemistry." Without the looming Regents, Benny had chances to show his abilities by doing labs and by creating projects. It was nice for once to see him celebrated for more than the tremendous effort he has learned to put forth, but also for the results of those efforts.

Now, Benny has a new-found confidence in himself and has begun, as he says, to "dig deeper" than his standby career of bus driver. He now wants to explore college. He is going to a one-week program at a local tech college this summer exploring the math and science behind transportation careers. By taking off the considerable edge of academic pressure related to conforming to rigorous tests, we have given him the freedom to find his strength. I wonder what would have happened had we moved to Vermont to begin with? Would they have held him to the high standards he was held to in New York? Or would he have been included, as is the norm, but held to a lower standard? Did we need this particular combination of academic experiences to maximize his abilities? Is it possible to create a school that can do both at the same time, that is, keep academic standards sky high and be flexible enough to allow a student to find themselves in the process? I'd like to think so.

Flexible Teaching and Assessment Practices

Throughout this chapter, we have described various ways in which to assess students. Even so, we would like to spend a little time emphasizing the need for teachers to be flexible in their approach. All suggestions in this chapter can be changed, adapted, modified, and customized (call it what you will—you get the picture) to support students in demonstrating what they can do. For educators who may find themselves scratching their heads when students hit a "roadblock" in their learning, Levine and Reed (1999) offer three broad and useful suggestions in the form of questions the teacher might ask herself:

1. How might you modify the rate, volume, or complexity of the assignment given? In considering rate, for example, how might you adapt time? Could you allow a student to finish the task for homework?
2. In contemplating volume, how might you increase (or decrease) certain aspects of the work expected? What could be pared down or extended within a student portfolio?
3. In thinking about complexity, how might you break down the multiple steps of an assignment, and provide critical support at the point it is needed? In what ways could you change the task for various students involved, perhaps to fit their learning styles, talents, or interests?

These questions can also be applied to writing assignments, from making lists to generating journal entries. In the teacher-friendly assessments and games, students can also have the opportunity to work with partners or in quads to generate a game of A to Z, or Switch. Matching games can be striated into card packs that are for beginner, proficient, and advanced levels. Note that these designations correspond not to students, but rather to their current level of functioning in relation to the acquisition of specific skills and content area. Likewise, vocabulary games can target the same vocabulary, but with packs containing different clues. Students who have difficulty writing may wish to ask the question orally. Shy students in Numbered Heads Together may wish to exert the option of using a "lifeline" to a friend. During a Gallery Walk, students might be given the option to write a word, phrase, or sentence—so long as they are willing to elaborate or explain their point orally when discussing the content as a class. As you can see, the options are potentially infinite ... and it is the teacher's judgment and flexibility, both in carefully planned instruction and "in the moment," that make students feel they can contribute to their class.

Teaching Responsibly without "Teaching to the Test"

Many educators rise to the challenge of teaching meaningful content and useful skills in creative ways while simultaneously preparing students for standardized tests. Teaching does not occur in a vacuum; it occurs in a climate, and that climate is always political. As educators, we do our best for our students, and that often involves a degree of compromise. Teachers often integrate skills and strategies (such as note-taking) within content area lessons to give students experiences that increase their proficiency and self-confidence. For example, a teacher can provide an outline of his lecture, introduce students to various shorthand symbols, invite a colleague to demonstrate on an overhead how he takes notes, model ways to categorize notes in preparation for a written response, invite students to create graphic maps to organize the lecture information and their own thoughts, and so on. In addition, the teacher can highlight and help students practice content-specific vocabulary, as well as give opportunities for "word attack" skills that improve comprehension

(Beck, McKeowan, & Kucan, 2002; Paynter, Bodrova, & Doty, 2005). In elementary-level literacy-based "progressive reading classes" in which children are immersed in literature (and are not required to participate in rote factual recall), researcher-practitioners begrudgingly concede to the need of giving careful, thoughtful attention to developing wise methods of test preparation. In many respects, progressive teachers may originally see test preparation as the enemy but come to see that it does not have to always resemble tests and that many innovative methodologies can be used, including teaching the test as a genre (Calkins, Montgomery, Santman, & Falk, 1998).

A Case for Multiple Forms of Assessment

In this chapter, we have examined multiple purposes of assessment within the classroom. Teachers are encouraged to be flexible and to contemplate using several forms of assessment to ensure that all students are able to demonstrate their knowledge and skills. Each option enhances the choice of teachers. All forms of assessment have potential value, yet we understand that teachers may have preferences based on different reasons, including how they were assessed, their own learning styles, time considerations, etc. For this reason, when the teacher is working collaboratively with another teacher in the classroom, assessment is one of the many topics that should be discussed in an ongoing manner. In the next chapter, we revisit assessment, along with many other aspects of teaching, within the context of a collaborative classroom.

Questions to Consider

1. What are some of the varied purposes of assessment?
2. Which of the options for ongoing assessment did you experience when in school? When in college?
3. If given the choice of how you are assessed, which methods do you think best represent your abilities? Which methods might obscure them?
4. If you were creating a test in a class, which formats would you consider using and why?
5. How might you use Bloom's taxonomy in different forms of assessment?
6. How might you use Gardner's multiple intelligence theory in different forms of assessment?
7. How might you use the principles of universal design in assessment?
8. What are some of the dilemmas, challenges, and contradictions associated with standardized testing?
9. What are some considerations to bear in mind when creating assessments for students with disability labels?
10. In what ways can you prepare students for standardized examinations without "teaching to the test" in a repetitive manner (that is likely to bore them)?

Notes

1 Title I is a federally-funded program (Special Revenue Grant) designed to provide additional basic skills in language arts and mathematics instruction for low-achieving students in all grades.
2 See http://www.gatesfoundation.org/UnitedStates/Education/ TransforminghighSchools/Related Info/SilentEpidemic.htm.
3 See http://schools.nyc.gov/Accountability/PromotionPolicy/default.htm.
4 See http://www.insideschools.org/st/ST promotion.php.
5 See "Narrating Disability: Pedagogical Imperatives," special issue of *Equity & Excellence in Education, 39*(2).

References

Beck, I., McKeowan, M., & Kucan, L. (2002). *Bringing words to life: Robust vocabulary instruction*. New York, NY: Guilford Press.

Bejoian, L. M. & Reid, D. K. (2005). A disability studies perspective on the Bush education agenda: The No Child Left Behind Act of 2001. *Equity and Excellence in Education, 38*(3), 220–31.

Berman, D. L. & Connor, D. J. (2017). *A child, a family, a school, a community: A tale of inclusive education*. New York, NY: Peter Lang.

Calkins, L., Montgomery, K., Santman, D., & Falk B. (1998). *A teacher's guide to standardized reading tests: Knowledge is power*. Portsmouth, NH: Heinemann.

Hehir, T. (2005). *New directions in special education: Eliminating ableism in policy and practice*. Cambridge, MA: Harvard Education Press.

Jimerson, S. R., Ferguson, P., Whipple, A. D., Anderson, G. E. & Dalton, M. J. (2002). Exploring the association between grade retention and dropout: A longitudinal study examining socio-emotional, behavioral, and achievement characteristics of retained students. *California School Psychologist, 7*(1), 51–62.

Kagan, S. & Kagan, M. (2001). *Multiple intelligences: The complete MI book*. San Clemente, CA: Kagan Publishing.

Levine, M. & Reed, M. (1999). *Developmental variation and learning disorders*. Cambridge, MA: Educators Publishing Service.

Paynter, D. E., Bodrova, E., & Doty, J. K. (2005). *For the love of words: Vocabulary instruction that works*. San Francisco, CA: Jossey-Bass.

Reif, S. F. & Heimburge, J. A. (1996). *How to reach and teach all students in the inclusive classroom*. New York, NY: Center for Applied Research in Education.

Udvari-Solner, A. & Kluth, P. (2008). *Joyful learning: Active and collaborative learning in inclusive classrooms*. Thousand Oaks, CA: Corwin.

8   Drawing upon the Power of Two

"What will happen if I am assigned to be a co-teacher?"

Cartoon #8 Making things grow

"Back in the day…" (meaning when we both started our careers in education), teaching was a solitary profession. A single person was expected to plan lessons, prepare materials, and know, teach, evaluate, and assess each student, while managing the whole class. This often translated into "make or break" experiences for many new teachers. Those who made it found hitherto unknown strengths, new depths of self-questioning, and a shift from imagined expectations to those grounded in actual experiences. In an effort to reach the maximum number of students in one fell swoop, teachers largely taught to the middle. This "typical" teacher profile is one of strength, hard work, and resolve in the face of thousands of daily decisions at the micro, meso, and macro levels. Despite the energy required, the sheer hard work, and seemingly countless tasks, teachers eventually grew to hone their efficiency. However, they simultaneously developed an insular view of teaching. As the old "in-house" education saying goes, "Once the classroom door is closed, a teacher can do whatever she wants."

In Darwinian terms, teachers adapted to their environment, largely becoming individual units within a large institution. As such, teachers came to view themselves as essentially solitary creatures who sometimes conferred, often commiserated, yet rarely collaborated. Often perceived by the administration as rugged individuals, they carved their turf within four walls and were singularly responsible for their lot. Given this history of how teaching has been traditionally organized in public institutions, the very idea of sharing space— indeed, a simple concept—posed major challenges to the existing educational landscape. A question of concern for all of us is this: "Can sharing a classroom be a good change?" While we understand some of the potential pitfalls and drawbacks of sharing, all in all, we argue, "Yes."

Returning to "back in the day" when no one co-taught, our worlds were rocked when special educators who taught in segregated spaces became assigned to classrooms in which "our students" with disabilities became mixed with "students of other teachers" in general education. Hence, we understand the many anxieties that may ensue, framed in questions such as: Whose kids do I teach? How do I teach with someone else in the room? Who is responsible for what? When and how will we plan on a regular basis? What if our styles are very different? What if I'm seen as the "bad cop" and my partner is seen as the "good cop"? Furthermore, our administrators had never team taught and were not quite sure how best to guide us. Not to mention that our graduate programs did not contain any information on team teaching! Thankfully, much has changed in the last two decades. Many administrators, once teachers, have experienced team teaching; some college courses now feature team teaching; student-teacher placements within inclusive classrooms are commonplace; a larger body of research on collaborative education exists[1]; and commercial materials are widely available (e.g., Friend, 2005). Within our own classes of graduate students who are already teaching full-time, at least one-third work within a team teaching environment.

We note that the fears and anxieties listed above are very real, and do not make light of them. However, on closer inspection, most of these concerns are initially about the teacher(s). It is worth calling attention to this central point: inclusive practices are grounded in the considerations of others. To state the obvious, of primary concern are children and youth being educated. In addition, consideration should always be given to one's teaching partner; it can be quite humbling to check one's ego at the door. Sharing a classroom has often been compared to a professional marriage. "But I didn't ask to be married!" a professional may complain. Once again, collaborative teaching is about what is good for children, not necessarily what teachers want or prefer. In fact, when it comes to actual matrimony, it is noteworthy that arranged marriages are statistically more successful than unions wherein both partners choose one another. We state this to emphasize that there is more than one way of successfully doing business.

In the next section, we further expand upon how inclusive education can benefit all constituents—general and special education teachers and general and special education students. In subsequent sections, we focus on ways in which professional relationships between teachers are formed, developed, and maintained.

Benefits of Collaborative Team Teaching

In this section, we outline the benefits of collaborative team teaching for general educators, special educators, general education students, and special education students.

Benefits for General Educators

Collaboration provides benefits in both directions, and general educators can acquire new knowledge and skills, such as:

1. *Opportunity to exchange knowledge with the special educator*
   Both teachers are able to understand each other's strengths and areas of expertise. As the grade levels rise, general education teachers are often content area specialists. Special educators, in turn, help the general educator to customize content to the needs of particular students.
2. *More time to focus on content and less on individual problems*
   Some teachers appreciate the possibility of primarily focusing on the content of their teaching, and for a stretch of time to be "freed up" from requests of individuals. The special educator can circulate and help all students on an as-needed basis.
3. *Twice as much opportunity to assist students*
   By the same token, both teachers can always be available to help all students. It is imperative that the initial feeling of "your students" and "my students" dissipates into the sense of "our students."
4. *Assistance to non-identified students who need more help*
   Oftentimes, students without disabilities need help. All classrooms have students variously labeled as "slow learners," "at risk," "English Language Learners," or "truant," who benefit from different levels of support based on a variety of factors that include learning styles, teaching format, content, personal interest, and so on.
5. *Awareness of different successful teaching strategies*
   The special educator is grounded in flexible pedagogy, ready to approach the task of teaching to students who need alternative methods, differently formatted materials, and opportunities to demonstrate knowledge in a variety of ways.
6. *Use of special education teachers to monitor organizational skills*
   While the general educator focuses on content, the special educator can primarily focus on aspects of organization, including student readiness, preparedness, ability to preplan assignments, ability to follow multi-step activities, and participation in collaborative group work.
7. *Use of special education teachers to coordinate and/or support home–school partnerships*
   The home–school partnership is of paramount importance in ensuring that all students receive support "at both ends." The special educator may take on the role of contacting parents, particularly to share good news about how their children are doing in school. In addition, the special educator can coordinate homework and inform parents how they can best help through practicing skills or reinforcing new content knowledge.

8. *Increased understanding of students with special needs*

    Given the segregated nature of their own schooling, including most teacher educa-
    tion programs (Young, 2008), and the public school system that in many ways is
    still bifurcated, some general educators feel they are not equipped to work with
    students who have disabilities.[2] When collaborating with another professional
    who is "at home" working with students with disabilities, the general educator
    comes to learn that these students are much more like students without disabil-
    ities than dissimilar from them. To be fair, at times, some teachers continue to
    struggle, realizing that there may be no quick or easy answers (Habib, 2008).

9. *Opportunity to become better equipped to help special education students*

    Collaboration gives general education teachers the opportunity to observe how spe-
    cial educators view, interact with, teach, and evaluate students with disabilities.
    For some, students with disabilities become demystified as they realize that few
    (if any) differences exist. Others, meanwhile, come to understand and appreciate
    human diversity: that is, the noticeable differences within our citizenry.

10. *Professional growth: greater personal satisfaction in teaching*

    Many educators assigned to teach in collaborative classes have come to recognize that
    sharing perspectives, responsibilities, hopes, fears, and questions with a trusted pro-
    fessional partner provides fertile ground for continued professional growth. Indeed,
    while staff development is often perceived as an add-on, collaborative team teaching
    provides the opportunity for professional development to occur every day.

Benefits for Special Educators

Special educators who have gone through teacher certification programs with little famil-
iarization in general education classes can reinterpret the paramenters of their roles
through collaboration. For example, it may provide:

1. *The opportunity to increase knowledge of one or more specific content areas*

    Special educators sometimes feel constrained by a skills-driven curriculum. Many
    teacher education programs continue to emphasize a "drill for skills" approach
    to teaching and learning, at the expense of content knowledge and methodology
    (Brantlinger, 2004). Keeping connected to content knowledge helps both teachers
    support their students.

2. *More opportunities to learn specialized skills*

    Although proficient in managing smaller groups of 6–12, or even individual students,
    special educators have traditionally had little or no experience in teaching and
    managing larger groups. Working in a general education classroom allows special
    educators to expand their skills in both pedagogy and classroom management.

3. *Awareness of daily life and expectations in a general education setting*

    It can be argued that special educators who enter the field without access to what
    happens in general education can grow to have a "distorted" sense of the academic
    levels and behaviors of students. Consequently, the everyday academic and behav-
    ioral standards in a general classroom can provide a yardstick of expectations for
    special education students.

4. *Exposure to general education students and curriculum, generating more realistic
    goals*

    Academic and behavioral goals for students with Individual Education Plans (IEPs)
    within collaborative classrooms are more in tune with the general education cur-
    riculum. Traditionally, IEP goals and objectives have been generic, pro forma,

and computerized—in brief, not individualized according to the original intent of the law.

5. *Mutual learning and appreciation of each other's expertise*

   Some special educators have reported feeling that they are seen as having a lower status than their general education colleagues, as well as experiencing incidences of being stigmatized because of their connection with disability. On the other hand, general educators are frequently characterized as preoccupied with pushing through "a mile-wide, inch-thick curriculum." Working together permits each educator to see up close how the other uses his or her expertise to ensure that students are taught the necessary knowledge and skills.

6. *Reward of seeing students succeed and establish friendships among their peers*

   Students with disabilities who have been taught in segregated settings are often teased or spurned by non-disabled peers (Goffman, 1963). If students with disabilities spend all of their time in segregated classes, then the majority, if not all, of their friendships will be with other disabled students. The inclusion of students with disabilities creates opportunities for friendships with non-disabled students to evolve naturally.

7. *Moral support from a colleague*

   Working together as a team provides much-needed moral support, especially when things do not go well. In addition, colleagues are there to share breakthroughs with children, and to celebrate what has been achieved. A trustworthy colleague with whom to swap ideas, check in at the end of class, compare notes, brainstorm, and develop plans can substantially lessen the pressures associated with teaching in isolation.

8. *Observation of improved student behavior*

   Granted, inclusion does not transform all students; however, it can have a significant impact on self-esteem, which, in turn, impacts behavior. Stereotypically, special education classes are often associated with misbehaving students. Ironically, students placed in special education classes sometimes misbehave because they believe they are expected to (Connor, 2008).

9. *Ability to spend more time and energy helping students develop motivation, effort, and responsibility for their own learning*

   While the general educator is teaching content, the special educator may home in on individual students, attending to their specific needs, customizing verbal feedback, or creating on-the-spot modified instruction.

10. *Opportunity to be not a content expert but a skills specialist*

    Special educators do not have to lose their identity. They can maintain a primary focus on targeted, individualized instruction as needed. Yet, at the same time, constant exposure to a rich, content-driven curriculum allows the special educator to actively implement skills in order to help students in the unpredictable arena of the classroom.

Benefits for General Education Students

General education students are often thought of as potentially suffering as a result of being in inclusive classrooms with their disabled peers. If numbers of students with and without disabilities are balanced, this is not the case. Potential benefits include:

1. *Better preparation for examinations*

   All students potentially benefit from the expertise of two educators. General education students in collaborative classrooms have been known to perform better on standardized tests because of the detailed care special educators take in analyzing tasks, providing scaffolded support, and using multiple approaches (Speece & Keogh, 1996).

2. *Availability of diverse learning techniques*

When given equal status with a general educator, a special educator can explain, discuss, and model various ways to teach and learn. In addition, both teachers can see which students succeed and which struggle, and can then adapt instruction accordingly for individuals, small groups, or even the entire class.

3. *Better understanding of students with different abilities*

Although diversity in terms of multiculturalism, gender, nationality, sexual orientation, and so on, are addressed to varying degrees throughout the K-12 curriculum, diverse abilities are not yet given equal weight. Cognitive, physical, emotional, and behavioral diversity, often understood beneath the broad (and contentious) umbrella of "disability," come to be known through real-life interactions and experiences of classmates. Misunderstanding and fear of disability can be undone by students learning together.

4. *More productive learning experiences*

"Two teacher heads together" can create a synergy that gives rise to new ways of teaching and learning. Both teachers and students benefit from the continual flow of ideas exchanged by two professionals who constantly monitor "how things are going" in terms of student learning.

5. *Strong emphasis placed on learning skills and organization*

As previously noted, general education classes may contain large numbers of students who are several grade levels behind or considered "at risk," "slow learners," English Language Learners, and so on. Once again, all students, but especially struggling learners (who can be in the majority or, in some cases, form the entire class) benefit from a clear focus on specific skills and organizational strategies and routines (Deshler, Schumaker, Harris, & Graham, 1999). Teaching and practicing organizational skills are considered time well spent by classroom teachers (Connor & Lagares, 2007).

6. *Opportunities for leadership through peer tutoring*

Students with disabilities are able to learn from non-disabled peers and vice versa. Depending upon the degree and severity of the disability, students can play active roles in peer tutoring and other socially-mediated strategies.

7. *More contact time with teachers for school and personal issues*

General education students who are interviewed about the benefits of having two teachers frequently cite knowing that they can always access a teacher at any time during class, for a variety of purposes such as clarification, re-explanation, contextualization, or "catch up" if they are late.

8. *Unique learning needs met to the greatest extent possible*

Circulating among all students, teachers can customize responses and support, regardless of whether or not a student has a disability label. Teachers also gain a shared knowledge of each child and can use their observations to co-plan future support.

9. *More time spent working cooperatively to acquire knowledge, and learning more about ways in which individuals can make positive contributions*

Cooperative learning is a staple teaching methodology used in inclusive classrooms. Through creating and supporting various groups, teachers provide multiple opportunities for students to problem solve and demonstrate their strengths to one another (Vernon, Schumaker, & Deshler, 1996).

10. *Flexible approaches used by two teachers*

All students are able to observe and experience how a partnership between adults— either personal (think marriage or partnership) or professional (think police

officers, surgeons, lawyers) is configured. Based on mutual respect and acknowledgment of give-and-take in everyday situations, students witness how responsibilities are shared and everyday problems resolved.

11. *Instruction maintained, even when one staff member is absent*
    Instructional time is paramount, and when a teacher is absent for good reason (sickness,
    emergency, family crisis) not only is time "lost," but re-entry into the curriculum
    can be difficult when momentum has been waylaid. With two teachers, one can
    always maintain a focus on the curriculum and provide consistency of instruction
    (with a substitute teacher for additional help).

Benefits for Special Education Students

Special education students who have been subjected in many ways to limitations imposed
upon them can benefit from being in general education classes in a variety of ways,
including:

1. *Raised expectations*
   A long-time and pervasive criticism of special education has been its lack of high
   expectations placed upon students with disabilities (Lipsky & Gartner, 1997).
   Many students with disabilities confirm that being in the general education environment makes them have higher expectations for themselves (Mooney & Cole,
   2000), including access to formal examinations that determine whether a student
   is eligible to apply for college.

2. *Improved self-esteem*
   Students with disabilities who are educated in segregated settings often feel they are
   "not good enough," "less than," or "inferior" when compared to students in general education classes (Mooney, 2008; Reid & Button, 1995). The majority of
   students feel a sense of accomplishment and a restoration to equal status when
   transitioned into general education (Gibb, Alfred, Ingram, Young, & Egan, 1999),
   although they still manage the stigma of disability to different degrees.

3. *Increased independence and responsibility*
   Students with disabilities who are supported in a general education classroom do
   not experience the "learned helplessness" that plagues students who have been in
   segregated settings for their entire school career. The climate in inclusive classes
   is also nurturing, but it cultivates participation in a more rigorous curriculum in
   which students work both for themselves and with other students.

4. *Strong emphasis on learning skills and organization*
   The focus for students with disabilities, like that of their non-disabled peers, is on content and organizational skills. In segregated classes, the emphasis is often upon
   "life skills," which are undeniably important and should be taught, but not at the
   expense of a rich, full curriculum of valuable knowledge.

5. *Better preparation for examinations*
   Before the passing of No Child Left Behind, students with disabilities were not
   required to take standardized examinations. The value of these exams is highly
   controversial, and many students are forced to sit them with little chance of
   passing. However, not being given access to exams is equally problematic, skewing
   national and local data through inflating scores by literally not counting all children (Allington & McGill-Franzen, 1992). The number of students with disabilities passing exams has risen marginally (Keller, 2000), yet the dropout rate of
   students with disabilities has not been adequately documented despite historically

poor results. Clearly, having high-stakes exams is a complex issue as they benefit some students while proving harmful to others.

6. *Exposure to students modeling appropriate behaviors and successful learning skills*
   The experiences of students in segregated settings are often limited by their exposure to other students with disabilities only. Thus students with disabilities are denied access to divergent ways of thinking and doing, problem solving and socializing. Learning and behavior can be significantly stultified in some segregated environments, and may even cause regression. In contrast, in the inclusive classroom, students demonstrating "inappropriate" behaviors are surrounded by peers modeling acceptable actions, and students with (and without) learning disabilities are able to recognize that there are different ways to understand and demonstrate knowledge.

7. *Realization that effort is recognized*
   Fairness is a concept that must be examined and discussed between teachers and among students in inclusive classrooms. It is important for all students to know that effort is valued and factored into student evaluations. Some students may never do what others are able to do, yet they need to be encouraged to always do their best and told that their efforts will be respected and counted.

8. *Increased contact with a variety of teachers*
   Segregated settings have traditionally signaled a lack of variety in teachers. It is not unusual for students in such circumstances to have the same teacher for all subjects, sometimes year after year. Obviously, the content knowledge of such a teacher cannot compete with the expertise of many who are qualified in a variety of areas.

9. *Opportunity to learn and grow in the least restrictive environment*
   Receiving an appropriate education in the least restrictive environment is a right afforded to all students with disabilities. However, the word "appropriate" has often been interpreted in terms of degree of segregation, and not the original intent of the law (Skrtic, 1991). To many advocates, it is a civil right of all students to have the chance to be educated in a general education classroom with non-disabled peers (Sapon-Shevin, 2007).

10. *Facilitation of friendships with non-disabled students*
    As mentioned earlier, students with disabilities are no longer ghettoized into separate settings, and the opportunity to make friends is optimized. Viewed from another angle, a student with a disability and a non-disabled student from the same neighborhood who are already friends can now attend the same class in school.

11. *Simulation of the real world*
    There is no special education world with separate shops, restaurants, workplaces, cinemas, and water fountains. The permanent segregation of students is an artificial structure that seems to benefit how schools are organized rather than accommodate the actual diversity of the population. Thus, inclusion with non-disabled peers is how students already experience the rest of the world outside of school.

Understanding the Relationship as a Process

Although wise administrators plan pairings with insight and knowledge about each educator's strengths, there is always the possibility that two people assigned to work together may be total strangers. Like personal relationships, professional pairings are complex phenomena full of nuances that are best viewed as works constantly in progress. Indeed, there are many parallels between personal and professional relationships, leading Gately and Gately (2001) to develop a useful framework consisting of three broad stages to help understand the process of initiating, developing, and maintaining a partnership. First, there is the beginning stage, in which guarded exchanges and careful communication occur as individuals get to know each other. Next is a compromising stage in which give and take is evident, with individuals accepting that they have to give up certain things in order to get others. Finally, there is the collaborative stage, in which the partnership has evolved into open communication and interactions demonstrating clear mutual respect.

Beginning Stage

In the beginning stages of co-teaching, two teachers often feel like separate entities placed together, sometimes experiencing awkwardness with one another, even anxiety. Others may immediately feel "open" to this arrangement and embrace it from day one. However, teachers have been enculturated to think of themselves as solitary creatures, and sharing (students, space, materials, responsibilities) may not always come easily. Communication, therefore, may start in a tentative way as individuals develop a sense of boundaries and begin a good-faith attempt to establish a professional working relationship. Interestingly, moving from a social to a professional relationship with a colleague may be difficult for some pairs of teachers. At first, some general educators may experience feelings of intrusion and invasion. Similarly, special educators may feel "out of place," uncomfortable, detached, and even excluded. During the beginning stage, teachers may tread more slowly as they work to determine role expectations. Communication may be polite, guarded, and infrequent. Unless there is a clear sense of the developmental process and the goal of collaboration is a mutual one, teachers may get "stuck" at this level. It can be argued that much of the dissatisfaction noted in the literature regarding co-teaching is expressed by teachers who continue to interact at the beginning level (Mastropieri, Scruggs, Graetz, Norland, Gardizi, & McDuffie, 2005).

Compromising Stage

In the compromising stage, teachers who have adequate work relationships come to be more open and interactive in their communication. Although students benefit from this increase in communication, teachers are still "finding their way," albeit with more confidence and a greater sense of self-knowledge. Compromise pervades at this level. In addition, the special education teacher may be taking a more active role in classroom teaching, but, in doing so, may have had to give up something in return (such as solely focusing on students with IEPs). The compromises made at this stage help the co-teachers to build a level of trust that is necessary for them to move beyond their current way of doing things to ultimately develop a more collaborative partnership. Open and honest "give and take" is the essence of the third stage.

Collaborating Stage

At the collaborative level, teachers openly converse and interact. Communication, humor, and a high degree of comfort are telling in their co-teaching. Teachers, students, paraprofessionals, and visitors to the classroom are able to recognize this high level of comfort. The two teachers work together and complement each other, one picking up where the other left off, adding additional information, and appearing intuitively "in tune" with one another, At this stage, it is often difficult for outsiders to discern which teacher is the special educator and which is the general educator. The ideal relationship is achieved through working hard to make it work. Some expert co-teachers have likened their skills to those of a doubles tennis team. Each teacher becomes in tune with the other to maneuver the ebbs and flows of classroom dynamics. Both are ready for whatever comes their way, though each has a designated area for which she has primary responsibility.

In addition to this framework for understanding the process of collaboration, Gately and Gately (2001) identified eight areas integral to sharing classroom life: interpersonal communication, physical arrangement of the room, familiarity with the curriculum, sharing curriculum goals and modifications, planning instruction, executing instructional presentation, classroom management, and assessment. In the following sections, we highlight how the beginning, compromising, and collaborating stages may look in each of these areas.

Contemplating how to work with these components is essential to a well-run partnered classroom. No two collaborative relationships are the same, as different components usually vary in importance for individual teachers. In addition, collaborative pairs may vary in different stages of the eight components. For example, teachers may be in the compromising stage for management and the beginning stage for assessment, Conversely, teachers may be in the collaborating stage for interpersonal communication but in the compromising stage regarding physical arrangement of the room. Some teachers fly from the start, while others need more time to take off. Occasionally, teachers do not want to venture beyond the beginning stage. It is important to remember that this is the choice of the individuals involved, and support from caring administrators, including ongoing professional development, can be a way for teachers to overcome initial resistance to an inclusive classroom.

Featured Voice of Keriann Martin

The Six Cs of Co-Teaching

One of the greatest gifts I have received in my career is the opportunity to work in a co-teaching classroom with a colleague who shares the same passion and philosophy in teaching. When looking back, it is easy to see that these years are also my most successful and memorable. Co-teaching is an amazing opportunity for teachers and students to learn, grow, and develop side by side, with the support of each other. In my experience, I found six key elements to be successful in a co-teaching team and classroom. I like to call these elements "The Six Cs of Co-Teaching." When these elements are embedded in the classroom of two well-matched teachers, the potential for success is limitless. They helped me to develop excellent co-teaching partnerships over the years.

Communication

Communication is key to any healthy relationship that we form and is at the heart of co-teaching. Teachers in a co-teaching class need to be able to effectively communicate with each other and their students regularly throughout the day. Communication should always be honest, constructive, and supportive in order to build and maintain trust and mutual respect among all members of the classroom community. Effective communication is not just expressing thoughts and opinions or discussing topics. It is being able to actively listen to what others have to say and demonstrating respect and appreciation for their thoughts and ideas.

Compromise

We all have ideas and ways in which we like to do things, but we can't always get our way. When working with a co-teacher, you need to be flexible with your thoughts and ideas and come to a consensus on every aspect of your classroom. This is when personal strengths and interests come into play.

Co-Planning

Every outstanding teacher is well-planned and prepared for the students sitting in front of him or her. In the co-teaching setting, you have to plan more intentionally. Both teachers need to have a comprehensive understanding of the lesson, the students, and their respective responsibilities for instruction. Co-teachers need to not only plan the lesson, but also discuss how they are going to differentiate the material for the range of students in their classroom, modifications that will enable students to access information, and the co-teaching structure(s) needed to deliver the instruction. In co-teaching classrooms, teachers need to set aside time in the morning to discuss plans before the day begins, time in the afternoon to reflect on the day and discuss modifications that need to be put into place the next day, and time at the end of the week to plan for the following week. Being well-planned is crucial to the success of teaching and learning. It's like my principal always tells us, "If you don't have a plan for your students, your students have a plan for you!"

Collaboration and Cohesiveness

For co-teaching to be successful for teachers and students, no teacher should ever be considered the lead or main teacher of the classroom and the other the assistant. Both teachers in the classroom need to receive the same level of respect and responsibility. The most successful co-teaching classrooms work as a unified team. The two teachers need to support each other throughout the day and work collaboratively, in order to show the students that they are a team and that both teachers in the classroom are equally important and equally responsible. You know that you have done a great job establishing this with your students when someone asks them who their teacher is and they say not one but both teachers' names. Students need to see that you work cohesively, and that what one teacher says or does is supported and repeated by the other. Both teachers are important to the success of the students in the classroom and there must be a significant amount of collaboration in order to maximize the success of the classroom and your co-teaching team.

Consistency

Consistency is key! If you say you are going to do something, be sure that you follow through so that your students know that they can trust your word and that you mean what you say. Students are much more successful when they have structure and routines because they know what to expect and are able to take the lead in their own learning.

Creativity

Be creative and be true to yourself! Don't become something that you are not or lose the special gifts and talents that you bring to the team. Be sure to showcase your talents and shine. Co-teaching is a truly wonderful experience and a work of art when both people are all in and don't hold back. You have the ability to think outside of the box and engage in activities and learning experiences that others may not because there are two people on deck at all times. Take advantage of this and let your creative sides flow!

"The Six Cs of Co-Teaching" is half of the equation in developing a good partnership. The other half is being flexible. It is important to understand that co-teaching is an ebb and flow of responsibility. We like to think that the workload and effort should be 50/50 all the time, but the reality is that this number fluctuates throughout the day, week, month, and year, depending on the tasks and events in front of you at the current time. Sometimes it will be 60/40, and at other times 30/70. It is important to remember that you are each other's support system and being flexible will allow your classroom to run smoothly. My most successful partnerships embodied all these elements and demonstrated the power of two!

"Push In" Model

"Push in" means that the special educator provides service in a general education classroom. This can be instructional or behavioral support and should be done in conjunction with the general educator. For example, the special educator may help students by focusing on organizational skills, note-taking methods, or problem solving in the context of curriculum (essay writing, lectures, math). A special educator who does this may work with several general educators during the course of a day. In these cases, the special educator must work on building multiple relationships simultaneously. The benefits of this "itinerant" model include the special educator's clear understanding of the scope and depth of the school's curriculum and the ability to help many students to different degrees, and the maintenance of a visible profile as a collaborative educator who supports struggling students. The downside may be that teachers can become overextended if spread too thinly and need to be proactive in negotiating schedules and expectations. Above all, they must still operate as the advocates and supporters of students with disabilities.

Box 8.1 Team Teaching Stages

	Interpersonal communication
Beginning stage	• Teachers treat each other in a guarded manner • Teachers seek to correctly interpret verbal and nonverbal messages • Possible lack of openness • Possible clash of communication styles • Possible dissatisfaction, stated or unstated
Compromising stage	• More open and interactive • Increase in amount of communication • Teachers begin to give and take ideas • Teachers develop respect for a different communication style • Increased appreciation of humor in classroom situations • Increase in own humor in communication

Collaborating stage	• Effective use of verbal, nonverbal, and social skills • Teachers use more nonverbal communication • Development of specific signals to communicate ideas • Positive role models of effective communication skills for students (students need to develop more effective social interactive skills) • Teachers model effective ways to communicate and solve problems • Effective communication between sexes is demonstrated

Physical arrangement of the room

Beginning stage	• May convey separateness • Students with disabilities sit together or close to one another • Little ownership of materials or space by special educators • Special educator doesn't feel free to access or share materials (asks permission) • Special educator brings own materials • In assigning space, the general educator may allot the special educator a place or a desk • Special educator elects to choose a separate space, e.g., back of the room • Feels like "a classroom within a classroom"
Compromising stage	• More movement and shared space • Materials are shared • Territoriality becomes evident • Special educator moves freely throughout the room but rarely takes center stage
Collaborating stage	• Student seating arrangements become intentionally interspersed through the classroom for whole-group lessons • All students participate in cooperative grouping assignments • Teachers are more fluid in their positioning within the classroom • Both teachers control space and are aware of each other's position in the room • The classroom is always effectively "covered" • Fluid movement is planned and natural

Familiarity with curriculum

Beginning stage	• Special educator may be unfamiliar with the content or methodology used by the general education teacher • Lack of knowledge creates lack of confidence • General educator may have limited confidence in the special educator and does not want to "give over the chalk" • The general educator's lack of confidence in the special educator makes it difficult for the special educator to suggest modifications
Compromising stage	• Special educator grows in confidence when engaging in the curriculum • General educator is more accepting of suggestions by special educator
Collaborating stage	• General educator grows in willingness to modify the curriculum and share in planning and teaching • Each teacher appreciates his or her partner's specific curriculum competencies

Curriculum goals and modifications

Beginning stage	• Programs are driven by textbooks and standards • Goals are test driven • Modifications and accommodations are restricted to students with IEPs • Special educator is viewed as "helper" • Little interaction takes place between teachers at this stage

Compromising stage	• Need for additional modifications and accommodations is observed and discussed, particularly for students with more "visible" or "evident" special needs • General educators interpret their acceptance of modifications as "giving up" or "watering down the curriculum" • Some teachers may still not appreciate that some students need modifications
Collaborating stage	• Both teachers differentiate concepts that all students must know from concepts that students *should* know • From this differentiation, modifications of content, activities, homework assignments, and tests become the norm for students who require them

Instructional planning

Beginning stage	• Often two types of service delivery are initially observed, related to two distinct and separate curricula being taught within the classroom to individuals or small groups of students • Separate curricula do not parallel each other and do not lend themselves to occasional large-group instruction • Special educator cast as "an assistant" • Shared planning time is essential; without it, the special educator does not know how the lesson is organized and how it will proceed
Compromising stage	• More give and take is evident in planning • More planning is shared
Collaborating stage	• Planning is ongoing and shared • Teachers continually plan outside of the classroom, as well as during the instructional lesson • Comfort level exhibited as "on the spot" change occurs in order to accommodate learners who may be struggling with the concept presented • Sharing of ideas becomes the norm

Instructional presentation

Beginning stage	• Teachers often present separate lessons • One teacher looks like "the boss" who "holds the chalk" (or likely more accurately commandeers the computer) and the other looks like "second fiddle."
Compromising stage	• Lesson structuring and presentation are shared • Both teachers may direct some of the activities in the classroom • Special educator may offer mini-lessons that clarify strategies that students could use
Collaborating stage	• Both teachers participate in the presentation of the lesson, provide instruction, and structure learning activities • The chalk (or computer for instructional purposes) passes freely between the teachers, because both are engaged in presentation and activities • Students address questions and discuss concerns with both teachers

Classroom management

Beginning stage	• Special educator sometimes assumes the role of behavior manager, so the other teacher can "teach"; this undermines the role of the special educator • The general educator may still assume the role of "chief behavior manager"

Compromising stage	• More communication • Mutual development of roles and routines for the classroom • May be some discussion of (and resistance to) individual behavior plans in favor of group management • May be some resistance to individualizing behavior expectations
Collaborating stage	• Teachers develop a common management system that benefits all students • Rules, routines, and expectations are mutually developed • Individual behavior plans are not uncommon • May include contracts, rewards, reinforcers—as well as community building

Assessment

Beginning stage	• Two separate grading systems, separately maintained by the individual teachers • Sometimes one grading system exclusively managed by general educator • Measures for evaluation tend to be objective in nature and solely examine the students' knowledge of content
Compromising stage	• Both teachers begin to explore alternative assessment ideas • Teachers discuss how to effectively capture students' progress • Number and quality of measures change, with more performance measures used
Collaborating stage	• Both teachers appreciate the need for a variety of options when assessing student progress • May include individualization of grading procedures for all students, specific progress monitoring, and use of objective and subjective standards for grading • Both teachers consider ways to integrate the goals and objectives written into student IEPs

Planning, Preparing, and Maintaining Collaborative Classes

We believe that teachers should be as prepared as possible before embarking on team teaching. Part of the preparation is to understand why team teaching exists as a means to include students with disabilities for the right reasons, such as ensuring access to a quality education with non-disabled peers (and not as a cost-saving measure). In addition, it is crucial that teachers recognize how the school administration will support them in this assignment, such as providing shared planning time.

Getting to Know Your Future Partner

It is recommended that you get to know your partner before sharing a classroom. This can be done by inviting your future partner to see you teach, and likewise suggesting that you visit her classroom. Together, you can put some time aside to compare your own teaching and learning styles, discuss similarities and differences, and identify your own strengths and weaknesses. Special educators can also discuss their level of personal comfort in a specific content area, and general educators can talk about their knowledge and experiences in working with students with disabilities, Indeed, the more educators discuss matters "up front," the more they are able to begin planning and preparing. Other recommended broad areas to discuss with a future partner might include:

- Prior team-teaching experiences.
- Belief systems about education.
- Perceptions of what constitutes equality between educators.
- Student variation.
- Adaptations and modifications used in the past.
- Most commonly-used strategies.
- Grading policy.
- Classroom management and rules.
- Potential student–teacher contracts.
- Knowledge base of team-teaching methodologies.
- Existing support systems for students.
- IEP goals and objectives (in general).
- Possible roles and responsibilities.
- Preparation of students for "re-entry."
- Planning time (establishing and honoring).
- Preparation for introduction to the class.
- Rules for teacher-to-teacher behavior while class is in session ("collaborative etiquette").
- Shaping classroom climate.
- Support from district/professional development.
- Reviewing curriculum.
- Designing customized materials.
- Personal quirks (What can't you stand? What don't you mind?).
- Problem solving.
- Flexibility.

Planning around Core Issues and Creating an Agreement with Each Other

As a result of your discussions, you can now plan around core issues in order to create an agreement with each other. Friend and Cook (1996) recommend that partners address the following issues:

1. *Instructional content*: What have you selected and why have you selected it?
2. *Planning*: What goals have you set?
3. *Instructional format*: In what ways will the content be taught?
4. *Parity*: How will you establish and maintain equality in the eyes of students?
5. *Space*: How will the room be arranged?
6. *Noise*: What will be the procedure when noise increases to unacceptable levels?
7. *Routines*: Who will do what? (Attendance, homework, notebook check, note-taking, etc.)
8. *Discipline*: What will be your mutually agreed-upon policy that must be adhered to?
9. *Feedback*: When and how will both teachers be able to discuss how the lesson went?
10. *Student evaluation*: In what ways will students be evaluated?
11. *Teaching chores*: Who will do the "nitty gritty" tasks such as cleaning the board?
12. *Confidentiality*: How can trust be established and maintained?
13. *Pet peeves*: What is a definite "no-no" for each of you?

Note that many of these issues can begin to be negotiated through co-planning (see Figure 8.1).

CLASS/SUBJECT AREA/SEMESTER _____

GENERAL EDUCATION TEAM MEMBER_____

SPECIAL EDUCATION TEAM MEMBER _____

WHEN IS YOUR WEEKLY PLANNING TIME SCHEDULED?

Monday Tuesday Wednesday Thursday Friday – From ___ to ___

HOW WILL TEACHER EQUITY BE ESTABLISHED IN CLASS?

_____

_____

_____

_____

NOTES:

TEXTBOOKS? _____

_____

INSTRUCTIONAL MATERIALS _____

_____

STUDENT RESPONSIBILITIES _____

_____

_____

CLASSROOM RULES _____

_____

_____

MANAGEMENT/DISCIPLINE PLAN _____

_____

_____

_____

PREFERRED TEAM TEACHING MODELS:

One teach, one observe	One teach, one assist	Alternative teaching
Station teaching	Parallel teaching	Tag team teaching

Primary responsibilities of general educator	Primary responsibilities of special educator
1.	1.
2.	2.
3.	3.
4.	4.
5.	5.

(Permission to copy for teachers)

Figure 8.1 Template: Planning to co-teach

Joint responsibilities

1.
2.
3.
4.
5.

INSTRUCTIONAL FORMATS: _____
_____
_____

STUDENT EVALUATION: _____
_____
_____

ARRANGEMENT OF ROOM: _____
_____

PEER FEEDBACK SYSTEM: _____
_____

This agreement should be reviewed periodically for necessary adjustments on a mutually agreed upon basis.

Figure 8.1 (Cont.)

"Checking-In" Daily about How Things are Going

Once the semester begins, time is always of the essence. For most teachers, even having 48 hours a day would not feel like enough time to do what is expected to be done. That said, collaborative teachers should always touch base with each other, even if briefly. Each day presents an opportunity to talk about new or ongoing issues, concerns, ideas, observations, and celebrations. It can be done before or after class starts. Some areas to touch base about may include these:

- Have you both honored the time set aside for co-planning?
- Have you both adequately prepared materials (texts, readings, cooperative learning structures, etc.)?
- Have you discussed individual students?
- Have you shared the responsibility for lesson planning?
- Have you clarified how selected points in the lesson are chosen?
- Have you established which format(s) of team teaching will be used?
- Have you clarified who will be grading, returning student work, and keeping records?
- Have you reminded each other (on an as-needed basis) of goals, objectives, previously made plans and decisions?

- On a particular day, have you decided who
  - (a) starts the class?
  - (b) reviews homework?
  - (c) reviews yesterday's lesson?
  - (d) initiates motivating questions or activities?
  - (e) maintains activities?
  - (f) clarifies or reemphasizes in an alternative manner?
  - (g) preps for a test?
  - (h) gives a quiz?
  - (i) takes which half of the debate group, etc.?

Recognizing the Importance of Ongoing Dialogue

In addition to daily check-ins, it is imperative to maintain ongoing dialogue that could take place during a set period of mutually agreed-upon co-planning time (for example, 3–4 p.m. every Thursday). Because collaborative education is a work in progress, committed teachers are always striving to improve co-planning, co-teaching, and co-assessing of all students. Many collaborative pairs are also willing to meet on an "as-needed" basis. Some examples of ongoing, open dialogue include:

- Prioritizing issues to talk about (e.g., student results, student behavior, individual students).
- Reviewing "how it went."
- Examining and discussing student work.
- Maintaining flexibility.
- Reflecting upon the things that went well and the things that could be changed for the better.
- Reviewing classroom protocols (e.g., a "correction" policy between teachers for occasions when one makes a mistake).
- Discussing commonplace issues such as student behavior, resistance, or motivation.
- Exploring possible responses for times when students use abusive language regarding gender, ability, race, ethnicity, or sexual orientation.
- Planning possible modifications and adaptations as needed.
- Monitoring to ensure that instruction is appropriate and differentiated as needed.

Collaborative teachers have a variety of teaching formats to choose from. Each team of co-teachers is able to explore various models to consider in relation to the specific goals and objectives of both educators. Six models were developed by Marilyn Friend that reflect instructional formats for co-teachers (Friend & Bursuck, 2002). Each one has advantages and disadvantages and should never be used all of the time. Instead, combining and alternating approaches provides for a rich and meaningful classroom where instructors are flexible in response to the needs of their students.

Friend's Six Models of Co-Teaching

The models briefly described below represent optional arrangements in co-teaching that many educators find to be useful:

- *Model 1. One teach, one observe*: One teacher teaches the content of the lesson while the other observes students as they respond to information and engage in work.

Teachers decide in advance what type of information they desire students to know and analyze the observational data together after class.

- *Model 2. One teach, one assist*: One teacher has a primary responsibility for teaching the content material while the other circulates through the room providing assistance to all students as needed.
- *Model 3. Station teaching*: In this co-teaching approach, teachers divide content and students. Each teaches the content to one group and subsequently repeats the instruction for the other group. If appropriate, a third "station" could give students an opportunity to work independently.
- *Model 4. Parallel teaching*: Teachers divide the class evenly in half and teach the same content simultaneously. This option allows for the sharing or comparing of information toward the end of the lesson, thus expanding the opportunity to cover more information.
- *Model 5. Alternative teaching*: In most class groups, occasions arise in which several students need specialized instruction. In alternative teaching, one teacher takes responsibility for the large group, while the other works with a smaller group.
- *Model 6. Teaming*: In this model, both teachers actively deliver the same information at the same time. It is a very fluid approach to teaching that requires the teachers to be synchronized but also somewhat spontaneous in delivery.

Good Things Happen in Co-Taught Classrooms

In this chapter, we have elaborated upon the benefits of a collaborative classroom for special and general educators, and for special and general education students. We have also emphasized that a collaborative relationship is an ongoing process that requires flexibility and openness to refining pedagogical practice. Working together with another teacher helps when interfacing with other professionals in many other school situations, including psychologists, counselors, occupational therapists, paraprofessionals, and so on. We realize that collaboration does not always come easily or even "naturally" to some educators but believe that the needs and rights of students come first—and all professionals should bear that in mind. We believe in teachers as problem solvers and creative thinkers who are willing to make changes from the way things are to the way things can be. Finally, the lesson plan in Figure 8.2 reflects many of the components that we have addressed thus far. It is but one example of how teachers can co-plan. We encourage you to develop a format that works best for your particular partnership and students.

Improving Collaboration: An Ongoing Process

Over the last decade, various researchers have weighed in regarding how best to continuously work on improving collaboration between educators. The work of Wendy Murawski (2008, 2009), in particular, has focused on helping teachers, administrators, and parents to maximize the possibilities within co-teaching. She has looked at international trends, implications for second language learners, and the effectiveness of engaging with culturally diverse families by understanding their cultural practices and expectations. In each instance, Murawski chronicled the benefits of responsible collaboration. Additionally, in relation to collaborating with colleagues (unsurprisingly!), she paid attention to the role of administrators in initiating, developing, and supporting their faculty members (Murawski & Deiker, 2013), as well as providing fair and constructive observations of co-teachers (Murawski, & Lochner, 2010). In *An Administrators Guide to Co-Teaching* (Murawski &

	Responsibility

DATE/DAY/CLASS: _____
STANDARD(S): _____
TEAM TEACHING MODEL(S): _____
 	
One teach, one observe   One teach, one assist   Station teaching
Alternative teaching   Parallel teaching   Tag team teaching
 	
OBJECTIVE(S):
  A. INSTRUCTIONAL _____
 	
  B. SOCIAL _____
 	
  C. BEHAVIORAL _____
 	
AIM: (Question form, starting with "How" or "Why" _____
 	
DO NOW   _____
MOTIVATION _____
MATERIALS   _____
 	
PROCEDURE   1. _____
               2.
               3.
               4.
               5.
               6.
 	
TYPES OF QUESTIONS? | Knowledge Comprehension Application Analysis Synthesis Evaluation |
 	
_____ ?
_____ ?
_____ ?
_____ ?
 	
GROUPING ACTIVITIES? | Individual   Pairs   Triads   Small Group   Large Group   Whole Class |
 	
INCORPORATION OF MULTIPLE INTELLIGENCES?
 	
| Language Math/logic Visual-spatial   Body-kinesthetic   Musical   Natural Interpersonal Intrapersonal |
 	
SUMMARY/MAJOR POINTS: _____
 	
INDIVIDUAL MODIFICATIONS: _____
 	
HOMEWORK: _____
NOTES: _____
 	
(Permission to copy for teachers)	

Figure 8.2 Template: Sample lesson plan

Berhardt, 2015), the following five areas are listed as essential to maintaining good collaborative co-teaching models in schools:

1. Providing professional development on inclusion, collaboration, and team teaching.
2. Establishing scheduling strategies.
3. Partnering the right teachers.
4. Supervising and evaluating strategically.
5. Improving, increasing, and institutionalizing co-teaching practices.

As can be seen from these recommendations, it is key for administrators to have high expectations in terms of collaborative teaching—including making it an expectation for all teachers. In addition, administrators should always have an eye toward making sure structures and systems are in place and that criteria for evaluation are clear and fair.

The provision of professional development for teachers (preferably *by* teachers, or at least featuring them) around collaborative teaching practices, actual students and the work they produce helps professionals by focusing on daily situations. As can be seen by the contents of this chapter, topics related to collaboration can be quite diverse. Having groups of teachers periodically share their daily practices among each other is conducive to the development of a responsive and reflective model for co-planning (Rood, Burnash, & Daviau, 2016). Revisiting commonplace topics such as IEPs in inclusive classes can be fruitful for all teachers, especially when viewed from a disability studies perspective. In her research analyzing IEPs, Kate McLaughlin (2016) calls attention to how their historical purpose has changed significantly and stresses that we need to be vigilant so that students and families can be more active in their customized development. She notes the implications of a shift in policies and politics:

> In contrast to the nascent intentions of the Education for all Handicapped Children's Act of 1975, the IEP is now centered on meeting standardized benchmarks and on the work required by professionals to ensure meeting those benchmarks rather than on the student's individual progress; on parent and student input; and on the importance of including students with their nondisabled peers as part of their progress.
>
> (p. 85)

This important point can help teachers remain grounded in the right/best thing to do for students and their families because "the IEP does not specifically prompt us to include the voices, opinions, and thoughts of the students, families, and other outside service agency providers or advocates[; rather], the document reflects the institution's needs rather than the goals of the student" (p. 97).

Playing Devil's advocate, I (David) spent many years providing professional development in schools focused on collaboration. I recall experiencing a range of emotions from teachers on this topic, from "Absolutely! This is the right thing to do" to "I don't want to listen to a word you have to say." What I learned fast was not to shy away from controversial topics, but rather to confront educators' concerns and work with them to explore solutions to perceived problems. In a recent work (Connor, 2016), I generated an amalgam of teachers' fears I had heard expressed over the years and crafted them into eight statements or questions with the purpose of playing Devil's advocate and casting a cynical eye on collaborative classes. I list them here:

1. I have been assigned to work with four co-teachers and four content-area lesson preparations.
2. I am working with a general educator who is never organized or prepared.
3. When teaching a lesson, I was publicly corrected and felt chastised by a co-teacher.
4. My general education co-teacher told me that, "My students do not belong in general education."
5. I have been placed in a large inclusive class without a general educator and spend most of my time disciplining students, worrying that I will not be able to get them to pass their state exams.

6. What happens if co-teaching is in place but not supported philosophically by administrators?
7. What happens if parents in the community do not support co-teaching?
8. What do I do when my co-teacher won't relinquish any of the control and is treating me like a paraprofessional rather than a teacher?

While mindful of considering "pushback," I have found that teachers want to genuinely engage with these serious issues, as they may reflect their own reality or that of a colleague, and grapple to find solutions that are as fair to all as they can be. At the same time, in my rhetorical written responses provided as examples to these eight statements or questions, I sought to provide teachers with a tool that would both help them feel a sense of control and enable them to be proactive in shaping the outcome. The tool was to allow themselves to process their initial reaction (often acknowledging how the position in which they have temporarily been placed is unfair), but then have them strategize and create short-, medium-, and long-term solutions, so they can thoughtfully and purposefully create a pathway out of the difficult situation and move toward a healthy relationship in which all students are the primary focus.

While career-long supporters of collaboration in general, and co-teaching specifically, we also know that there is no panacea to make every school function smoothly, every classroom run predictably, every educator to always behave professionally with peers, and every student to succeed academically and behaviorally. However, when done well, in good faith, with a disability studies/social justice disposition, and supported by administrators, everyone involved can benefit from sharing perspectives, making realistic suggestions, and continuing to learn with a view to always making situations better.

Questions to Consider

1. In your opinion, what are the most important of the many potential benefits resulting from collaborative team teaching for (a) general educators, (b) special educators, (c) students in general education, and (d) students receiving special education services?
2. Can you describe some professional experiences during which you came to recognize the value of working with a partner?
3. Broadly speaking, in what ways can a professional relationship be fostered?
4. How useful are Gately and Gately's (2001) ideas about eight areas and three levels of collaboration in outlining some of the complexities involved in collaborative teaching?
5. Which of Gately and Gately's eight areas would be your priority? In what areas might you anticipate potential "give and take"?
6. What explicit steps would you take to enable/establish collaboration with another teacher?
7. If you created an oral or written agreement with your potential collaborator, what might it look and/or sound like?
8. What are some good reasons to value and maintain an open dialogue with your teaching partner?
9. Of Friend's (2006) six collaborative models, which do you prefer? Why? Which might you have some reservations about trying? Why?
10. If you were to create your own lesson-planning template, in what ways might it be similar to and/or different from the one we presented?

Notes

1　See for example, "Collaborative Teaching: Successes, Failures, and Challenges," special edition of *Intervention in School and Clinic, 40*(5).
2　A poll by the American Federation of Teachers revealed that 78 percent of teachers thought that children with disabilities would not benefit from an inclusion policy and 87 percent stated that non-disabled children would not benefit either. See Leo (1994), p. 22.

References

Allington, R. & McGill-Franzen, A. (1992). Unintended effects of educational reform in New York. *Educational Policy, 6*(4), 397–414.

Brantlinger, E. (2004). Confounding the needs and confronting the norms: An extension of Reid and Valle's essay. *Journal of Learning Disabilities, 37*(6), 490–99.

Connor, D. J. (2008). *Urban narratives: Portraits-in-progress—life at the intersections of learning disability, race, and social class.* New York, NY: Peter Lang.

Connor, D. J. (2016). Analyzing school cultures and determining dynamics to enact co-teaching from a disability studies perspective. In M. Cosier & C. Ashby (Eds.), *Enacting change from within: Disability studies meets teaching and teacher education* (pp. 221–42). New York, NY: Peter Lang.

Connor, D. J. & Lagares, C. (2007). Facing high stakes in high school: 25 successful strategies from an inclusive social studies classroom. *TEACHING Exceptional Children, 40*(2), 18–27.

Deshler, D. D., Schumaker, J., Harris, K. R., & Graham, S. (Eds.). (1999). *Teaching every adolescent every day.* Cambridge, MA: Brookeline.

Friend, M. (2005). *The power of two* [video]. Alexandria, VA: ASCD. Retrieved from www.nprinc. com/the-power-of-2-3rd-ed/

Friend, M. & Bursuck, W. D. (2002). *Including students with special needs: A practical guide for classroom teachers.* Boston, MA: Allyn & Bacon.

Friend, M. & Cook, L. (1996). *The Power of 2: Making a difference through co-teaching—facilitator's guide.* Bloomington, IN: Elephant Rock.

Gately, S. & Gately, J. (2001). Understanding co-teaching components. *TEACHING Exceptional Children, 33*(4), 40–7.

Gibb, G. S., Alfred, K., Ingram, G. F., Young, J. R., & Egan, W. M. (1999). Lessons learned from the inclusion of students with emotional and behavioral disorders in one junior high school. *Behavioral Disorders, 24*(2), 122–36.

Goffman, E. (1963). *Stigma: Notes on the management of spoiled identity.* New York, NY: Simon & Schuster.

Habib, D. (2008). *Including Samuel* [video]. Retrieved from www.includingsamuel.com

Keller, B. (2000, April 12). More N.Y. special education students passing state tests. *Education Week.* Retrieved from www.edweek.org/ew/articles/2000/04/12/3lny.h19.html

Leo, J. (1994, June 27). Mainstreaming Jimmy's problem. *U.S. News & World Report, 116*(25), 22.

Lipsky, D. K. & Gartner, A. (1997). *Inclusion and school reform. Transforming America's classrooms.* Baltimore, MD: Paul H. Brookes.

Mastropieri, M. A., Scruggs, T. E., Graetz, J., Norland, J., Gardizi, W., & McDuffie, K. (2005). Case studies in co-teaching in the content areas: Successes, failures, and challenges. *Intervention in School and Clinic, 40*(5), 260–70.

McLaughlin, K. (2016). Institutional constructions of disability as deficit: Rethinking the individualized education plan. In M. Cosier & C. Ashby (Eds.), *Enacting change from within: Disability studies meets teaching and teacher education* (pp. 83–102). New York, NY: Peter Lang.

Mooney, J. (2008). *The short bus: A journey beyond normal.* New York, NY: Henry Holt.

Mooney, J. & Cole, D. (2000). *Learning outside the lines.* New York, NY: Simon & Schuster.

Murawski, W. (2008). 50 ways to keep your co-teacher. *TEACHING Exceptional Children, 40*, 40–8.

Murawski, W. (2009). *Collaborative teaching in secondary schools: Making the co-teaching marriage work!* Thousand Oaks, CA: Corwin.

Murawski, W. & Bernhardt, P. (2015). An administrator's guide to co-teaching. *Educational Leadership, 73*(4), 30–4.

Murawski, W. & Deiker, L. (2013). *Leading the co-teaching dance: Leadership strategies.* Arlington, VA: Council for Exceptional Children.

Murawski, W. & Lochner, W. W. (2010). Observing co-teaching: What to ask for, look for, and listen for. *Intervention in School and Clinic, 46*(3), 174–83.

Reid, D. K. & Button, L. J. (1995). Anna's story: Narratives of personal experience about being labeled learning disabled. *Journal of Learning Disabilities, 28*(10), 602–14.

Rood, C., Burnash, J., & Daviau, A. (2016). *Authentic collaboration: Developing a responsive and reflective model for secondary co-planning.* In M. Cosier & C. Ashby (Eds.), *Enacting change from within: Disability studies meets teaching and teacher education* (pp. 265–94). New York, NY: Peter Lang.

Sapon-Shevin, M. (2007). *Widening the circle: The power of inclusive classrooms.* Boston, MA: Beacon Press.

Skrtic, T. M. (1991). *Behind special education: A critical analysis of professional culture and school organization.* Denver, CO: Love Publishing.

Speece, D. & Keogh, B. (Eds.). (1996). *Research on classroom ecologies: Implications for inclusion of children with learning disabilities.* Mahwah, NJ: Lawrence Erlbaum.

Vernon, D. S., Schumaker, J., & Deshler, D. D. (1996). *The SCORE skills: Social skills for cooperative groups.* Lawrence, KS: Edge Enterprises, Inc.

Young, K. (2008). Physical and social organization of space in a combined credential program: Implications for inclusion. *International Journal of Inclusive Education, 12*(5–6), 477–95.

Part III

How Talk Changes Knowledge and Practice

9 Actively Challenging Normalcy
"How can I talk about disability in my classroom?"

Cartoon #9 Infusing disability

As urban teacher educators, we travel by bus, subway, taxi, and foot to classrooms across New York City to observe student teachers in action. Come along as I (Jan) visit a fifth-grade inclusive classroom. There is my student teacher, James, who has just announced a transition to writing workshop. The students gather on the carpet area designated for group instruction. James leans comfortably on a desk, a whiteboard by his side. He opens, "All week, we have been looking at feature articles—at the author's intent, what authors like to write about—basically reading and examining them. Today, I am going to share a feature article from *Time for Kids* called "Flying blind: Sightless dog sled racer hits the trail." He cues a student to turn on the smartboard and a copy of the article appears.

James reads aloud in an expressive and animated manner. He stops after a few sentences and says, "You know, we have been underlining sentences in the articles we have read. I think I will underline the sentence about the protesters." He underlines this sentence with a colored marker. Hearing that some people protested the inclusion of a visually impaired dogsled racer, a student comments, "I don't understand these people. She has every *right* to do it like anybody else!" Other students agree and add to the conversation. James returns to the article and reads the sentence, "Disability is not an inability." A student raises her hand and says, "I like that quote." James asks her to explain why. This invitation generates lively conversation among the students. James comments, "You are bringing up a lot of interesting points. And you will have time later to talk more about these topics."

James continues to read aloud. In response to a section of the article that mentions finding one's passion in life, students consider how the dogsled racer's disability does not interfere with the pursuit of her passion. They spontaneously brainstorm possible accommodations that would make it possible for a visually-impaired racer to participate. One student introduces the idea that the problem is not her disability, but rather the problem is other people. Another contemplates, "If I am in a wheelchair, do I have to be in wheelchair races only? Or could I race in a marathon?" The students thoughtfully reflect upon these questions.

James finishes reading the article. He asks, "What do you think made me choose this article?" The children consider his selection given what they have learned thus far about feature articles. James confirms that he is passionate about the topic of disability and comments, "I think that people with disabilities should have the opportunity to do whatever they want to do." He asks the students to think about whether this statement holds true within their own classroom and school. Following this conversation, students move into small groups to brainstorm passionate pursuits of their own that they might choose as topics for their feature articles.

Why Talk about Disability?

In the real-life scenario described above, James, a graduate student in special education, draws upon his coursework in disability studies to teach this writing workshop. Rather than present a "lesson" on disability, he infuses disability into the curriculum by selecting this particular text to model as an illustration of feature writing. It is worth noting that this is the *first* time that disability has been discussed within this class community. Given the opportunity to talk about disability, these fifth graders—with and without disabilities—engage openly and thoughtfully with the disability issues raised in the feature article. If we consider the depth of conversation generated out of just this initial introduction, imagine the impact that *systematic* infusion of disability issues across the curriculum might have upon our schools—an idea we return to later in this chapter.

Silence and Disability

During my first years as a special education teacher, I (Jan) learned to ask my middle school students to tell me why they were in my resource class (a "pull-out" service for one or two class periods per day). Almost without exception, they were unable to do so. No one had ever told them why. Some had been in resource classes since the primary grades. They never asked why because they feared it might be too terrible to know if no one could speak about it. Most were aware of their learning disability label and assumed this meant an inability to learn. Others believed deep down that they were dumb and teachers were just too kind to say so.

Let's fast forward to the present where students with disabilities are included within general education classrooms at increasing rates. In some classes, a paraprofessional may be assigned to a student with a disability. No one mentions the proverbial elephant in the room, but everyone knows it is never a good thing to have an adult "velcroed" to your side. Students without disabilities watch others leave the classroom for special services and wonder what one does to end up being one of those called and hope they never do whatever that is. No one talks about why some students leave or where they go, but others sometimes call them "the R-word" in the playground or on the bus.

If there are two teachers in a classroom, everyone knows that somebody has a disability. Everyone is suspect, but no one is talking. In schools where one class per grade level is designated for co-teaching, students with IEPs stay in those classes from year to year while students without IEPs shift from year to year. Sometimes students without disabilities do not want to be in a class that has co-teachers because they fear somebody might think *they* are the ones who have disabilities.

I am reminded of the silence that defined school integration for me as a student in the early 1970s (see Chapter 1). If our teachers could not speak about integration, we surely could not speak about it. We feared each other across the silence and sought refuge in others like ourselves. Moreover, we internalized the discomfort, anxiety, and tension that our teachers were unable to conceal. We walked on eggshells. After all, we did not know each other. We only knew what we knew and had no way to know differently. Silence erected a barrier beyond which we could not move.

Imagine if administrators and teachers had welcomed us as the inaugural generation of one of the greatest moments in civil rights history. What if the initiation of integration had been a grand celebratory event? How might things have turned out had we entered a school that hailed *Brown v. Board of Education* as a turning point in American society and invited us to contribute actively to its enactment? What if teachers had exuded enthusiasm and excitement about the possibilities before us? How might school and/or class forums have provided space for meaningful exchanges among students and teachers? What kind of community-building projects might we have envisioned for ourselves had we been given the opportunity? Perhaps it is naïve on my part to think that such a response could have emerged out of the intense political and social turmoil of that historical moment. But I do know that particular consequences resulted from the choices school personnel made during that time. And we are left to wonder how things might have turned out differently.

It does not take much of a cognitive leap to recognize that the integration of students with disabilities has followed a remarkably similar path to that of racial integration within public schools. Why *is* there silence around disability? If inclusion is about embracing diversity, why are we afraid to talk about disability in the classroom? It is sobering to acknowledge just how much our students reflect what we project as teachers. Children get messages about disability from somewhere and that somewhere includes teachers. If *we* are uncomfortable talking about disability, it stands to reason that students with and without disabilities will be too.

Silence and Shame

I remember devouring the Gothic romance novel, *Jane Eyre*, during one lazy adolescent summer. To this day, I can still see Bertha, the "insane" wife of Edward Rochester, imprisoned in the attic of Thornfield Manor, repeatedly escaping to wreak havoc upon the household. As a reader, I was pretty sure that Bertha's wild romps through the manor were meant to terrify me and arouse my compassion for the brooding and charismatic Edward. After all, poor Edward had no way of knowing that the beautiful and wealthy Bertha had madness lurking in her West Indian and Creole lineage (note the intersection of race and disability here), and now he was left to suffer under the burden of her care. But it was Bertha, not Edward, who drew my allegiance. I cheered for Bertha as she raced around madly, shattering the silence that rendered her invisible.

As discussed in Chapter 2, literature is rife with examples of characters with disabilities who embody the worst of human traits. While Bertha certainly fits this negative disability stereotype, what interests me most about the story is the destructive nature of silence. Edward desperately attempts to shroud Bertha's disability in silence and secrecy, yet she refuses to live unacknowledged. Bertha mesmerized me as a young adolescent. Perhaps it was her refusal to be dismissed as inhuman that I found so compelling. No matter how many times Edward locks her in the attic, Bertha emerges to reassert her powerful human presence. In a final act of defiance, she burns down the manor, killing herself in the process—an ending that the novelist, Charlotte Brontë, no doubt meant as a cautionary tale about the "evils" of insanity. Yet it was for Bertha that I mourned.

We might understand Bertha's story as an allegory for the destructive nature of silence. We need only look to our country's history of institutionalization to find the searing effects of silence and secrecy upon countless families (Blatt & Kaplan, 1966; Trent, 2016). The documentary, *Without Apology* (2004), uncovers one such story as told by filmmaker Susan Hamovitch, who resurrects her family's dark secret—the disappearance of her only sibling, Alan, at the age of eight, into a state institution in New York for persons with severe disabilities during the late 1950s. Alan's institutionalization remained a taboo topic within the Hamovitch family for decades. As a filmmaker, Hamovitch transgresses her family's code of silence to document the unending (and largely unspoken) pain of Alan's absence as experienced by each family member and the shame that separated and ultimately defined them all. Hamovitch's story is but one among thousands of stories from this era that remain untold.

Now think back to the metaphors expressed by the four special education teachers with learning disabilities whom we introduced in Chapter 4. The twin themes of silence and shame appear in each mosaic. Let's revisit these images of disability experience—a rat forced to run a maze, a forced walk through a jeering gauntlet of peers, a body burning at the stake, a face covered by hands, a caged rare species on display, a marked body surrounded by pointing fingers, a whispered taboo, a five-headed creature, a disease, undesirable bodies hidden in a closet. It seems the less we speak of disability, the more shameful it becomes.

Featured Voice of Kristen Goldmansour

Naming Biases and Having the Hard Conversations

I first worked as a public school teacher in New York City (NYC) before establishing my own business providing professional development in NYC schools. Some main guiding principles of my work (in no particular order) are:

- Teachers almost always truly care about their students.
- Teachers are very afraid to fail their students.
- There is a myth about special education: "There is a *special teacher somewhere else* who knows how to do something *very specialized* for *special students* that we can't do here in our co-teaching classroom."
- Change is scary and hard.
- A large part of being a successful inclusive educator actually means possessing a specific set of skills that can be learned—and I can teach you how to master them.
- Being committed to inclusive education is a matter of social justice and civil rights, so doing the hard and scary stuff is worth it and necessary.

How do we work as professional development providers? I remind my staff all the time, along with the teachers and administrators I work with: *We don't have fairy dust, we teach*. And so long as we *name* the teaching strategies, instructional choices and classroom structures, we can help teachers place inclusive teaching within context, and provide a rationale for appropriate choices. In turn, teachers feel supported, and over time, we build their independence and confidence in teaching inclusively so that they do not feel the need for a "special" teacher to do it. Part of our work is making room for people to fail while they are learning and to ask uncomfortable questions when they feel that their belief system is being challenged, particularly when they *really* believe there's a "special" place for students with disabilities that would be better than what they can provide.

Once we talk about what is feared and/or problematic—and, importantly, "name it"—most of the time we can learn about "it" and master the teaching skills to respond. It is my belief that effective inclusive teaching is deeply rooted in understanding the experiences and learning styles of our students. So often we hear that inclusive teaching is not effective. But it is more accurate to say that bad teaching is not effective. When teachers have a deep understanding of instructional barriers and how to identify and respond to them, they develop more independence and flexibility in their teaching and subsequently feel more successful. Always making sure that the underlying bias of an instructional design is *named* helps change the conversation in school communities. People start asking each other questions about making changes and creating access within their own community rather than talking about how to make certain kids go away to "special education land." And no one can do it alone. The whole school community needs to be a part of the conversation.

A couple of areas I'd like to focus on are (1) the invisible lines we create and sustain between general and special educators and why they should be visibly dismantled, and (2) the role of administrators as essential to the work of truly inclusive education. First, I have noticed that even in some of the most progressive inclusive classes there can still exist what I have come to call an imaginary line between the two teachers. In New York City, we have Integrated Collaborative Teaching Classes

(ICTs)—similar to other responses of local education authorities around the nation—to systemically organize, structure, and support inclusive education. However, it is common for teachers to talk of students with disabilities in these classes as "ICT kids," which sounds very much like a new way of saying "special education kids." Furthermore, many special educators still think inclusion "is not a good placement" for certain students with disabilities because they "need more support." I ask them to define "support" and probe for specifics. What I find is that special educators often self-identify with one or two disability categories (such as learning disabilities and behavior disorders) and do not think they can teach, for example, a student with autism or multiple and severe disabilities. I hear some special education teachers say something like, "I don't think he's an ICT kid." I respond by saying, "He's a second grader." I begin a conversation about the myth of a better placement that awaits him elsewhere, shifting the focus away from categories to instructional barriers (a phrase I use constantly) and what it is that they can do now and in the future.

In terms of administrators, I share that teachers need concrete strategies and language about instructional barriers that reflect the principles of universal design for learning (UDL). Based upon my observations in classrooms, it seems that many educators still do not have a working knowledge of or practice in using UDL, or even differentiated instruction (DI), for that matter. Unfortunately, in many schools, well-intended institutional responses by local school systems can end up diluting or co-opting important principles for instruction into what already exists, prompting some teachers to dismiss them as passing fads rather than career-long tools. To be fair to teachers, massive "roll outs" and "turn keying" approaches to teaching *without acknowledging the effective work being done by them* can be counterproductive. Bearing that in mind, administrators are in position to support, guide, and evaluate teachers in their daily work. I encourage them to keep the notion of instructional barriers in all of their conversations with, and evaluations of, teachers. They have to have deeper conversations with teachers to move beyond (while still including) student reading scores and behaviors. I also ask them to consider that building inclusive programming involves administrators thinking about not only "What to look for," but more specifically, "What to *listen* for." They have to be astute listeners to teachers' concerns and beliefs, and must be willing to ask them questions that help the conversation change. For example, if teachers say of a child, "He's so low" (in terms of academic performance) and utter the familiar refrain, "He needs so much support," they must also ask, "Support in what: self regulation, sustained attention, communication skills?" Teachers must then learn strategies and skills that can be taught to the child. The well-meaning practice of sitting next to the child is simply not an instructional strategy. All of the conversations between administrators and teachers can become linked to mutually-agreed areas in which teachers can informally and/or formally be observed. As educators, we are life-long learners and this inclusive work is both an important and an integral part of our job.

Dispelling Discomfort

There is no doubting our culture's legacy of silence regarding disability. Add to this legacy a healthy dose of ableism and minimal opportunities for interaction between people with and people without disabilities. Is it any wonder that teachers might not know how to talk about disability in the classroom? Most of us were taught early on not to point or stare at someone with a disability, much less mention the person's disability—as if he or she might suddenly recognize or remember that disability and hold us responsible for having pointed it out. Good manners require that we look away and pretend not to notice. We surely do not want to provoke a person with a disability by doing or saying the wrong thing. After all, we have read enough books and seen enough movies to know that people with disabilities can be a bitter and unhappy lot. (We are counting on your ability to read sarcasm here!) Or is it really about our own fears? Maybe we do not want to be reminded that a disability could befall us or those we love.

If we think about disability as simply natural variation among people rather than a pathology or tragedy, disability becomes one among many identity markers that people may claim. To pretend not to notice a person's embodiment in the world is to dismiss his or her "way of being" as too tragic to acknowledge. So now you are wondering just what it is that you are *supposed* to do. If conventional efforts at being polite may offend someone with a disability, how do we know *what* to do?

We begin by engaging in relationships with people who have disabilities and listening to what they tell us. Paul (who last appeared in Chapter 3) explains it this way. He wears two behind-the-ear hearing aids. Clear tubing runs from each hearing aid into a clear plastic earpiece that fits into each ear canal. It is easy to miss that he wears hearing aids. When young children notice, they immediately scramble closer to get a better look. They ask questions and show interest in what he has to tell them. He delights his young audience by taking out his hearing aids to explain how they work—a demonstration met with the universal response of "cool!" Adults, on the other hand, become visibly distracted upon noticing. They discreetly attempt to get a better look to confirm what they think they see (but not so discreetly that Paul does not notice), yet what they see is never mentioned. In response to this "appearing not to look while looking," Paul admits to sometimes amusing himself by making it just a bit more challenging for them to get a good look at his ears. Unlike well-intentioned adults who have been indoctrinated into "good" manners, what Paul observes in young children is a natural curiosity and interest about his way of being in the world. They readily acknowledge all of his humanity as valid, interesting, and worth knowing more about. And isn't that what all of us want?

Diversity as the Heart of Community

When we understand disability as *natural human variation* it becomes just another thread in the tapestry of diversity that defines an inclusive learning community. With diversity at the heart of inclusion, the building and sustenance of a strong community become *the* central classroom features. We start by engaging children in conversations about all of what makes us human. And from day one, the ongoing process of getting to know and appreciate one another is set in motion (see Chapter 5).

Think back to our imaginings about how school integration might have been approached. We have the opportunity to enact just such a vision for students with and without disabilities working together within inclusive communities. Let's welcome our students as the inaugural generation of the next great moment in civil rights history. Kick off the school year with an event to celebrate inclusion as a major step toward creating a just and equitable society. Hail the Individuals with Disabilities Education Improvement Act (IDEIA) as a turning point in American society. Include students in the process of learning how to live and work in an inclusive community. Exude enthusiasm and excitement about the possibilities of inclusion for everyone. Create space for meaningful exchanges among students and teachers. Invite students to envision and enact community-building projects to strengthen inclusivity within the classroom, school, and community. As a teacher, *you* have the choice to do things differently this time around for a better future. Take hold of this opportunity and make it possible.

In the last decade, books and materials on inclusion have exploded within the educational publishing market. It takes little time and effort in cyberspace to locate numerous and varied websites regarding inclusive practices. Avail yourself of the many resources at your fingertips. Mara Sapon-Shevin's book, *Because We Can Change the World: A Practical Guide to Building Cooperative, Inclusive Classroom Communities* (1998) remains a favorite of ours. Not only does Sapon-Shevin write elegantly about the hope and promise of inclusive practices, but she also draws upon her vast teaching experience to offer practical strategies for creating respectful and caring learning communities. The book is an invaluable resource for suggestions about cooperative games, children's literature selections and activities, and classroom songs to foster appreciation of diversity. We also recommend Julie Causton and Chelsea P. Tracy-Bronson's, *The Educator's Handbook for Inclusive School Practices* (2015). This volume is full of practical implementation strategies and classroom tools (K-12) based upon the authors' experience as successful inclusion teachers. Susan Baglieri's *Disability Studies and the Inclusive Classroom* (2017) is an excellent resource as a result of its treatment of critical practices for embracing diversity in the inclusive classroom.

Language and Disability

In an inclusive community, children become aware of how language shapes our thinking and actions. They learn to recognize and resist negative language about *any* kind of diversity. As pointed out in Chapter 2, the overt use of disability-related language within daily conversation typically is used with more abandon than references to race, ethnicity, gender, and/or sexual orientation. For example, children (and adults) freely use terms such as "lame," "retard," and "spaz" because our *culture* lacks awareness about the use of such language. The implication is clear. To be referred to as someone with a disability is the ultimate "put-down." Pay attention to the use of disability-related language in movies that target adolescent audiences. The number of disability references is staggering.

It is everyone's responsibility in an inclusive community to reflect upon language usage. Disability metaphors, similes, and expressions are rife within our everyday language, as in the following select examples: "She turns a blind eye when I try to talk to her"; "What are you, deaf?"; "That's like the blind leading the blind"; "Date him? He's like a midget!"; "… and then she just went *craaaazy*!"; "Dude, you are so retarded!"; "That is totally lame"; "Are you off your meds today?"; "What a moron!" As teachers and students raise their collective awareness about language and its impact upon how disability is perceived in society, it becomes a shared project to identify and resist the use of disability language. Ableist words, phrases, and metaphors function as shorthand for the *undesirability* associated with disability (thereby constituting an insult) and are so commonplace that they are hardly noticed. Developing awareness and skills within the classroom prepares teachers and students to promote positive disability language in their schools, families, and communities.

The Language of Neurodiversity

The term "neurodiversity" is an example of positive framing of disability that is gaining traction in media outlets as well as academic literature. Armstrong (2017) defines neurodiversity in this way:

Coined in the early 1990s by journalist Harvey Blume and Australian autism activist Judy Singer, the term *neurodiversity* can be defined as an understanding that neurological differences are to be honored and respected just like any other human variation, including diversity in race, ethnicity, gender identity, religion, sexual orientation, and so on.

(p. 10)

In other words, a neurodiversity perspective centers around identifying and capitalizing upon student strengths (Kluth & Schwarz, 2008; Mottron, 2011) within classrooms designed to support neurodiversity as opposed to traditional special education practice that focuses upon remediating students' identified deficit areas. Armstrong (2012) refers to the matching of classroom contexts to the needs of neurodiverse students as *positive niche construction* (p. 11).

The adoption of a neurodiverse perspective, typically applied to autism, learning disabilities, ADHD, and social and emotional challenges, shifts how a teacher understands difference within students. Back in Chapter 1, we suggested that what you believe and why you believe it = how you teach. What you believe and why you believe it profoundly influence how you understand and respond to students with disabilities in your classroom. While special educators certainly recognize and draw upon student strengths, it is significant to acknowledge that the institution of special education, grounded in a *deficit-oriented* perspective, influences how students are perceived and constructed by school personnel in ways that are taken for granted.

For example, I (Jan) continue to be dismayed by the negative responses of some general education teachers to the prospect of having a student with ADHD in their classroom. I adored my students with ADHD. I found them to be creative, eager, active, perceptive, and funny—what is not to love? The key is to identify and support their strengths within the classroom context. Equally important is helping students with ADHD understand themselves and their unique learning profiles as well as assisting them in developing effective strategies in executive functioning skills (see Chapter 5) that underlie most academic tasks. Moreover, I learned through experience that motor activity actually *enhances* concentration for students with ADHD. Stability balls, bouncy bands for chairs, standing desks, and wiggle seats are useful for students who need movement in order to concentrate (Armstrong, 2017).

Disability Representation

The women's movement of the 1970s and multiculturalism in the 1980s contributed to an increased representation of girls and children of color within the school curriculum. In comparison, there are far fewer representations of disability and the representations that do exist are variable in quality. For example, stereotypical ideas about disability persist within children's and young adult literature (Ayala, 1999) (see Chapter 2); however, notable books have appeared in recent years that portray disability in a more genuine and complex way. Perhaps the most well-known of these books is *Wonder* (2012), a *New York Times* bestseller by R. J. Palacio—so popular that Hollywood made a film version starring Julia Roberts and Owen Wilson (Chbosky, 2017). Featuring main character Auggie Pullman, a 10-year-old boy with a rare facial difference (mandibulofacial dysostosis), *Wonder* captures his thoughts and perspectives—as well as those of his family and peers—about his transition into public school. With its multiple perspectives on the meaning of difference, *Wonder* is an ideal choice for a class Read Aloud. Other books for "tweens" sure to generate rich class discussions about disability and/or difference are *Mockingbird* (2011) by Kathryn Erskine, *Stargirl* (2000) by Jerry Spinelli, *Out of My Mind* (2010) by Sharon Draper, and *Rules* (2008) by Cynthia Lord.

Beyond locating children's and young adult literature with positive portrayals of disability, we can also think about using stereotypical literature to teach children to read with a critical eye toward disability representation. Literature is a powerful avenue through which to spark meaningful conversations around disability. Moreover, we can challenge students to pay attention to the representation (or omission) of disability within media (e.g., television, animation, movies, newspapers, magazines, ads). Once awareness has been raised, students eagerly seek out and share media examples (positive and negative) with the class and school community.

Class Projects

As students grow in their disability awareness, class projects become a natural extension. Invite them to brainstorm about ways in which to increase awareness at the school level and within the larger community. For example, students might choose to create a hall bulletin board that features disability news; host a disability film festival for parents, administrators, teachers, and peers; write and perform a school play about disability assumptions and misconceptions; work with the school librarian to feature books with positive portrayals of disability; participate in National Inclusion Week; develop an exhibit for display outside the school office about the history of disability; work with the art teacher to highlight the work of disabled artists—the possibilities extend as far as the reaches of imagination.

Self-Advocacy

Inclusive communities validate all learners. Students understand that *every* individual has a particular set of strengths and challenges. There is a class ethos of collaboration rather than competition. Everyone contributes something unique to the learning community.

Disability, framed as natural human variation, loses the stigma of deficit and difference. Open discussions about disability dispel its mystery. When disability can be spoken about, it becomes part of everyday life and not the exception. Students with disabilities speak for themselves rather than having other people speak for them. And part of being able to speak for themselves has to do with understanding the laws that protect them. Thus, development of self-advocacy skills becomes an integral aspect of an inclusive curriculum.

Infusing Disability Studies into the Curriculum

As illustrated by the vignette that opens this chapter, disability studies can be infused quite naturally into the curriculum. Given that the human experience of disability is typically absent in current school curricula, it will be up to you to bring a disability perspective to classroom instruction. Much like the missing contributions of women and people of color in school curricula of years past, so it remains for people with disabilities. Just as girls and children of color once saw few and/or stereotypical representations of themselves in school curricula, so it remains for children with disabilities. How might we introduce a disability perspective into content areas? We can begin by asking students to consider disability-related questions within school curricula, such as:

- How has society's response to disability shifted over time, and why?
- What is the relationship between science and disability?
- How is disability represented (or not) in picture books? What messages are sent about disability through text and illustration?
- How is disability represented in the arts?
- How does disability function as a literary device in literature?
- How do wars contribute to society's response to disability?

To reinforce the notion of disability as human diversity, we might replace disability with race, class, and gender and ask the same questions again. In this way, we engage students in thinking about the ongoing intersections between race, class, gender, and disability.

Disability Curriculum

The Center on Human Policy (CHP) at Syracuse University (see http://thechp.syr.edu/) is perhaps the best online resource for teachers seeking disability studies curricula. The CHP is a policy, research, and advocacy organization involved in the national movement to ensure the rights of people with disabilities in the community. The center engages in a broad range of local, statewide, national, and international activities, including policy studies, research, information and referral, advocacy, training and consultation, and information dissemination. As part of its goal to disseminate information, the CHP website offers teachers downloadable lesson plans for integrating disability studies across areas of the curriculum. Although primarily focused upon grades six and higher, these lesson plans could easily be adapted to accommodate lower grade levels.

With permission from the CHP, we have reproduced a sampling of four lesson plans. Each plan identifies the curriculum content areas as well as the content standards addressed. Objectives, questions, resources and materials, and activities are also provided. We encourage you to access the CHP website for more lesson plans and further information.

Box 9.1 Lesson Plan: What's in a Name?

Subjects

Literature
Social Studies
Sociology

Overview of lesson plan

Students examine the different language used to refer to people with disabilities in American society.

Standards

1. Explain how information and experiences may be interpreted by people from diverse cultural perspectives and frames of reference.
2. Develop critical sensitivities such as empathy and skepticism regarding attitudes, values, and behaviors of people in different historical contexts.

3. Identify and describe the influence of perception, attitudes, values, and beliefs on personal identity.
4. Describe the role of institutions in furthering both continuity and change.

Objectives

1. Identify language used to refer to people with disabilities in different eras.
2. Understand the negative and positive implications of different language.
3. Recognize and understand that acceptable language used to refer to people can vary in different historical eras.
4. Recognize and understand how people with disabilities view language used to refer to them.

Questions to Consider

1. Why does it matter what we call people with disabilities?
2. Does changing language change attitudes?
3. Who should be able to decide what language is used to refer to any group of people?

Resources and Materials

Note: Some of these links may lead to external websites (see CHP website).

1. Excerpts from historical source materials: Dorothea Dix memorial (paragraphs 1–6); Gallaudet sermon (paragraphs 13–15); Education of Idiots, 1849 (p. 1 paragraphs 1–2); A Brief History of the American Asylum, 1893; Sketch of a Life 1863 (p. 1, paragraphs 1–2); Circus and Museum Freaks—Curiosities of Pathology, 1908 (paragraphs 1–3).
2. "Reassigning meaning"—excerpt from Simi Linton's *Claiming Disability.*
3. Excerpts from the articles of Steven Gelb, Scot Danforth, and Kevin Wals (published in *Mental Retardation*) on the name of the American Association on Mental Retardation.
4. "The language of disability: Problems of politics and practice," by Irv Zola.
5. "Terminology used to refer to deaf people," by Michael Schwartz.

Activities and Procedures

1. Students divide into three groups to review two historical source materials and identify language used to refer to people with disabilities. Each group writes terms on a blackboard. Teacher leads discussion. Which of these terms are still used today? What do these terms mean today? Are these terms positive or negative?
2. Students review the articles by Gelb, Danforth, and Walsh. Students have a class discussion or write one- to two-page essays on the following questions. How has the language used to refer to people with mental retardation changed over time? What terms were used in the past? What terms are used today? What might be better terminology? Does language matter? Will the negative meanings associated with old language eventually be associated with new language?
3. Students role play a meeting of the board of the American Association on Mental Retardation. The board is considering changing the name of the association. Students argue for or against the name change.

4. Students review Simi Linton's excerpt on language. Group discussion or one- or two-page essays. Compare and contrast the terms "afflicted," "handicapped," and "disabled." Do these mean the same thing? Does the acceptability of terms depend on who is using them? Should people have the right to decide what they want to be called? What euphemisms are used to refer to people with disabilities? What's wrong with these? Compare and contrast language used to refer to people with disabilities and language used to refer to other groups in society (based on ethnicity, race, or gender).

5. Students read the historical source materials and the essays and articles on language (Linton, Schwartz, Danforth, Gelb, Walsh). The class breaks into small groups. Each group is provided with a large sheet of paper. On a column on the left, students record outdated terms. On a column on the right, they record more acceptable terms for each of the outdated ones. If students are unsure of whether or not a term is acceptable, they record it on the bottom of the sheet. The class comes back together. Each group tapes its sheet to the blackboard or wall. The teacher leads a discussion comparing what the groups recorded.

Box 9.2 Lesson Plan: The Meaning of Disability

Subjects

Literature
Social Studies
Sociology

Overview of lesson plan

Students will be exposed to different definitions of disability, the stigma and stereotypes associated with disability, and the personal experiences of a person who lived in an institution.

Standards

1. Explain and apply ideas, theories, and modes of inquiry drawn from anthropology and sociology in the examination of persistent issues and social problems.
2. Develop critical sensitivities, such as empathy and skepticism regarding attitudes, values, and behaviors of people in different historical contexts.
3. Describe how people create places that reflect cultural values and ideals as they design and build specialized buildings.
4. Identify and describe the influence of perception, attitudes, values, and beliefs on personal identity.
5. Identify and interpret examples of stereotyping, conformity, and altruism.

Objectives

1. Recognize and understand the different ways of defining disability.
2. Understand the parallels between people with disabilities and other historically discriminated against groups.
3. Understand the stereotypes and stigma that can be associated with disability.

Questions to Consider

1. What are some of the different ways of defining people with disabilities?
2. What are the implications of different definitions of disability?
3. Should people have the right to decide what they should be called?

Resources and Materials

Note: Some of these links may lead to external websites (see CHP website).

1. "Reassigning meaning"—excerpt from Simi Linton's *Claiming Disability*.
2. "An insider's view"—excerpt from "The judged, not the judges" (Ed Murphy's life history).
3. "What is a disability?" by Steve Taylor.
4. "Communication barriers between the worlds of 'able-bodiedness' and 'disability,'" by Irv Zola.
5. Excerpt from Wolfensberger's "Origin and nature of our institutional models" (paragraphs 8–121).

Activities and Procedures

1. Students have small-group discussions on the various definitions of disability. Read Linton and Taylor.

   Questions:
   What are the various ways to define disability?
   Is disability an objective condition?
   What is the difference between a medical and a social definition of disability?

2. Students examine the stereotypes and stigmas associated with disability (essays or group discussions). Read Wolfensberger and Zola.

   Questions:
   What are the historical roles and stereotypes of people with disabilities? What are the implications of different roles and stereotypes?
   Do people with disabilities represent a minority group?
   In what ways are people with disabilities similar to or different from other minority groups?
   If you had a disability, would you try to hide it?

3. Read Ed Murphy's account of his life in an institution and write a brief essay on it (Grades 6–8, 9–10, 11–12).

   Questions:
   What does Ed think about labeling?
   Why did Ed end up at the state school?
   What opportunities did Ed miss by being at a state school?
   What does Ed's story tell you about mental retardation?
   Characterize Ed's "voice." Does he sound resentful or bitter?

Box 9.3 Lesson Plan: The Testing of the Feebleminded Immigrants

Subjects

Civics
History
Social Studies

Overview of Lesson Plan

Henry H. Goddard, an American psychologist, was one of the pioneers of intelligence testing. Goddard, best known for his work on the area of the inheritability of intelligence, believed that feeblemindedness was dangerous to society. He believed that it was dangerous for feebleminded people to reproduce, as they were, in his view, responsible for many crimes and other social problems. In this lesson, students will examine the beliefs and practices related to intelligence testing in the early 1900s and explore current criticisms of testing done in this era.

Standards

1. Apply concepts such as role, status, and social class in describing the connections between and interactions of individuals, groups, and institutions in society.
2. Analyze how science and technology influence the core values, beliefs, and attitudes of society, and how core values, beliefs, and attitudes of society shape science and technology.

Objectives

1. To identify at least one of the pioneers of American intelligence testing.
2. To explain the rise in the use of intelligence testing.
3. To explore how science can be used and misused to develop public policy and to influence public opinion.

Question to Consider

•   In what ways was early twentieth-century science used to develop public policy and influence public opinion?

Resources and Materials

1. Essay: *Testing at Ellis Island* (Kluth & Taylor, 2006).
2. "Two immigrants out of five feebleminded," *The Survey*, September 15, 1917.

Activities and Procedures

1. *Class discussion*: Have students read "Two immigrants out of five feebleminded" and ask them the following questions:
    (a) What were the Vineland staff members studying on Ellis Island? What might have been the motivation for conducting such a study?
    (b) Why did so many of the immigrants appear to be feebleminded? Were these individuals indeed of "low intelligence," as Goddard contended, or might there have been other explanations for the low scores?

(c) For what purpose do you think Goddard conducted these tests? How do you think the collected data were used?

(d) In the article, the author reports that even Goddard thought the number of immigrants testing as feebleminded was "startling." He did not, however, see this as an indication that the test might be faulty or problematic. Why do you suppose Goddard had so much faith in the tests?

(e) The author also reports that Goddard did not see the use of interpreters as a "*barrier* to efficient testing." How might the use of interpreters be a barrier to *effective* testing?

2. *Web search*: Now pass out copies of the essay, "Testing at Ellis Island," and allow students to do a web search on the topic of Henry Goddard and Ellis Island. The following websites are good places to begin a search:

(a) Human intelligence: Historical influences, current controversies, teaching resources: www.intelltheory.com

(b) The Vineland Training School: www.revolvy.com/topic/Vineland%20 Training%20School&item_type=topic

3. *Independent work and discussion*: Tell students they are going to create one-minute monologues based on the experiences of the immigrants tested at Ellis Island. Each student should create a character to represent. They should give their characters names, identities, and backgrounds (e.g., ethnicity, gender, country of origin, immigration experience). Then the students should research what a person with such characteristics might have experienced during his or her trans-atlantic crossing and processing at Ellis Island. For example, if the character is Italian, the student could research the Italian immigration experience and learn about the time period in which her character might have traveled, what obstacles he may have faced upon arriving in America, and what job he was trained to perform. Then consider what this character might have experienced upon being tested with Goddard's instruments. What might he have felt or thought? Write a one-minute monologue expressing the characters' thoughts about testing and being assessed by the Vineland staff. What did the testing look like from the perspective of the immigrants? When students finish writing their monologues, have them practice delivering the speech with a partner. Remind them that the monologue must last no longer than one minute. When students are finished writing, editing, and practicing, have them read their stories one by one to the entire class.

4. *Class discussion*: Conclude the lesson by having students discuss the monologues and share their thoughts on the Ellis Island testing. Ask:

(a) How did the Vineland staff understand or "see" disability?

(b) What do you suppose was the impact of Goddard's report? How do you think his findings shaped public opinion, policy, or practices of the time?

(c) How do the immigration and citizenship processes of the past compare with those of today? Are there practices that we employ today that might be considered bigoted?

Box 9.4 Lesson Plan: General Tom Thumb—Star or Spectacle?

Subjects

History
Social Studies
Sociology

Overview of Lesson Plan

Charles Sherwood Stratton (1838–83), American entertainer, was known to the American public as Tom Thumb. Stratton was a curiosity due to his size. Born in Connecticut in the 1830s, Tom Thumb was a person of short stature, or a little person. Stratton's parents were of usual size. He appeared normal at birth but stopped growing before he was a year old. At four years of age he was 25 inches tall. In 1842, P. T. Barnum exhibited Tom Thumb at Barnum's American Museum, a showcase for curiosities in New York City. Stratton became world-famous through his work with Barnum.

This lesson highlights Stratton's story. The activities are focused on Stratton's life as a celebrity and his fame. Students are asked to consider how differences have been viewed historically and to reflect on how Stratton is perhaps a "product of his times."

Standards

1. Apply an understanding of culture as an integrated whole that explains the functions and interactions of language, literature, the arts, traditions, beliefs and values, and behavior patterns.
2. Apply ideas, theories, and modes of historical inquiry to analyze historical and contemporary developments, and to inform and evaluate actions concerning public policy issues.
3. Analyze the role of perceptions, attitudes, values, and beliefs in the development of personal identity.
4. Describe the various forms institutions take and explain how they develop and change over time.

Objectives

1. To analyze the role of popular culture in American history.
2. To understand the ways images of people with differences were manipulated in freak shows and related venues to arouse public interest and curiosity.
3. To analyze the making of a celebrity.
4. To examine the ways people with disabilities or physical differences have been perceived, treated, and labeled over time.

Questions to Consider

1. Should "human curiosities" or "freaks" have been considered celebrities or exploited victims of manipulative showmen, or both?
2. How were the images of people who are different or have disabilities managed to arouse public interest?
3. What are the parallels between the freak shows and popular culture today?

Resources and Materials

Note: Some of these links may lead to external websites (see CHP website).

1. "Exhibiting people for money: Terminology," by Robert Bogdan.
2. "P.T. Barnum's American Museum," by Robert Bogdan.
3. "Love in miniature: Mr. and Mrs. Tom Thumb," by Robert Bogdan.
4. Visual stills: "Tom Thumb," "General Tom Thumb and Lady," "The Promenade," "The Reception," and "Mr. And Mrs. Tom Thumb with P.T. Barnum, Commodore Nutt and Minnie Warren."
5. "Sketch of the life … Charles S. Stratton," 1863 (paragraphs 2–5, 7–9, 11–25).
6. "The Life of P.T. Barnum" (paragraphs 184–91, 488–96).

Activities and Procedures

1. Ask students to share any information they have about people of short stature and other physical differences (e.g., those who use wheelchairs, those who are deaf, conjoined twins, those with albinism) and impressions they have of how those with physical differences are viewed by society. Then ask students to break into groups of three to four and have them name individuals or groups of people who have become famous for their physical differences (e.g., munchkins in *Wizard of Oz*).
2. Bring the group back together and introduce students to the story of Charles S. Stratton. Have students read or, for younger grades, read them Bogdan's "Love in miniature" (also the essays, "P.T. Barnum and the American Museum" and "Terminology," if Lesson 1 was not used), "Sketch of the life … Charles S. Stratton," and "The life of P.T. Barnum." Then show the visual stills. Again, ask students to return to small groups and discuss the passages from "Sketch of life" and "The life of P.T. Barnum" and the visual stills. Pose the question: What can be learned about Stratton from these materials (e.g., social class of Stratton, beliefs and norms of the time period)? Have one or two members from each group report on their discussion to the entire class.
3. Break the class into small groups. Each group will work with a different part of the "Sketch of the life … Charles S. Stratton" and "The life of P.T. Barnum." Assign each small group a few paragraphs of the document. Groups are responsible for presenting their passage to the rest of the class in some way. Allow them to use any of the following methods to share their passage with the rest of the class: perform a skit, do a dramatic reading, make a piece of impromptu art (e.g., collage, colorful timeline), or engage in some type of storytelling. Give students time to prepare their presentation and offer support and ideas as they work. Have students present Tom Thumb's (Stratton's) story to each other in chronological order (e.g., courtship, wedding). Offer clarifying comments as the story is presented. After the presentations, ask students to consider Stratton's story and present the following questions in a teacher-led discussion: How was Tom seen, perceived, and labeled by the public? By those close to him? By himself? Did Tom Thumb have a disability? Was Tom Thumb a celebrity? What makes someone a celebrity? How is celebrity achieved today? Was Tom Thumb exploited by Barnum? Did Tom Thumb think of his work with Barnum as exploitation?

4. Have students discuss Stratton's story in a historical and political context. Have them go back to their small groups and answer the following questions: Why was "Sketch of the life" written? What can be learned about the mid-1800s from Stratton's story? What were the entertainment options for people at that time? What was happening during this time period in America? How was Tom Thumb a product of the times?

5. Have students write a letter from Stratton (Tom Thumb) to those critics who believe he was exploited by Barnum. What would Stratton say to these critics? Students can choose to write to critics from Stratton's time or to those living today.

6. Have students design a project that compares Tom Thumb's work with Barnum to a situation today. For example, students might compare Barnum's display of Tom Thumb to the World Wrestling Federation (WWF) or a "reality" television program. Students might compare the two by creating a PowerPoint presentation, presenting a photo essay, writing a persuasive essay, or designing a collage or painting.

Try it … you can do it!

If we are to create inclusive communities, we must affirm human diversity within school curricula. In order to understand disability as a natural part of human diversity, children need to see disability represented in the same way that race, class, and gender are represented. Just as we include the contributions of women and people of color in school curricula, so must we include persons with disabilities.

We encourage you to get your feet wet. Wade in and try a single lesson. See what happens. Our bet is that your students will astound you and together you will grow in new and unexpected ways. Before you know it, you and your students will be on your way to joining the inclusion revolution!

Questions to Consider

1. How comfortable are you talking about disabilities? How comfortable are you when speaking to familiar or unfamiliar persons with disabilities?
2. How openly are disabilities talked about in your classroom, school, and community?
3. How well do your students understand their IEPs?
4. How well can your students describe their disabilities and what they need to learn? Are they comfortable doing so? How do you know?
5. Are you and your students aware of disability-related language used in your classroom, school, and community? How do you and your students respond (or not)?
6. What do you see as the consequences of silence around disability?
7. How well do your students without disabilities understand disability? How do you know?
8. Do your students with and without disabilities engage in conversations about disability? Why or why not?
9. How likely are you to try infusing disability studies into the curriculum? What might facilitate your willingness to try?
10. Do you think it is important to consider disability as another aspect of diversity (like race, class, and gender)? Why or why not?

References

Armstrong, T. (2012). *Neurodiversity in the classroom: Strength-based strategies to help students with special needs succeed in school and life.* Alexandria, VA: ASCD.

Armstrong, T. (2017). Neurodiversity: The future of special education? *Educational Leadership,* 74(7), 10–16.

Ayala, E. C. (1999). "Poor little things" and "brave little souls": The portrayal of individuals with disabilities in children's literature. *Reading Research and Instruction,* 39(1), 103–16.

Baglieri, S. (2017). *Disability studies and the inclusive classroom.* London: Routledge.

Blatt, B. & Kaplan, F. (1966). *Christmas in purgatory: A photographic essay on mental retardation.* Syracuse, NY: Human Policy Press.

Causton, J. & Tracy-Bronson, C. (2015). *The educator's handbook for inclusive school practices.* Baltimore, MD: Paul H. Brookes.

Chbosky, S. (Dir.). (2017). *Wonder* [film]. Santa Monica, CA: Lionsgate.

Draper, S. (2010). *Out of my mind.* New York, NY: Atheneum.

Erskine, K. (2011). *Mockingbird.* London: Penguin.

Hamovitch, S. (Dir./Prod.). (2004). *Without apology* [documentary]. Brookly, NY: One-eyed Cat Productions.

Kluth, P. & Schwarz, P. (2008). *Just give him the whale! 20 ways to use fascinations, areas of expertise, and strengths to support students with autism.* Baltimore, MD: Brookes Publishing.

Lord, C. (2008). *Rules.* New York, NY: Scholastic.

Mottron, L. (2011, November 3). Changing perceptions: The power of autism. *Nature,* 479, 33–5.

Palacio, R. J. (2012). *Wonder.* St. Louis, MO: Turtleback Books.

Sapon-Shevin, M. (1998). *Because we can change the world: A practical guide to building cooperative, inclusive classroom communities.* Upper Saddle River, NJ: Pearson Education.

Spinelli, J. (2000). *Stargirl.* New York, NY: Scholastic.

Stiker, H. J. (1999). *A history of disability.* Ann Arbor, MI: Love Publishing.

Trent, J. (2016). *Inventing the feeble mind: A history of intellectual disability in the United States.* Oxford: Oxford University Press.

10 Promoting Inclusive Beliefs and Practices
"What if my school is 'not there yet' in regard to inclusion?"

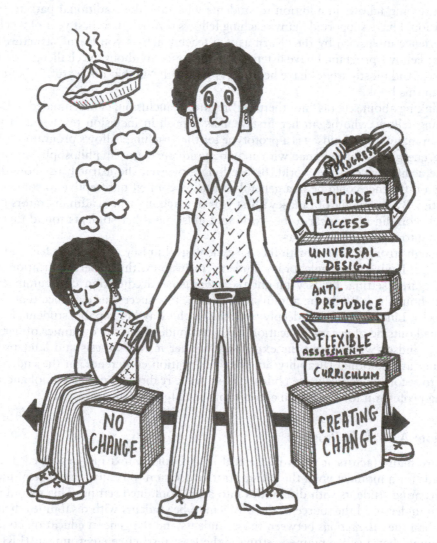

Cartoon #10 Pie-in-the-sky or civil right?

At the turn of the twenty-first century, New York City schools faced the largest teacher shortage in decades. In response to this crisis, as well as to the mandate for "highly qualified teachers" under No Child Left Behind (NCLB) legislation, the New York City Teaching Fellows program, an alternative teacher certification route, was established to attract professionals from other fields into teaching (see /www.nycteachingfellows.org). In light of its mission to recruit and prepare high-quality, dedicated persons to impact student achievement in high-need classrooms, it is rather unsurprising that special education was targeted as an area of high need. Every year since the turn of the century, large numbers of teaching fellows begin teaching in New York City special education classes while simultaneously attending graduate special education programs.

As a teacher educator at a university where teaching fellows are enrolled, I (Jan) have taught teaching fellows in addition to students who take the traditional path to teacher certification. I have supported many teaching fellows through their first year of teaching—an experience intensified by the "learn as you teach/teach as you learn" structure of the Teaching Fellows program. I have listened to their concerns about the challenges of special education. And mostly what I have heard has to do with "all that *other* stuff" about which we began this book.

In thinking about schools "not there yet" regarding inclusion, I am reminded of Lindsey, a teaching fellow, who began her first year as a push-in inclusion teacher at a middle school. In many ways, Lindsey is a prototype for the Teaching Fellows program—a bright, creative, energetic young woman with an undergraduate degree in philosophy and a desire to make a difference in the world. Before long, however, she learned just how difficult making a difference could be in a general education context unreceptive to students with disabilities. By the middle of Lindsey's first year of teaching, school administrators decided that inclusion did not appear to be working. Lindsey and her students found themselves resettled into a self-contained class.

Although strongly aligned with inclusive ideology, Lindsey admitted to feeling relieved at no longer having to struggle for her students' inclusion within general education. Within the segregated setting, Lindsey taught the *same* general education curriculum and her students flourished. While the administration took this success as evidence that segregation works, Lindsey remained deeply troubled by the way her capable students had been positioned outside of general education. To better understand the dynamics of her school context, Lindsey wrote about the experience for her master's thesis and later presented this paper at a national Disability Studies in Education conference. In the end, she was unable to reconcile her inclusive philosophy with the realities of public school and left the teaching profession for a career in a non-profit social justice organization.

Inclusion: A Work in Progress

There are many factors at work in the real-life school context just described. However, let's focus for a moment upon the administrative decision to resolve the issue of inclusion by segregating students with disabilities into a self-contained setting. This school administration understood the source of the problem to be students with disabilities themselves rather than the *interactions* between those students and the general education context. In determining that a self-contained setting is the least restrictive environment (LRE) for a *group* of students with disabilities (a response that falls outside of the tenets outlined in the Individuals with Disabilities Education Improvement Act but nevertheless implemented), the status quo is maintained and the structures that support general education remain unchanged. In other words, if we put students with disabilities where they "belong," we can get on with the business of education for everyone else.

As we have stated elsewhere, inclusion is a school-wide belief system in which diversity is viewed as a rich resource for everyone not a problem to overcome—or, as illustrated in the scenario above, a problem expediently resolved through segregation. Inclusion requires hard work on the part of administrators, teachers, and students. It is an organic process that requires systematic reflection and collective problem solving among everyone involved.

Nurturing Our Practice

Inclusion needs tending. It is not something we put into place structurally, then sit back and hope for the best. It is about everyone working consciously and collaboratively toward the common goal of nurturing a vibrant inclusive community. And achieving that goal requires shared leadership that routinely and thoughtfully takes stock of how actively its inclusive community pursues and enacts new knowledge and innovative practice. For example, we might ask ourselves questions such as the following:

- What kind of professional development opportunities are offered at school and district levels? How are faculty informed about such opportunities? Have faculty and/or administration attended professional development sessions? If so, how and with whom have they shared the information? Is release time available for faculty to attend professional development sessions? In what ways has professional development information and/or training been integrated into classroom practice?
- Are there opportunities for teachers to visit other inclusive classrooms and schools? If so, in what ways have these visits contributed to classroom practice?
- Are workshops about inclusion and co-teaching offered to parents at the school and district levels? If so, how are such opportunities communicated to parents? Have parents attended such sessions? If so, how and with whom have they shared the information?
- Are ongoing professional development opportunities offered to paraprofessionals (classroom aides)? If so, how has information about professional development been communicated? How many paraprofessionals have attended? In what ways has their professional development contributed to classroom practice in inclusive contexts?
- How do we continue to raise awareness among students with and without disabilities? What projects have students generated and carried out?

How Well are We Doing?

Now that we have thought about what it is that we are doing to nurture our practice, we need to consider how *well* we do inclusion. In other words, what outcomes have resulted from our practices? It is helpful to reflect upon questions such as these:

- Is disability spoken about in the classroom? What language do teachers, paraprofessionals, service providers, and administrators use when speaking about disabilities? What language do students use when speaking about disabilities? How do students with disabilities speak about themselves?
- How do students with and without disabilities engage with one another? What opportunities do students with and without disabilities have to interact meaningfully with each other? How well are students with and without disabilities performing (academically and socially)? How do we know? What do students say about inclusion? How well do students understand and appreciate diversity? How do we know? How often do students with disabilities remain within the general education classroom?

- How often do teachers collaborate with one another? In what ways is the general education curriculum differentiated? How effective are we in differentiating the curriculum? How do we know? Is diversity represented in the curriculum? How well? How do we know?
- What outcomes (positive and negative) did we not anticipate? What do these outcomes mean?
- What is the response of parents of children with and without disabilities to inclusion? How often do we communicate with parents? What do they have to tell us about our classroom practice? Do we have meaningful collaborations with parents? How do our collaborations with parents contribute to classroom practice?
- How do we communicate how well we are doing (e.g., newsletters, school websites, hallway bulletin boards, library displays, community meetings)? In answering such questions, the strengths and challenges of an inclusive school community will emerge, and goals can be set for moving even closer to inclusive ideals.

Advocating for School Change

Think back to Lindsey's school context. If administrators and teachers had asked themselves the questions above, no doubt their answers would have revealed little in the way of inclusive practices. Yet the "failure" of inclusion in this middle school is attributed to students with disabilities themselves, thereby absolving school personnel of accountability for their problematic implementation. We do not mean to suggest that Lindsey's experience is typical; however, we must acknowledge that such attitudes and practices do exist. What would happen if you found yourself, a new teacher like Lindsey, in a similar context?

What Is Your Stance?

Now that you have come along with us through these pages, how would you articulate your stance on inclusion? What beliefs have you reaffirmed? What beliefs have you reconsidered or acquired? What issues remain unresolved for you? Rest assured that none of us can claim to know with absolute certainty the *right* way to do inclusion. What we can do is commit to strive continually toward an educational vision that enacts social justice and educational equity for everyone.

As a new teacher, you can anticipate a career in which it is likely that you will teach in more than one school setting. Given that comprehensive changes in public education typically occur over time and at varying rates within local contexts, you may work in a school with a strong inclusion ethos, a school that is "not there yet" regarding inclusion, or a school somewhere in between. What remains constant is *you* and the beliefs you enact in your classroom. Remember—what you believe determines how you teach, which results in particular outcomes for students.

What Can You Do to Initiate School Change?

Recently I (Jan) initiated a discussion about the social construction of disability in a graduate education class comprised of mostly first- and second-year teachers in New York City schools. Two special education teachers who teach in segregated classrooms passionately argued that it does not matter what other people think about disability so long as special education students have the confidence and determination within themselves to succeed. As a lively class discussion ensued, these two teachers came to understand how a well-intentioned "pull yourself up by the bootstraps" stance (meant to inspire students toward success) is problematic in two ways: (1) the *reality* that students with disabilities experience (i.e., the assumptions and misconceptions that circulate within an ableist culture) is dismissed as nonexistent, irrelevant, and/or unimportant, and (2) responsibility for success is placed upon students with disabilities while the institutional structures that support ableism remain unchallenged and unchanged.

If we understand our work as teachers in terms of advocacy for all children, our stance on inclusion matters greatly, especially in school contexts that are "not there yet." Is it possible for a single teacher to facilitate a shift toward more inclusive practices? While we acknowledge the challenge of initiating change in any school culture, we offer the following ideas for your consideration:

- *Deepen understanding*: If we are to disrupt ableist thinking and practices, we must first reflect upon ourselves. No matter how deeply committed we are to inclusive ideals, we live within a culture where ableism seems right and natural. We are all susceptible to thinking and acting in ableist ways—no matter how informed we think that we are. Try to engage colleagues in an informal study group around disability studies, inclusion, and ableism (see the Appendices for a list of resources). If you are unable to gather such a group at school, reach out to friends and family to join you. After all, our culture has a long way to go in raising its awareness of ableism! Although you can certainly take up your own study, the benefit of a study group is the opportunity to engage with multiple points of view, pushing one another's thinking in new directions. Study groups might be formed around watching and engaging critically with cinematic representations of disability as well as documentaries that feature persons with disabilities (see Chapter 2); reading memoirs written by persons with disabilities (see Chapter 2); and/or studying media representations of disability (e.g., television news, magazines, advertisements, commercials, reality TV, newspapers).

- *Connect with like-minded colleagues*: It is easier to maintain focus and energy with the support of one or more like-minded colleagues. If you are new to your school context, pay careful attention to the way in which your colleagues talk about and respond to diversity among children. Connecting with even one colleague who shares a similar stance to your own is enough to start a meaningful collaboration. If, however, you are unable to find a like-minded colleague on your faculty, try to form collaborative relationships outside of your school context. For example, you may meet colleagues in graduate education classes or at professional development training sessions. You might also ask a professor or district consultant to recommend teachers with whom you might connect. The energy of others will sustain you—even if the relationship occurs via e-mail.

- *Disrupt ableism*: It is helpful to keep in mind that most people are unaware of ableist thinking and practices. If we are interested in change, we must acknowledge existing beliefs and work toward raising awareness among faculty and students. As discussed in Chapter 9, teachers and students can work together on projects for raising awareness in the classroom, school, and community. I had the privilege to see what came out of a stunning collaboration between Ronnie, a teaching fellow with a professional theater background, and his special education students in a "failing" high school slated for closure at the end of the school year. In response to his students' anger and frustration at having their school (and themselves by extension) publicly labeled as "failing," Ronnie challenged them to do something about it. His class joined forces with a general education English teacher and her students. The result was an original stage production written and performed by students with and without disabilities at an off-Broadway venue—a brilliant, wickedly humorous, and deeply poignant expression of life on the inside when "failure" defines who you are.

Negotiating the Special Education Process

Recently, a first-year co-teacher, Tanneka, expressed concerns to me about attending her very first annual review meeting for a little boy in her second-grade classroom. It seemed that there was something beyond the usual jitters about doing something new for the first time that she needed to say. It gradually emerged that something did not "seem right" to her about the process. She explained that the school guidance counselor had informed her that she needed to convince the mother to sign the paperwork agreeing to the placement of her son in a segregated special education class. This young teacher's instincts were on target. The law guarantees parents the right to *collaborate* with school personnel in educational decision making about their children; it does *not* give school personnel the right to coerce parents into agreement with unilaterally made decisions. If something does not "seem right" to you, most likely it is *not* right. Most new teachers are eager to cooperate and rely upon experienced colleagues for guidance. Based upon our experiences, we can tell you that not all school personnel accurately understand and implement the tenets of IDEIA. Special education law (not unlike many laws) can be challenging to understand. If you are to be an effective advocate for your students, you need to have a working understanding of the law.

IDEIA and You

Although we recommend that you consult more extensive resources about IDEIA, here we provide the main points for you as a quick reference. You will note that we have used boldface and type to highlight specific references to general education. The following principles constitute IDEIA.

Principle 1: Zero Reject and Child Find

- Local school districts cannot exclude students with disabilities from public schools due to the nature or degree of their disabilities.
- All students ages 3 through 21 must be located, evaluated, and provided with appropriate education programs.
- States are required to locate and evaluate children with disabilities between birth and 3 years of age.
- The 1997 reauthorization of IDEIA clarified that all students, *even those suspended or expelled*, must be provided with FAPE (free appropriate public education).
- Even students not yet identified could assert the protection of IDEIA in a disciplinary situation if school personnel had knowledge of the *potential* disability (e.g., the parent notified the school that the child was in need of special education, the child's behavior demonstrated the need for special services, the parent requested an evaluation, the child's **general education teacher** expressed concerns to special education personnel). All states are required to implement child find procedures to locate unserved children and inform parents of available services and programs for children with disabilities.
- Local school districts have annual early childhood screening programs in an attempt to locate unserved preschool children with disabilities.

Principle 2: Evaluation and Classification

- Discrimination in assessment is not allowed. Test instruments must not be culturally or racially biased. IDEIA states that, if students do not speak English, every attempt must be made to assess them in their native language. If students have disabilities, assessment instruments must not discriminate on the basis of the disability.

- The assessment must identify *all* of a child's educational needs, whether or not they commonly link to the child's disability category (e.g., social and emotional needs).
- Assessments must be comprehensive and use a variety of sources from a variety of professionals. The child must be assessed in all areas related to the suspected disability. Assessments must also gather functional and developmental information, include information from the parents, and include information related to helping the child be involved in and progress in the **general curriculum**. Assessments must be valid and reliable and administered by trained professionals.
- The rights of students with disabilities and their parents must be protected during assessment (e.g., parents must be notified in writing when their child is referred for an evaluation, receive information on parents' rights, give informed consent prior to evaluation, and participate in meetings when identification, evaluation, and educational placement of their child is discussed). The child's progress toward special education goals must be provided to parents **at least as often as in general education**, and a reevaluation must be conducted at least every three years.
- Children with disabilities must be included in **general education state and district-wide assessments**, with appropriate accommodations, if needed. For children who cannot participate, as determined by the IEP team, the team must write on the IEP why the assessment is not appropriate and how the child will be assessed.

Principle 3: Parental Rights

- IDEIA ensures that school districts cannot make unilateral decisions about the identification, evaluation, and placement of children with disabilities.
- Parents must give *informed* consent before their child is evaluated for initial consideration for placement in special education and before initial placement in special education.
- Parents are afforded the opportunity to provide information to the evaluation team and fully participate in decisions about a child's eligibility for special education, the IEP, and placement.
- Before the identification, evaluation, or placement of a child is changed, parents must be given the opportunity to participate in the decision-making process.
- Parents have the right to review and obtain all records concerning their child.
- If a parent disagrees with any decision, the parent has the right to challenge the decision through mediation and due process procedures.

Principle 4: Least Restrictive Environment

- *General requirements*: To the maximum extent appropriate, children with disabilities (including children in public and private institutions and other care facilities) are educated with children who are non-disabled. Special classes, separate schooling, or other removal of children with disabilities from the **general education environment** occurs only if the nature and severity of the disabilities are such that education in regular classes with the use of services and supplementary aids cannot be achieved satisfactorily.
- *Continuum of placements*: A continuum of placements must be available to students with disabilities—general education classes, special classes, special schools, home instruction, instruction in hospitals or institutions, and supplemental instruction to be provided in conjunction with **general education** placement.
- *Placements*: The child's placement is considered annually, is based on the child's IEP, and is as close as possible to the child's home. Children with disabilities may *not* be

removed from age-appropriate **general education** classrooms solely on the basis of needed modification in the **general education** curriculum.

- *Non-academic settings*: With respect to non-academic or extracurricular services, including meals and recess, children with disabilities are to participate with non-disabled children to the maximum extent possible.

Principle 5: The Individual Education Plan (IEP)

- The IEP consists of two parts: a meeting and a document. Required participants at an IEP meeting are as follows: the child's parents (or guardians); the **general education teacher**; the special education teacher; a district participant who is qualified to provide or supervise the provision of special education, knowledgeable about the **general education curriculum**, and knowledgeable about the availability of resources; a person who can interpret instructional implications of the child's education; others at the discretion of the parents and the school district; and the child (when appropriate).
- It is important to note that the parent is listed first in IDEIA regulations, indicating that parent participation is very important. Parents must receive copies of the IEP.

  The **general education teacher** must be present at IEP meetings to participate in the development, review, and revision of IEPs, including assisting in the determination of behavioral interventions, supplementary aids, services, and modifications for school personnel.

Components of the IEP

As a document, the Individual Education Plan contains many parts that are interrelated; for example:

- Present levels of performance.
- Annual goals.
- Short-term goals.
- Special education services to be provided (including related services, supplementary aids, and program modifications).
- Extent to which the child will participate in **general education**.
- Anticipated date for initiation, frequency, location, and duration of services.
- How child's progress toward goals will be measured and how parents will be regularly informed of progress.
- *Transition*: at age 14, statement of transition-service needs that focus on the child's course of study; at age 16, statement of needed transition services, including inter-agency responsibilities or needed linkages.
- Modification in administration of state and district assessments of student achievement (if not participating, tell why not and how the child will be assessed).

Note that IEPs must be accessible to the school district personnel responsible for their implementation. **General education teachers** must be informed of their specific responsibilities in carrying out IEPs.

Principle 6: Conflict Resolution

To protect children's rights, IDEIA regulates two types of conflict resolution: mediation and due process.

Mediation

In order to ensure "both sides" can come to an agreement before differences escalate, mediation is made available, whereby, in brief:

- All states must offer mediation as an option to resolve conflict.
- Mediation is a voluntary (and confidential) process in which an impartial third party assists the disputing parties in reaching a mutually satisfying agreement.
- Mediation focuses on creative problem solving, communication between all parties, and the future.
- Successful mediation results in a written agreement.

Due Process

Encompassed within a constellation of due process rights, a formal procedure of disagreeing with school recommendations about disability, placements, accommodations, modifications, and so on is guaranteed to parents. This form of due process is sometimes referred to as an "impartial hearing." In sum,

- Due process is a formal, adversarial procedure in which an impartial third party listens to evidence presented, including the examination and cross-examination of witnesses.
- Based on the evidence, the hearing officer renders a decision to resolve the conflict. This decision is binding unless it is appealed to the judicial system.
- During a hearing, there is a winner and a loser and the focus is mostly on the past.
- Both parents and school districts are usually represented by attorneys in due process hearings.
- During the hearing, the provision of **stay put** applies—i.e., the child stays in the current placement.
- Parents may be awarded reasonable attorney's fees by a court if they prevail in a due process hearing.

It is not uncommon for general educators to assume that it is special educators' responsibility to understand and respond to IDEIA. As evidenced by the number of times that general education is mentioned in the law, teaching students with disabilities is a *shared* responsibility between general and special educators. Ignorance is never an excuse under the law. If we are to guarantee the right of students with disabilities to a free and appropriate public education, *all* teachers need to understand and comply with IDEIA regulations. Keep in mind that you should be able to clearly articulate the law to both parents and students. The more parents and students know about the law, the better prepared they will be to participate meaningfully in a collaborative partnership with you. Your role as teacher advocate will contribute greatly toward building and sustaining an inclusive school environment.

Advocacy in Action

We have established that it is essential that general and special education teachers familiarize themselves with the tenets of IDEIA. Now we are going so far as to suggest that there is more required than mere knowledge. Successful inclusion requires that we pay active attention to the implementation of the law within our school contexts. We believe that teaching is an act of advocacy for each and every student as well as their families. Children do not exist in a vacuum. Families are *always* a highly significant aspect of teaching. All that we do should be in the best interest of moving children and their families forward. In every school context—a school with a strong inclusion ethos, a school that is "not there yet" with inclusion, or a school somewhere in-between—we believe that advocacy is an integral part of teaching. Thus, it is not enough to implement "the letter of the law"; advocacy means enacting "the *spirit* of the law." In other words, we are suggesting that you actively reflect upon the implementation of the law in your school and act on behalf of your students and their families in ways that "*feel* right." So what does advocacy look like in action? To illustrate, we highlight below two sections of the law: parental engagement (Principle 3) and transition (Principle 5).

Advocating for and with Parents (Principle 3 under IDEIA)

As referenced in Chapter 1, I (Jan) began my teaching career as a middle school resource teacher in the first year that states were required to implement the new special education law. In those early days, I observed tensions among administrators and teachers regarding implementation of the law, as well as an overall disconnectedness on the part of parents of children with disabilities. As I describe in *What Mothers Say about Special Education: From the 1960s to the Present* (Valle, 2009), my initial overtures to cultivate relationships with the parents of my students were met with responses that ranged from surprise to suspicion. After all, a phone call from a teacher typically signaled a problem at school. The law's mandated parent–teacher collaboration in regard to educational decision making was something new for parents *and* teachers. Moreover, I discovered that many of the parents of my students were not even aware of the new law much less the law's guarantee of parental rights.

In thinking about how to reconfigure my relationship with parents, I strategized with a fellow resource teacher to develop and offer a series of parent–teacher workshops. We reasoned that informal workshops held in our shared classroom could create a space for positive exchanges with and among parents, as well as provide a forum for much needed explanations about the new law. Given the reluctance of parents to engage with school personnel, we solicited the help of a few mothers with whom we had established a working relationship. These mothers reached out to other parents to explain the concept of the workshops, ask for topic suggestions, and generally stimulate interest.

Six years later, our workshop program had grown in ways we never expected. At the beginning of the project, we could not have imagined the degree of positive and productive energy that would emerge from parents and teachers coming together for the benefit of their *mutual* children.

Although we began with a small group of faithful mothers, participation in the six-session series (spaced throughout the school year to foster regular interaction) continued to grow year after year. Topics for discussion shifted with each school year, depending on the mothers' interests and needs (e.g., parents rights under the law, understanding the history and structure of the law, making sense of psychoeducational assessments, supporting learning disabilities at home and school, providing positive supports for homework, fostering organizational skills at home, developing strategies for ADHD at home and school, understanding the strengths of LD/ADHD, LD and giftedness, and preparing for high school and post-secondary options). After a few years, some fathers began to attend, as well as some extended family members (e.g., grandparents, aunts, in-laws). From the beginning, our students expressed interest in the workshops and urged their parents to attend. Before long, they asked if *they* could join the meetings—a thought that had not occurred to us initially. Their participation took the workshops to another level. This was a space where students could speak for and among themselves to their own and others' parents. The engagement among parents, teachers, *and* students became one of the most powerful aspects of the program.

I share my experience of the parent–teacher workshops as an example of *advocacy in action*. What began as a realization that parents did not have enough information about the law in order to meaningfully participate as educational partners laid the foundation for what would set the trajectory for my career in education. All that I learned from collaborating with parents during those early years has served as a guide in every educational context within which I have worked since. For example, during the mid-1980s through the mid-1990s, I worked at a developmental pediatrics clinic as an educational diagnostician on an interdisciplinary evaluation team. Parents began to report difficulties with school personnel considering and/or responding to non-district testing and recommendations—despite a parent's right under the law to secure independent testing. Thus, my role as an educational diagnostician expanded to include parent advocacy. Over the years, I accompanied countless parents to countless school meetings at every grade level in both public and private schools. As a former school district employee advocating from a position within the private sector, I gained a rich perspective on the dynamics of special education meetings. I did attend successful meetings in which participants engaged with one another in a respectful and collaborative manner; however, more often than not, I observed presumably well-intentioned school professionals engaging in coercive persuasion rather than collaboration—reflecting what Tanneka (earlier in this chapter) describes about a school guidance counselor instructing her to *convince* a parent to place her child in a more restrictive environment. Although parental rights exist under the law, it is clear that parents may need guidance and/or assistance to access the process.

What does advocacy look like in an inclusive context? Here are some simple strategies that go a long way toward establishing collaborative relationships with parents:

- Invite parents to *open the meeting* with what they need to say, need you to hear about their child, and/or need you to address in the meeting. Be explicit about your desire to establish a meaningful partnership in which you learn from each other.
- Be sure to schedule uninterrupted time to meet with a parent. Nothing inspires a lack of confidence more than a meeting in which teachers bounce in and out, loudly stating that they only have x amount of time.
- Always speak about the "whole child." Be descriptive about what you see in the classroom. Give concrete examples. Talk about the many ways in which you *delight* in their child.
- Acknowledge that parents hold a long-term perspective about their child in contrast to your comparatively "in-the-moment" perspective. Take time to learn what parents know and have to teach you about their child.
- Minimize the use of educational jargon and clearly explain any that you do use.
- Listen *carefully* to what parents have to say about what it is that they want for their child. All parents want the best for their children. Remember that seeing one's child struggle is an emotional experience for any parent. *Be very kind*.
- Dare to dream big. Open up as many possibilities as you can for a child. Try what a parent suggests. See what happens.
- Take notes and recap what has been talked about and agreed upon—other than what is written on the IEP. Send a follow-up email with these details and identifying who is responsible for what.
- Make yourself accessible to parents. Establish yourself as a team working in the best interest of the child you *share*!

Advocating for Quality of Life beyond K-12 (Principle 5 under IDEIA)

Cast your mind back, for a moment, to your last year or two in high school. Were you excited by the prospect of leaving it all behind, officially becoming a young adult, and planning to go to college or work? Did you know what you wanted to be? Or did you feel somewhat anxious that you'd be on your own, expected to do things independently and to prove yourself to a new group of people at college or in the workplace? Anthropologically speaking, graduating from school is a rite of passage within our society. Among their many purposes, K-12 schools are *a means to an end*, and that is to prepare young citizens to be employed for the majority of their lives. As twelfth grade approaches and arrives, students are increasingly aware that they are approaching a fork in the road and must make some important choices in life. Upon graduation, will it be college or work—and, how best to be prepared for either option?

Only a couple of generations ago, a minority of people were expected to attend college. However, the workplace has changed dramatically in the last half century, and now—and not without a degree of controversy—many educators and parents alike expect schools to prepare children and youth for college. Currently, over 84 percent of all students graduate from high school, with 69 percent of them entering college immediately (National Center for Education Statistics, 2017). In addition, there has been a steady annual growth in students with disabilities graduating from high school—currently, 65.5 percent do so (ibid.). Over the last 20 years, the number of students with disabilities in college has risen from 6 percent (Disabilities, Opportunities, Internetworking, & Technology, n.d.) to 10.9 percent (National Center for Education Statistics, 2016). So, while this shows promising growth in the right direction, it also obscures some important issues, including: preparing to graduate from high school for students with disabilities can feel more challenging, as can applying for colleges or jobs, than it does for their non-disabled peers; differences among racial groups with disabilities; sometimes a lack of flexibility at the college level to make accommodations; and higher college drop-out rates and longer degree completion times for students with disabilities compared to non-disabled peers. In addition, the 34.5 percent of students who do not graduate face greater challenges in terms of finding secure, well-paid work and are more likely to become part of the school-to-prison pipeline, a topic we will discuss later in this chapter.

At this juncture, we thought it would be interesting to share some recent statistics taken from the Institute on Disability, University of New Hampshire's Annual Report (2017) on citizens with disabilities in the U.S. in relation to employment across the lifespan:

- The percentage of people with disabilities varies greatly by state, as does the number of people with disabilities in employment. Data relating to poverty, earnings, and health behaviors also vary.
- In 2016, of the U.S. population with disabilities (12.8%), over half (51.0%) were people of working age (18–64), while 41.4% were 65 and older. Of the U.S. population as a whole, only 7.3% of children aged 5–17 were disabled and only 0.4% of children under 5 years of age.
- Of those people with disabilities aged 18–64 and living in the community, 35.9% were employed. In contrast, 76.6% of people without disabilities were employed.
- The employment gap between those with disabilities (35.9%) and those without (76.6%) was 40.7%.

- For people with disabilities, employment rates ranged from a high of 54.0% (North Dakota) to a low of 27.4% (West Virginia). For those without disabilities, the employment rate ranged from 70.8% (West Virginia) to 84.2% (North Dakota).
- In 34 states, the employment gap between those with a disability and those without was 40% or greater; only three states showed an employment gap of less than 23%.
- In 2016, the median earnings of people with disabilities aged 16 and over in the U.S. was $22,047, about two-thirds of the median earnings of people without disabilities, $32,479.
- An earnings disparity of over $10,000 in median earnings between those with and without disabilities continues a trend that has existed since at least 2008 and has increased in magnitude since 2013.
- States varied widely in terms of the earnings gap (the difference in median earnings for those with and without disabilities)—from a low of $5,242 in Idaho to a high of $23,144 in the District of Columbia.
- The poverty gap (the difference in earnings of those with and without disabilities), has ranged between 7.4–8.3% over the past eight years.

We have shared these statistics to underscore the "gap" in opportunities and general quality of life for people with disabilities when compared to non-disabled citizens, while also seeking to emphasize the importance of helping students transition from high school.

The Concept of Transition in Special Education Law

As part of the IEP process, students with disabilities are expected to be active members in creating a transition plan. The purpose of a transition plan is to help students plan for their future by focusing on their goals and ambitions. The IDEIA states that transition planning should begin at no later than age 14 (approximately when students enter high school), and by age 16 should be formalized into a concrete plan within the IEP. The plan can include a variety of components, including accommodations and supports needed, as well as plans for facing anticipated challenges or potential barriers. Encouraging self-determination is a key element of IEP transition planning, and is linked to the generation of short- and long-term goals developed with the IEP team that should include various school/agency personnel and parents. By involving additional agencies that may assist students, the team seeks to "connect the dots" among potential resources provided to citizens with disabilities.

In recent research I (David) conducted with a colleague, we foregrounded an example of an IEP meeting we observed that included what we agreed was an example of effective transition planning (Cavendish, Connor, & Rediker, 2016). What made the IEP/transition planning meeting successful was the teacher's ability to move from mere bureaucratic compliance with the law to facilitating meaningful involvement of high school students and their parents in an authentic planning process. Eva Rediker, the teacher, looked at the IEP meeting as having three components in which she engaged her student: (1) pre-meeting planning and strategizing; (2) during meeting facilitation; and (3) post-meeting follow up. We share her approach in Table 10.1 as we believe teachers can benefit from using it as is or following adaption.

As part of the same research project, we also interviewed 40 high school students with disabilities across three schools, discussing the topic of what schools are doing that helps

Table 10.1 Considerations for maximizing IEP meetings

IEP/transition meeting	Suggestions
Before	Developing student and family relationships: • Get to know students, their strengths and areas of need, their interests and desires, their short-term and long-term goals in life. • Get to know students' families so communication is expected. • Use technology to facilitate synchronous and asynchronous communication. • Conduct a student–teacher pre-IEP meeting to mentor the student so that they are able to take a lead role in the proceedings.
During	• Create opportunities for students to provide autonomy. This can take the form of: "(a) allow the students to review the notes made on the pre-IEP meeting protocols, (b) review their progress in goal attainment using academic artifacts and their portfolio, and (c) present their current goals to their parent(s) or guardian. Students often need gentle prompting by the special educator to lead the meeting and adhere to the procedure" (Cavendish, Connor, & Rediker, 2016, p. 4). • Include parental input on the IEP and write an initial draft of the goals and objectives collaboratively at the meeting.
After	• Meet with the student to debrief and provide (and ask for) feedback. • Provide follow up to the parents to: (a) provide a summary of the meeting; (b) summarize the teacher's next steps; and (c) create an opportunity for questions. • Communicate with the student's future teachers, providing them with information about their short- and long-term goals, and providing suggestions from former teachers to ensure student success.

them to graduate. Several areas were identified, and we share some of them here, using the voices of students:

1. Teacher's encouragement
   The support they give you. They push you. It's like teachers do get on your last nerve, but at the end of the day they're doing it for your best. For you to walk down that aisle.
2. Teacher's support one on one, both inside and outside class
   If we are failing a class just because of, of papers that we didn't turn in or homework that we didn't turn in, the teachers became more flexible and stayed more after school and so we can have one-to-one talks, and how can we fix that so we can actually pull through and graduate. I feel like I would tell them that they should have a period where they can meet with students one-to-one. Because, apart from class time, I feel like we should—the students should have more time for them to meet with one-on-one.
3. Teacher's willingness to be flexible and their availability after school
   I think if a teacher slows down if you need to slow down, or if they are there after school, available for extra help, I think that's actually an effective teacher, because if they are giving their time after school, then they actually care about what they are trying to teach you…
4. Counselor's availability and support
   If you wanna switch classes, she'll help you switch. And like if you don't feel comfortable in that class, she'll try her best to help you… Say if you were skipping class and you weren't in your right class, and you were just in the hallway sometimes too. If she

sees you, she will tell you, oh that this isn't good for your future, because you must be in class getting education so you can graduate and find a good job and just get out of high school.

5. Programs in school (e.g., after-school homework help, preparation for state examinations)
   We have prep at the end of the day… Yeah, that actually helps me.

6. Saturday "catch-up" classes, training to take SATs
   Something that the school has done in preparation for college is that they—they didn't do this before, and this is a really good change—they added in a SAT class, SAT math and SAT vocab. And that is really helpful because I feel like without that class I wouldn't have scored as high as I did on the SAT. That actually helped me and I learned a lot.

7. Programs out of School (e.g., internships)
   My mentor… We're always meeting. And she's always telling me to like do this, do that. She's always like helping me out with college applications and stuff like that.

8. School–family ties to maintain good communication
   Well, my mom, my mom… help with my… a lot. And she's constantly emails. Your teacher emailed me talking about, you didn't hand this in. And I'm like, "I'm gonna hand it in." The teachers here like email—they're like forever emailing parents about stuff. So parents here know what their child's doing. Assignments have been given, and they—we'll get the email and our parents get the email too. So like, if I got an email that's an assignment that's math or something, my mom's like "Well, you got this math that's due Friday." I'm like, "uh, okay." But, that's okay—and she's on top of it. She's like… "and your grade went down here, and I'm like…."

9. Career preparation
   School is basically preparing me how to work. [It] has different programs, like culinary arts, green carpentry… so it's like, they're just helping you out, how to work. And they'll look for the job for you and you just have to go to the interview. They actually help you out with like preparing you to work.

10. College preparation
    We have a college class once a week… We talk about like our essays and we try and fill out the common app, like the application process, and we like talk to seniors about what they did.

All of these seem relatively reasonable observations, including some straightforward requests from students. As we've mentioned many times, it's not easy being a teacher, particularly teaching a class of 30 or so high school students who all want to graduate with many of them struggling, in one form or another, to pass all subjects. In compiling a synthesis of research, I (David) compiled successful approaches for teachers to help students with learning disabilities and ADHD be more self-aware, focused, and better organized, with a view to concentrating in class, managing their work, passing required exams, and ultimately graduating from high school, and being prepared for college (Connor, 2012). We share a condensed version of them here as, like many strategies, they are pertinent to most (if not all) students in the same classroom:

1. *Be comfortable with the LD and/or ADHD classification*
   Many students still make negative associations with being labeled disabled. However, students who are able to shift this disposition and reframe their understanding come to see how their disability is not primarily an academic deficit but rather an integral part of who they are. The neurodiversity movement can be tapped as a resource, as

it has successfully shifted from a deficit-based perspective to one of human diversity, with benefits.

2. *Acknowledge strengths and areas of need*

   Teachers and parents can help guide students to identify the skills in which they are proficient and the content areas where they excel. This information should be counterbalanced with areas in which they struggle. By using skills in which they are proficient, students can hone their abilities to self-assess, self-strategize, and problem solve—in sum, self-manage.

3. *Learn about the college disability services office*

   All colleges that receive federal funding are required by law to have disability services on campus. A student's request for accommodations and support services is verified by this office, which then approves relevant support from a range of possibilities (e.g., priority registration, assistive technology, alternative testing arrangements, and so on). The campus disability services office also prepares a document notifying professors of accommodations required by the student, without disclosing the specific disability.

4. *Practice making decisions*

   One of the central goals for all individuals is to develop autonomy. Students should have multiple opportunities to practice their decision-making skills throughout high school, both in school and within their larger community. Students can ponder hypothetical scenarios about commonplace problematic situations, such as the pros and cons of selecting a course load, budgeting per semester, prioritizing choices in social situations, and learning to have a "Plan B."

5. *Read college success stories*

   Students with disabilities are experts on their own lives. Many have survived college and shared their experiences in the form of "how to" books that are informative, useful, and authentic—being from an insider's point of view. Students with significant difficulties in reading can get these books on tape or use a text-to-speech program.

6. *Know student rights before attending college*

   Students who have documented accommodations throughout their earlier school years can usually receive testing accommodations when taking college entrance exams such as the SATs. Generally speaking, these same accommodations can be obtained in postsecondary institutions through the campus disability services office. Students should be aware that any rights to accommodation during any form of testing does not preclude their own responsibilities in preparing for it!

7. *Know student responsibilities before attending college*

   With greater autonomy comes increased responsibility, but individuals with disabilities intending to go to college should know about the federal regulations that affect them, including what kind of assistance they personally require. The more specific, the better, along with the ability to provide documentation to substantiate their claims. Unlike school, the "burden of proof" is on the student to have his or her disability verified.

8. *Take a college course while in high school*

   If possible, taking a college class as part of a high school–college collaboration permits students to gauge the difference between typical high school work and expected levels of college work, helping them to meet higher standards. Such school-to-college links may influence high school students to select the college they have attended part-time, especially if they have developed personal contact with supportive staff and faculty there.

9. *Participate in pre-college academies*

   High school students with disabilities who visit college campuses describe these experiences as valuable because they enable them to understand the academic differences between the two settings. A visit can consist of an intensive, day-long schedule that includes time for students with IEPs to meet with personnel from the disability services office. Another option is for school faculty to arrange for students to visit freshman college classrooms as early as possible in their high school experience, with coordinated follow-up discussions between college students and faculty while on campus.

10. *Develop essential skills*

    Study skills taught and practiced in high school help prepare students for the increased rigor of college. Explicitly teaching students with disabilities in high school to organize when and how to complete assignments, in addition to managing time, can provide a strong foundation for the transference of these skills to college. These skills should be taught explicitly across all content area classes.

11. *Align study skills to specific classes*

    Although it is useful for students with disabilities to learn a variety of strategies, it is more important for them to develop the ability to match the best strategy to a specific assignment. Students who are able to actively determine what they need to do and why they need to do it are inclined to develop a strong sense of autonomy. For example, to help focus and reduce distraction when taking notes, they can employ the TASSEL strategy (Try not to doodle while taking notes; Arrive at each class fully prepared; Sit near the front of the classroom; Sit away from friends; End daydreaming; Look at the teacher).

12. *Make connections among classes*

    Just as strategies can be selected to match a specified task, they can also be generalized among courses. Once acclimated to the format and content of all their classes, students with disabilities can make connections among them and develop strategies to use in all or most of them. For example, test-taking strategies can be used consistently, including learning to prepare for tests by blocking time, creating a review plan, and using memory-based strategies for all courses.

13. *Utilize peer tutoring services*

    Campus disability services often offer the possibility of a peer tutor on a weekly basis. It is important to note that the most effective approach to peer tutoring is for students with disabilities to actively play a collaborative role in developing strategies guided by the tutor. For example, a student who may struggle in determining what is important in assigned readings should specifically identify this area to work on with his or her tutor, proactively sharing what methods have been successful and unsuccessful to date.

14. *Use informal peer mentors*

    Among many other things, college serves as a place to develop friendships with diverse people. Students can cultivate friendships with peers who understand their struggles in certain academic areas. Informal peer mentors have often proven invaluable for students with disabilities. Note that this can be a reciprocal arrangement, and students with disabilities who excel in different areas (academic subjects, arts, sports, and so on) can, in turn, mentor their peers.

15. *Access class notes*

    Many students face difficulties in taking detailed notes, and there are various ways to ameliorate this, such as using a digital tape recorder (including on phones), accessing notes from a note-taker, sharing or reviewing notes with peers, or requesting a copy of the professor's notes. In addition, by being proactive and requesting professors to post an outline of notes on the class webpage before class starts, students can guide faculty to help them understand ways of working together to provide maximum access to the curriculum.

16. *Evaluate a professor before taking the class*

    Students with disabilities may feel more anxious than their non-disabled peers when interacting with a professor, unsure of how a professor may respond to a request for accommodations. One way in which to deal with this issue is to have a direct conversation with possible professors to ascertain their levels of receptivity toward students with disabilities in their classes. Another way to find out more about professors is simply by being part of a network of students who inform each other of allies and potential obstacles.

17. *Access the benefits of technology*

    The paired concepts of teaching and learning within colleges and schools have been significantly impacted, and will continue to be so, by developments in technology. Students with disabilities can choose the types of classes they prefer, including online and hybrid courses that permit the completion of assignments asynchronously. In another example, students can use a variety of assistive technologies such as screen readers to help them process large quantities of text in auditory form.

18. *Consider the benefits of self-disclosure*

    Students with non-apparent (or "invisible") disabilities have the right to not disclose their status to any staff or faculty member. However, this may sometimes prove to be counterproductive if students try to go it alone only to discover later in the semester that, in order to succeed, they actually do need accommodations. There is a greater likelihood of success if students self-identify and register with campus disability services.

19. *Take responsibility for one's own education*

    Once registered, it is imperative for students with disabilities to maintain an ongoing relationship with the campus disability services office, and the advisers and counselors in these offices are often important allies. They can assist in many ways, including advising about course types and course loads, facilitating preferential registration and resolving problems with professors. Students should make an appointment with the coordinator of campus services, to introduce themselves with a view to building a relationship with those who can be their biggest supporters and advocates.

20. *Cultivate individual talent*

    College is also a place for students to grow in many ways, including cultivating abilities and talents. Oftentimes, the "dis" in disability can overshadow what a student can do. It therefore becomes vital for students with disabilities to continue nurturing their talents and gifts, receiving recognition and encouragement. After all, it is the student's talent that will significantly influence his or her career choice.

21. *Self-advocate*

    Students with disabilities who have a greater likelihood of succeeding in college are those who exhibit a strong sense of self-acceptance—including being comfortable with sharing their disability status with staff and faculty. The challenge is to develop specific attributes, such as being proactive, assertive, and self-determined, as these will serve students well in their pursuit of autonomy and increase the likelihood of their graduation. Additionally, experiences in school and college can serve as the basis for general advocacy for students across their lifespan, as well as impact the experiences of students with disabilities who will come after them.

Featured Voice of David I. Hernández-Saca

"It takes an inclusive village and spirit"—

Transitioning through Inclusion at the Intersections

My family and I emigrated to the U.S. in 1985 because of civil war in El Salvador. When we crossed the Rio Grande at the Mexico and Arizona border, my brother, Jose, carried me. I had a fever of 105 degrees. This fever, in conjunction with various sociocultural contexts, was to shape how I experienced childhood. My "disability," country of origin, economic status, immigration status, and spirituality intersected throughout the many transitions of my childhood.[1] As a child, I did not have the language to make sense of these experiences. However, I felt and continue to feel their effects on my sense of self.

Transitioning within Early Childhood

The high fever that I experienced led to seizures and convulsions. My family was central in alleviating my suffering. I was prescribed anticonvulsant medication by doctors (operating out of a "medical model of disability") who understood my "disability" as in need of "fixing." This medical response was limiting and left me "endrogado y sin vida [drugged and lifeless]," as my mom, Maria, described. My family and teachers helped me transition from a purely medical response to one of inclusion: *a social, psychological, emotional, and spiritual model of disability.*

As a child, I was self-aware about my disability experiences. I participated in remedies that my family and professionals advised. I did not realize then how much my family and professionals were aiding in my small "t" and big "T" transitions from my convulsions and seizures to a state of alleviating them. I do not recall the pain from the actual impairment because I would pass out. My convulsions and seizures shocked my body uncontrollably and threw my eyes to the top of my skull: "pausas [stops]," as my mom described. The negative stigma attached to "disability," however, hurt more. I was able to gain hope and relief after my mother removed me from anticonvulsants in favor of alternative Eastern remedies. Shortly after, my convulsions and seizures stopped and never returned. My mother's belief in Catholicism saved my life. My mom explained: "De repente, ya no mas, yo oraba mucho, y sesano [All of a sudden, no more, I prayed a lot, and you were healed]."

Transitioning within K-12

Due to my childhood convulsions and seizures, my "normal" progression of development was impaired and interrupted pertaining to literacy and basic psychological functioning. Later in school, I was labeled with an auditory learning disability (LD). I was placed in a self-contained special education setting from K-8th. In high school, I was in general education classes and resource room for study hall. During my freshman year, I was in a self-contained classroom for English. From sophomore to senior year, I had regular English courses. I sought out information about my auditory LD and my placement in special education during high school. I did not participate in my Individual Education Plan (IEP) meetings. I was tested for my auditory LD by the school psychologist and special education teachers. These experiences were not benign. They left life-long scars, post-traumatic stress, and psycho-emotional disablism (Hernández-Saca & Cannon, 2016).

Transitioning to College

One major event in my transitioning from high school to college was my immigration status. When my mother became a citizen, I did not automatically become one since I had already turned 18. My eligibility for a scholarship to my university of choice, UC Berkeley, was negatively affected. With the help of Carlos, my older brother and role model, I applied to several state schools in California. After I heard back from Berkeley, I became excited about college since Carlos went there. Due to my family's economic status, I could not afford the tuition. In consultation with my high school counselor, I applied for scholarships. One of the scholarships was for a full ride to Berkeley. After several months, I was notified I got the scholarship! After a couple of days, I was called to my counselor's office. My counselor informed me that due to my immigration status, I was not eligible for the scholarship. After hearing those words, a rush of sadness overwhelmed me. I immediately began to cry. My hard work was not recognized because I was not a legal citizen. This was unjust!

My high school responded to my financial needs in pursuit of my dream to become a teacher. In conversations with my special and general education teachers, school psychologist, and high school counselor, I realized that I loved learning and teaching. I wanted to give back to the world by becoming a teacher to others who had LDs. My high school was able to create scholarships to help me transition to college due to my academic and athletic achievements. My teachers and school psychologist encouraged me to seek the disability student services office at Berkeley. I received accommodations, which included a note-taker and additional time for test-taking. Being vocal about my auditory LD as well as audio-recording and listening to my class lectures assisted with my success in college. The initial disability disclosure to my professors was scary due to the disability microaggressions (that is, interpersonal violence and discrimination based on someone's inability) from some of my graduate school instructors and professors. I am aware of the psycho-emotional disablism inflicted on me. However, I used positive self-talk and awareness to combat such attitudes because I am important and valuable. The hope I chose to embrace, I believe lies in our ability to follow our spirit or will: our participation in self-determination and self-advocacy to meet our short- and long-term goals academically, socially, emotionally, and spiritually as human beings. Those issues combined with my immigration status were how my family, school community, and I navigated, so I could transition to college.

The World of Work

Of the 30 percent of students who graduate and do not go to university, many seek jobs immediately. Some enter technical college to learn a skill such as electrical repair; others go to beauty schools or barbershop training, are trained in healthcare or apply to government agencies such as the post office or the police force. These examples are some of the directions our own former students took. It is often thought that college is a far better choice than entering the world of work as, statistically speaking, the higher the degree obtained, the higher the salary. However, not all students are ready, willing, or able to attend college—for a myriad of reasons. Many graduates in this category often enter low paying positions until they develop a "skill" or stay at an organization for a period of time before they gain greater benefits and possibly promotion.

Governmental supports exist to assist people with disabilities in accessing employment opportunities, and these shift with the times. For example, since the first edition of this book was published in 2010, New York State has changed the name of its organization from the Vocational and Educational Services for Individuals with Disabilities (VESID) to the Adult Career and Continuing Educational Services (ACCES) whereby services for disabled and non-disabled citizens were merged. It is interesting to note that many graduates with high incidence disabilities tend to leave their label at school, not "claiming it," and therefore do not avail themselves of these services in the same way as graduates with low incidence disabilities.

Revisiting Dropouts/Pushouts

It has been a long-established fact that students with disabilities are more likely to drop out of school than their non-disabled counterparts. Currently, nationwide, 38.1 percent of students with disabilities leave school before graduating (www.diversityinc.com). The ubiquitous phrase "drop out," comes with connotations of failure, implicitly juxtaposed with the success of those who "rose" to the challenge of school. Some scholars have interpreted this phenomenon quite differently, viewing schools as sorting mechanisms that are likely to "push out" students who don't fit and/or literally can't make the grade (Bradley & Renzuli, 2011). A sad fact is that some schools *can be* inhospitable to some students, including students who have been identified as disabled. There are multiple reasons why almost four in ten students with disabilities don't "make it" to graduation, including: a rigid, high stakes test culture; school personnel misunderstanding the nature of their disabilities; lack of flexibility in instructional approaches; poor systems and structures; unwelcoming environments (we have visited many schools that seem more like prisons, complete with metal detectors, safety officers/guards, rooms without windows, or windows with bars). Poorly-resourced schools coupled with children and youth who struggle and/or are in crisis due to structural racism, poverty, family circumstances, poor housing, and so on make for bleak experiences for many students, vividly and consistently documented in the works of Jonathan Kozol with telling titles such as *Death at an Early Age* (1967), *Savage Inequalities* (1991), and *Shame of the Nation* (2005).

Youth with disabilities who leave school before graduation tend to have very limited options and experience high rates of unemployment or underemployment, at best, in what have become known as the "Six Fs," a point we wish to reiterate (Moxley & Finch, 2003). The Six Fs refer to food, flowers, filth, folding, fetching, and filing. Think fast food chains, food courts, cafeterias, restaurants, and institutional food services such as those provided in hospitals and schools; picking and selling flowers; supermarket cashiers; street, toilet, and office cleaning; retail; laundry; messenger work; and basic office/organizational work. These observations are not intended to diminish the status of workers in various roles, but rather to highlight the limited opportunities afforded to all citizens without a high school diploma, a situation exacerbated in particular for those with disabilities.

Revisiting the School-to-Prison Pipeline

An underbelly of the education system, in general, and deeply entrenched within special education is the phenomenon of what has been termed the school-to-prison-pipeline (StPP) (see Chapter 2). The StPP is the nexus between systems of education and incarceration that results in a disproportionate number of minors and youth from disadvantaged backgrounds being incarcerated, a process initiated by overly punitive school and local policies. For example, zero-tolerance polices (no excuses/reasons accepted for minor to major transgressions) have triggered greater numbers of suspensions and increased numbers of security officers both inside and outside of schools, resulting in schools reflecting law enforcement models. Zero tolerance and related policies have serious implications; for example, in the decade after their initiation in 1994, the suspension of black and Latino students increased by 12 percent while that of white students declined (Hoffman, 2014). Suspensions are a predictor of entry into the juvenile justice system, which, in turn, predicts the likelihood of further incarceration. There are many deeply troubling aspects of the StPP, including that the U.S. has the highest number of incarcerated people in the world and, further, that of these 61 percent are black and Latino (NAACP, 2018). Furthermore, according to the Office of Justice Programs (2018) in terms of incarcerated citizens:

- An estimated 32% of prisoners and 40% of prisoners reported having at least one disability.
- Prisoners were nearly 3 times more likely and jail inmates were more than 4 times more likely than the general population to report having at least one disability.
- About 2 in 10 prisoners and 3 in 10 jail inmates reported having a cognitive disability, the most common reported disability in each population.
- Female prisoners were more likely than male prisoners to report having a cognitive disability, but were equally likely to report having each of the other five disability types defined by the Federal Bureau of Prisons: hearing, vision, ambulatory, self-care, and independent living.
- Non-Hispanic white prisoners (37%) and prisoners of two or more races (42%) were more likely than non-Hispanic black prisoners (26%) to report having at least one disability.

More than half of prisoners (54%) and jail inmates (53%) with a disability reported a co-occurring chronic condition. Other estimates are far higher, especially when considering rates of illiteracy, reflecting that 85 percent of juvenile defenders have trouble reading and 60 percent of inmates cannot read (Literacy Project Foundation, 2017). We include these depressing statistics to highlight the need for awareness among educators regarding where they stand in relation to what has been called the prison industrial complex, and the school systems that are inextricably entwined with it. I (David) have asked the following question elsewhere: *Who is responsible for the racialized practices evident within (special) education and what can be done to change them?* (Connor, 2017). While this topic rarely seems discussed at the school level, it is debated in education classes, often leaving teachers lamenting, "What can we do?" Some suggestions offered here include what is actively within the teacher's locus of control: recognizing that overrepresentation is a historical legacy, while working against racism and against ableism. Teachers also must constantly examine their personal beliefs and self-reflect upon to what degree may teachers be complicit. How do they understand and respond to student diversity, a multicultural population, and culturally responsive pedagogy? How might they rethink behavior referrals, and work to consider shifting from "*what* is wrong" with students to looking at "*why* they behave in certain ways," thus allowing them to interact with students in more meaningful ways to problem-solve rather than adhere to zero-tolerance policies that flush students out without asking questions. In addition, how can teachers reconsider referrals to special education while learning to support the students in class? Support can mean using different forms of pedagogy, conferring with other teachers and/or counselors, case conferencing, outreach to families, team-teaching, and after school support. Another way to challenge the StPP is by explicitly supporting inclusive education, which means instead of assuming that, "The student can't do the work" or "This child doesn't fit here," teachers can ask, in the spirit of universal design, "How can I conceive of my classroom so that all students fit? What can I do to ensure that all students have access to, and will engage in, meaningful work?" Unfortunately, despite the increase in inclusive education models, special education remains conceived of by many as a place rather than a service, and a disability label signals more likelihood of a separate placement for black and Latino students. If a child is to remain in the same class, the necessity of a label can be reevaluated. Finally, teachers who can actively participate—without any punitive repercussions or potential tenure problems—in creating, implementing, and evaluating school policies can exert influence in general issues of equity and access, policies on referral for special education policies, academic expectations, referrals for discipline, and levels of support provided to students and families. For some more politically active teachers who have the opportunity, participating in the discussion and evaluation of district policies may be possible. Participatory, customized, and thoughtful school district policies are crucial to countering overrepresentation and the school-to-prison pipeline.

A Word on Theory, Research, Policy, and *Your* Practice

In full disclosure, we were tempted to write a whole chapter about the following thorny question: *What does theory, research, and policy* really *have to do with my daily practice?* This is because teachers, by definition, think in terms of anything related to education in terms of their teaching practice. The flip side of that is because a teacher's work can be demanding of time and all-absorbing ("I just need to get through the day!"), connections between practice and theory, research, and policy are often not given sufficient time for engagement. Although limitations placed on the length of the book meant we had to rein in some ideas such as this, we still wanted to at least plant a seed so that discussions could be had about the connections between theory, research, policy, and practice. It's a strange revelation, but the longer we spent in education, and the deeper we dug into many aspects, the more we began to see the connections among these four realms. As former classroom teachers we recall how closed off we felt in our rooms. Once the door shut, we were on our own and simply had to "make it work" by teaching. It seemed we were all in a cellular structure within a larger structure, feeling quite isolated at times (when things didn't go so well) and quite empowered during other times (when things were going well). Apart from attending our graduate classes in education, we rarely, if ever, thought about research, were wary of changing "official" policies, and knew of some theories but didn't talk about them among colleagues. Although collaborative teaching should make teachers feel less isolated these days, we understand that teachers may still feel isolated while being primarily interested in teaching and learning.

And yet, a teacher's practice is deeply connected to the other realms of theory, research, and policy. The more times we've circled around the educational table, the more we've seen that each one of these four realms serves as a leg of that table, equally important in maintaining its structure. Take one away and the concept of a table is incomplete; take two away and it can't function. One troubling aspect of education in general is that we all seem to identify with *one* realm—teachers, researchers, policy makers, or theorists—as if we "own" a separate piece. If we remain interested in, and cognizant of, only one realm, we limit ourselves in how we come to the table with a desire to make schools better places. It has taken us most of our careers to see the value of considering all four areas simultaneously in a discussion about anything of educational importance.

In terms of policy, teachers are required to implement federal policies that are interpreted by states and local education authorities (LEAs). These include all aspects of the Individuals with Disabilities Education Improvement Act (IDEIA), Response to Intervention (RtI), as well as state initiatives sponsored by Race to the Top, among others. Knowing *why* policies originate helps teachers understand their own role in the changes sought. In addition, there are many opportunities for teacher input in state and LEA-sponsored public forums and they can also have a voice through unions.

In terms of research, as a field we need to do better in bridging the well-known and often played down schism between educational researchers and teacher practitioners. Researchers have to do a better job at connecting their work to teachers' lives, daily practices, and interactions with kids. Even as doctoral students we found research—at first—to be quite intimidating. There were charts, tables, statistics, words we'd never heard before (and some, since). There were very few instances of teachers' lives, children's voices, classroom dynamics, and parental perspectives. "Interventions" based on quantitative, positivist investigations dominated research publications, but I never knew anyone who consistently read the journals let alone tried to implement what was being said "empirically." It became apparent, in our own understandings, that, unless they have been teachers themselves at some point, so many researchers do not quite understand schools and teaching. As we've mentioned before, research in the field of special education in particular proves to be particularly narrow. We have to ask researchers to make their work more teacher friendly and more directly and practically informative. Additionally, how can we encourage more teachers to be consumers of research, looking at it with a healthy, critical eye? Several journals feature "accessible" original research, such as *TEACHING Exceptional Children*, and/or features that cull from a synthesis, as in *Educational Leadership*. In addition, websites such as www.understood.org.en feature user-friendly information based upon research for parents, professionals, and students. Plus, it's always interesting to read a book on education that helps contextualize our work and either deepens or expands our original interest as educators.

In terms of theory, although it may sound like a fanciful word and more in the world of researchers and academics, nothing exists without it. Simply put, it's the system of ideas that forms the basis of how we think and, in turn, the actions that occur as a result of our thinking. Many theories are used within education, and it's useful to know how, why, and where they evolved and who developed them, and to consider who benefits the most and least from them. Each one of us as human beings, even before we think of ourselves as educators, has a world view, a position from which we speak, that informs how we perceive, interpret, think, and act. This cannot be divorced from our chosen profession, and how we conceive of teaching and learning in our classrooms.

In terms of practice, this is the bread and butter of teachers' professional lives. It's their responsibility to make sure the content and skills they teach are presented in an accessible and engaging way for a wide variety of learners. Well-rounded educators recognize that they're life-long learners and each group of children/youth/adults presents the possibility of new challenges and experiences to continue learning. In busy lives, it's not always easy to fit in professional conferences, yet these help to keep educators connected, stimulated, and apprised of new developments ranging from teaching methodologies to organization, policies to shifting cultural practices.

We know that contemplating all four realms of education is a lot to take on... and not quite what teachers signed up for as they purposefully chose or accidentally fell into teaching. But there's no getting way from it—they're all connected in some ways and will remain so. Take the concept of inclusive education, for example. If we look at policy, there has been a federal push for more and higher quality inclusive practices, and each state and

LEA continues to develop its responses. If we look at research, a plethora of information about inclusive classrooms exists, helping inform us of what can be successful and what to be cautious of. If we look at theory, we see frameworks that put forth equality, social justice, and civil rights. If we look at practice, we have decades of this work being done with various degrees of success, complete with recommendations.

Whatever we're thinking about in terms of inclusion (or any educational topic, for that matter), no matter how big or small, it's good to cull from all four areas in order to present a balanced picture and provide knowledge and information that inter-animates each realm. So, teachers in particular, but administrators too, we encourage you to push your existing boundaries and consider how what you do every day intersects with research, theory, and policy. And, in turn, how research, theory, and policy influence what you do every day.

Questions to Consider

1. Do you teach in a school that has a strong ethos of inclusion, a school that is "not there yet" regarding inclusion, or a school somewhere in-between? Explain.
2. What does your school do to nurture inclusive practices?
3. Using our questions for determining how well a school community is "doing" inclusion, how does your school fare? Do you find these questions to be a useful tool? Why or why not?
4. What is your stance on inclusion? What issues remain unresolved for you?
5. How might you go about "disrupting ableism" in your classroom, school, and community?
6. Would you try the idea of a study group on inclusion? Why or why not?
7. How might you collaborate with like-minded colleagues?
8. How comfortable are you with special education law? If you feel a need to learn more, how will you go about informing yourself?
9. Do you believe that the role of a teacher includes advocacy for children? Explain.
10. In what ways might you engage parents of children with and without disabilities regarding inclusion?

Note

1 Transition is "messy with paradoxes, and it is a process of continuous action, and thus, effort" Trainor, 2017, p. 1) and involves small "t transitions" and big "T transitions" and issues of power, privilege and difference at the intersections (Curry & Zabala, 2017. Small "t transitions" are those that we make every day and include from one activity to another or within activities and the interactions we have with self, other, and the environment. Big "T transitions" are those that mark major shifts in identity, age, and grade and lead to qualitatively different forms of participation with self, other and the environment. Within school contexts, students transition from home to kindergarten to elementary school to middle school to high school and to college (Curry & Zabala, 2017).

References

Bradley, C. L. & Renzuli, L. A. (2011). The complexity of non-completion: Being pushed or pulled to drop out of high school. *Social Forces, 90*(2), 521–45.

Cavendish, W., Connor, D. J., & Rediker, E. (2016). Strategies for engaging students and parents in transition focused IEPs. *Intervention in School & Clinic, 52*(4), 228–35.

Connor, D. J. (2012). 21 ways to help support students with LD and/or ADD prepare for transitioning into college. *TEACHING Exceptional Children, 44*(5), 16–25.

Connor, D. J. (2017). Who is responsible for the racialized practices evident within (special) education and what can be done to change them? *Theory into Practice, 56*(3), 226–33.

Curry, C. & Zabala, J. (2017, October 20). Preparing students to be AEM ready for postsecondary transition. Retrieved from www.closingthegap.com/conf-presentation/preparing-students-to-b/

Dávila, B. A. (2011). Negotiating "special" identities: Latina/o student experiences in special education (PhD thesis, University of California, Santa Barbara).

Disabilities, Opportunities, Internetworking, & Technology (DO-IT) (n.d.). Statistics. Retrieved from www.washington.edu/doit/statistics

Diversity Inc. (n.d.). Students with disabilities more likely to drop out of high school. Retrieved from www.diversityinc.com/news/students-with-disabilities-more-likely-to-drop-out-of-high-school

Hernández-Saca, D. I. & Cannon, M. A. (2016). Disability as psycho-emotional disablism: A theoretical and philosophical review of education theory and practice. In M. Peter (Ed.), *Encyclopedia of educational philosophy and theory* (pp. 1–7). New York, NY: Springer.

Hoffman, S. (2014). Zero benefit: Estimating the effect of zero tolerance discipline policies on racial disparities in school discipline. *Educational Policy, 28*(1), 69–95.

Institute on Disability. (2017). Annual report. Retrieved from https://iodannualreport.unh.edu/

Kozol, J. (1967). *Death at an early age.* New York, NY: Plume.

Kozol, J. (1991). *Savage inequalities: Children in America's schools.* Portland, OR: Broadway Books.

Kozol, J. (2005). *Shame of the nation.* Portland, OR: Broadway Books.

Literacy Project Foundation. (2017). www.literacyprojectfoundation.org

Moxley, D. & Finch, J. (Eds.). (2003). *Sourcebook of rehabilitation and mental health practice.* New York City, NY: Plenum Press.

National Association for the Advancement of Colored People (NAACP). (2018). Criminal justice fact sheet. Retrieved from www.naacp.org/criminal-justice-fact-sheet/

National Center for Education Statistics. (2016). Digest of education statistics, 2015, Table 311.10. Retrieved from https://nces.ed.gov/pubs2017/2017094.pdf

National Center for Education Statistics. (2017). Immediate college enrollment rate. Retrieved from https://nces.ed.gov/programs/coe/indicator_cpa.asp

Office of Justice Programs. (2018). Bureau of Justice statistics. Retrieved from www.bjs.gov/

Trainor, A. (2017). *Transition by design: Improving equity and outcomes for adolescents with disabilities.* New York, NY: Teachers College Press.

Valle, J. W. (2009). *What mothers say about special education: From the 1960s to the present.* New York, NY: Palgrave Macmillan.

A Final Note

The original manuscript, like most, was a long time in the making. Likewise, our second edition called upon us to make decisions on what to keep, cut, add, and change. We have lived with you, the reader, in our minds for quite some time now—so much so that we feel quite invested in you and your career.

We began this book by suggesting that what you believe has everything to do with how you teach, which then determines particular outcomes for students. We hope that you have been inspired to reflect upon the culture of public schools, the origins of your beliefs about difference, the nature of inclusive practices, and ways to promote inclusive school communities. Always remember, *you* possess the power as an individual teacher to initiate change—no matter how small or great—that can contribute to making public schools a better place for *all* children.

It is our hope that we have contributed in some significant way to your practice. Writing this book for you certainly improved our practice. We have borne in mind the value of using Disability Studies in Education as it has helped nurture optimism, sustain hope, and create innovative ways of thinking about and doing "business" for us, as career-long educators interested in disability. Douglas Biklen (2016) makes the same point in a different way:

> Disability studies has a transformative role to play... for it helps refine and democratize notions of difference, spawns new organizations and avenues of communication (especially electronic communication), engenders collaboration for challenging segregation-only schooling, creates platforms for people with disabilities to have a voice, and lends authority to the inclusive education agenda.

> (p. 329)

In closing, we thank you for having engaged in the ideas we have shared, and wish you the best whether you are newly taking your place in the family of public school educators or have been doing this work for years. We know how much teachers' efforts have influenced, and will continue to influence, generations of American schoolchildren.

Reference

Biklen, D. (2016). Finding the course, staying the course. In M. Cosier & C. Ashby (Eds.), *Enacting change from within: Disability studies meets teaching and teacher education* (pp. 315–33). New York, NY: Peter Lang.

Appendix A: Disability Studies in Education

American Educational Research Association

Given that, to date, there have been few alternatives to special education in contemplating education and disability, we believe it worthwhile for our readers to become familiar with the purpose and tenets of Disability Studies in Education, as posted on the website of the American Education Research Association (www.aera.net/Default.aspx?menu_id=162&id=1297) and featured in the *International Journal of Inclusive Education* (Connor, Gabel, Gallagher, & Morton, 2008).

Mission/Statement of Purpose

The mission of the Disability Studies in Education (DSE) Special Interest Group (SIG) is to promote the understanding of disability from a social model perspective, drawing on social, cultural, historical, discursive, philosophical, literary, aesthetic, artistic, and other traditions to challenge medical, scientific, and psychological models of disability as they relate to education.

The purpose of DSE is as follows: to provide an organizational vehicle for networking among Disability Studies researchers in education and to increase the visibility and influence of Disability Studies among all educational researchers.

Tenets

To engage in research, policy, and action that:

- Contextualize disability within political and social spheres.
- Privilege the interest, agendas, and voices of people labeled with disability/ disabled people.
- Promote social justice, equitable and inclusive educational opportunities, and full and meaningful access to all aspects of society for people labeled with disability/disabled people.
- Assume competence and reject deficit models of disability.

Approaches to Theory, Research, and Practice in DSE

Examples of approaches to *theory* and DSE may include:

- Contrasts medical, scientific, and psychological understandings with social and experiential understandings of disability.

- Predominantly focuses on political, social, cultural, historical, and individual understandings of disability.
- Supports the education of students labeled with disabilities in non-segregated settings from a civil rights stance.
- Engages in work that discerns the oppressive nature of essentialized/categorized/medicalized naming of disability in schools, policy, institutions, and the law while simultaneously recognizing the political power that may be found in collective and individual activism and pride through group-specific claims to disabled identities and positions.
- Recognizes the embodied/aesthetic experiences of people whose lives/selves are made meaningful as disabled, as well as troubles the school and societal discourses that position such experiences as "othered" to an assumed normate.
- Includes disabled people in theorizing about disability.

Examples of approaches to *research* and DSE may include:

- Welcomes scholars with disabilities and non-disabled scholars working together.
- Recognizes and privileges the knowledge derived from the lived experience of people with disabilities.
- Whenever possible, adheres to an emancipatory stance (e.g., working *with* people with disabilities as informed participants or co-researchers, not "subjects").
- Welcomes intradisciplinary approaches to understanding the phenomenon of disability (e.g., with educational foundations, special education, etc.).
- Cultivates interdisciplinary approaches to understanding the phenomenon of disability (e.g., interfacing with multicultural education, the humanities, social sciences, philosophy, cultural studies, etc.).
- Challenges research methodology that objectifies, marginalizes, and oppresses people with disabilities.

Examples of approaches to *practice* and DSE may include:

- Disability primarily recognized and valued as a natural part of human diversity.
- Disability and inclusive education.
- Disability culture and identity as part of a multicultural curriculum.
- Disability rights movement studied as part of the civil rights movement.
- Disability history and culture and the contributions of disabled people as integral to all aspects of the curriculum.
- Supporting disabled students in the development of a positive disability identity.

Future Possibilities

While Disability Studies stretches back for almost 30 years, DSE is a relatively new field, only a decade old. Bearing this in mind, scholars in DSE have articulated some areas of further potential study. These include:

- Constructing a new discourse of disability in education that emphasizes disability in its socio-political contexts and that is respectful of disabled people.
- Connections, overlaps, and dissonance between DSE and special education.
- Tensions, paradoxes, contradictions, and reticence within education toward conceptualizations of diversity that include disability.

- An intersectional approach to understanding disability at the interstices of class, race, ethnicity, gender, sexual orientation, nationality, etc.
- Explicit and tangible examples of ways in which DSE undergirds classroom practices.

Reference

Connor, D. J., Gabel, S. L., Gallagher, D., & Morton, M. (2008). Disability studies and inclusive education: Implications for theory, research, and practice: Guest editor's introduction. *International Journal of Inclusive Education, 12*(5–6),441–57.

Appendix B: Suggested Further Reading

Journals

Disability & Society
Disability Studies Quarterly (free online)
International Journal of Inclusion
Review of Disability Studies: An International Journal (free online)

The following is a broad selection of texts that we have found useful in relation to the study of disability. The authors may or may not self-identify as DS or DSE scholars. This list is not exhaustive but, rather, is representative of the scope of scholarship in these areas.

Books

Allan, J. (1999). *Actively seeking inclusion: Pupils with special needs in mainstream schools*. Philadelphia, PA: Falmer Press.

Allan, J. & Slee, R. (2008). *Doing inclusive education research*. Rotterdam, Netherlands: Sense.

Baglieri, S. & Shapiro, A. (2017). *Disabilities studies and the inclusive classroom: Critical practices for embracing diversity in education* (2nd ed.). New York, NY: Routledge.

Barnes, C., Oliver, M., & Barton, L. (Eds.). (2002). *Disability studies today*. Malden, MA: Blackwell.

Barton, L. (Ed.). (1996). *Disability and society: Emerging issues and insights*. London/New York: Longman.

Berman, D. L. (2009). *Beyond words: Reflections on our journey to inclusion*. Harrisburg, PA: White Hat Press.

Berman, D. L. & Connor, D. J. (2017). *A child, a family, a school, a community: A tale of inclusive education*. New York, NY: Peter Lang.

Biklen, D. (2005). *Autism and the myth of the person alone*. New York, NY: New York University Press.

Booth, T. & Ainscow, M. (2002–2011). Index for inclusion: Developing learning and participation in schools. Bristol: Centre for Studies on Inclusive Education.

Brantlinger, E. A. (Ed.). (2006). *Who benefits from special education? Remediating (fixing) other people's children*. Mahwah, NJ: Lawrence Erlbaum.

Campbell, J. & Oliver, M. (1996). *Disability politics: Understanding our past, changing our future*. New York, NY: Routledge.

Carrier, J. (1986). *Learning disability: Social class and the construction of inequality in American education*. New York, NY: Greenwood Press.

Collins, K. M. (2003/2013). *Ability profiling and school failure: One child's struggle to be seen as competent*. New York, NY: Routledge.

Connor, D. J. (2008). *Urban narratives: Portraits in progress—life at the intersections of learning disability, race, and social class*. New York, NY: Peter Lang.

Connor, D. J. (2018). *Contemplating dis/ability in schools and society: A life in education.* New York, NY: Lexington Books.

Connor, D. J., Ferri, B. A., & Annamma, S. (Eds.). (2016). *DisCrit: Disability studies and critical race theory in education.* New York, NY: Teachers College Press.

Connor, D., Valle, J., & Hale (Eds.) (2014). *Practicing disability studies in education: Acting toward social change.* New York, NY: Peter Lang.

Corker, M. & Shakespeare, T. (Eds.). (2002). *Disability/postmodernity.* London: Continuum.

Danforth, S. & Smith, T. J. (2005). Engaging troubling students: A constructivist approach. Thousand Oaks, CA: Corwin Press.

Danforth, S. & Gabel, S. L. (Eds.). (2007). *Vital questions for disabilities studies in education.* New York, NY: Peter Lang.

Danforth, S. (2009). *The incomplete child: An intellectual history of learning disabilities.* New York, NY: Peter Lang.

Danforth, S. (Ed.). (2014). *The best inclusive education: Stories and lessons of struggle and success.* New York, NY: Peter Lang.

Davis, L. J. (1995). *Enforcing normalcy: Disability, deafness and the body.* London: Verso.

Davis, L. J. (2002). *Bending over backwards: Disability, dismodernism, and other difficult positions.* New York, NY: New York University Press.

Dudley-Marling, C. & Gurn, E. (Eds.). (2010). *The myth of the normal curve.* New York, NY: Peter Lang.

Dunn, P. A. (2015). *Disabling characters: Representations of disability in young adult literature.* New York, NY: Peter Lang.

Erevelles, N. (2011). *Disability and difference in global contexts: Enabling a transformative body politic.* New York, NY: Palgrave Macmillan.

Ferri, B. A. & Connor, D. J. (2006). *Reading resistance: Discourses of exclusion in the desegregation and inclusion debates.* New York, NY: Peter Lang.

Fleischer, D. Z. & Zames, F. (2011). *The disability rights movement: From charity to confrontation.* Philadelphia, PA: Temple University Press.

Gabel, S. L. (Ed.). (2005). *Disability studies in education: Readings in theory and method.* New York, NY: Peter Lang.

Gabel, S. L. & Connor, D. J. (2014). *Teaching and disability.* Mahwah, NJ: Lawrence Erlbaum.

Gabel, S. L. & Danforth, S. (2008). *Disability and the politics of education: An international reader.* New York, NY: Peter Lang.

Gallagher, D. J., Heshusius, L., Iano, R. P., & Skrtic, T. M. (2004). *Challenging orthodoxy in special education: Dissenting voices.* Denver, CO: Love Publishing.

Garland-Thomson, R. (1997). *Extraordinary bodies.* New York, NY: Columbia University Press.

Goffman, E. (1963). *Stigma: Notes on the management of spoiled identity.* New York, NY: Simon & Schuster.

Goodley, D. (2010). *Disability studies: An interdisciplinary introduction.* London: Sage.

Goodley, D. (2014). *Dis/ability studies: Theorizing disableism and ableism.* London: Routledge.

Goodley, D. &Clavering, E. (2008). *Families raising disabled children: Enabling care and social justice.* London: Palgrave Macmillan.

Goodley, D. &Van Hove, G. (Eds.). (2005). *Another disability studies reader? People with learning disabilities and a disabling world.* Antwerp, Belgium: Garant Uitgevers.

Gould, S. J. (1981). *The mismeasure of man.* New York, NY: W.W. Norton.

Graham L. (2010). *(De)constructing ADHD: Critical guidance for teachers and teacher educators.* New York, NY: Peter Lang.

Hale, C. (2012). *From exclusivity to exclusion: The LD experience of privileged parents.* Rotterdam, Netherlands: Sense.

Haller, B. (2010). *Representing disability in an ableist world.* Louisville, KY: Advocado Press.

Harry, B. & Klingner, J. (2014). *Why are so many minority students in special education?* New York, NY: Teachers College Press.

Hehir, T. (2005). *New directions in special education: Eliminating ableism in policy and practice.* Cambridge, MA: Harvard University Press.

Hehir, T. & Katzman, L. I. (2012). *Effective inclusive schools: Designing successful school-wide programs*. San Francisco, CA: Jossey-Bass.

Keefe, E. B., Moore, V., & Duff, F. R. (2006). *Listening to the experts: Students with disabilities speak out*. Baltimore, MD: Paul H. Brookes.

Kozleski, E. & King Thorius, K. (2014). *Ability, equity, and culture: Sustaining inclusive education reform*. New York, NY: Teachers College Press.

Linton, S. (1998). *Claiming disability*. New York, NY: New York University Press.

Losen, D. & Orfield, G. (2002). *Racial inequity in special education*. Cambridge, MA: Harvard University Press.

Mooney, J. (2008). *The short bus: A journey beyond normal*. New York, NY: Henry Holt

Naraian, S. (2017). *Teaching for inclusion: Eight principles for effective and equitable practice*. New York, NY: Teachers College Press.

Nocella, A. J., Pramar, P., & Stovall, D. (2014). *From education to incarceration: Dismantling the school-to-prison-pipeline*. New York, NY: Peter Lang.

Oliver, M. (1990). *The politics of disablement*. Basingstoke: Macmillan.

Oliver, M. (1996). *Understanding disability: From theory to practice*. New York, NY: St. Martin's Press.

Rao, S. & Kalyanpur, M. (2015). *South Asia and disability studies*. New York, NY: Peter Lang.

Safford, P. L. & Safford, E. J. (1996). *A history of childhood and disability*. New York, NY: Teachers College Press.

Sapon-Shevin, M. (2007a). *Widening the circle: The power of inclusive classrooms*. Boston, MA: Beacon Press.

Sapon-Shevin, M. (2007b, May). All for one: Ten lessons from inclusive classrooms. *Scholastic Administrator*, 50–7.

Sapon-Shevin, M. (2010). *Because we can change the world: A practical guide to building cooperative inclusive classroom communities*. Thousand Oaks, CA: Corwin Press.

Shapiro, A. (1999). *Everybody belongs: Changing negative attitudes toward classmates with disabilities*. London: Routledge Falmer.

Shapiro, J. P. (1993). *No pity*. New York, NY: Three Rivers Press.

Shyman, E. (2013). *Beyond equality in the American classroom: The case for inclusive education*. Lanham, MD: Lexington.

Shyman, E. (2015). *Besieged by behavior analysis for autism spectrum disorder: A treatise for comprehensive educational approaches*. Lanham, MD: Lexington.

Skrtic, T. M. (1991). *Behind special education: A critical analysis of professional culture and school organization*. Denver, CO: Love Publishing.

Slee, R. (2011). The irregular school: Exclusion, schooling and inclusive education. New York, NY: Routledge.

Smith, P. (Ed.). (2010). *Whatever happened to inclusion?* New York, NY: Peter Lang.

Smith, P. (Ed.). (2013). *Both sides of the table: Autoethnographies of educators learning and teaching with/in (dis)ability*. New York, NY: Peter Lang.

Smith, R. M. (2014). Considering behavior as meaningful communication. In D. Lawrence-Brown & M. Sapon-Shevin (Eds.), *Condition critical: Key principles for equitable and inclusive education* (pp. 154–68). New York, NY: Teachers College Press.

Smith, T. J. (2007). *Teaching the students we fear: Lessons from the front*. New York, NY: Hampton Press.

Stiker, H. J. (1999). *A history of disability*. Ann Arbor, MI: Love Publishing.

Swartz, E. (1992). Emancipatory narratives: Rewriting the master script in the school curriculum. *Journal of Negro Education*, 61(3), 341–55.

Thomas, G. & Loxley, A. (2007). Deconstructing special education and constructing inclusion. New York, NY: McGraw-Hill.

Titchkosky, T. (2011). *The question of access: Disability, space, meaning*. Toronto, Canada: University of Toronto Press.

Tomlinson, S. (2014). *The politics of race, class, and special education: The selected works of Sally Tomlinson*. New York, NY: Routledge.

Tomlinson, S. (2017). *A sociology of special and inclusive education: Exploring the manufacture of inability.* New York, NY: Routledge.

Udvari-Solner, A. & Kluth, P. (2008). *Joyful learning: Active and collaborative learning in inclusive classrooms.* Thousand Oaks, CA: Corwin Press.

Valente, J. M. (2011). *d/Deaf and d/Dumb: A portrait of a deaf kid as a young superhero.* New York, NY: Peter Lang.

Valle, J. (2009). What mothers say about special education: From the 1960s to the present. New York, NY: Palgrave Macmillan.

Wappet, M. & Arndt, K. (2013). *Foundations of disability studies* (Vols. I & II). New York, NY: Palgrave Macmillan.

Ware, L. (2004). *Ideology and the politics of (in)exclusion.* New York, NY: Peter Lang.

Articles and Chapters

Classroom Practice

Bittman, F., Bikens, S., & Connor, D. J. (2014). Respecting and reaching all learners in ELA classes: A glimpse into a New York City high school. In S. Danforth (Ed.), *The best inclusive education: Stories and lessons of struggle and success* (pp. 269–84). New York, NY: Peter Lang.

Broderick, A., Mehta-Parek, H., & Reid, D. K. (2005). Differentiating instruction for disabled students in inclusive classrooms. *Theory into Practice, 44*(3), 194–202.

Burghstahler, S. & Corey, R. (2008). Moving from the margins: From accommodation to universal design. In S. L. Gabel & S. Danforth (Eds.), *Disability studies in education: An international reader* (pp. 561–81). New York, NY: Peter Lang.

Connell, B. R., Jones, M., Mace, R., Mueller, J., Mullick, A., Ostroff, E., …Vanderheiden, G. (1997). *The principles of universal design.* Retrieved from http://design.ncsu.edu/cud/about_ud/udprinciples.htm

Connor, D. J. & Bejoian, J. (2006). Pigs, pirates, and pills: Using film to teach the social context of disability. *Teaching Exceptional Children, 39*(2), 52–60.

Connor, D. J. & Bejoian, L. (2007). Cripping school curricula: 20 ways to re-teach disability. *Review of Disability Studies, 3*(3), 3–13.

Connor, D. J. & Lagares, C. (2007). Facing high stakes in high school: 25 successful strategies from an inclusive social studies classroom. *Teaching Exceptional Children, 40*(2), 18–27.

Elder, B. C., Damiani, M. L., & Oswago, B. O. (2016). From attitudes to practice: Utilizing inclusive teaching strategies in Kenyan primary schools. *International Journal of Inclusive Education, 20*(4), 413–34.

Ferguson, P. M. (2001). On infusing disability studies into the general curriculum: On point… brief discussions of critical issues. Special Education Programs (ED/OSERS). Retrieved from www.urbanschools.org/pdf/OPdisability.pdf?v_document_name=On%20Infusing%20Disability%20Studies

King Thorius, K. A. & Simon, M. (2014). Multidisciplinary collaboration to support struggling readers: Centering culture in concerns about process and outcomes. *Journal of Educational and Psychological Consultation, 24*(2), 165–82.

Culture

Bal, A. (2016). From intervention to innovation: A cultural historical approach to the racialization of school discipline. *Interchange, 47*(4), 409–27.

Bal, A., King Thorius, K., & Kozleski, E. (2014). *Culturally responsive behavior support matters.* Tempe, AZ: Equity Alliance.

Waitoller, F. R. & Thorius, K. A. K. (2016). Cross-pollinating culturally sustaining pedagogy and universal design for learning: Toward an inclusive pedagogy that accounts for dis/ability. *Harvard Educational Review, 86*(3), 366–89.

Inclusion

Biklen, D. (2010). Constructing inclusion: Lessons from critical, disability narratives. *International Journal of Inclusive Education, 4*(4), 337–53.

Brown, P. A. & Brown, S. E. (2006). Accessible information technology in education: Addressing the "separate but equal" treatment of disabled individuals. In S. Danforth & S. Gabel (Eds.), *Vital questions facing disability studies in education* (pp. 253–70). New York, NY: Peter Lang.

Connor, D. J., Gabel, S., Gallagher, D., & Morton, M. (2008). Disability studies and inclusive education: Implications for theory, research, and practice. *International Journal of Inclusive Education, 12*(5–6), 441–57.

Gartner, A. & Lipsky, D. (1987). Beyond special education: Toward a system of quality for all students. *Harvard Educational Review, 57*(4), 367–95.

Hehir, T. (2003). Beyond inclusion. *School Administrator, 60*(3), 36–9.

Sapon-Shevin, M. (2000). Schools fit for all. *Educational Leadership, 58*(4), 34–9.

Sapon-Shevin, M. (2007, May). All for one: Ten lessons from inclusive classrooms. *Scholastic Administrator, 6*(7), 50–7.

Slee, R. & Allan, J. (2001). Excluding the included: A reconsideration of inclusive education. *International Studies in Sociology of Education, 11*(2), 173–92.

Valle, J. W., Connor, D. J., Broderick, A., Bejoian, L., & Baglieri, S. (2011). Creating alliances against exclusivity: A pathway to inclusive educational reform. *Teachers College Record, 113*(10), 2282–308.

Waitoller, F. R. & Annamma, S. A. (2017). Taking a spatial turn in inclusive education. In M. T. Hughes & E. Talbott (Eds.), *The Wiley handbook of diversity in special education,* (pp. 23–44). Malden, MA: Wiley.

White, J. (2011). Policy matters: Law, policy, practice, and their relationships to inclusivity. In P. Jones, J. Fauske, & J. Carr (Eds.), *Leading for inclusion: How schools can build on the strengths of all learners* (pp. 29–44). New York, NY: Teachers College Press.

Intersectionality

Ben-Moshe, L. & Magaña, S. (2014). An introduction to race, gender, and disability: Intersectionality, disability studies, and families of color. *Women, Gender, and Families of Color, 2*(2), 105–14.

Bjornsdotir, K. & Traustadotir, R. (2010). Stuck in the land of disability? The intersection of learning difficulties, class, gender, and religion. *Disability & Society, 25*(1), 49–62.

Broderick, A. & Leonardo, Z. (2016). What a good boy: The deployment and distribution of "goodness" as ideological property in schools. In D. Connor, B. Ferri, & S. A. Annamma (Eds.), *DisCrit: Critical conversations across race, class, & dis/ability* (pp. 55–69). New York, NY: Teachers College Press.

Cioè-Peña, M. (2017). Who is excluded from inclusion? Points of union and division in bilingual and special education. *Theory, Research, and Action in Urban Education: Special Issue on #BlackLivesMatter, 5*(1). Retrieved from https://blmtraue.commons.gc.cuny.edu/2017/02/24/

Cioè-Peña, M. (2017). The intersectional gap: How bilingual students in the United States are excluded from inclusion. *International Journal of Inclusive Education, 21*(9), 906–19.

Erevelles, N. (2006). How does it feel to be a problem? Race, disability, and exclusion in educational policy. In E. A. Brantlinger (Ed.), *Who benefits from special education? Remediating (fixing) other people's children* (pp. 77–99). Mahwah, NJ: Lawrence Erlbaum.

Erevelles, N. & Minear, A. (2010). Unspeakable offenses: Untangling race and disability in discourses of intersectionality. *Journal of Literary & Cultural Disability Studies, 4*(2), 127–45.

Ferri, B. A. (2009). Changing the script: Race and disability in Lynne Manning's "Weights." *International Journal of Inclusive Education, 12*(5–6), 497–509.

Ferri, B. A. & Connor, D. J. (2014). Talking (and not talking) about race, social class, and dis/ability: Toward a margin-to-margin approach. *Race Ethnicity & Education, 17*(4), 471–93.

Freedman, J. & Ferri, B. A. (2017). Locating the problem within: Race, learning disabilities, and science. *Teachers College Record, 19*(5), 1–28.

Hernández-Saca, D. I., Kahn, L. G., & Cannon, M. A. (2018). A look inside: How intersectional educational research reveals the multidimensional construction of (dis)abled experiences. *Review of Research in Education, 42*(1), 286–311.

Leonardo, Z. & Broderick, A. (2011). Smartness as property: A critical exploration of intersections between whiteness and disability studies. *Teachers College Record, 113*(10), 2206–32.

Petersen, A. J. (2009). "Ain't nobody gonna get me down": An examination of the educational experiences of four African American women labeled with disabilities. *Equity & Excellence in Education, 42*(4), 428–42.

Normalcy

Baglieri, S. & Knopf, J. (2004). Normalizing difference in inclusive teaching. *Journal of Learning Disabilities, 37*(6), 525–29.

Baglieri, S., Bejoian, L, Broderick, A., Connor, D. J., & Valle, J. (2011). [Re]claiming "Inclusive Education" toward cohesion in educational reform: Disability studies unravels the myth of the typical child. *Teachers College Record, 113*(10), 2122–54.

Baker, B. (2002). The hunt for disability: The new eugenics and the normalization of school children. *Teachers College Record, 104,* 663–703.

Brantlinger, E. A. (2004). Confounding the needs and confronting the norms: An extension of Reid and Valle's essay. *Journal of Learning Disabilities, 37*(6), 490–99.

Cioè-Peña, M. (2017). Disability, bilingualism and what it means to be normal. *Journal of Bilingual Education Research & Instruction, 19*(1), 138–60.

Connor, D. J. (2017). Questioning "normal": Actively undoing dis/ability stereotypes through teaching a critical analysis of films. In J. Stoddard, A. Marcus, & D. Hicks (Eds.), *Teaching difficult history through film* (pp. 199–218). New York, NY: Taylor & Francis.

Gallagher, D. (2010). Educational researchers and the makers of normal people. In C. Dudley-Marling & A. Gurn (Eds.), *The myth of the normal curve* (pp. 25–38). New York, NY: Peter Lang.

Mutua, K. & Smith, R. M. (2006). Disrupting normalcy and the practical concerns of teachers. In S. Danforth & S. Gabel (Eds.), *Vital questions facing disability studies in education* (pp. 121–33). New York, NY: Peter Lang.

Smith, P. (2008). Cartographies of eugenics and special education: A history of the (ab)normal. In S. Gabel & S. Danforth (Eds.), *Disability and the politics of education: An international reader* (pp. 417–32). New York, NY: Peter Lang.

Parents and Families

Bacon, J. & Causton-Theoharis, J. (2013). "It should be teamwork": A critical investigation of school practices and parent advocacy in special education. *International Journal of Inclusive Education, 17*(7), 682–99.

Ferguson, P. M. & Ferguson, D. (2006). Finding the "proper attitude": The potential of disability studies to reframe family/school linkages. In S. Danforth & S. Gabel (Eds.), *Vital questions facing disability studies in education* (pp. 217–35). New York, NY: Peter Lang.

Valle, J. W. & Aponte, E. (2002). IDEA and collaboration: A Bakhtinian perspective on parent and professional discourse. *Journal of Learning Disabilities, 35*(5), 469–79.

Perspectives of Disabled Adults, Youth, and Children

Annamma, S. A. (2014). Disabling juvenile justice: Engaging the stories of incarcerated young women of color with disabilities. *Remedial and Special Education, 35*(5), 313–24.

Ashby, C. & Causton-Theoharis, J. (2009). Disqualified in the human race: A close reading of the autobiographies of individuals identified as autistic. *International Journal of Inclusive Education, 13*(5), 501–16.

Ferri, B. A., Connor, D. J., Solis, S., & Volpitta, D. (2005). Teachers with LD: Ongoing negotiations with discourses of disability. *Journal of Learning Disabilities, 38*(1), 62–78.

Ferri, B. A., Hendrick, C., & Gregg, N. (2001). Teachers with learning disabilities: A view from both sides of the desk. *Journal of Learning Disabilities, 34*(1), 22–32.

Gonzalez, T., Hernández-Saca, D. I., & Artiles, A. J. (2016). In search of voice: Theory and methods in K-12 student voice research in the US, 1990–2010. *Educational Review, 69*(4), 1–23.

Hamre, B., Oyler, C., & Bejoian, L. B. (2006).Narrating disability: Pedagogical imperatives [Guest editors' introduction]. *Equity & Excellence in Education, 39*(2), 91–100.

Murphy, R. F. (1995). Encounters: The body silent in America. In B. Instad & S. R. White (Eds.), *Disability and culture* (pp. 140–57). Berkeley, CA: University of California Press.

Narian, S. (2008). Institutional stories and self-stories: Investigating peer interpretations of significant disability. *International Journal of Inclusive Education, 12*(5–6), 525–42.

Olander, L. (2016). Rethinking "those kids": Lessons learned from a novice teacher's introduction to in/exclusion. *Bank Street Occasional Papers, 36.* Retrieved from https://educate.bankstreet.edu/occasional-paper-series/vol2016/iss36/4/

Valente, J. M. & Danforth, S. (2016). Disability studies in education: Storying our way into inclusion. *Bank Street Occasional Papers Series, 36.* Retrieved from https://educate.bankstreet.edu/occasional-paper-series/vol2016/iss36/1/

Zola, I. K. (1982). *Missing pieces: A chronicle of living with a disability.* Philadelphia, PA: Temple University Press.

Politics of Disability

Ashby, C., Jung, E., Woodfield, C., Vroman, K., & Orsati, F. (2015). "Wishing to go it alone": The complicated interplay of independence, interdependence and agency. *Disability & Society, 30*(10), 1474–89.

Connor, D. J. (2012). Common confusions with inclusion. In B. Cooper, C. Strax, & M. Strax (Eds.), *The politics of special education: Problems, promises, and progress* (pp. 101–22). Lanham, MD: Rowman & Littlefield.

Connor, D. J. (2014). The Disability Studies in Education Annual Conference: Explorations of working within, and against, special education. *Disability Studies Quarterly, 34*(2).

Connor, D. J. & Baglieri, S. (2009). Tipping the scales: Disability studies asks "How much diversity can you take?" In S. Steinberg (Ed.), *Diversity: A reader* (pp. 341–61). New York, NY: Peter Lang.

Danforth, S. (1997). On what basis hope? Modern progress and postmodern possibilities. *Mental Retardation, 35*(2), 93–106.

Danforth, S. (1999). Pragmatism and the scientific validation of professional practices in American special education. *Disability and Society, 14*(6), 733–51.

Danforth, S. (2006). From epistemology to democracy: Pragmatism and the reorientation of disability research. *Remedial and Special Education, 27*(6), 337–45.

Ferguson, P. M. (2002). Notes toward a history of hopelessness: Disability and the places of therapeutic failure. *Disability, Culture and Education, 1*(1), 27–40.

Ferguson, P. & Nusbaum, E. (2012). Disability studies: What is it and what difference does it make? *Research and Practice of Persons with Severe Disabilities, 37*(2), 70–80.

Gabel, S. L. (2008). A model for policy activism. In S. Gabel & S. Danforth (Eds.), *Disability and the politics of education: An international reader* (pp. 311–31). New York, NY: Peter Lang.

Gordon, B. O. & Rosenblum, K. E. (2001). Bringing disability into the sociological frame: A comparison of disability with race, sex, and sexual orientation statuses. *Disability & Society, 16*(1), 5–19.

Grace, E. J. (Ibby). (2014). Practitioner inquiry and community engaged research. *i.e.: Inquiry in Education, 5*(1), 1–2.

Hahn, H. (2002). Academic debates and political advocacy: The US disability movement. In C. Barnes, M. Oliver, & L. Barton (Eds.), *Disability studies today* (pp. 162–89). Cambridge: Polity Press.

Kliewer, C., Biklen, D., & Petersen, A. J. (2015). At the end of intellectual disability. *Harvard Educational Review, 85*(1), 1–28.

Kudlick, C. J. (2003). Disability history: Why we need another "other." Retrieved from www. hostorycooperative.org

Ladson-Billings, G. (2006). From the achievement gap to the education debt: Understanding achievement in US schools. *Educational Researcher, 35*(7), 3–12.

Peters, S. (1996). The politics of disability identity. In L. Barton (Ed.), *Disability and society: Emerging issues and insights* (pp. 215–46). London/New York: Longman.

Peters, S. (2000). Is there a disability culture? A syncretisation of three possible world views. *Disability & Society, 15*(4), 583–601.

Reid, D. K. & Valle, J. (2004). The discursive practice of learning disability: Implication for instruction and parent–school relations. *Journal of Learning Disabilities, 37*(6), 466–81.

Reid, D. K. & Knight, M. G. (2006). Disability justifies exclusion of minority students: A critical history grounded in disability studies. *Educational Researcher, 35*(6), 18–23.

Union of the Physically Impaired Against Segregation [UPIAS]. (1975). *Fundamental principles of disability.* Retrieved from www.leeds.ac.uk/disabilitystudies/archiveuk/UPIAS/fundamental%20 principles.pdf.

Race

Annamma, S., Morrison, D., & Jackson, D. (2014). Disproportionality fills in the gaps: Connections between achievement, discipline and special education in the school-to-prison pipeline. *Berkeley Review of Education, 5*(1), 53–87.

Blanchett, W. J. (2010). Telling it like it is: The role of race, class, and culture in the perpetuation of learning disability as a privileged category for the white middle class. *Disability Studies Quarterly, 30*(2), 1230–77.

Migliarini, V. (2018). "Colour-evasiveness" and racism without race: The disablement of asylum-seeking children at the edge of fortress Europe. *Race Ethnicity and Education, 21*(4), 438–57.

Smith, P. (2004). Whiteness, normal theory, and disability studies. *Disability Studies Quarterly, 24*(2). Retrieved from http://dsq-sds.org/article/view/491/668

Racial Overrepresentation

Beratan, G. D. (2008). The song remains the same: Transposition and the disproportionate representation of minority students in special education. *Race Ethnicity and Education, 11*(4), 337–54.

Blanchett, W. (2006). Disproportionate representation of African American students in special education: Acknowledging the role of white privilege and racism. *Educational Researcher, 35*(6), 24–8.

Connor, D. J. (2017). Who is responsible for the racialized practices evident within (special) education and what can be done to change them? *Theory into Practice, 56*(3), 226–33.

Ferri, B. A. & Connor, D. J. (2005). Tools of exclusion: Race, disability, and (re)segregated education. *Teachers College Record, 107*(3), 453–74.

Ferri, B. A& Connor, D. J. (2010). "I was the special ed. Girl": Urban working-class young women of colour. *Gender and Education, 22*(1), 105–21.

Gabel, S. L., Curcic, S., Powell, J., Khader, K., &Albee, L. (2009). Migration and ethnic group disproportionality in special education: An exploratory study. *Disability & Society, 24..* Retrieved from www.tandfonline.com/doi/abs/10.1080/09687590903011063.

Representation of Disability

Ayala, E. C. (1999). "Poor little things" and "brave little souls": The portrayal of individuals with disabilities in children's literature. *Reading Research and Instruction, 39*(1), 103–16.

Blaska, J. K. & Lynch, E. C. (1998). Is everyone included? Using children's literature to facilitate the understanding of disabilities. *Young Children, 53*(2), 36–8.

Broderick, A. & Ne'eman, A. (2008). Autism as metaphor: Narrative and counter narrative. *International Journal of Inclusive Education, 12*(5–6), 459–76.

Christensen, C. (1996). Disabled, handicapped or disordered: "What's in a name?" In C. Christensen & F. Rizvi (Eds.), *Disability and the dilemmas of educational justice* (pp. 63–77). Buckingham: Open University Press.

Danforth, S. & Kim, T. (2008). Tracing the metaphors of ADHD: A preliminary analysis with implications for inclusive education. *International Journal of Inclusive Education, 12*(1), 49–64.

Danforth, S. (2007). Disability as metaphor: Examining the conceptual framing of emotional behavioral disorder in American public education. *Educational Studies: A Journal of the American Educational Studies Association, 42*(1), 8–27.

Danforth, S. (2008). Using metaphors to research the cultural and ideological construction of disability. In S. Gabel & S. Danforth (Eds.), *Disability and the politics of education: An international reader* (pp. 385–400). New York, NY: Peter Lang.

Darke, P. (1998). Understanding cinematic representations of disability. In T. Shakespeare (Ed.), *The disabilities studies reader: Social science perspectives* (pp. 181–97). London: Cassel.

Meyers, C. & Bersani, H. (2009). Ten quick ways to analyze children's books for ableism. *Rethinking Schools, 23*(2), 52–4.

Rice, N. E. (2006). "Reining in" special education: Constructions of special education in *New York Times* editorials, 1975–2004. *Disability Studies Quarterly, 26*(2).

Safran, S. P. (1998). Disability portrayal in film: Reflecting the past, directing the future. *Exceptional Children, 64*(2), 227–38.

Safran, S. P. (2002). Using movies to teach students about disabilities. *TEACHING Exceptional Children, 32*(3), 44–7.

Shakespeare, T. (1994). Cultural representations of disabled people. *Disability and Society, 9*(3), 283–99.

Worotynec, S. Z. (2004). Contrived or inspired: Ability/disability in the children's picture book. *Disability Studies Quarterly, 24*(1).

School-to-Prison Pipeline

Annamma, S. A. (2015). Disrupting the school-to-prison pipeline through disability critical race theory. In L. Dowdell Drakeford (Ed.), *The race controversy in American education* (Vol. 1, pp. 191–214). Santa Barbara, CA: Praeger.

Annamma, S. A. (2015). Innocence, ability and whiteness as property: Teacher education and the school-to-prison pipeline. *Urban Review, 47*(2), 293–316.

Karagiannis, A. (2000). Soft disability in schools: Assisting or confining at risk children and youth? *Journal of Educational Thought, 34*(2), 113–34.

Social Model(s) of Disability

Abberley, P. (1987). The concept of oppression and the development of a social theory of disability. *Disability, Handicap, and Society, 2*(1), 5–19.

Bjarnason, D. S. (2008). Private troubles or public issues? The social construction of "the disabled baby" in the context of social policy and social technological changes. In S. Gabel, & S. Danforth (Eds.), *Disability and the politics of education: An international reader*. New York, NY: Peter Lang.

Bogdan, R. & Bicklen, D. (1977). Handicapism. *Social Policy, 7*(5), 14–19.

Bogdan, R. & Taylor, S. (1989). Relationships with severely disabled people: The social construction of humanness. *Social Problems, 36*(2), 135–47.

Connor, D. J. & Valle, J. W. (2015). A socio-cultural reframing of science and dis/ability in education: Past problems, current concerns, and future possibilities. *Journal of Cultural Studies of Science Education, 10*(2), 1103–12.

Finkelstein, V. (2003). The social model of disability repossessed. Retrieved from www.leeds.ac.uk/disability-studies/archiveuk/finkelstein/soc%20mod%20repossessed.pdf

Gabel, S. L. & Peters, S. (2004). Presage of a paradigm shift? Beyond the social model of disability toward a resistance theory of disability. *Disability and Society, 19*(6), 571–96.

Gabel, S. L. & Connor, D. J. (2009). Theorizing disability: Implications and applications for social justice in education. In W. Ayres, T. Quinn, & D. Stovall (Eds.), *Handbook of social justice in education* (pp. 377–99). New York, NY: Routledge.

Humphrey, J. C. (2000). Researching disability politics, or, some problems with the social model in practice. *Disability & Society, 15*(1), 63–85.

Linton, S., Mello, S., & O'Neill, J. (1995). Disability studies: Expanding the parameters of diversity. *Radical Teacher, 47*, 4–10.

Priestly, M. (1998). Constructions and creations: Idealism, materialism and disability theory. *Disability & Society, 13*(1), 75–94.

Shakespeare, T. & Watson, N. (1997). Defending the social model. *Disability & Society, 12*(2), 293–300.

Shakespeare, T. & Watson, N. (2001). The social model of disability: An outdated ideology? In S. Barnartt & B. Altman (Eds.), *Exploring theories and expanding methodologies: Where we are and where we need to go* (pp. 9–28). Oxford: Elsevier Science.

Thomas, C. & Corker, M. (2002). A journey around the social model. In M. Corker & T. Shakespeare (Eds.), *Disability/postmodernity* (pp. 18–31). New York/London: Routledge.

Social Justice and Disability

Connor, D. J. (2012). Diversifying "diversity": Contemplating dis/ability at the table(s) of social justice and multicultural education. *Disability Studies Quarterly, 32*(3).

Gabel, S. & Connor, D. J. (2009). Theorizing disability: Implications and applications for social justice in education. In W. Ayers, T. Quinn, &D. Stovall (Eds.), *Handbook of social justice* (pp. 377–99). New York, NY: Lawrence Erlbaum.

Special Education Divide

Andrews, J. E., Carnine, D. W., Coutinho, M. J., Edgar, E. B., Forness, S. R., Fuchs, L. S., Jordan, D.,... & Wong, J. (2000). Bridging the special education divide. *Remedial and Special Education, 21*(5), 258–67.

Baglieri, S., Valle, J., Connor, D. J., & Gallagher, D. (2011). Disability studies and special education: The need for plurality of perspectives on disability. *Remedial and Special Education, 32*(4), 267–78.

Brantlinger, E. A. (1997). Using ideology: Cases of nonrecognition of the politics of research and practice in special education. *Review of Educational Research, 67*(4), 425–59.

Causton-Theoharis, J., Theoharis, G., Orsati, F., & Cosier, M. (2011). Does self-contained special education deliver on its promises? A critical inquiry into research and practice. *Journal of Special Education Leadership, 24*(2), 1–78.

Connor, D. J. & Ferri, B. A. (2007). The conflict within: Resistance to inclusion and other paradoxes within special education. *Disability & Society, 22*(1), 63–77.

Gallagher, D. J. (1998). The scientific knowledge base of special education: Do we know what we think we know? *Exceptional Children, 64*(4), 493–502.

Gallagher, D. J. (2001). Neutrality as a moral standpoint, conceptual confusion and the full inclusion debate. *Disability & Society, 16*(5), 637–54.

Gallagher, D. J. (2006). If not absolute objectivity, then what? A reply to Kauffman and Sasso. *Exceptionality, 14*(2), 91–107.

Gallagher, D., Connor, D. J., & Ferri, B. A. (2014). Beyond the far too incessant schism: Special education and the social model of disability. *International Journal of Inclusive Education, 18*(11), 1120–42.

Heshusius, L. (1989). The Newtonian mechanistic paradigm, special education, and contours of alternatives: An overview. *Journal of Learning Disabilities, 22*(7), 403–15.

Heshusius, L. (1995). Holism and special education: There is no substitute for real life purposes and processes. In T. M. Skrtic (Ed.), *Disability and democracy: Reconstructing (special) education for postmodernity* (pp. 166–89). New York, NY: Teachers College Press.

Wang, M. C., Reynolds, M. C., &Walberg, H. J. (1986). Rethinking special education. *Educational Leadership*, 44(1), 26–31.

Teacher Education and Professional Development

Blaser, A. (2003). Awareness days: Some alternatives to simulated exercises. Retrieved from www.raggededgemagazine.com/0903/0903ft1.html

Cosier, M. & Ashby, C. (Eds.) (2016). *Enacting change from within: Disability studies meets teaching and teacher education*. New York, NY: Peter Lang.

Cowley, D. M. (2011). Teacher education for inclusion: Changing paradigms and innovative approaches. *International Journal of Disability, Development and Education, 58*(3), 332–34.

Iano, R. (1986). The study and development of teaching: With implications for the advancement of special education. *Remedial and Special Education, 75*(5), 50–61.

Iano, R. (1990). Special education teachers: Technicians or educators? *Journal of Learning Disabilities, 23*, 462–65.

Lalvani, P. (2013). Privilege, compromise, or social justice: Teachers' conceptualizations of inclusive education. *Disability & Society, 28*(1), 14–27.

Lalvani, P., Broderick, A. A., Fine, M., Jacobowitz, T., & Michelli, N. (2015). Teacher education, InExclusion, and the implicit ideology of *Separate but Equal*: An invitation to a dialogue. *Education, Citizenship and Social Justice, 10*(2), 168–83.

Rauscher, L. & McClintock, J. (1996). Ablesim and curriculum design. In M. Adams, L. A. Bell, & P. Griffen (Eds.), *Teaching for diversity and social justice* (pp. 198–231). New York, NY: Routledge.

Ware, L. (2001). Writing, identity, and the other: Dare we do disabilities studies? *Journal of Teacher Education, 52*(2), 107–23.

Ware, L. (2006). Urban educators, disability studies and education: Excavations in schools and society. *International Journal of Inclusive Education, 10*, 145–68.

Ware, L. (2006). A "look" at the way we look at disability. In S. Danforth & S. Gabel (Eds.), *Vital questions facing disability studies in education* (pp. 271–88). New York, NY: Peter Lang.

Young, K. S. (2008). Physical and social organization of space in a combined credential programme: Implications for inclusion. *International Journal of Inclusive Education, 12*(5–6), 477–96.

Appendix C: Useful and Interesting Websites

Resources for children with disabilities in New York City: www.resourcesnycdata base.org/

Illinois's response to inclusion in LRE: http://projectchoices.org/

Pennsylvania-based organization on LRE issues: http://kidstogether.org/

Teachers of students with learning disabilities: http://teachingld.org/about/

New York City Kids Project, using puppets to teach about disability, friendship, and bullying: https://nyc-kidsproject.squarespace.com/programs/

Social and emotional learning for students preschool to high school: www.casel.org

Focus on teacher collaboration: www.powerof2.org/

Special education and civil rights: www.civilrightsproject.harvard.edu/research/specialed/specialed_gen.php

Council for Learning Disabilities: www.cldinternational.org/

Disability-related films (commercial and documentary): www.disabilityfilms.co.uk/

Center on Disability Studies, Hawaii: www.cds.hawaii.edu/

Disability Studies seminars at Columbia University, open to the public: www.columbia.edu/cu/seminars/seminars/cultural-studies/seminar-folder/disability-studies.html www.dsq-sds.org/

Disability Studies, quarterly electronic journal: www.dsq-sds.org/

Issues related to abuse of disabled people: www.bioethicsanddisability.org/abuseof disabledpeople.htm

Disability studies for teachers (curricula and materials): www.disabilitystudiesfor teachers.org/

Society for Disability Studies: www.uic.edu/orgs/sds/links.html

Disability is Natural: www.disabilityisnatural.com/

Inclusion Press: www.inclusion.com/inclusionpress.html

Disability studies information and resources: http://thechp.syr.edu//Disability_Studies_2003_current.html www.lrecoalition.org/

Least Restrictive Environment Coalition of NYC: www.lrecoalition.org/

Technical assistance center on disproportionality of students of color in special education: https://steinhardt.nyu.edu/metrocenter/center/technical_assistance/program/disproportionality

Cooke Center for Learning and Development: www.cookecenter.org/index.html

Inclusion Daily Express, International Disability Rights New Service: www.inclusion daily.com/

Disability Rights Commission (UK): www.drc.org.uk/ www.ragged-edge-mag.com/0903/0903ft1.html

Alternatives to disability simulations: www.ragged-edge-mag.com/0903/0903ft1.html

Building the legacy of IDEA: http://idea.ed.gov/

Disability World webzine: www.disabilityworld.org/

Website of Jonathan Mooney, author and public speaker with LD and ADHD: www.jonathanmooney.com/

National Center for Learning Disabilities: www.ncld.org/content/view/752/456/

Whole Schooling Consortium: www.wholeschooling.net/

Disability History Association: http://dha.osu.edu/

Museum of Disability: www.museumofdisability.org/

Index